The
Revival
of American Socialism

The
Revival
of American
Socialism

Selected Papers of the Socialist Scholars Conference

Edited by GEORGE FISCHER

Associate Editors: ALAN BLOCK
JOHN M. CAMMETT
RICHARD FRIEDMAN

NEW YORK   OXFORD UNIVERSITY PRESS   1971

Preface

At no time did socialism show the strength in the United States that it did in most of Europe and the Third World. This is true whether we look at ideas, social movements, or parties that seek power; a communal and ultimately egalitarian alternative to capitalism remains outside the imagination of most Americans. Within this special kind of American underdevelopment, socialism has known high points as well as slumps. The main high points were the Debsian "golden age" prior to World War I and the heyday of the Communist Party in the unionizing and anti-fascism of the mid-1930's. Now, after two decades of Cold War, socialism in the United States again appears to be gathering strength, to be undergoing a significant revival. This book throws light on the start, the first years, of the current revival of American socialism.

The revived socialism differs as much from the Popular Front Communism of Earl Browder as that differed from the all-American socialism of Eugene V. Debs. Currently, no single group or party or system of ideas embodies socialism. Rather, the revival of socialism is found in various key areas of The Movement—that novel and loose Left amalgam born in the 1960's of the civil rights, anti-war, campus, feminist, and other struggles. In each of these areas of protest and subsequent radicalization, significant groups—Students for a Democratic Society, the Black Panthers, much of Women's Liberation—moved toward a socialist perspective as they came to realize that their specific demands were also condemnations of capitalism. In the realm of ideas a number of neo-Marxist and Third World figures—Marcuse, Fanon, Che—enjoy a following in this country inconceivable half a dozen years ago. Most important, there emerged alternative modes of living, thinking, and organizing.

At first glance, the reader may question the existence of a resurgent socialism in the United States today. Its many critics and foes seldom speak of the present-day Left in these terms. Nor do most of those active on the Left make much of their commitment to an over-all socialist alternative to existing institutions. What accounts for the limited acknowledgment thus far of the revival of American socialism?

The main reasons, probably, are the historical weakness of socialism in the United States; the lack of enthusiasm within the Movement for the more familiar present-day embodiments of socialism, in Western as well as Eastern Europe; plus perhaps some shying away from the semantic overkill characteristic of both McCarthy-type redbaiting and orthodox Marxism. For all these reasons, the socialist label still seems to lack meaning or appeal in this country outside of small circles of followers and opponents. It remains to be seen under what circumstances more people will come to see the present-day Left as constituting a significant resurgence of American socialism, or call it socialist.

The beginning of a socialist revival can be put in the middle of the 1960's. The evolution of the early Students for a Democratic Society— the New Left, in a strict sense—makes that clear. Thus, in the mid-sixties the rejection of liberalism by the SDS became anti-capitalist as well. It was at this time that its radicalism turned into socialism, and militant reformism gave way to a search for revolutionary strategies.[1]

The Socialist Scholars Conference, the source of the materials in

---

[1] The fullest treatment so far comes from younger leaders, theorists, and historians within the Movement. The interested reader will find these recent works useful: Ronald Aronson and John Cowley, in *Socialist Register 1967*, New York: Monthly Review Press, 1967; James O'Brien, *A History of the New Left, 1960–1968*, a pamphlet of the New England Press based on three articles in *Radical America* in 1968; Staughton Lynd's introduction to *The New Left*, Boston: Porter Sargent, 1969; Carl Oglesby's introduction to *The New Left Reader*, New York: Grove Press, 1969; Massimo Teodori's introduction to *The New Left*, Indianapolis: Bobbs-Merrill, 1969; *Liberation*, special issue on the Movement, August-September 1969; James Weinstein and David W. Eakins's introduction to *For a New America*, the anthology of *Studies on the Left*, New York: Random House, 1970; and *The Movement Toward a New America*, edited by Mitchell Goodman, New York: Knopf, 1970. Also useful are *Alternative Press Index*, launched in 1970 by the Radical Research Center at Carleton College in Minnesota, and a serial, *Guide to the American Left*, compiled by Laird M. Wilcox (United States Directory, Kansas City, Missouri).

this book, was an active agent in starting the current revival. Like the revival as a whole, the SSC began in the mid-1960's. Though limited in the main to annual meetings in or near New York City, the SSC served as the main face-to-face intellectual forum for the renewal of socialism. The life of the SSC can tell us much about recent changes in the Movement as a whole.

In 1964 a number of young faculty members at Rutgers University and the Polytechnic Institute of Brooklyn, all historians, concluded that enough Left academics could now be found to meet at a conference discussing areas of radical scholarship; at the time, few if any of these areas were discussed at conventions of the established professional organizations in the social sciences and humanities. In December of 1964, four historians at Rutgers—John M. Cammett, Lloyd Gardner, Eugene D. Genovese, and Warren I. Susman—sent out a call for a Labor Day meeting.[2] While the founders agreed to set up an organization and name it a scholars conference, the qualifying adjective was a matter of some debate. In 1964 it was still a difficult decision to use the socialist label.

From the start, the forum was to be open to all socialists. Therefore it avoided identification with any Left party or group. Unaffiliated Marxists, Socialist Party members, Communists, a variety of Trotskyists, independent radicals of any persuasion—all these could work together, it was held, but only in an organization which avoided taking positions on any political issue. The SSC maintained this difficult stand, ecumenical and non-partisan, by putting its focus on the sometimes elusive goal of socialist scholarship.

The organization used "socialist scholarship" in a very broad sense to mean any intellectual work carried out by someone who regards himself a socialist. Only once did the SSC deviate from the nonpartisan stand: in 1968 it sent a telegram supporting the Czechoslovak people in the face of Soviet occupation.

All along, the SSC served as an ecumenical forum for ideas that might be called both scholarly and socialist. This stand brought the organization a good deal of buffeting. The buffeting came from those who would see the organization purify its scholarship of all active political and social concerns and also from those who would see it put

---

[2] The first two chairmen of the SSC steering committee were Helmut Gruber and Louis Menashe, historians at Brooklyn Polytechnic. They were followed by Genovese and then Cammett. Most recently, the main officers were also historians: William Miller and Michael Greenberg, both associated with Rutgers.

forward scholarship which addresses itself to the ongoing problems of the Movement. The three-cornered debate among both of these orientations and those favoring a middle course began almost with the birth of SSC and has gained in force and turbulence ever since.

The organizers of the first conference felt certain that they would attract at the most several hundred people and that there were perhaps fifty scholars in the United States who might have contributions to make. The actual number of participants exceeded all expectations. Also unexpected were the various constituencies represented at the first and all subsequent meetings. The founders of the SSC saw as its constituency a handful of Left intellectuals in and out of universities, plus a then still small group of graduate students who in the early sixties were becoming intellectually radical and politically active. The large turnout at the first conference indicated that the Left felt the need for an organization that could provide an open forum for discussions of new ideas, a place to meet old friends and new comrades, and perhaps a way to affirm a socialist identity.

As became clear at the following conferences, many of those in attendance desired something quite different from the small-sized and studious meetings the founders had in mind. For in addition to the scholars and would-be scholars, the SSC continued to draw to its meetings sizable numbers of people representing other constituencies: union, professional, and business people active in the Communist and Socialist parties in their youth and still attached to the Left; at least as many under-thirty white-collar workers such as school teachers, social workers, and media technicians; and a large number of college students. The additional constituencies adhered to Old as well as New Left positions, but without political affiliation or scholarly pretensions. It is these constituencies, every bit as much as the academic ones, that contributed to the debates and strains within the SSC over the organization's task on the Left. It became clearer as the sixties progressed that these strains in the SSC were characteristic of the strife-ridden growth of the entire Left and of the differentiations taking place within the Left.

Originally, the first conference was scheduled to take place at Rutgers, the state university of New Jersey. But in the meantime, one of the conveners of the conference, Eugene Genovese, had become a highly controversial figure in that state's ongoing gubernatorial campaign. During the Rutgers teach-in in spring 1965 Genovese had said: "Those of

viii

you who know me know that I am a Marxist and a socialist. Far from fearing the impending Viet Cong victory, I welcome it." The Republican candidate for governor played a tape of that speech as a preface to radio advertisements in which he promised to "rid Rutgers of reds." The Democratic candidate came out for civil liberties and academic freedom, and won the election in November. Meanwhile, however, the SSC decided it would be more politic to hold the first conference out of New Jersey. At the last minute arrangements were made to meet at Columbia University.

About a thousand people converged on Columbia's Macmillan Theatre over the weekend of September 11–12, 1965. The first conference consisted of four panels, an organizational meeting, and a keynote speech on literature and the Cold War, by Maxwell Geismar.

No university facilities could be found for the second annual meeting, and it was held at the Hotel Commodore in New York on September 9–11, 1966. More than 2000 attended the meeting. This meeting, with eleven panels, was marked by a major speech by Isaac Deutscher and a keynote address by Conor Cruise O'Brien.

The third annual meeting was the largest. On September 9–10, 1967, almost 3000 went to the New York Hilton to hear nineteen panels and a keynote speech by Owen Lattimore. Cognizant of a rapidly growing political upheaval in the Third World, and in this country among blacks, students, intellectuals, clerics, and hippies, the SSC that year launched panels on all these contemporary themes. For an organization founded and led mainly by academic historians, the presentation of such non-academic or at least non-traditional material was an experiment that caused some difficulty. A scholarly analysis of hippies was followed by a memorably unacademic presentation by Abbie Hoffman, who stressed that he resented being discussed as if he were an object. Ivanhoe Donaldson of the Student Nonviolent Coordinating Committee commented in the same vein on a paper on Black Power. In 1967 the world around the SSC was becoming more explosively political, exacerbating the built-in tension between its scholarship and political commitment.

The fourth annual meeting sought to ease this tension by reducing the size and concentrating on active, methodical participation by all those present. On the weekend of September 6–8, 1968, some 600 people made their way to the New Brunswick campus of Rutgers University. Six panels were held, and Ernest Mandel gave a much-discussed keynote speech. The last panel was a special one, on the preconditions in the United States for a mass socialist party.

In 1969 the fifth annual meeting took place at Hofstra University on Long Island from September 5 through 7. The meeting was similar to the preceding one, but a bit larger and with a more sizable representation of "movement people." About 800 people came to take part in eleven panels and hear a keynote address by Robin Blackburn, an editor of *New Left Review* of London. A workshop and major panel were held on Women's Liberation, while Susan Sontag and Sol Yurick set forth a radical analysis of American literature. The fifth meeting concluded with an all-day panel on technical methodological aspects of neo-Marxism, highlighted by Trent Schroyer's paper which appears in this volume.

During the Thanksgiving weekend of 1969, the SSC co-sponsored a special program at Town Hall in New York, on Agencies of Social Change. A thousand people attended the day-long program. This volume includes a paper James R. O'Connor delivered at that meeting.

The sixth—and last—annual meeting of the SSC took place on June 13–14, 1970. It was held in I. S. 70, a junior high school in downtown Manhattan, with nineteen panels and some 600 people attending. Marlene Dixon gave a keynote speech on Women's Liberation, and the last annual SSC meeting gave this subject the most attention. By the end of 1970, the Socialist Scholars Conference ceased to exist.

Just as the history of the SSC throws light on how American socialism began its current revival, so do the papers presented here. In deciding which papers to include in the volume, the editors' main consideration was to choose the most significant papers available from among the meetings sponsored by the SSC. Two other considerations loomed large for the editors. We wanted to demonstrate the wide range of political orientations for which the Socialist Scholars Conference served as a forum. Further, we decided to focus this volume on the broader, more general issues of social theory and analysis.

Often the choice was not an easy one, and unfortunately some of the most notable contributions were not available. Some authors had not put their papers in final publishable form, others had already made arrangements to publish them elsewhere, while still others wrote papers too specialized or descriptive for this volume. If within these limits the present collection of essays tells much about the start of the socialist revival, it does so both through its content and through its omissions.

Like earlier highpoints of socialism, such as the Debsian party or the Popular Front, the current revival is conceptually distinctive in its goals and concerns. Hence Part One of *The Revival of American Socialism* singles out three new paths to socialism. In the first paper, Martin Nicolaus argues that the main difference between the present and the past lies in the changing and deepening crisis of capitalism, and in the new theory, strategy, and tactics consequently called for. To some extent the second paper develops this argument further. What becomes necessary today, according to James O'Connor, is a coming together of historical consciousness, rooted in thought, with a self-consciousness of feelings. A third new path, presented by John Cammett, has to do with the relationship between socialism and participatory democracy, in the classic sense of workers' control. All these new paths start from current themes, debates, and imagery.

Part Two of this book, on contemporary or late capitalism, brings together quite divergent views on the social order of the United States, ranging from Irving Howe to Harry Magdoff. Particular emphasis is put on a traditional theme in socialist theory, the working class. Paul Sweezy and Ernest Mandel offer general Marxist analyses of the working class, while Norman Birnbaum and Stanley Aronowitz deal with the much-discussed issue of a white-collar New Working Class. Also related to this theme is a study by Richard Hamilton of empirical data on racism in the United States. The author takes issue with established sociologists who picture workers as being more authoritarian than the middle classes, and more racist. A piece by Christopher Lasch on another recurring problem of socialist theory, the relationship of intellectuals to politics and to culture, ends Part Two.

Part Three contains five papers on some major figures of neo-Marxism. While the figures discussed are all either German or American —to the exclusion of interesting counterparts in France, Italy, Yugoslavia, Poland, and Britain—the essays give a sense of the reconstruction of classical and orthodox Marxism that has been taking place in the West since World War II. Part Three moves from an essay by Irving Zeitlin on C. Wright Mills to Trent Schroyer's on the Frankfurt school of critical sociology. With each of the figures examined, the author combines a knowledgeable appreciation with a critique which is far removed from hero worship or mere exegesis.

The reader will note that most of the contributions to Part Three deal with a single figure, Herbert Marcuse. A seeming imbalance results, and this may call for a word of explanation. In the current American exposure and response to Western neo-Marxism, Marcuse occupies a unique place. Whether one likes this fact or not, it makes extensive consideration of Marcuse not only desirable but essential in a volume of socialist scholarship. All the contributions here stem from the new generation of scholars who first came on the scene in the sixties. Each paper approaches the subject from quite a different vantage point.

The first paper on Marcuse, by Martin Jay, offers an academic comment of a kind frequently presented to the Socialist Scholars Conference. The other two comments, by Ronald Aronson and Paul Breines, shift the focus from primarily academic analysis to the Movement, and to how the Left should respond to Marcuse's ideas. On another level, the papers differ from each other in how their authors judge the thought and impact of Marcuse. The first two papers reach some quite negative conclusions, while Breines puts forth a far-reaching defense.

If this collection of papers can be said to reflect the present state of American socialism, some parts of the picture stand out less clearly than others. As a crucial case in point, the volume lacks analysis of the Movement itself—those active among working people and the young, women and homosexuals, the poor and the non-whites, servicemen and draft resisters. Also missing is analysis of the forces in the United States that may now seek to crush the Left. One important reason for such gaps is that, like the SSC meetings from which it draws, the volume dwells in the main on themes rooted in established academic training and institutions. As yet few Left scholars (and few others, for that matter) engage in a serious intellectual dialogue about the Movement—few consider systematically where it's at, and where it can and should go.

No less important is the long-standing dependence of American socialist thought on foreign models. Whether one thinks of classic Marxism or anarchism, or of the orthodox Marxism of present-day Communists and Trotskyists, or of the Western neo-Marxism singled out in this volume, or of the writings of Mao or Che or Fanon or Castro—in almost every instance ideas from abroad tend to mold and dominate much of the thinking among American socialists. Up to now no native school or alternative political culture has emerged to break this striking "colonial" pattern. That pattern, too, helps to account for the difficulty, reflected in the present volume, of making a close, live link between general concepts and the ongoing situation in the United States.

Finally, a big internal shift dominates the Left of late—a cross-cutting process of differentiation, in the sense of specializing and drawing apart. The half dozen years this volume covers were marked by an increasingly clear-cut and often acrimonious differentiation between parts of the Movement. This far-reaching differentiation took varied and overlapping forms. For one, in the mid-sixties Left academics and "movement people" were much closer to each other—they were more often the same people—than came to be true at the very end of the sixties. Black Power, the splits in SDS, the rapid growth and separatism of Women's Liberation—all these developments accelerated and intensified the process of differentiation. Nor does that process seem to slow down with a great national upheaval like the May 1970 protests against the Cambodia invasion and the killing of students at Kent State and Jackson State College.

Another facet of this differentiation emerged at the turn of the seventies. Here the differentiation tends to set apart linear descendants of the New Left from younger converts to the Old Left, partisans of cultural revolution from partisans of political revolution, and libertarians from what might be called neo-Leninists.[3] On one side of this hazy but conceivably crucial divide stand those who uphold the primacy of individual liberation and communal democracy. On the other side stand those who believe that the struggle for basic change cannot succeed without a systematic world view or rigorous discipline and organization.

Of special significance to the SSC, and to its demise in 1970, is one more aspect of what already sets the seventies apart from the sixties, the crystallization of a group of Movement theorists. Often these theorists,

---

[3] In different ways, the "neo-Leninists" are now represented by the Weatherman and Progressive Labor remnants of Students for a Democratic Society, by the Black Panther Party, and by the weekly *Guardian* of New York. Two statements typify the libertarian orientation in the Movement: Murray Bookchin, *Listen, Marxist!* (special issue of *Anarchos*, May 1969) and Tom Hayden, *Trial*, New York: Holt Rinehart, 1970. So does *Critical Interruptions, New Left Perspectives on Herbert Marcuse*, edited by Paul Breines, New York: Herder and Herder, 1970. For a critique of both orientations by other socialists in the United States, see *Beyond the New Left*, edited by Irving Howe, New York: McCall, 1970. Paul Goodman voices misgivings about the youth culture as a whole throughout his *New Reformation* (New York: Random House, 1970), and in Chapter 10 he argues against the way young radicals now combine "anarchist" and "Leninist" notions.

xiii

in the main younger intellectuals, have become distinctive enough to stand apart from full-time Movement organizers. At the same time, they have few ties to established scholarship or academic institutions. Nor were most of them close to the SSC. This third aspect can be seen in the birth of new theoretical journals within the Movement: *Anarchos, Leviathan, Radical America, Root and Branch, Socialist Revolution, Telos.*

The recent internal shifts on the Left go far to account not only for gaps in this book but also for the demise of the Socialist Scholars Conference. Year by year, those active in the intentionally undifferentiated SSC turned from it to other spheres of academic life or other spheres of the Movement. Some made their peace with the established academic centers, associations, and journals, now less inhospitable to Left scholarly activities than when the SSC was launched. Most others combine college teaching with work in Left journals, the radical caucuses of their professions, or the New University Conference.

In the 1960's, the United States experienced a swift rise of both rejection of the status quo and its defense by repression. The same decade gave birth to broad movements for social change, and with it began a revival of American socialism. The story of how that revival started is told in part by the Socialist Scholars Conference and this sampling of its best work.

The Editors

Contents

3 Neo-Marxism

1

New
Paths to
Socialism

1

MARTIN NICOLAUS

The Crisis
of Late Capitalism

Martin Nicolaus has taught sociology at Simon Fraser University and now lives in San Francisco as a free-lance writer. In 1969, he was awarded the first Isaac Deutscher Memorial Prize for two widely discussed essays on Marx.

1967

Today, the influence of Marx's thought around the world is greater than ever, but his most important prophecy appears farther than ever from fulfillment. Marxism as an ideology has grown faster and influenced history more deeply perhaps than any other body of thought in the history of civilization. Yet its central doctrine—that the industrial workers would arise to overthrow the capitalist system—has failed to find even a single clear and unambiguous confirmation. This is the paradox I would like to explore in light of the crisis of late capitalism.

Two main approaches are possible. On the one hand it would be interesting to know how Marxism as a movement has survived its apparent failure as a predictive theory. Marx hoped that his own ideas would seize the minds of the masses and become themselves a material force. Apparently the material force, the socialist movement, has traced a course of its own, relatively oblivious to the theory which it originally incorporated. One might trace this divorce between the movement and the idea in the works of, for example, Michels, Sorel, or Bernstein. On the other hand, one can approach this problem by focusing primarily on the original theory rather than on the movement. I propose here to adopt the latter course. If Marx was mistaken in his prediction of a

3

workers' revolution, then is his entire analysis of the political economy of capitalism wrong? If there is to be no workers' revolution, must it be concluded that the capitalist order is impermeable to fundamental change? Is there in advanced capitalist society a contradiction with revolutionary implications? What approximate form must socialist theory take to expose and to sharpen such a contradiction? Are there concrete signs that contemporary capitalist society is entering a critical phase, and that a movement out of which a new and higher stage of civilization may emerge is in formation? It goes without saying that no claim can be made to provide definitive answers to any of these questions. I merely hope to suggest lines of analysis on the basis of which further investigation and action might fruitfully proceed.

A consensus is emerging among Marxists themselves that the industrial proletariat in advanced capitalist countries is no longer a potentially revolutionary force. In part this consensus manifests itself by default. With the possible exception of a small group of French and Italian Marxists, notably André Gorz and Lelio Basso, the major topics of discussion in the international socialist currents of ideas no longer concern the working-class revolution, or indeed the working class at all. No significant enumeration or over-all appraisal of the working classes has appeared in Marxist writing in the last fifty years, and Marx's own proposal for an international questionnaire survey of the condition of the working class has never been carried out. Most of the ideas socialists espouse today about the actual form which a working-class revolution might take are of the sort that might be heard in a Victorian parlor. No book has tried to show how the political-economic laws of motion of advanced capitalist society must result in a workers' revolution. The prophecy has been transformed into an article of transcendental faith, not a concrete part of socialist strategy.

One can trace a decline in the belief in the prophecy very early within Marxism. Marx and Engels themselves berated the English working class—in which they had at first placed their hopes—for its stubborn adherence to bourgeois ideology. The theory of false consciousness was originated chiefly by Engels to account for the absence of revolutionary spirit in the proletariat. German Social Democracy experienced its great intellectual crisis over this issue in the Bernstein controversy on how much faith to put in non-revolutionary politics. Lenin's theory of the vanguard party is based on the explicit avowal that the mass of workers will never achieve revolutionary capabilities in the normal course of capitalist development. His theory of imperialism, too, is (among other and more important things) an attempt to explain why the prophecy of working-class revolution would not necessarily be fulfilled. Today, spokesmen of the Chinese and Cuban wings of socialist thought specifically deny the revolutionary potential of the urban industrial working class and of the organizations based on it. The two most prominent independent Marxist economists of post-war America, Paul Baran and Paul Sweezy, have written off the revolutionary potential of the American working class. In short, except for a scattering of unreconstructed Fabians, isolated Communist Party ideologists, and a panoply of sectarian splinter groups, the body of Marxist thought has implicitly or explicitly given up on the industrial working class as an agency of socialist revolution.

The question now is: how could Marx have been so wrong? The most balanced answer I can give to this question is that Marx, the political economist who laid bare the laws of motion of capitalist society, was not very far wrong at all. But Marx the revolutionary pamphleteer and agitator was certainly mistaken. It is an unfortunate fact that Marxist movements, as well as individuals whether they call themselves Marxists or not, have derived most of their knowledge of Marx's thought from his pamphlets and agitational literature. Most of this literature and all of Marx's most cataclysmic pronouncements on the working-class revolution were written in Marx's youth, *before* Marx had studied the political economy of capitalism and before he had made his own important contributions to it. For example, Marx's proclamation of the inevitability of proletarian revolution comes in a philosophical tract written at the age of twenty-five. Only then did Marx make an initial foray into the economic literature of his day (chiefly Adam Smith and Ricardo). From this venture he learned enough to refute the monetary quackeries of Proudhon, but little more. He was thirty when he wrote the *Communist Manifesto* with Engels, but not until he reached forty did he achieve the theoretical breakthrough on which his mature economic work is based. To be sure, he wrote pamphlets and newspaper articles in full maturity, took the lead in organizing the first socialist international association of workers, and never flagged in his support for the proletarian cause. Still, in the eight tomes which contain his political-economic analysis of capitalist society, the proletarian revolution is mentioned in scarcely half a dozen passages, and usually *en passant*. Often

5

he speaks simply of transition to a higher form of civilization, or speculates about the nature of a future communist society. The most famous passage in *Capital I* ("The integument is burst asunder. The knell of capitalist property sounds. The expropriators are expropriated!") is so brief and so out of context that its organic relation to the rest of the work is not apparent. Most important, there is in Marx's political-economic work no consistent theory of economic crisis and ultimate breakdown, no adequate discussion of the conditions under which proletarian revolution appears possible or probable. This is a gap which has given rise to extensive and bitter disputes among later Marxists, and about which there is still no substantial agreement.

In short, Marx never succeeded completely in welding his pamphleteering and his serious political-economic analysis into an organic, coherent whole. Most glaring among the disjunctures remaining in his work between agitation and analysis is his theory about the fate of the working class.

A great many theories have been offered since Marx to explain why a proletarian revolution need not occur. But I think it is possible to show that Marx's *own* political-economic system does not lead to proletarian revolution as a *necessary* conclusion.

In the first volume of *Capital,* Marx makes a distinction between two stages of capitalist development. The first stage was characterized by what he called the extraction of *absolute* surplus value.* The rate and volume of surplus value are low. The enterprise exploits its labor intensively: female and child labor are common, speed-ups are the rule, and the working day is stretched up to and beyond the physically endurable limit. This is the stage of capitalist production which we associate with the image of the sweatshop.

The second stage is characterized by the extraction of a *relative* surplus. Now the output of the workers is increased and multiplied by the introduction of advanced machinery. Productivity rises rapidly, and with it rise the rate and volume of surplus value. In order for the capitalist to realize a greater surplus, it is no longer necessary for him to sweat and whip his workers to death. The worst abuses of female and child labor are abolished. Speed-ups are recognized as inefficient. The capital-

---

* In brief, "surplus value" is that part of the output of a factory (or other productive enterprise) which remains after the wages of the workers have been paid. Thus, surplus value includes the capitalist's profit, interest and dividends, rent, and the salaries of managerial and other unproductive personnel.

ist class gradually yields to labor demands for a working day standardized at ten or eight hours.

This distinction has several consequences for the working class. In the first stage, the rate and volume of surplus value being low and productivity being low, every increase in surplus value must be taken out of the hides and wages of the workers. If the capitalist wishes to raise his profits, he must lower wages or lengthen hours or intensify the work in proportion. At such a time, workers have strong and obvious motivations to demand a betterment in their living and working conditions. The trend of their living standard is downward. At precisely the same time, the low rate and volume of surplus value leaves the capitalist class with a very narrow margin, a thin reserve, from which workers' demands can be met if necessary. Every wage raise demanded threatens to put the enterprise out of business. During this stage of capitalist development, workers' demands for better living and working conditions can pose a revolutionary threat simply because the capitalist class is incapable of granting what is demanded, while the working class has nothing to lose.

Marx held that the length of this stage depended in part on the vigor with which pre-capitalist economic formations resisted the rise and dominance of capitalism. Thus we might expect the capitalist system in largely pre-capitalist Tsarist Russia to have been particularly brittle and vulnerable.

Barring a major upheaval in the early stage, the capitalist system soon passes on to the advanced stage of *relative* surplus extraction. At this point, increases in surplus value derive from increases in productivity, and not necessarily from decreases in wages. The rate and volume of surplus value rise; the real or potential reserves possessed by capitalists grow enormously. The point is that the capitalist class can grant increases in the real wages of workers without damaging its profit position. What Marx called the rate of exploitation (the rate of surplus value extraction) can escalate higher and higher, while the real wages of the working class can continue to rise higher also. There is no contradiction in Marx's scheme between a rising rate of exploitation and a rising standard of living for the working class. It is my hypothesis—an hypothesis I think consistent with Marx's economics—that the working classes of the advanced capitalist nations have made no revolution because their past has always been a little worse than their present, and their future has promised to be a little better yet.

One can extend this hypothesis into a more general principle. The probability of a working-class revolution varies inversely with the rate of exploitation. The higher the rate of exploitation, the bigger the margin of surplus controlled by the capitalist class. The bigger this margin, the more easily can labor demands be satisfied. The more easily they can be satisfied, the less of a threat they represent to the capitalist system, and the smaller is the probability that the working class will sacrifice whatever gains it has made in order to make a bid for power. In short, the higher the rate of exploitation, the lower is the probability of revolution.

But what of Marx's famous law of increasing impoverishment? Despite the interpretations given this "law," chiefly by Soviet-oriented Marxists in the 1930's and early 1940's—and unfortunately this bastardized orthodoxy still exercises a subtle and powerful influence— Marx did not hold that the living standards of the working class must suffer an absolute decline over time. He stated explicitly that an increase in real wages was compatible with capitalist accumulation, and even in his well-known catalogue of the misery into which the working classes would sink, he is careful to add that this eventually will occur "whether their wages are high or low." What Marx is referring to is clearly *relative* impoverishment. Compared with its own past, the working class has bettered its condition; but compared with what its condition would be if the volume of surplus value absorbed and variously wasted or consumed by the capitalist system were to be appropriated by its producers— by this relative standard—the condition of the working class continues to deteriorate abysmally even when its absolute condition remains stable or rises.

These considerations amount to the statement that the contradiction between the capitalist class and the working class can no longer pose a revolutionary threat to an intelligently managed capitalist system. Because the surplus at the disposal of the modern corporation system is so vast, no realistically conceivable proletarian demand for higher wages or for any other quantifiable goal is likely to raise the specter of revolution. Struggles over wages and conditions may be fought quite bitterly, but there is little probability that anything more than bitterness will emerge from them.

There is a further reason why this contradiction is no longer potentially explosive. The great advances in automation technology which have been achieved in the last two generations have made the elimination of most industrial jobs—and of many service and managerial functions—a distinct technical possibility. It must not be supposed that automation will arrive automatically. Its actual pace has lagged far behind technological potential, and there are good reasons for supposing that the rate of technological advance in producer goods in a monopoly capitalist economy tends to approach stagnation. It is a great irony that working-class action may stimulate the capitalist economy to do what it would not have done otherwise; for the greatest stimulus to automated production is undoubtedly the rising cost of wages. Faced with membership pressure for higher wages from below, and the threat of automation from above, the established leadership of organized labor can be expected to move farther in a conservative direction. It seems reasonable to expect that more rather than fewer labor unions will establish a variety of restrictive practices designed to protect the fading privilege of being exploited.

There is a danger that a favorite analogy of Marxist thought, the analogy between the overthrow of the feudal nobility and the overthrow of the capitalist bosses, will gradually reveal its darker side. The feudal nobility, after all, was not overthrown by its own proletariat, its own working class. The feudal serf engaged in a great many revolts, but was finally eliminated from the scene because the form of production which had created him had been surpassed. The fate of the industrial working class in capitalist society may well be similar. Thus, Marxists who stand fast in their expectations of the working class risk having the social rug pulled out from under them.

Does this mean that capitalist society, having survived the contradiction between capital and labor, will survive forever, world without end?

It seems to me that quite the opposite conclusion follows. Capitalist society has survived the contradiction between capital and labor, but it appears doubtful whether it can survive the gradual disappearance of this contradiction. The system has entered the phase in which it is torn by a still greater conflict, namely, the contradiction of capital with itself. As the mature Marx wrote: *"Capital is its own contradiction."* I will attempt to put these somewhat cryptic remarks in a plainer form.

In Marx's scheme of thought, the term "capital" always refers to two different aspects of the same entity. On the one hand, capital is a thing, a *productive force* expressible as so many dollars' worth of machinery capable of a given output over a period of time. Viewed from this perspective, capital as a productive force "does not care" to whom the output is distributed; this productive capability can equally well be applied to the manufacture of clothes for school children or uniforms for soldiers or fancy dresses for executives' wives. But on the other hand, capital is also a *social relationship*. It forms the basis of an entire social system in which one class profits from the labor of another class. Viewed from this perspective, it is of crucial relevance that the output of production become the property of the capitalist class, and that the yield of capital be reinvested to yield more profits, and so on. On the one hand, capital is so many machines; on the other hand, capital is the categorical social imperative that the operation of those machines must yield a profit for a specific class. When Marx wrote that capital will enter into contradiction with itself, he was referring to this duality. Capital as a productive force is in contradiction with capital as a social relationship.

Let me take this argument one step closer to concreteness. It is a frequently stated truism that the capitalist system in the most advanced industrial nation, the United States, has developed the powers of producing material wealth to unprecedented heights. The productive potential of the U.S. is generally conceded, and sometimes boasted, to be virtually unlimited. Yet at least half the population, by official estimates, lives below the level officially defined as adequate for minimum comfort, and the existence of areas of extreme misery is too well known to require further comment. Why cannot the enormous productive potential of the American economy be applied to the rapid alleviation of this misery, poverty, and substandard life? The answer is that there is not enough profit in such an undertaking. The capitalist system must make a profit, and in order to make a profit it has to sell its products to people who can afford to pay for them. But the poor cannot afford to pay for them, by definition. Therefore, we may say that capital as a social relationship, capital as the categorical profit imperative, prevents the utilization of capital as a productive force for the benefit of the majority of the population.

To refine the issues involved, I would like to state the contradiction once more by using the concepts of political economy. Here I shall be drawing heavily upon *Monopoly Capital,* the joint work of Paul Baran and Paul Sweezy. Together, these two political economists have been responsible for working out whatever significant Marxist analysis of con-

10

temporary capitalism there is today. Using as their starting point the fact that the amount of economic surplus generated by the American business system is larger than ever before and continues to rise, they go on to ask to what employment this surplus is put. A significant portion of it, they find, pays the cost of advertising, marketing, and selling the product; other studies have shown, for example, that these distribution costs now make up a greater portion of the price of a commodity than the actual manufacturing costs.

Apart from the cost of transporting commodities from place of manufacture to place of final retail distribution, Baran and Sweezy classify these distribution costs as capitalist waste. More accurately, they are the costs of capital as a social relationship. Without the social imperative of profit, these products could be distributed to the consumer free of charge, thus making the cost of advertising and the salaries of all sales personnel superfluous. Secondly, they find waste of productive potential in all of the elaborate packaging and styling for which American automobiles are especially notorious. They cite studies showing, for example, that if annual style changes and similar expenditures for what economists refer to as "product differentiation" were eliminated, then the consumer could have today a decent-looking vehicle of comparable performance, superior safety and durability, for less than $800.

Accordingly, they classify the remainder of the price of the automobile as capitalist waste. Again, this is waste owed to the necessities of capitalist competition and profit, waste imputable to the *social* imperatives of capitalist production. Finally, Baran and Sweezy point to the tremendous expenditure of resources for the military establishment, whose chief reason for existence is the maintenance of toleration for capitalist social relationships throughout as much of the world as possible. Adding together all of these modes of surplus on the basis of available statistics, they offer the conservative estimate that at least 56 per cent of the Gross National Product in 1963 was expended for purposes of maintaining the social order of capitalism, and represented productive forces of which the population at large was deprived. In other terms, the real income of about half the population could have been nearly doubled, and the work week cut to twenty hours for everyone.

Whenever a social system suffers from a contradiction of this magnitude, one would expect to find present within it a number of currents, both ideological and political, which aim at the resolution of that contradiction. From Marx's viewpoint, the existence of a contradiction between a society's forces of production and the social relationships of production signaled the beginning of the end of that social order, and its imminent replacement by another. If this generalization, perhaps the most sweeping statement on social change which Marx permitted himself, is correct, then the image of a new social order should be visible, however dimly, underneath the forces of repressive social relationships which attempt to contain its growth.

Unfortunately, the type of sociological perception which Marxism has inherited from Soviet communism of the 1930's is particularly unsuited to the present contradiction. Soviet-inspired Marxism—and indeed all Marxisms originating in countries which have still to win their battles against material scarcity—still prides itself on wanting to turn all society into a factory. It sees unemployment and underemployment as anachronisms to be abolished in a rational organization of production, and proclaims the universality of labor as its guiding principle. Its goal is to spread the compulsion to work, the necessity of earning one's living by the sweat of one's brow, evenly throughout all of society. "He who does not work shall not eat" is its slogan, and the equitable distribution of scarcity is its highest practical goal.

The great majority of those in America who call themselves Marxists, especially the generation over fifty which controls the ideological establishment of Marxism, such as it is, have not progressed significantly beyond this world view. Yet it should be apparent after any inspection of the productive forces now available in American capitalism that such an outlook is as obsolete and unexplosive as the demand for nationalization of basic industries. Radical social ideas are radical not because they express the demand for some imagined desirable society, not because they protest against some inequity in the order. Their radicalness derives from their ability to express the *repressed potential* of the *present* social order, from their accuracy in pointing to the possibilities which the status quo *negates*.

Seen from this perspective, the 1930's vision of a world of universal labor and equitable distribution of scarcity points to no repressed potential, no stage of civilization higher and in some sense more humanly desirable and practically attainable than the present. Are these principles the only ones to which the vision of Marx extends? Is Marxism incapable of envisioning anything other than a world of universal labor? Quite the contrary. At the very nucleus of Marx's thought—from philosophical youth to political-economic maturity—lies the consistent vision that the liberation of mankind will be achieved only when mankind is *liberated from labor.* The realm of freedom begins, he wrote in *Capital,* only where the realm of labor ends. The vision which fully grasps and points out the present contradiction between capital as a productive force and capital as a social relationship, between growing surplus value and growing surplus population, is the vision of a world without work. "Everyone should eat, nobody should work"; everyone can be free to consume, nobody need be *forced* to produce. These are the principles that underlie what Marx meant by a true classless society, a genuine communist social order. And these are also the principles which express the repressed potential of the social order of advanced capitalism.

To what extent are these somewhat abstract observations verifiable in social reality? Can we cease speaking of contradictions, a category of logic, and begin speaking of conflict, a category of sociology? I would like to suggest briefly here that two movements of current interest in American society, the hippie movement and the ghetto rebellions, can be usefully interpreted as protests against and demands for the resolution of the contradiction of advanced capitalist society.

It is beyond my purpose and abilities to present an adequate description of the hippie subculture. However, certain distinguishing features can, I think, be described at this point. First, one must peel away an entire massive layer of commercialism and faddism. Then one must work past the drug issue. In this regard, "straight" society insists that the use of drugs in an escape from reality, while spokesmen for the hippie subculture insist with equal firmness, though more gently, that the use of drugs is a means of exploring reality more effectively. It may be that neither point of view is valid. My own informal observations lead me to think that use of drugs serves as little more than an esoteric rite, a badge of identification to demarcate this subculture sharply from the larger culture and to promote internal solidarity, much like the Semitic refusal to eat pork or the secret handclasps of fraternal orders.

Once past the drug issue, what remains of the hippie subculture can be summarized under two headings. First, the hippie refuses to work for a living if at all possible (though he may work, typically in artistic forms, for pleasure and self-satisfaction). Second, the hippie ethos denies the importance of the relationship between men and commodities, and asserts the primacy of direct relationships among human beings. These two principles amount to the assertion, so offensive to capitalist

13

society and those who share its ethos, that there are more important things in life than earning one's living. Variously subsisting on the surplus income of middle-class parents, on the waste products of the economy, or on handouts from any source available (rarely are hippies able to receive welfare payments), the hippie subculture asserts that the era of material scarcity is or should be over, and declares that the time has come to abolish the compulsion exercised by economic relationships over genuine human relationships.

I do not intend to suggest that the hippie subculture is or will become a revolutionary force, in the sense that it will develop the power to alter the basic political and economic structure of capitalist society. It is possible, however, that it will have the effect of seriously undermining the fundamental value system which is essential to the smooth functioning of capitalist society. As Antonio Gramsci wrote, the ultimate subjugation of the oppressed occurs in the ideological or cultural realm; a social system can maintain its repressive effectiveness only so long as the oppressed share the fundamental ethos of the oppressors. This, I take it, is what Gramsci implied in the notion of *hegemony*. In the history of the two great revolutions of the modern world, the French and the Russian, we may observe a long preliminary process during which the culture and the ethos of the dominant class were challenged and undermined by an antagonistic world view. It may well be that the hippies are to be *philosophes,* Allen Ginsburg and Abbie Hoffman and Paul Krassner the Rousseau and the Diderot and the Voltaire, of a new American revolution. The present style and appeal of the hippie subculture may well fade away, but the vision of a practical culture in which man is free from labor, free to begin at last the historic task of constructing truly human relationships, probably has been permanently launched and will continue to haunt capitalist society as the specter of its own repressed potentialities. The official attempt to suppress and crush the hippie subculture must be viewed as an effort to commit social infanticide.

Ecologically not far removed from the refuges of the hippie subculture in many cities lie the ghettos of the involuntarily unemployed. Because the American economy has always had a racist edge to it, Negroes are the first to be cut off the job rolls and the first to feel the general deterioration of all public services which has been observable in American cities over the last two decades. Neither the conditions of oppression nor the response to them, however, have been exclusively aligned along racial divisions. In the Boston police riot of 1967, for example, an integrated squad of police forcibly removed from the steps of the municipal building a group of Negro welfare mothers demanding higher payments and more dignified treatment from an integrated welfare bureaucracy. In Detroit in 1967, white as well as black people looted stores, and a few whites were among the snipers. In Newark, white members of a community organizing project (NCUP) walked the streets unmolested during the phase of the 1967 rebellion which preceded the arrival of massive police reinforcements. Many observers have noted the high rate of unemployment among Negro youths in the ghettos, and the low purchasing power of the ghetto population in general is too obvious to require emphasis. It needs to be mentioned, however, that the cities in which these outbreaks of revolt occurred were not so long ago considered primary centers of capitalist production, mainsprings of the nation's prosperity. And it should be remembered that the major corporations which still operate in and around these cities report unprecedented financial prosperity. Here again, in other words, we are confronted with the contradiction between growing surplus capital and a growing superfluous population.

The outbreaks of systematic and general looting which characterized all these revolts must be understood in the framework of this contradiction. In economic terms, what the looters were doing was to solve the problem of effective demand under capitalism in the only way open to them. They represent the surplus population appropriating the surplus wealth. They broke through capitalist social relations—the profit imperative—by appropriating commodities which they had not labored to earn. They were demanding that the right to consume must not be measured in terms of labor time; they were demanding by their actions that labor time as a measure of wealth be abolished. In unmistakable language they were asserting that everyone must have the right to consume and that no one should first be forced to produce. In short, they were practicing—now illegally and by force—the right which is fundamental to an advanced communist system. It is perhaps for that reason that the looting was carried on, by all accounts, in an atmosphere of great joyfulness and with a profound sense of liberation—until the guardians of capitalist social relations appeared, *en masse,* on the scene.

It would be inappropriate to conclude this survey of social conflict imputable to the contradiction of advanced capitalism without attempting to assess the significance of these currents and movements for the study of sociology, in particular for Marx-inspired social theory.

To begin with, the contradiction of advanced capitalist society, if

15

I have identified it correctly, underlies the urgency of acquiring more and better knowledge of the functioning of *communities* as units of internal and external conflict. Many observers have noted, for example, the declining importance of *work* unions as foci of conflict and the rising of *community* unions. If it is correct to say that the main contradiction lies between surplus product and surplus population, between unemployed capital and unemployed people, then it follows that community unions must be a more appropriate form of polemic organization.

For Marxist theory, this poses the problem of rethinking the entire labor-union tradition, even the entire class-struggle notion, in order to discover exactly what role the concept of community in addition to the concept of class can play in social change models. There are interesting precedents. For example, the rise of the bourgeoisie within feudal society can be seen either as the rise of a new class or, perhaps better, as the rise of a counter-society or counter-community. As another example, it may be of interest to note that when Marx wrote that the "dictatorship of the proletariat" had come briefly into existence, he was referring not to a labor union but to the Community Union, or Commune, of Paris in 1871.

These considerations seem to me to pose problems of special importance for the study of communities as political systems. What is involved is, on the one hand, a breakdown of legitimacy. On the other hand, it is an example of social change partly determined by the motion of the economic structure. From either approach it is necessary to rethink the entire concept of the state and its function. For example, David Easton's definition of government (subtly refined from Lasswell's earlier view) as the system of authoritative value allocations, represents a step in a fruitful direction. Where it falls short, however, is in its restricted definition of the term "values." Indeed, it is startling to find that in political systems analysis, where extensive use is made of terms which have become part of the economic vocabulary, such as input and output, there is hardly a single reference to that most important of all values which the government authoritatively allocates, namely, taxes. The history of the French and Russian revolutions, by contrast, shows that the fiscal structure of the state is one of the first areas in which government impotence and a breakdown of legitimacy make themselves felt. In both cases, the state found itself in a cruel political-fiscal dilemma. Its tax structure was oriented to the maintenance of the old order, an order which had become increasingly expensive and required increasingly heavy taxation. Yet the growing burden of taxation increasingly eroded the state's legitimacy among the lower strata, without whose support or at least passive acceptance the old order became politically impossible. In short, the maintenance of the old social relationships became too expensive.

Something very much like this process has been observable for the last thirty years in the United States. In order to meet the social costs of private enterprise, chiefly militarism, welfare and unemployment, and what is daintily referred to as "urban decay," government at all levels has been going deeper and deeper into debt. Municipal governments in the United States (as well as in Canada) have already ceased to be effective economic units, and are often completely at the mercy of outside financial interests and/or the national government. It goes without saying that this functional bankruptcy has greatly impaired the ability of local governing authorities to respond flexibly to local problems, thus creating a virtual, though hidden, power vacuum. Segments of the local population who address their demands to the local authorities are told repeatedly that there is no money and that control over funds lies elsewhere. It would be interesting to know at what point this power vacuum may contribute to the creation of a counter-community, with a parallel power structure at the local level. Government at the national level, the last resort, is also finding itself affected by the same fiscal drain. The national government must spend for military, space, or other unproductive production in order to maintain effective demand and prevent economic implosion, yet it must also spend more heavily for welfare and urban renewal programs to prevent social explosion. It is caught in the contradiction between surplus capital and surplus population, between capital as a productive force and capital as a social relationship. Both sides of the contradiction drain it of resources, and it in turn bleeds the population. Thus the impoverishment of the population, which Marxists still expect to arrive via the paycheck, is more likely to arrive instead via the tax bill. If present trends continue, fiscal impotence at the top will lead to a generalized power vacuum, to a corresponding loss of legitimacy, and to the rise of a variety of counter-communities within. In sum, the contradiction of advanced capitalism is propelling contemporary industrial societies relentlessly toward a classic generalized crisis.

Whether the outcome of this crisis, however, will be the conquest of the productive power of capital by new social relationships or the ultimate triumph of capitalist social relationships at the sacrifice of its productive potential—a higher stage of civilization or a new medieval millennium—is a question which can be answered only through the determined, conscious efforts of those who see and understand.

1970

The chief delight in seeing this paper of 1967 republished now is in being able to say that nearly everything in it is wrong. Apparently uninformed of the "consensus among [certain] Marxists" that it was finished, the working class in France demonstrated in 1968 that it was still very much alive and kicking. In the process it cheerfully brushed aside these and many other cobwebs. Let that be a lesson! He who writes off the working class, writes off.

Let me add that the lesson is good enough to be worth learning properly. Those who took the initiative in France in 1968 were the students. Among them were many, and not the least of them, who thought approximately as I did. Did they *plan* to spark an upheaval of ten million workers? Did they even consider it possible? Discounting the professional jumpers-on-bandwagons, who will modestly admit today that they or their organization foresaw and planned it all, the fact is that little was farther from their minds. What a motley, glorious mess they were, these initiators! If they had read Marx, it was under a Communist schoolteacher along with Corneille and Racine, and in the same category of experience. They were "anarchists," these human sparks, and "elitists" and "bourgeois adventurists"; they were, terrible word: "anti-working class"! And wrong to be so, those who were. But right they were, beautifully correct, to regard all the labels that were pressed on them from every side as so many—cobwebs.

What a lesson! People whose theory was a thousand times wrong brought the workers out of their factories and out of their houses, and while the others, whose theory was a thousand times "proletarian" and "orthodox," dragged the workers back into the embraces of Capital and State.

There is "theory" and theory, "orthodoxy" and orthodoxy. Back in 1901, in Russia, one hundred and eighty-three students were drafted into the army as punishment for academic protest. They were sons of noblemen, of bourgeois, of bureaucrats. What did the most orthodox and theoretical among Russian revolutionaries do? Did he call on the students to "ally with the workers," did he preach to them the pettiness of their grievances? Just the contrary. He called on the *workers* to rally to the *students'* cause. And had his knuckles rapped for it, too, in the name of "leading role of the proletariat" and "class analysis." Only— those who put Lenin down for calling on workers to ally with students turned out shortly and forever thereafter to be the purest Mensheviks, opportunists, reformists, Bernsteineans under the skin.

And so it was in France, and so it has been in the United States. A few exceptions apart, the student uprisings of the 1960's were sparked, led, and carried by the so-called "anti-working class" elements. These were magnificent pages of revolutionary history. Let the blockheads "prove" a thousand times that the theory was wrong, that the demands were petty, and that "anyway" nothing "permanent" was "gained" by it. Nonsense. Hundreds of fresh revolutionaries were gained by it, and the images of proper revolutionary action were engraved and stored away for future use in tens of millions of minds. When the picket line and the walk-out are finally outgrown by the current generation of workers in the United States, can they forget that it is not enough to occupy the factories but that they must also seize the *administrative buildings?* It is an old lesson, to be sure, from the Paris Commune; it has been preserved in a handful—too small a handful—of history books. But it will have been the student movement and not the books who transmitted that lesson, and many others, fresh and alive to the working class.

Our "orthodox" meanwhile specialized in "proving" that without the workers nothing significant could be done, that the workers alone could make history, that nothing is revolutionary which is not proletarian. To attack them on the "theoretical" grounds that the "old" proletariat was out and the "new" proletariat was in, was mostly wrong. Even there a few things were gained or restored, but mostly it was a waste of time. Correct was to say to these fine "orthodox": very well, comrades, we too believe in "the working class"! Only we are not satisfied with your historical and rhetorical workers, bring some flesh-and-blood workers! And be quick about it! Bring the workers, as Lenin did, and we will welcome them and you with open arms, assign them the leading role and take your class analysis for real. Only meanwhile be so good either to give us a hand or else get out of our way. But whenever such a glove was thrown to the "orthodox," they became veritable Thomas Edisons at inventing excuses. Is it any wonder that among the

19

best of the actual leaders of the 1960's student movement there are many who were turned by such experiences into inwardly hardened and embittered "anti-working-class" people?

None of this excuses in the least the errors in this paper. Instead of listing all that is wrong, which would require another paper at least as long, let me summarize what is sound in it. Correct it is to recognize that in the industrially advanced countries of capitalism, a rising rate of relative exploitation and a rising standard of living are not contradictories, and that these phenomena, where and as long as they obtain, explain a great deal about the lack of revolutionary (as opposed to economistic) action by workers in many industrially advanced capitalist countries.

Greatly wrong, on the other hand, was to have restricted the eye to the industrial countries only. Seen within the framework of the entire capitalist production sphere, the industrial advance of the imperialist powers will be found to be based on a rising rate of absolute exploitation of the oppressed ("underdeveloped") countries within that sphere, and to be sustainable only so long as the latter tolerate their condition. The "retirement" of the working class in the metropoles from productive labor cannot come about, not even for many decades after the revolution, and not even then entirely, and only within the framework of a universal shortening of the working day, through automation. That "retirement" is a technocratic fantasy, as it stands. It could theoretically come about only if the people of the "underdeveloped" countries were to accept the burden of all productive work, allowing the American proletariat to live at their expense like idle, parasitic retainers, as Hobson long ago envisioned. Happily the colonized and imperialized people have other ideas. As they rise, so must the degree of absolute exploitation in the metropolis; and so it has been doing.

Correct it was to point to the hippie life style (that was back in 1967) as an effort to break through alienated labor; that became plain to all in People's Park in Berkeley. Correct was the defense, in Watts and Detroit, of looting as a form of primitive communist accumulation; more correct would have been to add that in a less primitive situation, in planned and organized revolutions—insofar as they ever are—looting would be wrong. Correct also, but only in a primitive sense, was to argue that point-of-production organizing was insufficient by itself. The Paris Commune certainly is the model of dictatorship of the proletariat, not the labor union, as Marx, Engels, and Lenin never tired of repeating.

20

Much would have been added, however, by a warning to the effect that "community unions" by themselves are also insufficient, and that to reject point-of-production organizing is a great mistake. Finally, the same erroneous either/or spirit pervades the section on the bankruptcy of the state. Instead of counterposing impoverishment via paycheck to impoverishment via tax bill, that section should have said both.

On the contradictions of late capitalism, these are the major points that seem worth saving now. The remainder of the 1967 essay is not.

2

JAMES R. O'CONNOR

Merging Thought with Feeling

James R. O'Connor is an associate professor of economics at San Jose State College and an editor of *Socialist Revolution*. His publications include *Origins of Socialism in Cuba* (1970).

Orthodox Marxists argue that the need for revolution is produced by the worsening of production relations arising from economic crisis, depression, and breakdown. Of late, some other Marxists believe that economic crisis does no more than "shake up the base," to use Henri Lefebvre's expression, and that "only an action-critique of superstructures (ideologies and institutions) transforms the economic crisis into a general crisis." What we need to do now is to merge the material base with the superstructure—and, by the same token, merge historical consciousness with self-consciousness or thought with feeling.

By themselves, crisis and depression do not generate an *all-inclusive* critique of capitalism, but rather a definite and limited one. Economic crisis forces people to question a specific bourgeois policy—for example, balanced budgets—or, at most, the ability of the bourgeoisie or a section of it to exercise economic rule in traditional ways. Economic crisis produces the need for jobs, minimum wages, unemployment insurance, and so on, not the need for revolution. The reason is that economic crisis makes the proletariat aware of unemployment, low wages, the shortage

Deep thanks and appreciation are due the members of the Editorial Board of *Socialist Revolution,* not only for helping to develop the general framework for the analysis of revolution in the developed capitalist countries, but also for contributing to the formulation of some of the specific ideas presented in this paper.

of consumption goods—but not aware of alienated labor itself. A man or woman who is involuntarily out of work seeks one thing—a job; that is, consciously or unconsciously the unemployed worker seeks to alienate his labor and himself. And a capitalist whose profit margins are thin or non-existent because of excess productive capacity or obsolete equipment seeks new markets or an expansion of productivity. These aims are not mutually exclusive or contradictory; in fact, during crisis and depression in the past they have complemented one another.

Historically, economic crisis forces proletariat and capital alike to develop and implement political programs for increasing material production and employment through the expansion of aggregate demand, foreign trade and investment, productivity, and the state sector of the economy. Crisis and depression soften and temporarily reconcile class antagonisms. Capitalist breakdown in the developed poles of the world capitalist system has led to, first, the survival of both capital and proletariat; second, the political containment of the proletariat; and, third, the consolidation of the bourgeois social order as a whole.

Economic crisis does not produce a critique of alienated labor itself, or practical revolutionary activity around the issues of the relations between men and objects (including nature), the relations between men and other men, and the relations that men have with themselves. These issues do not rise to the center of man's consciousness, nor do they become the core of a revolutionary program. Quite the contrary, the analysis of alienated labor does not develop beyond the level of a theoretical critique, and consists of the cultural dissent of a handful of intellectuals, artists, poets, clergymen, and critics.

Material survival, in the strict sense, is not a revolutionary issue in the advanced capitalist countries. The revolutionary issues are those that the early Students for a Democratic Society called "quality of life" issues, those that affect the course of daily life.

People in advanced capitalist countries experience daily life in two conflicting ways—their lives consist of a tension between two competing consciousnesses—one established and developed long ago by bourgeois society, another struggling to be born.

First, there is the tension between that part of us that remains oblivious to the rape of the natural environment and the production of wasteful and destructive objects and that part that is re-evaluating our relations with nature, the work process, and production itself.

Second, there is the tension between that part of us that is making no effort to escape from the oppressive social relations of daily life and that part that is attempting to develop new social relations within the womb of bourgeois society.

Third, there is that part of us that is still afraid to question our ideas, value, and needs, and to get closer to our feelings and that part that is trying to subject our own lives to critical examination.

More and more, we are resolving these personal conflicts in favor of the new consciousness, and against the old, and transforming personal antagonisms into experiment and political conflict. The divided self is becoming a divided nation, consisting of two cultures, structures of feeling, modes of thought, and kinds of people. The nation reconstitutes itself into political divisions—imperialists and anti-imperialists, racists and anti-racists, male chauvinists and anti-chauvinists, authoritarians and anti-authoritarians.

These divisions run through the proletariat as a whole and between the ruling class and the proletariat. On the one side, the ruling class is homogeneous, experiences daily life in similar ways, and has similar needs. On the other side, the American working class is highly variegated, experiences daily life in many different ways, develops many different kinds of needs, and engages in many different kinds of politics —politics that today divide the proletariat from itself, but which contain the possibility of dividing the proletariat from the ruling class.

Today the ruling class is more united than divided and the proletariat is more divided than united. Revolutionary strategy seeks to unite the proletariat and divide the ruling class. The point of revolutionary strategy is therefore to dissolve the divisions between proletarian imperialists and anti-imperialists, racists and anti-racists, male chauvinists and anti-chauvinists, authoritarians and anti-authoritarians, and reconstitute them into the primary division—capitalists and anti-capitalists.

I am not saying that the traditional divisions between rich and poor do not exist, nor denying that capitalism produces a stratum of wealthy capitalists, managers, and professionals, on the one side, and a subproletariat of the poor, on the other. I am not saying that the poor do not have material needs that even advanced capitalism can not fulfill. I am saying that this division is no longer of basic significance, and that the fundamental antagonism is between those who are re-examining their lives and redefining their needs, those who are deciding that they do not want to have the kinds of needs produced by advanced capitalism, and those who accept the needs of daily life.

24

The main tendencies of twentieth-century capitalist development are threefold: first, the expansion of surplus value has required both an expansion of the proletariat and the general technical and cultural upgrading of the proletariat. On the one hand, the quantitative growth of the labor force has required the uprooting of the rural population, the mass migration of the Southern black and poor white population to the cities, the destruction of small-scale industry and farming, and the mass entry of women into factory and office employment. Twentieth-century capitalism has proletarianized the great majority of the population. On the other hand, the expansion of surplus value has required rapid advances in productivity, which in turn has required an increasingly economically sophisticated proletariat. Advanced capitalism has produced not only a larger working class, but also a new working class—not primarily in the form of a stratum of technical workers or "mind workers" but rather in the form of an entire work force educated to sophisticated techniques of production and social control. Advanced capitalism requires the development of new productive and synthetic processes, rational forms of work organization, rational control of raw material supplies, a "systems" approach to production, distribution, and social control. In turn, these require an expanding, educated proletariat. In short, capitalism becomes more rational, defining rationality by efficiency, productivity, and profitability criteria.

Second, the realization of surplus value has required new expanding markets, and the substitution of values in exchange for values in use, both domestically and internationally. In nineteenth-century capitalism, production was oriented to meeting those needs of the proletariat that were formed in production itself. The market consisted of the demand for investment goods and *wage goods,* the latter satisfying the needs of the worker *as* a worker. Today, the market consists of the demand for goods by the state, the demand for *consumer goods,* and, of least importance, the demand for investment goods. Consumer-goods production does not satisfy the needs of the worker *as* a worker alone, but also as a consumer, as a homeowner, a householder, a husband, a wife, an individual with leisure time.

The problem of realizing surplus value requires that the ruling class make the proletariat more aware of its needs—for example, modern advertising makes people keenly aware of their need for accomplishment, status, even love. It also requires that the ruling class manufacture new needs by increasing the level of expectations. And this requires product differentiation, advertising, sales, public relations, entertainment, sports —industries and activities that are need-producing. Realizing surplus value requires surveys of consumer behavior, motivational research, psychological depth studies, a greater emotional knowledge of the proletariat, the use of mass media to educate the proletariat that commodities will satisfy their deepest emotional needs. Modern capitalism produces a kind of sensitivity, the sensitivity of the salesman, the copywriter, the sports promoter, and the film director.

Both of these tendencies—the expansion and upgrading of the proletariat and the search for new markets—have led to the interpenetration of the economic base and superstructures, not merely to an expanded role of the government in the economy but also to the integration of all secondary institutions into production itself.

The home, the state, and especially the education system, are all sources of labor power and markets. Recreation, leisure-time, and culture are all markets. And following the spread of commodities and commodity culture into all spheres of life is the spread of social antagonisms from direct production into the secondary institutions.

The third major tendency of twentieth-century capitalism is the development of a political economic system designed to maintain the social order as a whole, engendering even more rationality and kinds of sensitivity. Keynesian planning is impossible without cost-of-living indexes, budgetary control, balance of payments analyses. Social planning is impossible without city planners, social workers, "humanistic" approaches to child care, education, not to speak of family counseling, school psychologists, and psychotherapy. Military planning is impossible without a science apparatus. And all of these activities rest on the development of an information industry, an information explosion, which includes "presentation depots" and "interpretation networks."

All of these tendencies taken together have produced a new kind of man. First, "rational man," with an ability to conceptualize, analyze, and synthesize, who can potentially identify well-being with the production and distribution of objects for human ends. Second, "sensitive man," who needs more intimacy and full social relations, and who can potentially identify well-being with a social order in which man can afford to be intimate and develop full social relations. Advanced capitalism produces awareness, partial and distorted as it is, including the potential awareness of the irrational character of capitalism itself.

By educating itself to the operation of the economy and society,

26

the ruling class, at times deliberately, and at times inadvertently, educates the proletariat as well. These tendencies produce a skilled, aware, curious, understanding, bright proletariat, a proletariat that is equipped to rule. Simultaneously, the ruling class further consolidates its own rule by concentrating economic power, monopolizing the science apparatus, running the education system, seizing control of the state budget from the Congress.

Capitalism educates man to new consumption horizons, and then shortens these horizons by producing wasteful and destructive objects. It teaches man that production is rational, and then hires man to waste and destroy. It programs man in school to perform as "human capital," and then hires man to create systems approaches to production, sales, and social problems, and to design, build, program, and control machinery.

Bourgeois thought teaches man that material production is the definition of well-being, and then the bourgeoisie orders the production of objects whose usefulness is subordinated to the need to sustain aggregate demand, to maintain the corporate liberal social order at home, and to maintain the imperialist system abroad. Bourgeois thought teaches man to respect nature, and then capitalist development wastes and destroys the productive forces by polluting the air and water, fouling the land, poisoning the food, the wild life, and man himself.

Advanced capitalism produces new experiences for which it has no satisfactory explanation, new promises of personal liberation and happiness that can not be fulfilled, new hopes that it shatters, a new rational, sensitive man reproducing himself in an environment in which there is less and less space to exercise rationality. It teaches that man is a historical subject, and treats man as an object. More and more, it defines man as an end, and treats man as a means. Needing historical understanding, the proletariat finds ideology, which constrains its intellectual development and historical consciousness. Needing emotional understanding, the proletariat finds manipulation and coercion, which constrains its emotional development and self-consciousness.

We are arguing that advanced capitalism has insinuated itself into every corner of daily life and has created a new proletariat and a new proletarian culture. It has spread into the home, leisure, recreation, culture, and education. The penetration of capital into the secondary institutions has transformed the social relations, the needs, the expectations, and the values of the proletariat. In general, the proletariat experiences

27

social relations as more impoverished—in the sense that there exists a greater discrepancy between bourgeois thought and promise versus perceived reality—more antagonistic, more alienated. Capitalism has created a social, physical, and ecological environment in which it is impossible for the masses of the people to establish trusting, loving, collective social relations.

Integral to the process of capitalist development, the "traditional" proletarian cultures made during earlier phases of capitalism in both urban and rural society have been destroyed. The candy store gives way to the drive-in; the neighborhood block to the "strip"; the ethnic neighborhood to the homogeneous suburb; the rural sharecropping culture to the urban black ghetto; the village and town to the metropolitan area. Modern capitalism has disintegrated earlier cultures and reintegrated culture around commodity production and consumption.

For these reasons, there exist fewer traditional avenues of escape from alienation in production. The humane, albeit conservatizing milieus of the family, neighborhood, village, and town have been all but fully destroyed. It literally becomes true that "you can't go home again."

When men and women escape the rule of commodities, the traditional conservatizing environments of the past disappear. The breakdown of neighborhood and community structures, and the growth of the super-organizations of capital and the state, combine to overwhelm large sectors of the population. At a time when escape from alienation becomes more necessary, it becomes impossible in bourgeois daily life.

A vast, variegated proletariat lives in isolation, its life outside of work organized around commodity consumption; its emotional survival dependent upon the establishment of new relations with objects, nature, and each other. As capital offers more and more distractions in the form of new and different commodities, these distractions become less and less involving. As the proletariat is promised personal liberation and fulfillment through commodities, it becomes more confused, irritated, and angry. Students rise up against authoritarian institutions; blacks burn the cities; street people reject alienated labor and attempt to establish their own turf in the streets; dropouts seek escape in the intimacy of personal encounter, mysticism, rural communes; the majority search for meaning in new wives and husbands, sexual excitement, escapist travel, television, and the heroism, controlled violence, and military precision of professional sports. Antagonistic social relations in the most chaotic, distorted, self-deceptive, and violent forms are displaced from

28

the factories and offices into the streets, the schools, the state, and the home.

Capital tries to contain the chaos in the only way it knows how. It attempts to turn these forms of escape, these outbursts, these new experiments in living, into more capital. Eye-drops are sold to "solve" the problem of air pollution; depressants to solve the problem of anxiety; stimulants to solve the problem of depression; objects for "homemaking" to solve the problem of broken families; "programs for urban reconstruction" to solve the problem of the black ghetto; "systems" approaches to solve the problem of control in the schools; "psychedelic items," pro football, and films which begin and end with the individual "doing his own thing" to solve the problem of a barren culture; and, probably, a decade from now, individual helicopters to solve the problem of transportation in Los Angeles County. And, simultaneously, capital attempts to explain these outbursts and this disintegration in terms of new but still mystified theories of human behavior.

When distractions no longer distract, and explanations no longer explain, capital is compelled to fall back on force, dehumanizing social relations still further. And the critique is extended into the courts, the jails, the army stockades, as well as the entire "corrections" system— relations with school principals, probation officers, social workers. In short, capital produces anger and rage and then produces commodity and fear to suppress this anger and rage. The effect, however, is a deepening of the anger and rage.

The new proletariat created by twentieth-century capitalism experiences alienation in many different ways, some which engender radical, potentially revolutionary political movements, some which do not. On the one hand, the majority of the white proletariat becomes confused and angry faced with "forces" that seem to be out of control—wages, inflation, taxes, youth questioning the meaning of patriotism, blacks questioning the meaning of Americanism. By and large, this majority is still preoccupied with "bread and butter" issues; it continues to define the good life as the acquisition of more things. One problem in particular bewilders this "middle America": the people in the working-class suburbs of Paterson, Detroit, and San Jose cannot understand why higher wages and income and the accumulation of more material objects do not make them happy, but instead more dissatisfied. They do not understand that they are workers producing not only the objects they buy to satisfy their needs, but they are also producing the needs that the objects satisfy. They are not aware that wage struggles and wage advances have helped to force capital to raise productivity, introduce new commodity lines, new production processes, exploit new raw materials, find new uses for existing raw materials, establish new industrial location patterns—and, in general, constantly modify and change the physical, ecological, and social environment. They are not aware that every advance in wages is paralleled by an expansion of needs. Yet today they are not as convinced as they were in the past that higher wages is the answer to their problems; nevertheless, they will strike for higher wages and continue to be preoccupied with quantitative issues until they understand fully that they are producing their own needs themselves, needs that they might not want to have.

On the other hand, there is a minority of the proletariat that experiences alienation in ways that lead to redefinitions of well-being, redefinitions of needs, and radical political movements. This minority consists of growing numbers of black people, youth, and women, and also includes a small but significant number of older white men—artists who no longer wish to sell their art, professionals, teachers, and intellectuals who are becoming indifferent to their careers, social service workers who are trying to serve the people and not the state administration or their higher-ups, and others who are redefining their jobs, their social relations, and their entire social existence in small, marginal, but potentially significant ways.

The most important critical practice today—the critique that takes the form of visible, organized action—consists of the struggle against the alienated social relations in the secondary institutions around the issues of imperialism, racism, male chauvinism, and authoritarianism. The traditional relations between black and white, women and men, and youth and age are disintegrating, and are being reintegrated along new lines. The process of the disintegration of alienated social relations and their reintegration around new principles, values, and needs—the process that we may call "de-alienation"—is rooted in the structure of capitalist production. Alienated labor and private property itself—the pillars of the capitalist mode of production—determine both the process of de-alienation in the secondary institutions, and the limits on this process.

Imperialism is experienced by the young in obvious ways—the mobilization for war, the draft, the tracking system, the army, repression by the police and the courts, all forms of alienated social relations outside of production itself. Imperialism is produced by capitalism in less obvious ways. The basic cause of modern imperialism is the need to expand and realize surplus value. As capitalism spills over national boundaries and creates a world division of labor, more people and physical resources are integrated into world capitalism as a whole. Economic integration requires social and political integration in forms that are consistent with private property relations. One expression of these new forms of social integration is the international conglomerate corporation; the other is the modern state, including the international organizations, militarism, and a world-wide military network.

The creation of a world proletariat, economic underdevelopment, colonialism and neo-colonialism, these are the pre-conditions for revolutionary wars around the themes of national liberation and economic development. Revolutionary wars engender counter-revolutionary, imperialist attacks—that is, capitalism in its final stages produces a revolution of the weak against the strong, wars of the strong on the weak, wars in which the weak win against the strong. Vietnam is the great watershed. Previous wars were fought between soldiers of nations; the Vietnamese war is fought between the army of one nation and a whole people.

The youth of advanced countries experience war, and the preparation and mobilization for war, not as a patriotic necessity but at the least as a nuisance and at the most as a heinous crime. War is not seen as meaningless, old-fashioned, but as meaningful only to capital.

These aspects of modern imperialism produce an anti-imperialist political movement, and figure in the revolt in the army, the draft resistance, the mass demonstrations, and the insurgency in the schools. The revolt produces more repression, and repression produces more revolt. And, finally, the revolt, because it is not informed either by a high level of theoretical understanding (historical consciousness) or emotional understanding (self-consciousness) begins to express the distortions of bourgeois society within itself—in the form of intolerance, insistence on the correct line, the outburst of rage and anger against all symbols of authority irrespective of rational strategic and tactical considerations, authoritarianism, chauvinism.

Like imperialism, *racism* is not specific to capitalism, but its present forms are specific to advanced capitalism. The expansion and realization of surplus value reshapes and reconstitutes the black population in two important ways. First, the mechanization of Southern agriculture provides new markets for Northern capital, and new efficiencies for capitalist

31

agriculture itself. Second, the great wars produced a serious labor shortage, which led to the uprooting of large sections of the Southern proletariat, both black and white. Blacks were pushed North by mechanization and pulled North by war: in these ways, capitalism proletarianized a largely rural black population. The white population, practicing its racism—partly pre-capitalist, partly produced by the slave South, partly integral to capitalist production—then ghettoized the black population.

Blacks are a permanently ghettoized proletariat in a society that has institutionalized racism—this fact is crucial for any understanding of the black movement against white racism. The general reason is that black people have been socialized into capitalist society, not in the earlier industrial capitalist stage but in the state capitalist stage—that is, at a time when the proletariat as a whole has acquired an abundance of expectations and needs. For blacks, even the illusion that these needs can be satisfied and expectations fulfilled is impossible: first, opportunities for upward mobility into independent business, professional, and farm careers are few and far between in the present era of corporate capital and corporate farming. Second, opportunities for geographical mobility, the acquisition of a little land, a home, and a small savings account—opportunities seized upon historically by the white proletariat, and ones that played an important role in conservatizing the white proletariat—are limited by institutionalized racism itself. Third, opportunities for well-paid jobs in the private sector of the economy are few; in fact, the private sector provides fewer and fewer jobs for blacks, who today are dependent upon the state for employment, welfare, and material help of all kinds.

The disparity between the high expectations of the modern working class and the perceived experience of the working class is thus greatest among black people. Although racism in the United States has been institutionalized for a very long time, it is only in the current era that blacks experience racism in all its varied, subtle, and cruel forms. Blacks experience daily life as proletarians, as a group that is partially integrated, but one that under capitalism can never be fully integrated into all institutions—business, unions, local government, schools, the state.

Again, the black revolt produces more repression, and repression produces more revolt. Again, black leaders acquire the need for a higher degree of historical consciousness and self-consciousness, the only insurance against the danger that the movement against white racism itself will reflect the distortions and impoverishment of bourgeois society. The development of the Black Panther Party—an anti-racist and anti-capitalist party—signifies a great leap forward not only for the black movement, but also for the proletariat as a whole.

Paralleling, and partly developing out of, the anti-imperialist and anti-racist political movements is anti-*authoritarianism,* which is the guiding idea for the development of an organized movement in the schools, and which is a strong tendency in the home. Again, we must try to show that the ways in which youth experience authority today generates an organized, political movement, rather than personal or cultural dissent.

As we have seen, expanded surplus value has meant the creation of a new proletariat, one which is socialized to capitalist society not in the factory but in the schools and colleges, which have become part of the productive apparatus. The schools retain their older function of socializing individuals into the acceptance of bourgeois values and thought; they still try to structure experience to produce a personality adaptable to bourgeois society. But they also take on two new functions: first, a technical function—the production of technical/administrative knowledge, research, and development, and other functions necessary for modern capitalist production. Second, the schools structure experience to produce a complex of feelings that are needed for survival not only in bourgeois society as a whole (for example, patriotism, racism), but also in work itself. In work, the manipulation of ideas, symbols, and people is increasingly important; in the "technostructure" of large corporations, in the state bureaucracy, in teaching and social work, in the hierarchy of labor unions, in sales and public relations, in entertainment and sports, modern employment requires men and women skilled in all phases of personal and ideological manipulation—that is, people schooled in the art of alienation.

With these goals primary, capitalism requires the streamlining of school organization on the basis of efficiency and rationality criteria. Time is rationed and programed; the teacher's flexibility is lost, as are individuals and individual differences. The authorities see the student population in urban America as a problem in mass social control. The contradiction between the bourgeois idea of individualism and personal fulfillment and the open and subtle repression of the individual deepens. With the introduction of tracking, specialization of functions and division of labor, teaching machines, closed-circuit television, and the rest of the paraphernalia of modern education introduced to control, mold, and produce a certain kind of personality, the school is transformed into a protofactory.

Like workers in the past, the students are forced to organize themselves to realize their own individuality, a difficult and subversive act, because one of the main lessons of the school is that youth should look to authority to settle their differences and resolve their conflicts. Now the youth are beginning to organize themselves, in radical student unions in the high schools and a host of organizations in the colleges. Faced in school with a specific kind of authority, which amounts to a synthesis between the authority of the parent and that of the factory, the students experience authority as a social phenomenon not a personal one, and one which necessarily has social solutions.

Like imperialism, racism, and authoritarianism, *male chauvinism* today expresses itself in forms that engender an organized, anti-chauvinist movement. As we know, capitalism requires an expanded proletariat to expand surplus value and new markets to realize surplus value. Increasingly, women supply the expansion in labor power and the new markets.

On the one side, the development of capitalism in the twentieth century would not have been possible without the integration of women into higher education, the use of women in electronics and other industries in which the work process consists of light assembly operations, retailing, insurance, military and other non-productive sectors that require masses of clerical and sales workers, and the state sector, which requires millions of teachers, social workers, and other non-manual employees.

On the other side, the exploitation of women in production requires the substitution of mass-produced commodities for those values traditionally produced in the home without pay. Women have helped to produce the commodities that fill the home and leisure time and also have helped to produce the need for those commodities.

The expanded role of women in the labor force and the penetration of commodities into the home is one general process, one which has placed women in an impossible situation. On the one hand, women enter the labor force in search of "satisfaction in work," "creative jobs," and "the opportunity to acquire things for home and self." Or all three. On the other hand, bourgeois society continues to sanctify the family and attempts to convince women that their basic social role consists of maintaining a happy, comfortable home. Women learn to be "high need

34

achievers" and to adapt themselves to the male bourgeois ethic of personal ambition and success and simultaneously learn that they must subordinate their own aspirations to their primary role as homemaker. The mass media, the women's magazines, the government, and business propaganda promise "productive careers" and "creative homemaking" through commodities, and simultaneously drum away at the theme of women as submissive to men and as the mainstay of the home. This theme repeats itself in the entreaties and demands of the husband, who wants to escape alienated labor in leisure, to be taken care of, who believes that he needs a passive, dependent mate.

Women experience life as a series of conflicting demands, feeling bitterness and anger toward men and themselves after experiencing the frustrations and disappointments of alienated labor. They seek a kind of liberation in work, find alienation, and become more dependent on men. They feel ambivalent toward commodities and work-saving devices, wanting them and depending on them but resenting them because they threaten any creativity that women may have experienced in relation to their homemaking tasks. Their job is alienating, and there is less and less necessary work in the household; both factors combine to force women to find their identities through men and dependence on men. Still more expectations are acquired via the identification with "male ambition," which engenders still more dependency. The fact that for most women jobs are temporary and sex-typed, that the stereotyped characteristics of women that exist prior to their entering the labor force are maintained and reinforced in work, inhibit the development of a proletarian consciousness, and also serve to force women back to a dependency on men.

These tendencies combine to produce a need for an awareness on the part of women themselves as a definite, oppressed social category. The women's liberationist experiences male chauvinism as a social phenomenon, not only as an individual one, and learns that she can find her individuality only in a collective endeavor. Quarrels in the home, disappointment, hurt, self-hate, and rage—these emotions that follow the curve of the growth of material production—are experienced as feelings requiring social solutions. She replaces the older, social redefinition of herself with a new one. Free to leave her man and not starve, she requires a total transformation of her relations with men, and of her dependence on the social milieu of the family. And this project again

35

requires the further development of historical and self-consciousness and the transformation of all alienated relations, including alienated labor, or runs the risk of certain defeat.

All of these movements—by blacks, women, and youth—link up their action-critique of social relations with a critique of production itself. The draft resister opposes the allocation of the largest part of the federal budget for military spending. The black militant begins to link racism with the utilization of public funds for business-oriented urban renewal, rather than for the needs of the black community. The women's liberationist sees male chauvinism in all advertising and all fashions. The youth begins to see the school-as factory, the teacher-as-foreman, and the book-as-industrial raw material. The radical teacher opposes the fiscal starvation of the school; the radical social worker the fiscal starvation of the welfare budget; the radical scientist the rape of nature; the radical industrial worker and technician the production of unsafe, wasteful, useless objects. All in the opposition mount demands for a reorientation of production—free abortions, free client-controlled child care centers, more classrooms, black-controlled ghetto redevelopment, curbs on the automobile industry, the oil industry.

All of these critiques and demands reflect a certain stage in the development of the American proletarian consciousness. When critiques of this depth and scope express themselves in action, the demands of the people seem to the ruling class to be chaotic and "irrational." In fact, these demands and this action, however distorted, uninformed, and misinformed, are *total*. At a certain point, the ruling class can no longer contain the proletariat, and social democracy and corporate liberalism cease to be possible.

I have been arguing that the crucial subject for revolution in advanced capitalist countries is the development of historical consciousness and self-consciousness, theoretical understanding and emotional awareness. Why is this such a crucial subject? Because in the advanced capitalist countries the bourgeoisie rules by ruling consciousness, and because we inherit no useful programs from the ruling class. Our program is not economic development but rather the construction of a different society with different social relations. We do not want to structure experience in order to maximize the work effort, productivity, and production. We want to structure experience in order to maximize the free development of the individual and his social relations.

36

We are not utopians. We cannot create the good society out of our heads. Rather, we must identify those movements that are out of necessity reintegrating social relations around emerging principles, values, and needs. We must work with them, encourage them, and struggle with them.

A pre-condition for this is an understanding of how capitalism forms not only a bourgeois consciousness, but also an anti-bourgeois consciousness. It is not that social relations today are "objectively" more brutalizing, cruel, and inhumane. If anything, the opposite is true. It is rather that capitalism has produced new needs and expectations which it cannot fulfill, and which demand political solutions.

It follows that the individual needs to understand his social condition, social relations, and himself. Capitalist production impoverishes social relations, yet continues to identify the good life with material abundance. The individual who cannot find satisfaction in either work or consumption lives not in the role of slave or serf or nineteenth-century factory hand, but in the context of a society that prides itself on its rationality and efficiency and which demands an explanation for everything.

Advanced capitalism attempts to provide explanations for the emptiness, boredom, deception and self-deception, coercion, and terror of modern life through psychoanalysis and antiquated definitions of "human nature." These explanations run from Freud through Fromm and Spock, from social Darwinism to modern social psychology, from the bohemian poets of the 1920's to Tim Leary. All of these explanations of the human condition are ideological.

These ideas, and the men who put them forward, are trusted, but prove to be untrustworthy. The practice of the ideas of a Kennedy does not end imperialism, but obfuscates it. The practice of the ideas of Booker T. Washington and Martin Luther King does not end racism, but frustrates efforts to end and understand it. The practice of the ideas of Ben Spock does not alleviate the anxiety of parents about child-raising, but intensifies it. The ideas of the women's magazines, that work and homemaking around commodity consumption produce a happy, stable home, do not remove the antagonism between men and women but expand it.

Advanced capitalism thus produces not only more needs in general, but specifically the need for more explanations and a different practice, the need for trustworthy ideas, and a trustworthy practice. Ultimately,

37

capitalism produces the need for Marxism, a class analysis, one which roots the experience of social relations in alienated labor itself. One which leads an individual to realize that his social relations are impoverished not because the individual is a youth, a woman, or black alone, but because the individual is a proletarian. An individual who no matter how successfully he fights alienated relations in the impersonal secondary institutions still faces racism, authoritarianism, and male chauvinism in production itself. An individual who is saying "no" to those who oppress him or her in the secondary institutions but is still compelled to say "yes" to those same people in production, in the work experience.

I conclude with what might be called a morphology of consciousness, a historical categorization of degrees of consciousness.

First, I think the "movement" today encompasses all those who engage in the theoretical and practical critique of bourgeois social relations in secondary institutions. It encompasses blacks who say to whites, "I am not an object. I am a man. I am a woman"; women and youth who are intellectually and emotionally aware that their social condition is not explicable in terms of sex or age alone, but in terms of their social relations with men and women. In short, it encompasses all those who have obtained a degree of historical consciousness, and who are acting upon it.

Second, I think the "revolutionary movement" encompasses all those who engage in the theoretical critique of bourgeois production relations. It encompasses blacks who say to whites *and* blacks, "It is not a question of race alone, but of class"; blacks who are intellectually aware that their social condition is not explicable in terms of their "blackness" and social relations with whites alone, but in terms of their production relations with capital. It encompasses youth who say to their elders *and* other youth, "It is not a question of age, but of class"; youth who are intellectually aware that their social condition is not explicable in terms of their age and their social relations with their elders alone, but in terms of their production relations. It encompasses women who say to men *and* other women, "It is not a question of sex, but of class"; women who are aware that their social condition is not explicable in terms of their sex and social relations with men alone, but in terms of their production relations. In short, it encompasses all those who have obtained a high degree of historical consciousness, but not a corresponding degree of self-consciousness.

38

Third, there is the "uncritical revolutionary movement," largely invisible, because it is unorganized, spontaneous. It encompasses all those who engage in a critique of bourgeois production relations through their own practice at work; all those in production who say to themselves, "I am not an object. I am a man. I am a woman"; workers who are emotionally aware that their condition is not explicable in terms of their race, age, sex, or social relations in secondary institutions alone, but in terms of their immediate production relations. It encompasses all those who have attained a high degree of self-consciousness, but remain unselfconscious historically, which defines and limits the significance of their actions. It encompasses the auto worker, for example, who feels confused, angry, fearful, and who strikes back through sabotage—as an individual act, a self-deceptive form of struggle, one which is potentially murderous or suicidal.

Fourth, what might come to be called in the future the "socialist revolution" encompasses all those who engage in a theoretical and practical critique of bourgeois production relations, those who mount an action-critique against production as well as the superstructures. It encompasses workers who say to their supervisors, "I am not an object. I am a man. I am a woman," and who say to other workers, "It is not a question of you and your supervisor, it is a question of wage labor and capital, a question of alienated labor, a process which you actively participate in." It encompasses workers who are intellectually and emotionally aware that their social condition is explicable only in terms of the production relations, that is, capitalism itself, and who are practicing the de-alienation of labor.

Socialist revolutionary thought and practice must widen and deepen both historical consciousness and self-consciousness—it must dissolve in theory and practice the secondary contradictions to force the struggle into the primary contradiction itself: capitalism as a system. Revolutionary socialist thought and practices must develop alternatives to a social order based on alienated labor, alternatives based on the development of social planning. It includes the understanding that machines do not control men, but capital does. It includes the feeling that alienated labor does not consist of a particular kind of work, but rather working in an alienated state.

It also consists of the giving back to capital the anger and rage that blacks feel toward whites, women toward men, youth toward age—the

39

rage and anger that at present the proletariat has displaced and turns on itself, but that should be expressed against capital in production.

It consists of the opening up of psychic space, emotional space, for the development of human relations within the proletariat, in order that the struggle against capital intensify, as the proletariat develops a capacity for more solidarity, more trust.

Socialist revolution is a process that simultaneously negates bourgeois society and creates a new society, a process in which the struggle for humanity is inseparable from the struggle against the bourgeoisie. In the process, the proletariat recognizes its two enemies, the bourgeoisie and itself, its own self-alienation.

In the struggle, the proletariat ceases to alienate itself, and alienates the bourgeoisie. The proletariat puts back its anger on the bourgeoisie, forcing on the bourgeoisie instrumental relations, hateful relations, relations embodying the anger that was once the proletariat's toward itself. The confidence and self-assurance of the bourgeoisie become the confidence and self-assurance of the proletariat. The "restlessness" of the proletariat becomes the "restlessness" of the bourgeoisie. And the cry in the land, "don't fuck me over, don't fuck over my body and mind!" becomes the cry of the bourgeoisie.

3

JOHN M. CAMMETT

Socialism and Participatory Democracy

John M. Cammett is Professor of History at the John Jay College of Criminal Justice, City University of New York. While teaching at Rutgers University in the mid-1960's, he was one of the founding members of the Socialist Scholars Conference. Since then, he has continued to serve as a member of the SSC Steering Committee. His best known work is *Antonio Gramsci and the Origins of Italian Communism* (1967).

The relation between socialism and democracy is not a new concern, either for American socialism or for socialist movements elsewhere. Nor is the core issue one of direct rule, of self-government at the grass roots. In the socialist tradition, participatory democracy was discussed most often with regard to workers' control. Few have related workers' control to socialism more suggestively, and few today enjoy as much influence on a new generation of socialists, as the great early leader of the Italian Communist Party, Antonio Gramsci. Both in theory and in practice, his work on the creation of "Italian Soviets" (in 1919) stands out as a notable answer to a most contemporary question: what is the place of working men in a free, non-repressive socialism?

According to Gramsci, the socialist state "already exists potentially in the institutions of social life characteristic of the exploited working class." The basic condition of this new state was that all the workers enter the framework of socialist institutions, for only so could the whole

41

class become aware of its role. None of the existing institutions of the working class could meet this condition. The party was hardly in a position to assimilate the entire working class in a short period of time. The trade unions spoke only for the organized members of specific trades and, in any case, proposed only limited goals, such as improvements in wages and hours; hence, the future did not lie with them.

It was necessary to create another institution, which could organize the proletariat to "educate itself, gather experience, and acquire a responsible awareness of the duties incumbent upon classes that hold state power." The new institution should also contain, in itself, the model for the proletarian state (p. 11).* The soviet, and more particularly the factory-shop committees, as developed in Russia, met both of these requirements. Gramsci regarded the internal committee as a potential soviet.[1]

On October 31, 1919, the first general assembly of the Turin factory commissars discussed and approved a program of general concepts and specific regulations for the further organization of factory councils. The "Program," of which Gramsci was the chief editor, is especially noteworthy for the importance which it attributes to the education of the working class. The commissars were responsible for organizing, within the factory, a school for increasing the workers' skills in their own trades or industrial functions. In addition to these "Labor Schools," *Ordine nuovo* established a "School of Culture and Socialist Propaganda" in December 1919, attended by both university students and workers.[2]

---

* All page references in the text are to the ninth volume of Gramsci's collected works: *L'Ordine nuovo, 1919–1920* (Turin: Einaudi, 1954). Translations into English are by the author of this paper.

[1] Gramsci reprinted or commissioned a goodly number of articles for *L'Ordine nuovo* by Russian and other foreign communists on the nature of the Russian soviet. Cf. especially John Reed, "I Commisari di reparte nella Rivoluzione russa," *L'Ordine nuovo*, I, 23 (October 25, 1919).

[2] "Il Programma dei commisari di reparte" (November 8, 1919), *L'Ordine nuovo*, p. 194. It is interesting to compare the earlier Russian "Resolution of the Factory-Shop Committees" (June 1917) with Gramsci's later "Programma." For the most part, the Russian document concentrates on the administrative aspects of worker control over production, but Article Five does refer to the role of the Committees in changing the mentality of the worker. "Only Workers' Control over capitalist enterprises, cultivating the workers' conscious attitude toward work, and making clear its social meaning, can create conditions favorable to the development of a firm self-discipline in labor, and the development of all labor's possible "productivity" (The Resolution" as given in the "Appendix" to John Reed, *Ten Days That Shook the World,* New York: Modern Library, 1935, p. 330).

Gramsci, Togliatti, and other socialist leaders gave frequent lectures there, as did several professors from the University of Turin.[3]

For Gramsci, the point of this and other educational activities undertaken by the *Ordine nuovo* group was twofold: (1) to convince the working class through the councils "that it is in their interest to submit to a permanent discipline of culture, to develop a conception of the world and the complex and intricate system of human relations, economic and spiritual, that form the social life of the globe" (p. 447), and (2) to prepare for the technical aspects of the seizure of power. This task was primarily one of training the workers to become autonomous producers. The commissars were therefore required to study "bourgeois systems of production" and whenever possible to suggest ways of accelerating production by eliminating unnecessary work. If technical innovations—even those proposed by management—seemed useful in production, the workers should be urged to accept them, even at the cost of "temporary damage" to their interests, provided that the industrialists were also willing to make sacrifices (p. 198). In this way, the worker would begin to think of himself not as a wage earner but as a producer, with an awareness of his precise place in the process of production "in all its levels, from the factory, to the nation, to the world" (p. 46).

By now it will be apparent that the Gramsci of this period did not focus his attention on the political party as such. The very inadequacies of the political party, as Gramsci had experienced it during this critical period in the history of Italy, led him to attribute to the workers' councils many of the functions which he would later attempt to incorporate in a new type of party. Still, even at this time, Gramsci laid the firm foundations for his later and much more sophisticated view of what the political party of the working class can and must do. Consider, for example, the following judgment, written in July of 1920:

> . . . in an historical period dominated by the bourgeois class, all the forms of association (even those which the working class has built to carry on its struggle) inasmuch as they are born and develop on the terrain of liberal democracy, are necessarily inherent to the bourgeois system and the capitalist structure. Since they are born and developed

[3] Paolo Spriano, ed., *L'Ordine nuovo, 1919–1920* (Turin, Einaudi, 1963), p. 37, n. 1. Also Togliatti, "Creare una scuela" (November 15, 1919), *ibid.,* pp. 358–62.

with the birth and development of capitalism, they therefore decay and become corrupt with the decay and corruption of the system in which they are incorporated (p. 140).

On the other hand, says Gramsci, the factory council is "original" precisely because it arises where the "political relations of citizen to citizen" do not exist, where "democracy and freedom" do not exist for the working class but rather the naked economic relations of exploiter to exploited.

The *contingent* character of the trade union has been recognized as far back as the *Communist Manifesto* itself. But Gramsci saw even this problem from a fresh angle. The trade union, he says, originated in reaction to hostile historical conditions (*imposto*) rather than as an autonomous formulation of the workers (*proposto*). Dependent as the trade union was upon capitalist laws, it did not have a "constant and predictable line of development"; hence, it was incapable of embodying a positive revolutionary movement (p. 15).

The trade union was limited in freedom of action by its increasing observance of strict legality in relations with the propertied class (pp. 131–133). Indeed, its legalism was the best guarantee of its ability to perform its proper task, the negotiation of labor contracts. Increasing size and the development of a centralized bureaucracy had gradually detached the trade unions from the masses. But this ostensible weakness was the real strength of the trade-union movement. Its detached bureaucracy was beyond reach of the tumultuous masses; therefore, it was able to contract pacts and assume obligations.

Nevertheless, industrial legality was a temporary compromise, justified only in circumstances unfavorable to the working class. Unfortunately, however, the trade-union movement often viewed industrial legality as a *perpetual* compromise. In this event, clashes with the frankly revolutionary institutions of the working class were inevitable.

The factory council negated industrial legality, since its primary purpose was to educate the working class for the seizure of power through control over production; whereas the union, to guarantee continuity of labor and wages to the workers, insisted upon the maintenance of industrial legality. "The council tends, because of its revolutionary spontaneity, to unleash the class war at any moment; the union, because of its bureaucratic form, tends to prevent the class war from ever being unleashed."

44

Gramsci's ideas on the relationship of the Socialist Party to the factory council were based on the same premise used in his analysis of the trade union; namely, that the development of the party into a revolutionary organ was hindered by its origin in a capitalist society as an organ of competition with the bourgeoisie. The rules of the game were determined for the Socialist Party too by the basic principles of bourgeois democracy (pp. 98 and 141).[4] The organizational "form" of the Socialist Party, like that of other parties, was the "general assembly" of its members. The aim was to conquer a majority of votes "by the method proper to democracy—by displaying before the electorate programs as generic as they are muddled (and promising to realize them at any cost)." Like those of other parties, the meetings of the Socialist Party produced their share of "irresponsibility, incompetence, volubility, and tumult," defects which were repaired by the equally traditional method of "bureaucratic imposition by the executive officers" (p. 141).

But according to Gramsci the party could avoid the dangers inherent in this situation by encouraging the development of a strong council movement. This would root the party in the *economic life of the working class itself.*

The party, as the "vanguard of the proletariat," was composed of the most class-conscious and disciplined members of the working class. It stood above the transient interests of that class in order to direct the long-range struggle for the conquest of power. With its superior discipline, knowledge of the "laws" of historical development, close analysis of contemporary events, and intimate awareness of conditions among the laboring masses, it was equipped to delineate the strategy and tactics of the class struggle (especially pp. 67–71).

The council, on the other hand, was charged with the economic and political education, of the whole laboring mass, to be achieved

---

[4] A possible source for Gramsci's ideas on the nature of the Socialist Party under capitalism is Daniel De Leon's *Socialist Reconstruction of Society* (New York: Labor News, 1930), a speech delivered at Minneapolis in July 1905. De Leon says, for example, "Socialism is the outgrowth of the higher development from capitalism. As such, the methods of the Socialist movement on its march toward Socialist society are perforce primarily dictated by the capitalist shell from which Socialism is hatching" (p. 39). And again, "The reason for a political party, we have seen, is to contend with capitalism on its own special field—the field that determines the fate of political power. It follows that the structure of a political party must be determined by the capitalist governmental system of territorial demarcations" (p. 46).

through control over production. Ultimately, the councils would replace the State as the organ of government. Nevertheless, Gramsci recognized the possibility that many councils would support for a time the non-socialist ideologies of the proletariat, particularly syndicalism and anarchism. This was so because the unqualified democracy of the council reflects the momentary interests and tumultuous desires of the masses (pp. 59–60).

The party had no control over the course of events among the masses unless the masses gave their allegiance to the party. But complete identity of party and working class was possible only after a long period of education. In the meantime the council, which was capable of organizing the entire working class, could attempt to control the revolutionary process. The council, in turn, could facilitate and discipline the revolution only so long as it was completely responsive to its workers —that is, truly democratic. For this reason the party was urged not to impose its own judgments and beliefs upon the councils, lest they lost contact with the mood actually prevailing among the masses. According to Gramsci, the German revolutionary movement in 1919 failed because the Social Democrats attempted to impose councils controlled by their own men upon the workers; hence, the revolution was "shackled and domesticated" (p. 68). In such a case the revolutionary movement would certainly continue, but it would no longer be subject to any control, because the council, the only body immediately responsive to the mood of the workers, would no longer truly represent their desires.

Gramsci was unyielding on the question of absolute representativeness in the councils, even in the face of a torrent of criticism from other socialist leaders. At the same time that he was subjecting anarchism to devastating theoretical criticism,[5] he defended the presence of anarchists in the councils and even included one libertarian on the staff of *Ordine nuovo*.

Gramsci's defense of members of the Catholic party (*Partito popolare italiano*) as council members was even more courageous in those days of notorious priest-baiting, long before anyone dreamed of a Marxist-Christian "dialogue." The Popular Party, said Gramsci, is a necessary phase in the development of the Italian proletariat toward communism. It creates "associationism" and solidarity where socialism at present could not, that is among the peasantry (pp. 284–86). To

[5] Cf. J. M. Cammett, *Antonio Gramsci and the Origins of Italian Communism* (Stanford, Calif.: Stanford University Press, 1967), pp. 123–28.

socialist fears that some councils might fall under the control of Catholics Gramsci responded, "Should Bergamo [a stronghold of the PPI] be put to fire and sword? Should those workers and peasants who politically follow the left wing of the Popular Party be extirpated from Italian soil?" Gramsci asserted that Italian socialism would have quite enough to do with its civil war against reaction without also beginning a religious war. Socialists must recognize that the Vatican did exist in Italy, that Catholicism was a real political force. The workers' State, like the liberal State, would be obliged to find a system of equilibrium with the spiritual force of the Church (pp 475–476).

Gramsci so emphasized the obligations of the party and trade union to the council that his words frequently sound as though he believed in the possibility of a "spontaneous" revolution of the working class without the political direction and discipline afforded by the party. We have seen that Gramsci's theoretical judgment of political parties as such was not really so negative; however, he had become increasingly aware that the Italian Socialist Party had far too many shortcomings to direct the course of the revolution successfully. In 1919 he believed that the party could be renewed from below by the construction of the councils, but the failure of the Italian Revolution in 1920 convinced him that only a reorganization of the party could ensure the success of the councils. Meanwhile, Gramsci's experience in the council movement led him to an abiding awareness of two fundamental principles: the need for an autonomous party of the working class, unbeholden in any way to the bourgeoisie, and the related need for that party to be completely responsive to the workers, to practice internal democracy.[6]

In September of 1920, the factory council movement in Italy was crushed. In the meantime, foreign invasion and white reaction had destroyed the Hungarian Soviets, while Karl Liebknecht and Rosa Luxemburg had become the martyrs of the abortive German revolution.

---

[6] The Gramscian notion of autonomy might be applied to the current debate on "black power." The germ of reality in the latter is the attempt of a social group to retreat temporarily in order to prepare a later advance from a position of greater "autonomy," not to struggle within the framework of the "political relations of citizen to citizen." This is the terrain marked out by the ruling class, and it is perhaps no better adapted to the black masses than purely parliamentary struggle was to the socialist movement. True enough, "black power" is ultimately no more than an aspect of "workers' power." But in the short run, the former is not identical with the latter.

Still, the Bolshevik regime managed to overcome all obstacles in Russia. Failure in Central and Western Europe and success in Russia. This was the supreme reality for Marxists in the early 1920's.

As usual, Lenin anticipated everyone else in distinguishing the problems of revolution in backward countries from those in advanced countries. In his speech on "War and Peace" of March 7, 1918, Lenin insisted that the European revolution "will not come as quickly as we expected . . . we must be able to reckon with the fact that the world socialist revolution cannot begin so easily in the advanced countries as the revolution began in Russia—the land of Nicholas and Rasputin, the land in which the overwhelming majority of the population were quite indifferent to the conditions of life of the people in the outlying regions. In such a country it was quite easy to start a revolution, as easy as lifting a feather. But it is wrong, absurd, without preparation to start a revolution in a country in which capitalism is developed, which has produced a democratic culture and has organized every man." [7]

Very few communist leaders showed Gramsci's originality in developing these ideas. His analysis is important, for upon it depended not merely the tactics and strategy of revolution but also his theory of the political party itself. In a discussion of 1923 on the united front policy of the Communist International, a policy which Gramsci viewed favorably, he observed that "Three years of experience have taught us, not only in Italy, how deeply rooted are social-democratic traditions, and how difficult it is to destroy the residue of the past with simple ideological polemics. A vast and detailed political action is necessary to distintegrate this tradition by disintegrating the organism that personifies it." [8]

The following year Gramsci raised his analysis to a much higher level. Amadeo Bordiga, the leader of the left wing of Italian communism, had argued that the Russian revolution was "not determined by the historical situation." On the other hand, Bordiga believed, in the spirit of what might be called "conventional" Marxism, that in the more advanced countries "the historical mechanism functions according to all

[7] *Selected Works,* Volume VII; *After the Seizure of Power, 1917–1918* (New York: International Publishers, 1946), pp. 294–95. This speech was not published until 1923. Even today it deserves careful study as a model of how a revolutionary leader behaved in an apparently all but hopeless situation.

[8] Gramsci, Letter of May 18, 1923, in Togliatti (ed.), *La Formaziono del gruppo dirigente del PCI nel 1923–1924* (Rome: Riuniti, 1962), p. 65.

the Marxist sacraments." There the task of revolution would be much simpler, no more than the organization of a "proper" Communist Party to help the revolution along.

Gramsci disagreed. He argued that the development of capitalism in Central and Western Europe had not only produced a large mass of proletarians "but also created an upper stratum, the working-class aristocracy with its annexes of trade-union bureaucracy and social-democratic groups. The direct determinism that moved the Russian masses in the streets to revolutionary assaults was complicated in Central and Western Europe by all the political superstructures created by the greater development of capitalism; it rendered mass action slower and more cautious, and therefore demands from the revolutionary party a system of strategy and tactics much more complex and long-range than those used by the Bolsheviks between March and November 1917.[9]

In a report of 1926 to the Central Committee of his party, a report first published in April 1967, Gramsci sharpened his analysis by distinguishing between general conditions in those capitalist states which are "the keystone of the bourgeois system" and those states on the "periphery" of the capitalist world: ". . . in the countries of advanced capitalism the ruling class possesses political and organizational reserves which it did not have, for example, in Russia. That means that even the most serious economic crises do not have immediate repercussions in the political field. Politics always runs behind, and greatly behind, the economy. The state apparatus is much more resistant than is often thought and in moments of crisis succeeds in organizing forces more faithful to the regime than the depth of the crisis would indicate. . . . In the peripheral states such as Italy, Poland, Spain, and Portugal, the state forces are less efficient. But in these countries we have a phenomenon of the greatest importance. . . . in these countries between the proletariat and capitalism there is a broad stratum of intermediate classes which wishes to and in a certain sense succeeds in carrying out its own politics with ideologies which often influence broad strata of the proletariat but which have a special effect on the peasant masses.[10]

Gramsci illustrated the political anomalies of the second group of countries by reference to developments in Italy in the 1920's: "In 1919

[9] Letter of February 9, 1924, ibid., pp. 196–97.
[10] Gramsci, "Un rapporto inedito al partito (Relazione alla riunione del Comitato direttivo del PCI del 2–3 agosto, 1926," Rinascita, XXIV, 15 (April 14, 1967), 23.

and '20 the military and political formations of the middle classes were represented in Italy by primitive fascism and by D'Annunzio. It is well known that in those years both the fascist movement and D'Annunzio's movement were also prepared to align themselves with the revolutionary proletarian forces to overthrow Nitti's government which appeared to be the intermediary of American capitalism to subjugate Italy. . . . The second phase of fascism—1921 and '22— was clearly reactionary. From '23 there began a molecular process by which the most active elements of the middle classes moved from the reactionary fascist camp to the camp of the Aventine opposition." (We might add that this phase ended three months after Gramsci delivered this report.) Significantly, Gramsci referred to this pattern of phases in Italy as "classic and exemplary" with regard to "almost all" the peripheral countries of capitalism.

For him, the principal meaning of this situation was that, under certain circumstances, it permitted more radical political action of the working class toward certain elements of the middle class. For us, it has, I think, some larger meanings. This analysis helps us to understand why a multi-party system is normally possible in such "peripheral" countries. In weak capitalist states it is much harder to establish "organic" unity of the middle classes, except when the element of force imposes such a unity (use of force toward this end is the ultimate meaning of fascism). Moreover the "peripheral" countries of capitalism are no longer for the most part in Europe but rather in the Third World. Gramsci's distinctions might be very useful in developing more adequate Marxian ideas on the political and revolutionary possibilities in these newly emerging countries. Under what concrete circumstances can a so-called national bourgeoisie play a revolutionary role? And what conditions impell it to reaction?

In any case, Gramsci's general theory of revolution in Central and Western Europe encouraged him to regard the political party as a much more *creative* instrument than it had been hitherto regarded by Marxists. Lenin was of course the primary inspiration for Gramsci's views, but in some respects the Italian leader was even more "voluntaristic" than the Russian. Gramsci gave little importance to the "objective conditions" for revolution, such as the existence of a great economic depression. In any case "objective conditions for the proletarian revolution have existed in Europe for more than fifty years." The principal requisite was to "be more political, to know how to use the political element, to be less

50

afraid of making politics." [11] Now for Gramsci, at least, politics do not merely "come out of the barrel of a gun." Political action must also be an act of "persuasion." Gramsci's theory of hegemony was grounded in this conviction. It is probably his most important contribution to the theory of the political party.

In his elaboration of the concept of hegemony, Gramsci made use of an old distinction in the history of political thought: that between "political society" and "civil society." The former is made up of public institutions and organs of coercion (the army, the courts, the State bureaucracy); the latter is the totality of private institutions (Church schools, political parties).[12] The relevance of this distinction to the problem of hegemony will soon become clear.

A British student of Gramsci's thought has provided us with a useful introductory definition of the problem: hegemony is "an order in which a certain way of life and thought is dominant, in which one concept of reality is diffused throughout society in all its institutional and private manifestations, informing with its spirit all taste, morality, customs, religious and political principles, and all social relations, particularly in their intellectual and moral connotations." [13] It follows that a hegemony is the predominance, obtained by consent rather than force, of one class or group over other classes. Hegemony is therefore achieved by institutions of civil society.

In its general sense, hegemony refers to the "spontaneous" loyalty that any dominant social group obtains from the masses by virtue of its social and intellectual prestige and its supposedly superior function in the world of production. Thus the Italian bourgeoisie exercised an almost unchallenged hegemony over the workers and peasants from 1870 to 1890, following its successful conclusion of Italian unification and before the birth of the Italian Socialist Party, with a competing and "autonomous" ideology.[14] In a more restricted sense, Gramsci uses the term "hegemony" to refer to projected alliances of a predominant

[11] Athos Lisa, "Discussione politica con Gramsci in carcere," *Rinascita*, XXI, 49 (December 12, 1964), 20.

[12] *Gli Intellectuali e l'erganizzazione della cultura* [Opere di Antonio Gramsci, III] (Turin: Einaudi, 1949), p. 9. Cf. also *Passato e presente*, pp. 164–65.

[13] Gwynn A. Williams, "Gramsci's Concept of *Egemonia*," *Journal of the History of Ideas*, XXI, 4 (October–December 1960), 587.

[14] *Gli Intellettuali*, p. 9.

working class with other "subaltern" but "progressive" social elements, especially the peasantry, parts of the petty bourgeoisie, and the intelligentsia. Even in a socialist state, the term "hegemony" would still be useful to indicate the social (or civil) form of the workers' state based on consent—in contrast to the "dictatorship of the proletariat," based on force, which would be the state's political form.[15]

The development of hegemony depends on the "level of homogeneity, self-consciousness, and organization" reached by a given social class. Mere awareness of economic interests is not sufficient: the class must be convinced that its "own economic interests, in their present and future development, go beyond the corporative circle of a merely economic group, and can and must become the interests of other repressed groups. This is the most purely political phase, which marks the passage from structure to the sphere of complex superstructures." At this point, the class has truly become a party, and it must now fight for its intellectual and moral values, as well as its economic and political ends. The leading class must also coordinate its interests with those "allied" classes. In this new equilibrium the "interests of the dominant group will prevail," but not to the point of fully achieving only its own "crude" economic interests.[16]

The fundamental assumption behind Gramsci's view of hegemony is that the working class, before it seizes state power, must establish its claim to be a ruling class in the political, cultural, and "ethical" fields.[17] The founding of a ruling class is equivalent to the creation of a *Weltanschauung*."[18] This idea, of great theoretical importance for the development of socialism, was basic to Gramsci's work at least as far back as the days of *Ordine nuovo* and the factory-council movement. For Gramsci, a social class scarcely deserves the name until it becomes *conscious* of its existence as a class; it cannot play a role in history until it develops a comprehensive world-view and a political program.[19]

---

[15] Cf. Vezio Crisafulli, "State e società nel pensiere di Gramsci," *Società,* VIII (December 1951), 593.

[16] *Note sul Machiavelli, sulla politica, e sullo Stato moderno* [*Opere di Antonio Gramsci,* V] (Turin: Einaudi, 1949), pp. 45–46.

[17] Cf. *Il Risorgimento* [*Opere di Antonio Gramsci,* IV] (Turin: Einaudi, p. 70.

[18] *Il Materialismo storico e la filosofia di Benedetto Croce* [*Opere di Antonio Gramsci,* II] (Turin: Einaudi, 1948), p. 75.

[19] Cf. Serafino Cambareri, "Il Concetto di egemonia nel pensiere di A. Gramsci," *Studi gramsciani* (Rome: Riuniti, 1958), p. 91.

The "orthodox" school of Marxism, in the late nineteenth and early twentieth centuries, was riddled with "economism" and materialism, a climate that left no room for problems of hegemony. For Gramsci, it was Lenin who revived Marxism as a creative philosophy: Lenin, "in opposition to various 'economistic' tendencies" reaffirmed the importance of hegemony in his conception of the State and gave the cultural "front" as much emphasis as the economic and political fronts.[20] Lenin's struggle against "economism" and "tailism" (or "spontaneity") led him to stress the necessity of educating the masses in a revolutionary sense. Moreover, his theory of the political party was founded on the conviction that conscious organization was essential for victory. Perhaps most important of all, he insisted on establishing a "hegemonic" relationship between working class and peasantry as a prerequisite for the revolution.

Still, Gramsci seems to have doubts about Lenin's thoroughness in examining the hegemony of the working class and the "cultural front." In reality, Gramsci went far beyond Lenin in seeing hegemony as a political and cultural predominance of the working class and its party aimed at securing the "spontaneous" adherence of other groups.[21] Hegemony—rule by consent, the legitimatization of revolution by a higher and more comprehensive culture—is the unifying idea of Gramsci's life.

In his later work Gramsci stressed the problem of "civil society," hegemony, over the problem of "political society," which is—for Marxists—the dictatorship of the proletariat. The shift in emphasis was caused by Gramsci's increasing awareness of differences between the Russia of 1917 and Western Europe after 1923. Problems of hegemony, said Gramsci, become particularly important in periods that follow a phase of revolutionary activity. Gramsci believed that the class struggle then

[20] *Il Materialismo storico,* pp. 201, 189, 32, 39.

[21] Most communist writers have tended to identify the views of Gramsci and Lenin on hegemony, whereas non-communist writers have tended to emphasize Gramsci's originality. For the first group, see Emilio Sereni, "Antonio Gramsci e la scienza d'avanguardia," *Società,* IV (January–March 1948), 28, and Togliatti, "Il Leninismo," in *Studi gramsciani,* p. 34. For the second group, cf. Williams, *op. cit.,* Nicola Matteucci, *Antonio Gramsci e la filosofia della prassi* (Milan: Giuffré, 1951), p. 76, and Giuseppe Tamburrano, *Antonio Gramsci* (Manduria: Lacaita, 1963). But see the very recent article by the communist Luciano Gruppi, "Il Concetto di egemonia," *Critica marxista—Quaderni no. 3* (1967), p. 85. Gruppi makes a sharp distinction between Lenin's *Materialism and Empiriocriticism* and some ideas in Gramsci's *Materialismo storico.*

changes from a "war of maneuver" to a "war of position" fought mainly on the cultural front.[22] The *Quaderni* were written during such a period, and this partly accounts for their emphasis on hegemony.

In the united front policy Lenin himself, said Gramsci, indicated the need to shift from a war of maneuver, which had succeeded in Russia in 1917, to a war of position, "the only possible one in the West." [23] But the shift was the responsibility of Western communist leaders because of certain fundamental differences between Russia and Western Europe. "In the East the State was everything, and civil society was primordial and gelatinous; in the West there was a correct relationship between the State and civil society." However unstable the State might have appeared to be, behind it stood "a robust structure of civil society." [24] Under these conditions, the seizure of power by a new class is unlikely to succeed without a prior victory in the area of civil society; hence, the struggle for hegemony, for cultural and moral predominance, is the main task of Marxists in the advanced countries of the West.

Gramsci placed a high value on the political party in the life of modern states. There is nothing conspiratorial or sectarian in his view; the party is above all an instrument of education and civilization. Among other things this includes discipline, and party discipline is important to Gramsci. Yet it is certainly not a passive and supine acceptance of orders, a mechanical execution of assignments (though even that would sometimes be necessary: during an already decided and initiated action, for example), but a conscious and clear understanding of the aims to be realized. "Discipline in this sense does not annul individual personality . . . but merely limits the will and irresponsible impulsiveness." In evaluating the role of party discipline, everything depends on the "origin of the power that enforces the discipline": "If the authority is a specialized, technical function, and not an 'arbitrary' force or an external imposition, discipline is a necessary element of democratic

---

[22] *Il Materialismo storico,* p. 194.

[23] *Note sul Machiavelli,* p. 68.

[24] *Loc. cit.* Cf. also, in this connection, Gramsci's note on "State-idolatry": "For some social groups, which before their rise to an autonomous State life did not have a long period of independent cultural and moral development . . . a period of State-idolatry is necessary and even opportune. . . . However, this 'State-idolatry' should not be left to itself. Especially it should not become theoretical fanaticism and be conceived as 'perpetual'" (*Passate e presente,* pp. 165–66).

order and freedom. A specialized technical function exists when the authority is exercised within one socially (or nationally) homogeneous group; when it is exercised by one group over another group, discipline will be autonomous and free for the first, but not for the second." [25]

One other aspect of the political party was of extreme interest to Gramsci, given the conditions under which he wrote the *Quaderni*: the assurance of his party's survival. More generally, the question might be: "What are the conditions that historically justify the existence of any political party?" First, the party must have a solid base in a particular social group (parties as the "nomenclature" of classes). In addition, the organization must have a political tradition, a sense of historical continuity similar to the kind of permanence normally identified with the State itself (*spirito statale*). Each member must be aware of intangible forces, "which are nevertheless felt to be operating and active, accounted for as if they were 'materially' and bodily present." The solidarity of a movement depends upon consciousness of its historical continuity: "We must feel solidarity with the old men of today, who represent the past still living among us, with which we must come to terms, and also with the children and growing generations, for whom we feel responsible." [26]

A party justifies its historical existence when it develops three basic elements: (1) the rank and file, "a diffuse element of ordinary men whose participation is characterized by discipline and faith, not by a creative or organizational spirit"; (2) leadership, "the principal cohesive element, centralized in the national field and developing efficiency and power in an ensemble of forces that are worthless individually"; (3) party cadres, "a middle element that articulates the first with the second element by putting them in contact 'physically,' morally, and intellectually."

Gramsci emphasizes that a party cannot exist with the rank and file and the cadres alone; leadership is of primary importance: "We speak of captains with an army, but in reality it is easier to form an army than to find captains. It is surely true than an already existing army will be destroyed if it lacks captains; whereas a group of captains, cooperative and in agreement on common ends, will not be slow in forming an army, even where none exists." [27] Thus the presence of

[25] *Passate e presente,* p. 65.
[26] *Note sul Machiavelli,* p. 19.
[27] *Ibid.,* pp. 23–24.

leadership will ensure the existence of a whole party structure. Competent leaders must be able to demonstrate "that necessary and sufficient conditions already exist so that certain tasks can, and therefore should, be resolved historically (*should,* because any failure in one's historical duty increases disorder and prepares graver catastrophes)."[28] Gramsci denies that immediate economic crises produce revolutions directly. They can only create a more favorable environment "for the diffusion of certain ways of thinking." [29] Competent leadership is responsible for exploiting this more favorable environment.

Here we have characteristic examples of the dialectical unity of objective and subjective factors in Gramsci's historical analysis. Many of Gramsci's contemporaries regarded him as a champion of idealism or "voluntarism," in opposition to an older Marxist tradition that was supposedly a form of "historical determinism." Gramsci himself merely thought he was further developing the "anti-economistic" ideas of Lenin.[30] Gramsci was definitely a Leninist, but he emphasized "voluntarism" in his analysis of the political party more consistently than Lenin did.

Gramsci insisted on a thoroughly non-mechanical interpretation of party doctrine: "Ideology" or doctrine should be considered not something artificially superimposed ("like a suit, and not like the skin, which is organically produced"), but something historical, developing through incessant struggle. A party must integrate three elements: its doctrine, the specific historical nature of its personnel, and the "real historical movement," the dynamics of the particular culture in which the party operates. "The first and second elements can be controlled by the associated and deliberating will [the party]. The third element constantly reacts with the other two and causes an incessant struggle, theoretical and practical, to raise the organism [the party] to ever more elevated and refined collective consciousness." [31]

But if doctrine must be continually developed in ever-changing circumstances, then we cannot expect any "specific conception of life

28 *Ibid.,* p. 32 (emphasis mine).

29 *Ibid.,* p. 48. After having read Mathiez's account of the causes of the French Revolution, Gramsci asserted that revolution did not occur for "mechanical" economic reasons, but because of "conflicts superior to the immediate economic world, connected to class 'prestige' (future economic interests) and to a stimulation of the feelings of independence, autonomy and power." On this point, cf. Lisa, *op. cit.,* p. 20.

30 Cf., for example, *Il Materialismo storico,* p. 199.

31 *Note sul Machiavelli,* p. 294.

and the world to have an *intrinsically* superior capacity for foresight."
This statement seems a striking admission of futility, coming from a
Marxist theoretician and communist political leader—a negation of
Gramsci's own views on the importance of the creative will in history.
However, Gramsci's interpretation of foresight is far from either futility or determinism: "Foresight means nothing but clearly seeing
the present and past as movement: that is, precisely identifying the
fundamental and permanent aspects of the process. But it is absurd
to imagine a purely "objective" foresight. The man with foresight has,
in reality, a definite program in mind; and foresight is an aid to reaching that goal. This does not mean that foresight must always be arbitrary and gratuitous, or always tendentious. Indeed, one may say that
the objective aspects of foresight are really objective only insofar as
they are connected with a goal: (1) because only passion sharpens the
intellect and cooperates to render intuition clearer; (2) because reality
comes from applying human will to the society of things (like a ma-
chinist and his machine); ignoring any voluntary element, or calculating
only *another's* will as an objective element in the process, mutilates
reality itself. Only he who strongly wills identifies the elements necessary to realize his will." [32] This judgment led Gramsci to condemn the
popular idea of the realistic politician as one who deals only with
"effectual reality," and not reality as it "ought to be." A true states-
man has a program; he wishes to create new relations of forces, and
therefore must consider what ought to be. He bases himself on effectual
reality—but what is effectual reality? It is not something static or im-
mobile, but a pattern of forces continually moving and changing equilibrium. A man must apply his will to create a new equilibrium of concrete
forces, selecting the force he sees as progressive and working to strengthen
it; then he is working with effectual reality, but is able to dominate it.[33]

Gramsci's political ideas were not abstract reflections, but derived
from his own political experience before his imprisonment; and opposition to the reformist point of view was a constant stand in his political
and intellectual life. The reformist, asserts Gramsci, does not conceive
of the socialist movement as independent and autonomous, but as
part of a larger movement, bourgeois democracy, in which its task is
reforming "certain presumed or real evils." [34] He assumes, in effect, that
a "natural" political order exists, which needs no more than adjustment

[32] *Ibid.*, p. 38.
[33] *Ibid.*, p. 39.
[34] *Ibid.*, p. 28.

or retouching. In a crisis, as in 1921–22 in Italy, the reformist leaders return to their "real" party (the party representing the "natural" order) and leave the masses, who have very different political interests, disoriented and ineffective. Therefore Gramsci insists—in the light of his "theoretical truth" that every class has one unique party—that a party should be founded on a "monolithic" basis, and not on secondary questions, "on the basis of an autonomous conception of the world and the role of the represented class in history."

Here Gramsci suggests why there was no adequate defense against fascism. The reformist leaders were paralyzed by their "fatalistic and mechanical conception of history," and did not recognize the *autonomous* interests of the class they presumably represented. In reality, they had "no comprehension of its fundamental needs, its aspirations, its latent energies." As far back as 1917 reformist leaders had accused Gramsci of voluntarism, in opposition to their own declared determinism. However, Gramsci noted that if reformism were opposed to voluntarism, it ought to appreciate "spontaneity," that is, the unpremeditated political action of the masses. Instead, the reformist leaders regarded the " 'spontaneous' as an inferior thing, not worthy of consideration, not even worthy of being analyzed." For Gramsci, "spontaneous" events, especially those in 1919–20, clearly proved the ineptness of the PSI in those years. The very spontaneity of these events, and their repudiation by the party leadership, induced the climate of "panic" that enabled the ruling classes to unite in a more effective repression of these and other events. Gramsci asserted that "pure" spontaneity did not really exist. In the "most spontaneous" movements, the "elements of 'conscious leadership' are merely invisible. They have not left any ascertainable traces." [35]

Gramsci's long struggle with Bordiga also led him to consider the effects of "extremism" (or "sectarianism") on political parties. Many of his remarks on reformism are also applicable to extremism. Extremism, however, is rigidly averse to compromise because of its "iron conviction that there are objective historical laws, similar to natural laws"; this combines with an almost religious fatalism. If one believes that favorable conditions must inevitably develop, then of course "any voluntary initiative aimed at arranging these situations according to a plan" is useless, perhaps harmful. This view is a form of "economism," the

[35] *Passato e presente*, pp. 59, 60, 66.

belief that economic conditions irrevocably determine the human situation. Yet this thinking was fallacious precisely because it did not take account of the "real economy," the mass ideological facts that always lie behind mass economic facts. Political initiative is always needed to "free the economic thrust from the shackles of traditional politics," to change the political direction of certain forces that must be absorbed in order to form a new "economic-political, historical bloc, without internal contradictions." [36] Gramsci condemns "economism," a form of sectarianism, in "economic" language: if consciousness follows economic realities, then the politician must repair the gap by raising the level of consciousness.

The sectarian confuses the party's "technical organization" with the needs of the real historical movement of which the party is merely an instrument.[37] Thus "the sectarian will extol the petty internal events [of party life]," whereas the historian or politician will "emphasize the real efficiency of the party . . . in contributing to events, or even in preventing other events from occurring." [38] The irresponsible sectarian neglect of the represented class's actual condition causes a wholly unwarranted optimism: "One looks on the 'will to believe' as a condition of victory, which would not be mistaken if it were not conceived mechanically and did not become a self-deception" (that is, confuse mass and leaders and lower the leader to the level of the most backward follower). Characteristic of this self-deception is a tendency to "belittle the adversary." But, asks Gramsci, if this adversary presently dominates you —although you are "superior" to him—"then how did he succeed in dominating you?" [39]

Finally, the sectarian politician is all too ready to resort to arms, although this tendency would seem contradictory to the deterministic sectarian view. The answer is that the extremist believes that the "intervention of the will is useful for destruction, but not for reconstruction." A little push, as it were, will facilitate the final victory of underlying currents. While coercion is certainly unavoidable in some cases, Gramsci did not view it as even theoretically desirable in creating a fusion of related forces: "The only real possibility is a compromise; force may be employed against enemies, but not against a part of oneself that one

[36] *Note sul Machiavelli*, pp. 36, 37.
[37] *Passato e presente*, pp. 70–71.
[38] *Note sul Machiavelli*, p. 23.
[39] *Passato e presente*, p. 7.

wants to assimilate rapidly and from whom 'good will' and enthusiasm are required." [40]

"Precisely because the American socialist movement is one of the most backward and feeble in the world," averred an editor of *Studies on the Left,* "it possesses what Veblen called 'the advantage of the borrower,' the possibility of utilizing the most advanced concepts of the European Left without also inheriting the dead weight of the past under which European socialism must labor."[41] Antonio Gramsci's work is the inspiration for one of the most successful socialist movements of the capitalist world. But it is our heritage too. Specifically, Gramsci has much to say to those who today see in participatory democracy an essential new path to socialism.

[40] *Note sul Machiavelli,* pp. 36–37.
[41] John Cowley, "Crisis of the European Left," *Studies on the Left,* VII, 2 (March–April 1967), p. 12.

2

Late Capitalism

4

IRVING HOWE

The Welfare State

Irving Howe is Professor of English, Hunter College and Graduate Center, City University of New York. He is also a founder and editor of *Dissent,* and a prolific writer on culture and politics. His best known books include *Politics and the Novel* (1957) and *Steady Work* (1966).

THE ABSTRACT MODEL

Ferment, conflict, innovation, violence, a measure of madness—all these and more characterize the American scene. The image of social stability, which dominated both liberal and conservative thought only a decade ago, has proved to be an illusion. The welfare state in which we live is strained by tension and clash. But before examining these, let's look at the welfare state as an idea or model in order to gain some historical perspective. A model is not a picture, either still or moving; it lacks, and in order to serve its purpose it must lack, the dynamics of reality. It may articulate skeletal structures but it cannot describe either the processes of change or idiosyncratic traits.

Among current models of contemporary society the most useful, I think, is that of the welfare state. By the welfare state one signifies a capitalist economy in which the interplay of private and/or corporate owners in a largely regulated market remains dominant but in which the workings of the economy are so modified that the powers of free disposal by property owners are controlled politically.

The welfare state is constantly being reconstructed. The model we advance for it may suggest an equilibrium, but in the actuality from which the model is drawn there persist serious difficulties, conflicts, and

63

breakdowns. If the welfare state could reach, so to say, a point of internal perfection, the point at which it would all but approach its "ideal type," it would comprise a system of regulated conflicts making for pluralist balance and stability. But this point of perfection cannot be reached, if only because the welfare state appears within a given historical context, so that it must always be complicated by the accumulation of problems provided by a capitalist economy and a specific national past; complicated, further, by concurrent international conflicts which, as we now see, can crucially affect and distort its formation; and complicated, as well, by a series of pressures, ranging from status ambition to moral idealism, which it is not, as a society, well equipped to handle.

Within certain limits having to do with basic relations of power and production, the welfare state remains open to varying sociopolitical contents, since it is itself the visible evidence of a long and continuing struggle among classes and groups for greater shares in the social product. That the welfare state exists at all is due not merely to autonomous processes within the economy, or enlightened self-interest on the part of dominant classes, or moral idealism, as over decades it has stirred segments of the population into conscience; no, the welfare state is importantly the result of social struggle on the part of the labor movement. If the working class has not fulfilled the "historic tasks" assigned to it by Marxism and if it shows, at least in the advanced industrial countries, few signs of revolutionary initiative, it has nevertheless significantly modified the nature and softened the cruelties of capitalist society.

In a curious way—the analogy need not be stressed—the welfare state has served a function similar to that of Communism in the East. I do not mean to suggest an equivalence in value, since for myself, as a socialist, there can be no question that it is immensely more desirable to live in a society that allows political freedom and thereby organized struggle and independent class action. Yet, from a certain long-range perspective, one could say that both the welfare state and the Communist societies have had the effect of raising the historical expectations of millions of people, even while offering radically different kinds of satisfaction and sharing in common failures. Both have enabled previously mute segments of society to feel that the state ought to act in their behalf and that perhaps they have a role in history as active subjects demanding that the state serve their needs. The contrast with earlier societies is striking, for in them, as Michael Walzer writes, the dominant conviction was that

. . . the state always *is* more than it *does.* Pre-welfare theorists described it as a closely knit body, dense and opaque, whose members were involved emotionally as well as materially, mysteriously as well as rationally, in the fate of the whole. The members ought to be involved, it was said, not for the sake of concrete benefits of any sort, but simply, for the sake of communion. Since loyalty was a gift for which there was to be no necessary return, it could not be predicated on anything so clear-cut as interest. It depended instead on all sorts of ideological and ceremonial mystification. . . . The state still does depend on ideology and mystery, but to a far less degree than ever before. It has been the great triumph of liberal theorists and politicians to undermine every sort of political divinity, to shatter all the forms of ritual obfuscation, and to return the mysterious oath into a rational contract. The state itself they have made over . . . into a machine, the instrument of its citizens (rather than their mythical common life) devoted to what Bentham called "welfare production." It is judged, as it ought to be, by the amounts of welfare it produces and by the justice and efficiency of its distributive system.[1]

What occurs characteristically during the growth of the welfare state is a series of "invasions," by previously neglected or newly cohered social groups demanding for themselves a more equitable portion of the social product and appealing to the common ideology of welfarism as the rationale for their demands. (Again an analogy with Communism: the dominant ideology is exploited and violated by the ruling class, yet can be turned against its interests.)

In its early stages, the welfare state is "invaded" mostly by interest groups—economic, racial, ethnic—which seek both improvements in their condition and recognition of their status. An interest claim that is made through norms the entire society says it accepts is harder to reject than one which sets up new norms not yet enshrined in the society's formal value system—and that, in passing, is one reason it is today easier to press for desirable domestic legislation than to affect foreign policy. In its later stages—which I believe we are just beginning to approach in the United States—the welfare state is subjected to a series of pressures that morally are both more grandiose and more trivial than those of the usual interest groups; since now it becomes possible for claims to be entered with—and against—the welfare state by those who yearn

[1] Michael Walzer, "Politics in the Welfare State," *Dissent,* Vol. 15, No. 1, January–February 1968.

forward to what they hope will be a splendid future and those who yearn backward to what they imagine was a golden past.

This course of "invasions" is by no means completed in the United States and indeed is scandalously frustrated by racial and social meanness. As long, however, as there are groups trying to break in and powers trying to keep them out, we can be certain that the welfare state will be marked by severe conflict, even though the "invading" groups may differ from decade to decade. Nor is there any certainty whatever that the welfare state will prove receptive to all the claims likely to be made by groups largely outside its system of dispensation. It is possible that the legitimate demands of the Negroes will not be met and that this would, in turn, lead to the virtual destruction of the welfare state as we know it; but if that were to occur it would not, I believe, be the result of an inherent dynamic or ineluctable necessity within the welfare state as socioeconomic system, but rather it would be the result of a tradition of racism so deeply ingrained in American life that it threatens to survive, and overwhelm, any form of society.

This process of "invasion" is one that a good many of the younger American radicals find troublesome and concerning which I find a good many of them confused. Except for a few who have developed a snobbish contempt for the working class, they recognize the justice of the claims made by deprived groups trying to gain a larger share of power, goods, and recognition; but they fear that once this happens there must follow among the once-insurgent groups an adaptation to detested values and a complacent lapse into material comfort. In part, the young radicals are right. At a particular moment, a once-insurgent group may settle for what seems too little—though we ought to be suspicious of contemptuous judgments made by people who have not shared in past struggles or have merely grown up to enjoy their rewards. At a particular moment, a once-insurgent group may move from the drama of popular struggle to the politics of limited pressure. Right now, for example, the trade unions seem relatively quiescent; having won major victories, they may for a time content themselves with minor adjustments; but with time they are likely to raise their horizons of possibility and again come into conflict with the existing order; and in any case, it takes a peculiarly sectarian mentality to doubt the tremendous potentialities of the mid-sixties UAW demand for something approaching a guaranteed annual wage for blue-collar workers.

Simply to stop at the point where formerly rebellious groups are "absorbed" into society is to miss the point. For what the young radicals fail sufficiently to see is that when a major social group breaks into the welfare society, then—even though full justice is by no means done—the society nevertheless undergoes an important betterment. The United States after the "absorption" of the labor movement is a different and, on the whole, better society than it was before. By a certain judgment the unions have succumbed to the system, though we should remember that only rarely had they claimed to be its intransigent opponents. Yet even in their relative quiescence of the last few decades, the unions have performed an extremely valuable function: they have maintained a steady pressure, more than any other institution, in behalf of domestic social legislation which benefits not only their own members but a much wider segment of the population.

If—it is a large if—the Negroes succeed in establishing themselves within the society to the extent that the labor unions have, there will occur changes which can only be described as major and perhaps revolutionary—though there will not have occurred that "revolution" which various kinds of ideologues hope the Negroes will enact for them. Were such victories to be won by the Negroes, there would probably follow a certain relaxation among them, a settling-down to enjoy the fruits of struggle, such as occurred earlier among trade unionists. But if past experience is any guide, there would follow after a certain interval a new rise in social appetites among the once-insurgent group, so that it would continue to affect the shape of society even if no longer through exclusively insurgent methods.

Is there, however, a built-in limit to this process of "invasion"? Almost certainly, yes; and by habit one would say the point where fundamental relations of power seem threatened. But we are nowhere near that point; a large array of struggles await us before reaching it, and we cannot even be sure, certainly not as sure as we were a few decades ago, that this point can be located precisely. The history of the Left in the twentieth century is marked by a series of dogmatic assertions as to what could not be done short of revolutionary upheaval; the actuality of history has consisted of changes won through struggle and human will which have in fact achieved some of the goals that were supposed to be unattainable short of apocalypse.

Some Other Models

The model of the welfare state I have been using here is of course an extrapolation from the complexities of history, and even if we are to content ourselves with it we must acknowledge the presence in our society of elements it cannot account for and which, indeed, conflict with it. Even the traditional *laissez-faire* model of capitalism, which by common consent is now obsolete, retains some importance. There are aspects of the society—certain segments of the economy, certain sectors of the country, certain strands of our ideological folklore—in regard to which the traditional model of capitalism retains much relevance, so that in discussing the welfare state, or welfare capitalism, one must bear in mind the earlier historical form out of which it emerged. More immediately, however, there are several models which should be looked at, not merely or even so much as competitors but rather as supplements, necessary complications, to the welfare state model.

The Garrison State
The war economy is like a parallel structure, a double aorta, of the welfare state, at some points reinforcing it through an economic largesse which a reactionary Congress might not otherwise be willing to allow, and at other points crippling it through sociopolitical aggrandizement such as we can observe at this very moment. In consequence, we can never be free of the haunting possibility that if our military expenditure were radically cut there would follow a collapse or a very severe crisis in the welfare state. Nor can we be sure that gradually the military arrangement will not overwhelm and consume welfare. But these, I would stress, are matters of political decision and thereby of social struggle; they will be settled not through some mysterious economic automatism but through the encounter of opposing classes and groups.

The Mass Society
This theory proposes a model of society in which traditional class antagonisms and distinctions have become blurred and in which there occurs a steady drift toward a bureaucratic, non-terrorist and prosperous authoritarianism, with a population grown passive and atomized, "primary" social groups disintegrated, and traditional loyalties and asso-

ciations become lax. Herbert Marcuse writes: "Those social groups which dialectical theory identified as forces of negation are either defeated or reconciled within the established system." In simpler language this means that the working class which Marxism assigned to revolutionary leadership seems either unwilling or incapable of fulfilling the assignment. That there is a tendency in modern society toward a slack contentment it would be foolish to deny. But I think it sentimental to slide from an abandonment of traditional Marxist expectations to a vision of historical stasis in which men are fated to be the zombies of bureaucratic organization, zombies stuffed with calories, comfort, and contentment; or to slide from the conclusion that revolutionary expectations no longer hold in the West to a Spenglerian gloom in which we must yield the idea of major social change and indulge ourselves in compensatory fantasies about the last "pure" revolution of the third world.

More fundamentally, the trouble with the "mass society" theory is that, if pushed hard enough, it posits a virtual blockage of history. Yet the one thing that history, including the history of the last several decades, teaches us is that, for good or bad, such an eventuality seems most unlikely. Even in what seems to some disenchanted intellectuals the murk of stability, change is ceaseless. Twenty years ago who would have supposed that Russia and China would be at each other's throats, or that the seeming monolith of Communism would disintegrate? That a conservative French general would succeed in ending a colonial war in Algeria after both the liberal and radical parties failed? That in the United States Catholic students would be picketing Cardinal Spellman's residence? That a silent generation would appear, to be followed by a remarkably articulate one, which in turn . . . well, who knows? What looks at a given moment like the end of days turns out to be a mere vestibule to novelty.

One interesting offshoot of the mass-society theory, popular in some academic and student circles, declares that in a society where revolution is impossible and reform ineffectual, the only remaining strategy of protest is a series of dramatic raids from the social margin, akin to the guerrilla movements of Latin America. Insofar as this strategy draws upon the American tradition of individual moral protest, it has a decided respectability if only, I think, a limited usefulness. Insofar as it is meant to satisfy an unearned nostalgia, it is utterly feckless. Raising hell is a fine American habit, and if hell is even approximately identified, a useful one. But in contemporary society there is always the danger that the desperado exhausts himself much sooner than he discomfits society, and then retires at the ripe age of thirty and a half muttering about the sloth of the masses. Or he may be crushed in the embrace of a society always on the lookout for interesting spectacles.

A far more serious and honorable version of this strategy is that of absolute moral conscience, for example, that of the young people who, while not religious, refuse the Vietnam war on moral grounds. Their protest is to be respected. If they are simply bearing witness, then nothing more need be said. If, however, it is claimed that they stir other, more conventional and sluggish segments of the mass society into response, then we have abandoned the ground of moral absolutes and moved to the slippery terrain of effectiveness and expediency—and then what they do must be scrutinized as a political tactic, open to the problem of consequences both expected and unexpected.

Liberal Pluralism

This theory, associated with the name of Daniel Bell, sees the society as a pluralist system in which competing pressure groups—some reflecting socioeconomic interests and others refracting the aspirations of status groups—tacitly agree to abide by the "rules of the game" and to submit their rival claims to the jurisdiction of technical experts. Superficially, this approach is congruent with the one I have here outlined, insofar as it traces the effects of political clash within a given society; fundamentally, it is divergent from the approach I have taken, insofar as it accepts the society as a given and fails to penetrate beneath political maneuver to the deeper contradictions of social interest. Still, whether we like it or not, this theory helps describe a good part of what has been happening in the United States these last few decades, especially when one confines oneself to the local texture of political life. I think, however, it is a theory inadequate on several counts:

It fails to consider sufficiently that within the society there remain long-range economic and technological trends threatening the stability, perhaps the survival, of the pluralist system: that is, it asserts a state of equilibrium too readily.

It fails to recognize sufficiently that even when the society is operating at a high degree of efficiency and what passes for a notable benevolence, it does not satisfy human needs and instead gives rise to new kinds of trouble with which it is poorly equipped to deal.

70

It fails to acknowledge sufficiently that the very "rules of the game" are prearranged so as to favor inequities of power and wealth.

SOME COMPLICATIONS OF REALITY

The welfare state does not appear in a vacuum; it arises at a certain point in the development of capitalist society and must therefore confront the accumulated tradition and peculiarities of that society. In Britain it comes to a society where serious problems remain of a pre-modern and pre-democratic kind, difficulties having to do with aristocracy and status. In France it comes to a society where the necessary industrialization has just been completed. In Sweden it comes to a society with a minimum of historical impediments or world political entanglements and therefore functions best of all—though here, as Gunnar Myrdal describes it, the welfare state tends to break down organs of rural and village self-government. In the United States it comes at a time of severe historical and moral tensions: the former concerning our role as a world power and the latter a long-term shift in the country's pattern of values. Let us glance at the second.

For some decades now there has been noticeable in this country a slow disintegration of those binding assumptions which, operating almost invisibly, hold a society together and provide its moral discipline. These values can hardly be evoked in a phrase but we can at least point to a few: a creed of individualist self-reliance linked with a belief that the resultant of unrestrained struggle among private persons (atomized economic units) will prove to be to the common good; a conviction that the claims of conscience, seriously entertained, and the promptings of will, persistently accepted, are in fact equivalent; a belief in work as salvation and therapy; a steady devotion to privacy, rigor, control, and moral sobriety. In short, the whole American mythos which we have inherited from the nineteenth century and which in retrospect has been remarkably successful in unifying the country.

During the last few decades, however, this creed has proven inadequate to the American reality, with the evidence ranging from the crisis of urbanization to the gradual decay of religious belief. Perhaps the most striking evidence has been the way in which the WASP elite has slowly been losing its hegemony in American society. So far as I can tell, this loss of hegemony, accompanied by a decline in self-confidence, has occurred more on the social surface than at the economic base, but with time it is bound also to affect the latter.

The American creed served to unify a nation that in its earlier years had largely consisted of a loose compact of regions. Once these regions were gradually melted into a nation, the unifying ideology began to lose some of its power and the sociocultural elite articulating the ideology began to decline. Precisely the unification of the country through the cement of this ideology gave an opportunity for new interest groups and competing moral styles to press their claims.

This process could not, of course, act itself out autonomously. It was always intertwined with social struggles. And as it slowly unfolded itself at the center of society there occurred crisis reactions at the extremes: on the right, a heartfelt cry that morality is being destroyed, religion mocked, our way of life abandoned; on the left, an impatience to be done with old ways and to plunge joyously, sometimes merely programmatically, into experiment. The earnest suburban middle class which only a few years ago was shaking with indignation at the collapse of standards, and the hippies of Haight-Ashbury and East Village—these form symmetrical polarities along the spectrum of American moral life, each reacting to the gradual decay of American convictions and neither absorbed by the kind of pluralistic moderation and maneuvering encouraged by the welfare state. Both the little old lady in tennis shoes and the young hippie in sandals are demonstrating their hostility to the "role playing" of the current scene. Both provide complications of response which our increasingly rationalized and rationalistic society finds it hard to handle. For in a sense, the kind of issues raised by Barry Goldwater and the SDS are symmetrical in concern, if sharply different in moral value. Both of these metapolitical tendencies were reacting to long-range historical and cultural developments at least as much as to immediate political issues.

What then are the political consequences of this gradual deterioration of the American value system?

The traditional elite can no longer assert itself with its former powers and self-assurance. One reason Adlai Stevenson roused such positive reactions among intellectuals was that it seemed to them that he was a figure in the old style, for which, in their conservative disenchantment, they had developed a sudden fondness.

The image of America inherited from folklore, textbooks, and civic rhetoric proves unusable, and the result is an enormous barrier of intellectual and emotional fog which prevents people from apprehending their true needs.

At the margins of the welfare state there spring up apocalyptic movements and moods, seemingly political but often in their deepest impulses anti-political (they want not a change in power relations but an end of days). Reflecting the pressures of the fading past and the undiscovered future, these movements confound, yet sometimes also refresh, the politics of the welfare state.

INNER PROBLEMS OF THE WELFARE STATE

It is not only the distinctive American setting which affects our version of the welfare state; there are also certain characteristics which seem to be intrinsically dysfunctional or at least unattractive. A few of them:

Especially in America, the welfare state fails to live up to its formal claims. At best it is a semi-welfare state; at worst an anti-welfare state. It allows a significant minority, the chronic poor, to be dumped beneath the social structure, as a *lumpen* deposit of degradation and pathology.

The welfare state may gratify the interests of previously deprived minorities and thereby benefit the society as a whole; but while doing this, and perhaps because of it, the welfare state tends to dampen concern with such larger values as justice, fraternity, equality, and community. At least for a time, one consequence is that fundamental issues of power are muted; for better or worse—I think for worse—the system as such is hardly an issue in public debate.

Yet here again we ought to beware of a sin prevalent among intellectuals: the sin of impatience with history. For even in its brief existence, and with its own "historical tasks" far from fulfilled, the welfare state has witnessed the growth of an enormous body of social criticism, as well as the appearance of the militantly idealistic young, both of which insist that we pay attention to precisely the larger issues. If the welfare state lulls some groups into acquiescence, it also grants a succeeding generation the relative affluence to experiment with its life-styles and cry out against the slumbers of their elders. The crucial question, to which no answer can yet be given, is whether this concern will remain limited to a tiny segment of the population, driven wild with frustrated reachings toward transcendence.

In its own right, the welfare state does not arouse strong loyalties. It seems easier, if no more intelligent, to die for King and Country, or the Stars and Stripes, or the Proletarian Fatherland than for Unemployment Insurance and Social Security. The welfare state makes for a fragmentation of publics and, at a certain point, a decline in political participation. By one of those accursed paradoxes history keeps throwing up, the welfare state seems to undercut the vitality of the democratic process even while strengthening both its formal arrangements and its socioeconomic base.

But again a word of caution. It should not be assumed that in a country like the United States, despite the rise of group interest politics and the atomization of social life, the traditional claims of the nation no longer operate. For they do, even if in a muted and more quizzical way. Millions of people still respond to the call of patriotism and the rhetoric of democracy, even in their corniest versions. The centrifugal tendencies set into motion by the welfare state must always, therefore, be seen against a background of historical traditions and national sentiments which lie deeply imbedded in collective life.

The welfare state cannot, within the limits of the nation-state, cope with the growing number of socioeconomic problems that are soluble only on an international level or do not really fit into the received categories of class or group conflict. As Richard Titmuss says:

> it [is] much harder today to identify the causal agents of change—the microbes of social disorganization and the viruses of impoverishment—and to make them responsible for the costs of "disservices." Who should bear the social costs of the thalidomide babies, of urban blight, of smoke pollution, of the obsolescence of skills, of automation, of the impact of synthetic coffee, which will dispense with the need for coffee beans, on the peasants of Brazil? [2]

The welfare state provides no clear or necessary outlook concerning the role of the nation in the modern world. It is almost compatible with any foreign policy, despite our too-easy assumption that domestic liberalism is likely to go together with restraint in foreign policy. The welfare state can be yoked to a foreign policy which saves Titoist Yugoslavia and destroys Vietnam, which provides food to India and shores

[2] Richard M. Titmuss, "Social Welfare and the Art of Giving," *Socialist Humanism,* edited by Erich Fromm (New York: Doubleday, 1965), p. 346.

up dictators elsewhere in Asia, which proclaims and begins the Alliance for Progress and sanctions the Dominican intervention. The consequences are severe dislocations within the welfare state, splits between groups oriented primarily toward the improvement of their own conditions and groups oriented primarily toward improving the place our society occupies within the world. Of this, more later.

Within its terms and limits the welfare state finds it very difficult to provide avenues of fulfillment for many of the people whose conditions it has helped to improve—the workers displaced by automation, the Negroes given the vote but little else, the young seeking work that makes sense. That is why there now appear new formations, such as the sub-culture of the alienated young, responding primarily to their felt sense of the falseness of things. If the revolt of the radical right was, in Richard Hofstadter's phrase, an outburst of status politics—the anxious need of an insecure segment to assert itself in the prestige hierarchy—then the revolt of the alienated young is, among other things, an anti-status outburst—a wish to break loose from the terms of categorization fixed by the society. That, in the course of this effort, the young sometimes settle into categories, styles, and mannerisms quite as rigid as those against which they rebel, is something else again.

POLITICS OF THE WELFARE STATE

The politics of the welfare state extends back into the early twentieth century, through a variety of parallel and competing traditions—the labor movement, the Socialist movement, the various liberal groups, the moral pressures exerted through Christian action, the increasing role of the Jews as a liberal force. But for our present purposes we can date the beginning of welfare-state politics as a style of coalition to the early thirties and perhaps even more precisely to the election of 1932, one of the few in American history which marked a major realignment of political forces. In that election the unions began to play the powerful role they would command during the next few decades; large numbers of Negroes began their historic switch to the Democratic party; the city machines found it expedient to go along with Roosevelt's policies. And soon significant numbers of intellectuals would begin their entry into practical politics. This coalition would remain a major force in American life during the next three or so decades. When all or most of its component parts could be held together, formally or informally, and it could command the practical issues and/or moral appeals to win a good cut of the middle-class vote, this coalition could often win elections on a national scale and in many industrialized states. When there were group defections, victory went to the right. In general one can say that this coalition was most successful whenever it managed to link strong economic interests with moral urgencies, the politics of pressure with the traditions of American liberalism and populism. I believe that this lesson still holds, despite sharply changed circumstances.

What specific forms did this coalition take? It could be one or more of the following:

a bloc of organizations and movements cooperating for a legislative or electoral end;

a long-range concurrence in electoral behavior, so that certain expectations could reasonably be inferred—e.g., that even if we do not have self-conscious classes or disciplined publics there are at least certain fundamental recognitions of common interest;

intermittent activization of class and interest groups when aroused by specific issues—e.g., "right to work" laws, Negro rights, etc;

various electoral and political arrangements within and across the political parties.

Now one way of looking upon recent American politics is to conclude that in recent years the liberal-left coalition has gradually disintegrated and, with the Vietnam war, seems virtually to have come to an end.

There are plenty of signs. The electoral blocs seem to function with less assurance and predictability than ten or twenty years ago. Workers reaching a measure of affluence are less likely to follow the signals of their union leadership; they may veer off into middle-class styles or lapse into racialism. Still, when certain issues are clearly drawn along class lines, as for example during the 1964 presidential election or the earlier struggles around "right to work" laws, the labor vote can still cohere into a major force.

Similar signs of change seem to be occurring among the Negroes, where the massive commitment to the Democratic party may—though it certainly has not yet—come to an end. And among younger people there is a growing inclination to respond to politics as if group interest were somehow vulgar or even reprehensible and what mattered most were political "styles" and moral, or pseudomoral, appeals rising above socio-economic concerns.

Why then has this coalition devoted to defending and extending the welfare state come to a condition of crisis? A few answers suggest themselves:

As the interest groups become increasingly absorbed into the welfare state, their combativeness decreases, at least for a time. They develop a stake in the status quo and become economically and psychologically resistant to new kinds of insurgency. Thus, while a general case can and should be made for a community of interests among the unions, the Negroes, and the unorganized poor, these groups will often clash both in their immediate demands and their basic political styles.

What I would call the "rate of involvement" among the interest groups and moral-issue groups is likely to be sharply different at various moments, and the result is unavoidable friction. When the unions were surging ahead in the thirties, they received little help from the churches; it did not even occur to anyone at that time to expect much help. The Catholic Church in particular was regarded as a major center of political reaction. Today we witness the astonishing and exhilarating rise of ferment within the Catholic community, while the unions, though still fierce guardians of yesterday's gains, are not notable as centers of innovation.

Ideally there ought to be cooperation between those committed to a politics of pressure and those committed to a politics of insurgency; but in practice the latter often tend to define themselves through dissociation from the former (perhaps on the "principle" that you strike out most violently against your closest relatives) while the former feel their survival and even their honor to be threatened by the latter. As long as the wretched Vietnam war continues and social stagnation consequently characterizes our domestic life, this conflict is likely to be exacerbated.

The programmatic demands advanced by the liberal-left groups for domestic reforms during the thirties have by now either been mostly realized or require merely—but that's *some* merely!—quantitative implementation. By itself this does not yield a dramatic or inspiring perspective; it does not excite the young, it barely arouses those in whose behalf it is advanced, and it proves more and more inadequate for coping with the new problems we all experience more sharply than we can define.

There has occurred over the Vietnam war a split between groups focusing primarily on domestic issues, mostly the unions, and the groups focusing primarily on foreign policy, mostly the middle-class peace organizations and radical youth. During the twentieth century, with the possible exception of the 1916 election, foreign policy has never played a decisive role in American elections; or, to modify that a bit, disputes over foreign policy, such as the interventionist/isolationist quarrel in the thirties, did not threaten the survival of the liberal coalition. Today this is no longer true, and cannot be true—even though I am unhappily convinced that in an electoral showdown the moral protestants, among whom I wish to include myself, would prove to be a very small minority. Never in the past has it been possible to rally a successful liberal-left movement on issues of foreign policy alone or predominantly. Whether it can be done today remains very much an open question.

We are living through an exhaustion, perhaps temporary, of American liberalism. It is not, at the moment, rich in programmatic suggestions. It has lost much of its earlier élan. It has become all too easily absorbed into establishment maneuvers, so that it shares a measure of responsibility for the Vietnam disasters and ghetto outbreaks. It has not developed new leaders. In short, as its most intelligent spokesmen know, it is in a state of moral and intellectual disarray.

Yet in fairness one should add that pretty much the same difficulties beset most or all other political tendencies in the United States. One of the remarkable facts about our political life is the paucity of specific proposals to come from the far left or far right. A comparison with the thirties is instructive, for whatever else was wrong with American radicalism (almost everything) at that time, it did advance specific proposals for legislation and thereby agitation. Today that is hardly the case. "Participatory democracy" may be a sentiment as noble as it is vague, but even its most ardent defenders cannot suppose it to be a focused proposal for our national life. And by a similar token, it is interesting that Governor Reagan did not really try to dismantle the welfare state against which he had mock-raged during his first campaign.

I think that for the next period we shall have to live and work within the limits of the welfare state. There is only one possibility that this perspective will be invalidated, and that is a racial conflict pitting white against black—a tragedy which even the most puerile advocates of "nose-to-nose confrontation" must recognize as utterly disastrous. Unless we are to delude ourselves with the infantile leftism of the talk

78

about "Negro revolution" (sometimes invoked most fiercely by guerrillas with tenure), the first point on the political agenda must be a
renewed struggle for the fulfillment of the claims advanced by the welfare state. And that, in turn, means a simultaneous struggle to end the
Vietnam war and to bring large-scale economic help to the Negro
ghettos.

A Word About the Future

If one could view the present moment with detachment, one might say
that we are witnessing the breakdown of the old political coalition which
helped usher in the welfare state and perhaps the slow beginnings of a
new coalition to improve and transcend the welfare state. In this new
coalition the labor movement would still have—it would have to have—
a central role, but no longer with the decisive weight of the past. The
churches would matter a great deal more, and so would the American
"new class," that scattered array of intellectuals, academicians, and technicians. Issues of foreign policy would occupy a central place in the
program of such a coalition, as would those concerning "quality of life"
—though, I am convinced, the immediate major domestic concern remains the realization of the welfare-state expectations for the American
Negroes. In such a coalition there might come together the tradition of
moral protest and the bearing of witness with the tradition of disinter-
ested service. All of this could occur only through a radicalization of
American liberalism: a politics unqualifiedly devoted to democratic norms
but much more militant, independent, and combative than the left-
liberalism of today.

Whenever in the past American radicalism has flourished somewhat, it has largely been in consort with an upsurge of liberalism. There
have been two major periods of radical activity: first during the years
immediately preceding World War I and then during the thirties. The
notion that radicalism can grow fat on the entrails of liberalism is a crude
error, an absurdity.

But all of this remains hope and speculation. Before such a new
coalition emerges, if ever it does, there is likely to be severe tension and
conflict among its hoped-for component parts. The Vietnam war stands
as a harsh barrier, political and psychological, which must be broken

down in order to take care of our business at home—which is by no means to accept the quietistic and reactionary argument that until the war is ended nothing can or should be done at home.

Even the full realization of the "idea" of the welfare state would not bring us to utopia or "the good society." The traditional socialist criticisms in respect to the maldistribution of power, property, and income would still hold. But to continue the struggle for such a realization is both a political and a human responsibility. And through the very struggle to realize the "idea" of the welfare state—if I may offer a "dialectical" observation—it is possible to gain the confidence, strength, and ideas through which to move beyond the welfare state. Unfortunately, American intellectuals do not seem well equipped for keeping to this dual perspective: they either lapse into a genteel and complacent conservatism or they veer off into an ultimatistic and pseudo-utopian leftism. Yet, when one comes to think of it, why should it be so difficult to preserve a balance between the struggle to force the present society to enact the reforms it claims to favor and the struggle to move beyond the limits of the society? Tactically, to be sure, this creates frequent difficulties; but conceptually, as a guiding principle, I think it our only way.

5

RICHARD F. HAMILTON

Class and Race
in the United States

Richard F. Hamilton is a professor of sociology at McGill University. His
writings include *Affluence and the French Worker in the Fourth Republic*
(1967) and *Class and Politics in the United States* (forthcoming).

In recent discussions it has been claimed that manual workers are more
"authoritarian" than the middle classes. Specifically, the claim has been
made that the workers are less tolerant of racial, ethnic, and religious
minorities; that they are less tolerant of political minorities; and that
they are less likely to support democratic rules of procedure.[1] The
leading presentation of this thesis makes an extended discussion of the
experiences of those raised in the working class, experiences which might
plausibly produce "rigid and intolerant approaches to politics." Among
the experiences mentioned are "low education, low participation in political or voluntary organizations of any type, little reading, isolated
occupations, economic insecurity, and authoritarian family patterns. . . ."
The end product of such "training" is a "greater suggestibility, absence
of a sense of past and future . . . [an] inability to take a complex view
. . . [they have] greater difficulty in abstracting from concrete experience,

---

[1] The leading formulation is that of Seymour Martin Lipset, "Working-class
Authoritarianism," Chapter 4 of *Political Man* (New York: Doubleday, 1960).
Some statements appeared even earlier, in Nathan Glazer and S. M. Lipset, "The
Polls on Communism and Conformity," pp. 141–65 of Daniel Bell, ed., *The New
American Right* (New York: Criterion Books, 1955).

81

and lack imagination." Their training "predisposes them to view politics as black and white, good and evil."[2]

Discussions in earlier decades made the same claims about the "lower-middle class." This ill-defined group was viewed as a "dangerous" class, as a group which, potentially at least, could provide the mass support for radical rightist, reactionary movements. It was this group, so it is said, which gave the Nazis their mass electoral base. The sources of their "reaction," then and now, are to be found in their strained position, their apparent loss of status relative to workers, their isolation and anomie, their helplessness in the face of events and lack of effective control of their own life conditions. They, like manual workers, have been portrayed as having little education and little involvement in voluntary associations. Small shopkeepers, for example, work in isolated occupations; they are competing against other small shopkeepers and at the same time are being ground down by big chain stores and so on. They are, therefore, subject to considerable economic insecurity. Within small shops one also finds more authoritarian family patterns. Children are enlisted to work in the family enterprise at an early age and are continuously subject to the rule of an anxious and increasingly desperate father. Unreasoning obedience is demanded; children growing up in this context are "broken," they are made into dependent submissive beings. As adults, they later become willing followers of "tough" and "dynamic" leaders who offer easy (and, therefore, unreal) solutions. Since they have no effective organized way of dealing with their strained social position, it is to be expected that they would develop hostility toward any easily identifiable groups which might be viewed as the source of their difficulty. Such hostilities would also be directed toward groups viewed as getting ahead at their expense. Given their low level of education and understanding, they come to be willing followers of "demagogues" who appear from time to time proffering easy solutions and defining stereotypically the "enemies."

In short, the lower-middle class is also thought to be authoritarian. They, too, are felt to be intolerant of racial, religious, and ethnic minori-

[2] Lipset, *Political Man,* pp. 98, 100, 109, 115. The Lipset position contains two basic elements; first, the claim of a greater "authoritarianism" among workers, and second, an explanatory claim linking the orientation to deprivation and child-rearing practices. For a fuller discussion and detailed documentation of this and other points raised in this paper, see Chapter 11 of the author's forthcoming book, *Class and Politics in the United States* (John Wiley and Sons).

ties, to distrust political minorities, and to lack commitment to the "democratic rules of the game."

Given the plausibility of the argument, given the expectation that "authoritarianism" follows from such life experiences, it is not surprising that these views are widely accepted by members of the upper-middle-class intelligentsia. These views have also gained widespread acceptance because there is a range of supporting evidence. The acceptance of the claim has, in turn, provided the basis for an "appropriate" political response, namely, a retreat to elitism. The inverse of these views of authoritarianism is the supposition of upper-middle-class and elite virtue. These groups come to be portrayed as tolerant, as "moderates," as those who are interested in and willing to protect minority rights, as guarantors of due process, and as capable managers of the social and economic enterprise. Capable management, it is said, will "pay off" in the long run with increased income, education, and security for everyone, thus ushering in a universal good life for all citizens. It is a contingent necessity, however, that the political-economic mechanism not be disturbed or disrupted by either the lower-middle-class or working-class authoritarians. For those interested in maximizing such development, as well as for those interested in maintaining and protecting minority rights, it therefore seems clear, there is a need for "containment" of the dangerous, erratic, unpredictable, and un- or even anti-democratic masses.

These claims thus provide the basis for a definition of appropriate political strategies, strategies which seriously undermine conventional views of democracy. Hence it is clearly a matter of the greatest importance to explore once again the empirical support for the view.

WHITE ATTITUDES AND THE RIGHTS OF BLACKS: MANUALS AND NONMANUALS

Distribution of response to questions in four national studies (dated 1956, 1964, and two from 1965) are shown in Table 1. Contrasting first non-Southern manuals and nonmanuals, we find very little difference between the two groups.[3] The greatest difference in favor of the received

[3] The 1956 and 1964 studies are those of the Survey Research Center of the University of Michigan. They were made available through the Inter-University Consortium for Political Research. The 1965 studies were conducted by the Amer-

hypothesis amounts to only 8 percentage points. There is one difference of 6 percentage points. As for the remaining six questions, there is *no difference* between the white non-Southern manuals and the non-manuals.

TABLE 1   WHITE ATTITUDES TOWARD BLACK RIGHTS: BY CLASS AND REGION
(married, employed)

	Non-Southern		Southern	
	Manual	Nonmanual	Manual	Nonmanual
	Per cent tolerant (of those with opinion)			

1956   "If Negros are not getting fair treatment in jobs and housing, the government should see to it that they do."

PER CENT AGREEING	73	74	63	64
N =	(348)	(315)	(90)	(123)

1956   "The government in Washington should stay out of the question of whether white and colored children go to the same school."

PER CENT DISAGREEING	52	54	30	31
N =	(349)	(315)	(111)	(137)

1964   "Should the government in Washington . . . see to it that Negroes get fair treatment in jobs [or] . . . leave these matters to the states and local communities?"

PER CENT FOR WASHINGTON ACTION	47	45	32	33
N =	(229)	(273)	(60)	(120)

1964   "Do you think that the government in Washington should see to it that white and Negro children go to the same

ican Institute for Public Opinion (Gallup) and were made available through the Roper Center, Williamstown, Massachusetts. I wish to express my appreciation to both research organizations and to both distributors for making these studies available.

The manual workers are those falling into one of the following U.S. Census categories: craftsmen, operatives, laborers, or service. The nonmanuals are those falling into one of the following: professionals, managers, officials, proprietors, sales, and clericals. For more details, see my *Class and Politics.*

It will be noted that the categories being used are those developed in Weimar Germany which stem largely out of the work of revisionist Marxism. These categories have been taken over and incorporated in much of contemporary American social science. They are being used here so as to address the claims which have beein derived from this framework.

	Non-Southern		Southern	
	Manual	Nonmanual	Manual	Nonmanual

Per cent tolerant (of those with opinion)

schools [or] . . . stay out of this area as it is none of its business?"

PER CENT FOR WASHINGTON

ACTION	54	60	19	36
N =	(230)	(282)	(64)	(128)

1964   "Which of these statements would you agree with? White people have a right to keep Negroes out of their neighborhoods if they want to. Or, Negroes have a right to live wherever they can afford to, just like white people."

PER CENT FOR OPEN HOUSING	72	80	38	41
N =	(247)	(293)	(63)	(123)

1965   (Asked of those with children in schools)
"Would you, yourself, have any objection to sending your children to a school where . . . half of the children are colored?"

PER CENT SAYING THEY

WOULD NOT OBJECT	74	72	29	39
N =	(250)	(256)	(96)	(66)

1965   "If colored people came to live next door, would you move?"

PER CENT SAYING NO	64	67	46	40
N =	(506)	(530)	(221)	(168)

1965   ". . . do you think that private organizations such as country clubs and college fraternities and the like should or should not have the right to exclude otherwise qualified Negroes from membership?"

PER CENT SAYING NO	54	52	22	14
N =	(654)	(573)	(214)	(183)

Among the white Southerners, a somewhat more complex pattern appears. There is again no difference between manuals and nonmanuals in the responses to many of the questions, e.g., to the 1956 jobs and housing question, to the 1956 school question, and to the 1964 jobs question. With respect to the 1964 school integration question, there is a fair-sized difference, one of 17 percentage points. There is also a middling difference, of 10 percentage points, in the response to the 1965 question on school integration. For the rest, the pattern is again one of essentially no difference in the responses to four questions and rather small differences in two cases.

On the whole, the evidence presented here yields only very restricted support for the claim of "working-class authoritarianism." In six of the eight comparisons of the non-Southern groups there is basically no support for the claim. In the remaining two comparisons, the maximum difference amounts to 8 percentage points. In the South, there is again no support in six of the eight comparisons. In the Southern responses to the school integration questions of 1964 and 1965, there is some support for the claim; the maximum difference is 17 percentage points.

If one were talking about sharp contrasts, where all or nearly all of the members of group A possess trait X and none or only few of the members of group B possess the trait, one would be justified in referring to the X-ness of group A. If, on the other hand, the case were similar to the one we are considering, in which one group is somewhat more likely (by a few percentage points) to possess a trait, then the attribution of X-ness to the entire group would not be justified. Rather than asking why one group and not the other has the characteristic, the data presented here indicate that the appropriate line of inquiry is to discover the sources of intolerance *within each* of the groups. Particularly outside the South, it is clear that "class" is not a significant factor and that it is necessary to look for that "something else" which may either stimulate or support intolerance in both classes.

WHITE ATTITUDES AND THE RIGHTS OF BLACKS: LOWER-MIDDLE AND UPPER-MIDDLE CLASSES

Taking the same questions and exploring the pattern within the white-collar ranks, we find a solid basis also to be lacking for the second of the received hypotheses: that the lower-middle class is more "authoritarian" than the upper-middle class (Table 2). Looking first at the non-Southern middle-class populations we find the lower middles on the whole to be somewhat *more* tolerant than the upper middles.[4] This is the case in five

[4] The division of the nonmanual category into upper middles and lower middles was on the basis of an arbitrary income break. For the 1964 and 1965 studies a family income of $10,000 or more was taken as "upper middle" and those below that as "lower middle." In the South, allowing for somewhat lower income levels, a $7,500 figure was used.

86

TABLE 2   MIDDLE-CLASS WHITE ATTITUDES TOWARD BLACK RIGHTS:
BY REGION

(*married, employed*)

	Non-Southern		Southern	
	Lower Middles	Upper Middles	Lower Middles	Upper Middles
	Per cent tolerant (of those with opinion)			
1956	Jobs and housing			
PER CENT	82	64	68	63
N =	(162)	(137)	(34)	(86)
1956	School integration			
PER CENT	58	50	14	37
N =	(155)	(144)	(36)	(96)
1964	Fair treatment in jobs			
PER CENT	45	44	35	33
N =	(146)	(116)	(48)	(70)
1964	School integration			
PER CENT	60	61	31	40
N =	(153)	(117)	(51)	(73)
1964	Housing			
PER CENT	79	80	31	47
N =	(159)	(118)	(48)	(75)
1965	School integration			
PER CENT	80	56	25	39
N =	(153)	(94)	(16)	(44)
1965	Family next door			
PER CENT	71	61	45	38
N =	(365)	(164)	(62)	(104)
1965	Private organizations			
PER CENT	54	48	16	10
N =	(348)	(210)	(107)	(68)

of the eight comparisons, the differences ranging from a low of 6 percentage points to a high of 24. This difference occurs in response to the school integration question, that is, whether one would object to sending one's children to a school where half the children were "colored." Only one in five of the non-Southern lower-middle class say they would object as opposed to some 44 per cent of the upper-middle category. There are three comparisons which do not show the lower-middle-class respondents to be more tolerant than those from the upper-middle class.

They are, however, cases involving almost no difference between the lower- and upper-middle classes. The responses reviewed here, in short, provide no support for the conventional position—that is, that the lower-middle class is especially intolerant and that the upper-middle class is tolerant.

In the South, the pattern is again somewhat more complicated. In four of the eight comparisons the Southern lower-middle class proves to be slightly more tolerant than the upper-middle, although all differences are small (ranging from 2 to 7 percentage points). An equal number of differences in the opposite direction support the conventional viewpoint. These differences are somewhat larger, ranging from 9 percentage points to 23.

The idea of upper-middle-class moderation and lower-middle-class immoderation receives only very limited support. Nowhere do sharp differences between these classes justify a claim about contrasting class-specific propensities. Outside of the South, the imputed view of a "dangerous" lower-middle class gains no support whatsoever, most comparisons in fact showing greater tolerance in the lower-middle class. Other comparisons show no difference. In the South, as indicated, the pattern is more complex, but it still does not show clear support for the prevailing view.

If that view were valid, one ought to find consistent and fair-sized differences between the lower- and the upper-middle classes. In twelve of the comparisons presented here that is not the case. In some of these the pattern is just the opposite of the expected one. The best that can be said for the conventional hypothesis is that there are four instances of support out of a total of sixteen. All four of these, it must be noted, involve the Southern population.

Thus far, so as to address the two conventional claims, we have presented either combined or truncated results. By piecing together data from the previous two tables, we may now see, simultaneously, the state of tolerance in all three class levels. For this purpose, the 1964 results of the Survey Research Center will be presented. We find the following percentage tolerant in the population outside the South:

	Manuals	Lower Middles	Upper Middles
Jobs	47	45	44
Schooling	54	60	61
Housing	72	79	80

It will be noted that the over-all differences are, as is to be expected, very small. While there is a slight positive relationship between class and tolerance with respect to schools and housing, the opposite is the case with respect to jobs. Once again, the lesson is clear: outside the South, class is no significant predictor of tolerance.[5]

Parallel percentage measures of toleration in the South are:

	Manuals	Lower Middles	Upper Middles
Jobs	32	35	33
Schooling	19	31	40
Housing	38	31	47

Here, once again, the result is rather erratic. With respect to the job question there is essentially no difference. With respect to the school integration question there is clear support for both of the received hypotheses. With respect to housing we find the lower-middle class the least tolerant, the upper-middle class the most tolerant, and the working class in between.

It should be noted that a presentation which did *not* make a separation by region would show an over-all pattern of working-class intolerance. A similar result would appear in an over-all comparison of lower- and upper-middle classes. The separation makes it clear that whatever support there is for the hypotheses about greater intolerance among manual workers as well as the lower-middle class is to be found, not across the nation, but only in the South.

Another fact must be considered here—namely, the peculiar "Southern-ness" of the United States' manual workers. The non-Southern white manual ranks have a somewhat higher percentage of Southern-reared members than the equivalent nonmanuals. The Southern non-manual ranks, by comparison, have a higher proportion of persons reared outside of the region than the Southern white manuals. In the course of migration some of the Southern bigotry is transferred into the non-Southern manual ranks, and some of the relatively moderate outlooks of the North are transferred into the Southern middle-class ranks. This sug-

[5] It should be kept in mind that the first two of these questions have a mixed focus. The questions on jobs and schooling involve a federal government role in enforcement. The housing question focuses directly on rights.

gests that in part the above results are due to interregional migration patterns rather than to any class-specific training or deprivation.[6]

The original formulation of the "working-class authoritarianism" claim focused on class-specific experiences in "explaining" the "fact" of worker intolerance. An alternative worth considering, another line of inquiry into the components of the classes, into the outlooks and relative sizes of the various class segments, involves the socio-religious factor. This is to suggest that there are distinctive patterns of training which are independent of class and specific to the major socio-religious communities.

It should come as no surprise that Jews in the United States are overwhelmingly in favor of equal rights. Not so well known, but also important, is the fact that white Catholics are generally more tolerant than white Protestants (Table 3). The lowest levels of tolerance, of willingness to recognize Negro rights, is found among white Protestants. On the whole, this distribution of outlooks is to be expected. It is clearly in the *interest* of minorities, ideal considerations apart, to be supportive of equal rights. For a dominant majority such considerations are not likely to be pressing. Moreover, a long history of "nativism"—white

TABLE 3   CLASS, RELIGION * AND TOLERANCE: NON-SOUTHERN WHITES
(*married, employed*) 1964

Per cent tolerant (of those with opinion)

Manuals	Jobs	N =	Schools	N =	Housing	N =
Protestant	46	(142)	49	(142)	70	(154)
Catholic	51	(75)	61	(75)	73	(79)
Lower Middles						
Protestant	41	(80)	56	(90)	78	(92)
Catholic	47	(53)	65	(51)	77	(53)
Upper Middles						
Protestant	37	(63)	55	(60)	75	(65)
Catholic	53	(38)	61	(38)	88	(34)

* There were too few Jewish respondents to justify presentation.

[6] The manual ranks are disproportionately located in the South. One study shows 31 per cent (N=1023) of the economically active male manual workers to be located in the South as compared to 23 per cent (N=701) of the nonmanual. These figures are derived from Samuel A. Stouffer's study, *Communism, Conformity and Civil Liberties* (New York: Doubleday, 1955).

Protestant hostility to immigrants, outsiders, newcomers, etc.—would undoubtedly leave some contemporary residues. For the influential and powerful groups within the majority, one might well expect an opposite commitment—namely, an emphasis on the special rights, the special prerogatives of the gifted, the capable, the elect, the talented, the "fittest."

One might assume that the white upper-middle class in the United States would be disproportionately Protestant. That, however, is not the case. There is a slight inverse relationship existing, the white Protestant percentage in the non-Southern upper-middle class being 54 and among the equivalent manual workers, 62. The Catholic proportion runs at about one-third in all three class levels. The Jewish percentage increases with the class level.

For three reasons the over-all picture initially presented tends to misrepresent the relative tolerance of the classes in question: because of the disproportionate presence of Southerners in the white working class, because of the disproportionate Protestant representation in the white working class, and because of the disproportionate presence of Jews in the upper-middle class. Were we to take the non-Southern white Protestant majority and exclude the Southern-reared segment, it is clear that the relationship shown above would be shifted in the direction of relatively greater working-class tolerance.

Considerations of the composition of various classes do not alter the facts about the distribution of attitudes by class shown in Table 1. Rather, they provide some basis for interpreting the significance of that original relationship. This examination of the component segments indicates the unimportance of class-specific training, of low education, and of economic deprivation as far as attitudes toward blacks are concerned. The traditional focus, in short, is misleading; it causes one to overlook a fact of greater significance, namely, socio-religious background and, presumably, the training associated with "growing up" in the Catholic or Jewish as opposed to the white Protestant context.

One other lesson is clear. In some respects, the Southern working class proves to be less tolerant than the Southern middle class. A presentation without regional analysis would suggest support for the working-class authoritarianism thesis. Specification by region, however, makes it clear that the tendency is not found in the entire class but only in its Southern segment.

91

RACISM: PERSONAL AND INSTITUTIONAL

It is worthwhile noting the relevance of the above data to the potency of "race" as an issue for "cutting across" the ranks of the economic liberal majority and thus making possible a "conservative victory. In recent years it has been claimed, with increasing frequency, that the United States is a "racist" society. There are two divergent views of this, the "white racism" problem. One holds that there is widespread personal, individual hostility felt by whites toward the black population. The other maintains the existence of "institutional racism," in which the personal position of whites may be tolerant, but, because there are institutions which segregate, the personal position has little effect on realities which involve separate and very unequal conditions.[7]

The difference is an important one. If the racism were "personal"— that is, if it were widespread, open, aware, and committed intolerance— the problem of social change would be a formidable one. It would involve going against the will of a sizable and committed majority. If the majority attitude were tolerant, the possibilities for change would be much greater. Change, however, would involve the transformation of institutions. The willingness to recognize the rights of others is one thing, the willingness and capacity to make major institutional changes is another.

Available evidence offers very little support for the notion of widespread personal intolerance. The basic trend in recent decades has decisively been in the opposite direction, toward ever greater tolerance.

The willingness to recognize equal rights, at least to the extent of a verbal commitment, is indicated by data in this paper. The "purest" statement of rights is the 1964 question on housing, that is, whether Negroes "have a right to live wherever they can afford to." As shown in Table 1, some 80 per cent of the non-Southern middle-class whites favor that right. Among the manual workers the figure is 72 per cent. Corresponding percentages for the South, expectedly, are considerably lower, 41 and 38 respectively for nonmanual and manual workers. The majority support for equal housing outside of the South does not guarantee social peace. Intolerant minorities, the 20 and 28 per cent respec-

[7] A useful account of the implications of institutional racism appears in Louis L. Knowles and Kenneth Prewitt, eds., *Institutional Racism in America* (Englewood Cliffs: Prentice-Hall, 1969).

tively who do not support the right to live where one pleases, represent tens of millions. The possibility of racist reaction from these millions, or some minorities within that minority, is obviously enormous. The possibility and actuality of such "disturbances" (which loom so large in the headlines) should not, however, lead one to overlook or misrepresent the character of majority sentiment.

Other responses in the 1964 study show lower "tolerant" percentages. The questions, however, involved two elements, the question of the rights of blacks and the question of a federal government role. It seems likely that some people who would favor the equal rights position would not favor "government intervention." The unwillingness to use that political vehicle is one of the reasons for a relative absence of personal racism and a simultaneous persistence of racist institutions—in schools, with respect to job opportunities, and with respect to private clubs and organizations.

AGE AND ATTITUDES TOWARD BLACKS

Previous research has indicated that younger people are more tolerant, more willing to recognize the equality of other groups, than are older generations.

It would be easy to assume that increasing education, greater media attention, more "cosmopolitan" experience, and organized campaigns to build tolerance have brought this about. The implication is that massive intolerance within the white population existed at some time in the past (judging from the oldest cohorts, at the turn of the century) and that new "educational" efforts have succeeded in "converting" younger generations to a more amicable position. An alternative possibility is a changed composition hypothesis. We have seen that white Protestants are less "tolerant" than Catholics and Jews. It has been also shown that the older age cohorts are disproportionately white and Protestant.

A separate consideration of the three major groups, the white Protestant, Catholic, and Jewish "communities," yielded a rather complicated picture. Taking first the white Protestants and using five age categories, we found, with respect to the job rights and school integration responses, that the oldest cohort, those fifty-five or more, were markedly less in favor of government intervention than the younger groups (Table 4). There was little systematic variation between the four younger age

93

groups. With respect to the less complex question of a right to a free choice in housing, there was a consistent increase in tolerance among younger age groups.

TABLE 4   AGE AND CIVIL RIGHTS QUESTIONS:
NON-SOUTHERN WHITE PROTESTANTS AND CATHOLICS
(*married, employed*) 1964

	Age				
	To 24	25-34	35-44	45-54	55 or more
WHITE PROTESTANTS	Per cent liberal (of those with opinion)				
Jobs	43	48	41	46	29
N =	(37)	(66)	(78)	(68)	(42)
Schools	53	48	58	55	40
N =	(38)	(65)	(81)	(65)	(47)
Housing	87	83	73	67	67
N =	(39)	(70)	(95)	(73)	(39)
WHITE CATHOLICS					
Jobs	45 *	52	52	59	32
N =	(11)	(62)	(42)	(27)	(25)
Schools	58 *	63	58	65	67
N =	(12)	(59)	(41)	(34)	(21)
Housing	85 *	88	76	61	74
N =	(13)	(59)	(51)	(28)	(19)

* Small number of cases.

A similar pattern appeared among white Catholics. The oldest cohort was least favorably disposed to government intervention to guarantee job rights, but otherwise there was no clear variation. There was no variation at all with respect to the school integration question, all age categories being more or less equal in their willingness to accept a government role. Again, with respect to the housing question there was a fairly consistent pattern of increased tolerance among the younger age categories. There was little variation by age within the Jewish group. All age groups with few exceptions were "tolerant."

There does appear to be a consistent tendency toward enhanced equalitarianism indicated by the responses to the housing question. With respect to the more complex questions, those on jobs and schooling, involving both equalitarian principles and a government role, the picture is not so simple. The oldest cohort considered was less willing to accept a government role than the other cohorts. There is a decisive break between this older group and all the younger groups. Otherwise there is no shift indicated.

In the South, taking only the dominant white Protestant group, we found no consistent variation at all by age with respect to the two questions on a government role. With respect to the housing question, there was, once again, a fairly consistent tendency toward increased equalitarianism in the younger generations.

In both the South and the rest of the country there appears to be a secular trend toward increasing acceptance of the equalitarian principle. That trend exists within both white Protestant and Catholic subgroups and is enhanced by a shift in the relative proportions of these two groups in the non-Southern population. Although there is an increase in willingness to recognize equality, with the exception of the oldest cohort, a corresponding development of willingness to use the federal government as an instrument to guarantee equality does not seem to occur.

If there is a trend toward the principle of equality, as we have argued, this would again suggest a diminution of the potential for radical rightist movements based on racist appeals. The nucleus of anti-black sentiment appears among older white Protestants. It is clear that with the passing of the years, due to declining participation and the obvious facts of demography, the importance of that group will be steadily reduced.

The most frequently propounded claim about the trend is that "education" brings about tolerance. This assumes that "education" either directly involves the teaching of tolerance or, alternatively, has an indirect impact by bringing people into social and economic circumstances which then engender more "moderate" outlooks.

The assumption of a direct liberalizing influence, while perhaps applicable to the contemporary scene, is not so appropriate as an explanation of the past. Much of education then, particularly higher education, taught a lesson of special privilege for the "fit," for those of "good stock," for the gentry trained for leadership. This "pre-modern" educational orientation is demonstrated by the oldest of the cohorts, for their education-tolerance relationship shows a slight inversion, the least educated tending to be the somewhat more tolerant.

The education-tolerance relationship, as indicated by the responses to the housing question, is positive in the three younger cohorts considered here. If this result is due to education, it would again suggest a continuing erosion of the basis for any racist demagogic appeal. With respect to the questions of a federal government role, on the other hand, the relationship is erratic. Particularly in regard to a government role in guaranteeing job equality, the finding varies strikingly with conventional expectations. In the youngest cohort equal percentages of both grade school educated and college educated favored the government role. In both cohorts the high school educated, by a small margin, were most favorably disposed. Again, a lack of correspondence is indicated between acceptance of the principle of equality and willingness to make use of the most effective guaranteeing agency.

The question of a possible reaction may be approached more directly. The 1964 Presidential campaign contained an intentional effort at generating a white "blacklash," that is to say, a reaction away from the majority Democratic party. This was supposed to occur among the economically depressed or marginal whites, those who felt themselves threatened by the advances being made in the black revolution. Here we may explicitly link the "reaction" to both the personal, financial situation and to the attitude toward the rights of blacks.

The percentage of Republican votes was lowest among those who said they were not satisfied with their financial situation. The largest percentage of Republican votes was to be found among those who were "more or less" satisfied, although even here the differences are not very large. Perhaps the best conclusion is that the individual economic condition had very little to do with Republican voting among the white workers. It is clear that sensed deprivation was *not* a factor in creating Republican voting; those who were dissatisfied were clearly *less* likely than other workers either to vote for or to favor the Republican candidate.

A more fruitful line of analysis would begin with party identification. That is to say, here as elsewhere, the key factor may be a traditional allegiance. Part of the result reported in the above paragraph, for example, is due to the fact that those who are "not at all" satisfied (21 of 24) happen to be Democratic identifiers.

The overwhelming majority of Democratic identifiers remained with their party in 1964. Those voting came out for their traditional party and those who did not vote also were loyal to that party. None of the Democratic identifiers, incidentally, who were dissatisfied with their financial situation defected. By comparison, again as indicated previously, there was a substantial counter-defection among the white working-class Republicans. The reaction to the attempt at generating a backlash among the white workers, in short, was a net gain for the Democrats. Most of the defecting Democrats, as is to be expected, opposed a federal government role in guaranteeing job equality for Negroes. There was, however, a counter movement among the Republican workers who favor the government guaranteeing role. Even among the white Republican workers who opposed the federal role, the defection involved one in three.

A peculiar feature of the white Republican working class is that they are, in comparison to their Democratic peers, relatively opposed to federal government intervention in the areas of schooling and jobs. There is virtually no difference between the two groups in the responses to the housing question, suggesting that the division is not on the equality principle but rather involves the question of the proper role of government.

The absence of "consistency" in these attitudes points up a difference in behavior and outlooks of liberal and radical intelligentsia, on the one hand, and of the general population on the other. The liberal and radical position in respect to the three questions used here is that one should be for the equal housing option and for a government role in guaranteeing both job and school equality. At the other extreme, there is an expectation of some kind of core racism (thought to be very widespread) which would involve a preference for the three opposite positions. It is easy to sort out white workers into the "pure liberal" and the "pure racist" categories. When that is done, it turns out that only a smallish minority of the non-Southern white workers display such consistency. Most of those who were consistent happened to be consistent liberals, the distribution being as follows: consistent liberals, 20 per cent; mixed cases, 71 per cent; and consistent racists, 9 per cent.

Sizable majorities of all three working-class groups are Democratic identifiers. Both Democratic and Republican liberals came down overwhelmingly for the Democratic candidate in 1964 voting and in nonvoter preferences. Surprisingly, most of the racists who were Democratic identifiers, eleven out of twelve, also remained with the Democratic party. Most of the defection (both directions) is found among those with mixed positions on these issues.

There are a number of lessons of special interest to be observed here. The first is the absence of widespread committed racism within the working class such as would be indicated by consistent intolerant responses to these three questions. The most frequent case is one involving a "mixture" of outlooks. Within that "mix," one important cluster involves an acceptance of the equal housing principle with a simultaneous refusal to use government enforcement potential in the other two areas. Another large group responded with "don't knows," "it depends," and "no interest" with respect to the questions and issues raised. It is to be noted that these responses do not indicate opposition to the black demands but suggest, if not openness, at least an "uncommittedness" which might be channeled in either direction.

A second lesson involves the consistent liberals. The coherence of viewpoint of the liberal intelligentsia (or of the radicals) stems from exceptional circumstances and exceptional training. It comes from being raised in a milieu sharing those outlooks. Within such a milieu a continuous informal process of education takes place, a process of refinement, correction, and improvement in the outlook of those in the setting. The "mature" outlook is far from being a "natural" development. It means, too, that expecting a "pure" position from those who have not had the advantages of that "training" is somewhat unrealistic.

BLACK-WHITE CONTACTS AND ATTITUDES

The discussion to this point has been somewhat abstract because comparisons have been of the attitudes of large aggregates of the white population. By themselves, these attitudes do not make events (or prevent their occurrence). Of central importance to the development of black-white relations in general are the attitudes of those actually present at the points of contact between blacks and whites. As a consequence of migration patterns and segregation, a large percentage of manual workers and an even greater percentage of nonmanual workers have no significant contact with blacks either in their neighborhoods or in their workplaces (Table 5). The greatest amount of contact is found among large-city manual workers. Roughly two out of three are employed in a shop with at least some blacks, and roughly one-third live in a neighborhood with at least some blacks.

In terms of the two conventional hypotheses on the subject, we ought to find among workers in the integrated settings the greatest hostility toward blacks, specifically, we should find the most intense competition for jobs, and we should find the most formidable struggle to keep blacks out of the neighborhood.

It was possible to sort out the non-Southern white workers by integration settings so as to allow some testing of these expectations. The re-

TABLE 5   NEIGHBORHOOD AND WORKPLACE INTEGRATION
BY SIZE OF PLACE AND CLASS

(*non-Southern employed whites*)

	Size of Place								
	Large City			Middle-Sized			Small Town		
Class:	Working	Lower-Middle	Upper-Middle	Working	Lower-Middle	Upper-Middle	Working	Lower-Middle	Upper-Middle
Neighborhood:									
All-white	68	77	72	79	92	92	87	93	91
Mostly white	21	17	25	21	8	8	13	7	9
Half and half, Mostly black *	11	6	3	—	—	—	—	—	—
N =	(133)	(81)	(75)	(82)	(61)	(39)	(82)	(54)	(23)
Workplace:									
All-white	34	51	52	71	74	70	62	74	70
Mostly white	49	42	43	26	25	24	37	21	30
Half and half, Mostly black *	18	7	5	3	2	6	—	4	—
N =	(113)	(73)	(61)	(77)	(57)	(33)	(72)	(47)	(20)

* The overwhelming majority of these say "half and half."

spondents were initially divided into three categories: those living in all-white neighborhoods and working in all-white shops, those who have all-white neighborhoods and integrated workplaces, and those who have both integrated neighborhoods and workplaces.[8] Contrary to the popular hypothesis, those in integrated neighborhoods and jobs also had the most favorable attitudes with respect to both the job-rights and equal-housing questions. The least favorable attitudes with respect to the job-rights question are found among those in the segregated milieu. There are no sharp differences between the segregated and the mixed settings with respect to the residential segregation question, both running slightly behind the integrated group in their level of tolerance. In short, contrary

[8] In what follows, the term "integrated" is used to refer to those reporting at least some Negroes in the workplace or neighborhood, that is, it includes all those categories from "mostly white" to "all Negro."

to the image of competition and struggle in the transitional areas on the edges of the ghetto, those settings actually contain the most positive attitudes to be found in the working class.

Those questions indicate the attitudes with respect to rights. Perhaps more decisive is a question on interracial friendships. It is, of course, to be expected that there will be very few friendships mentioned by those in the segregated or mixed settings. If competition and conflict were the case in the integrated neighborhoods, one would also expect to find very few friendly contacts there. People might live side by side but they would have little to do with each other. The reports from those living in the integrated settings, however, indicate an opposite picture, namely, one of much friendly contact.

These findings suggest that the conventional view of ruthless struggle at the point of contact is not accurate. This point is even more significant in view of the fact that the whites in the integrated neighborhoods, on the whole, are poorer, older, and are more likely to be immigrant or first-generation American.

All of this suggests that another line of analysis might be more appropriate. One simple, straightforward hypothesis present in the sociological literature is the claim that continuous and sustained contact, particularly as status equals, will lead to feelings of friendliness and solidarity. It is this kind of contact which is present in the integrated neighborhoods and, conceivably, has created this favorable outlook. By comparison, those whites who happened to be born, raised, and living in small towns have never had that kind of contact and their orientations are likely to have been formed out of the remnants of a nativist tradition together with some more recent stereotypes fashioned out of episodes and fragments from the mass media. That would suggest that the "competition for jobs" and the concern with housing prices in middle-sized and small communities is of little importance.

This alternative to the competition-hostility hypothesis assumes that there is a change in attitude associated with integration. The data presented here, it will be noted, do not justify that conclusion. One would need a before-after study in order to show such a *change* in attitude. Another possible explanation for the observed finding might be self-selection. It might be, for example, that what we are looking at in the integrated urban setting is a kind of "residual" white community, the one which is left over after the most intolerant whites have moved out.

In short, the positive attitudes of those living in the integrated neighbor-hoods might result not from attitude change but rather from a change in the location of the intolerant populations. It is also clearly a possibility that both factors are involved, that there may be both self-selection, a choice to move out, and also a conversion on the part of those remaining. At minimum, however, it is clear that the points of contact are not, as has been frequently assumed, characterized by widespread hostility felt by the white population living there. Greater hostility to the equal rights of the blacks appears among those who live some distance away and who have little contact with the black population.

The Housing Question

The major concerns which presumably lead white working-class persons to be hostile toward blacks are centered in the areas of housing and jobs. The movement of blacks into a neighborhood presumably reduces the value of housing there, causing financial loss to families ill-equipped to pay such costs. The threat of such losses gives rise to hostilities or else aggravates those already present.[9]

The over-all result suggests some support for this expectation. The non-Southern white working-class home-owners do show less support for the equal-housing option than do the renters. At the same time, it ought to be noted that a majority of the owners, two-thirds of them in fact, favor the open-housing option and that the difference between the owners and the non-owners amounts to only 13 percentage points.

The picture is complicated by a number of related factors. Home-owners tend to be older than the renters. Then, too, the proximity to blacks varies considerably by city size so that the large-city owners face the "threat" of reduced house values, but those in middle-sized cities and small towns, on the whole, do not. It might be that the greater tolerance of the renters is purely a function of age, they having been reared in a more tolerant era than is the case with a majority of the owners. A limited control for both age and city size, however, still shows the owners to be less approving than the renters. The most positive atti-

[9] This is a claim which has been challenged by some empirical studies of the question, for example, the work of Luigi Laurenti, *Property Values and Race: Studies in Seven Cities* (Berkeley: University of California Press, 1961).

101

tudes are found among the younger renters. The least positive attitudes are found among older owners. In the case of the older owners, however, the division is still fifty-fifty, not one of overwhelming opposition.

There are two alternative possible readings of this result. One is that the older generation is less tolerant, that different attitudes were instilled in times past. The other alternative is that people change their outlooks over the years; they are tolerant early in their careers but with increasing age, as their equity increases and their earning power declines, they come around to a "defensive" intolerant outlook. There is very little one can do to resolve the matter at this point. A contrast with the older renters is difficult because there are very few cases of older working-class renters in this sample.

Another complicating factor is the religious one. In the large cities, older working-class home-owners are disproportionately white and Protestant. A majority of the younger white working-class home-owners, by comparison, are Catholic. A separate examination within the two religious communities still showed the home-owners to be less tolerant than the renters in all comparisons. At the same time, however, it should be noted that with one minor exception all groups of home-owners have tolerant majorities.

Implicit in the above results is another complicating factor. A majority of the large-city manual workers living in mixed neighborhoods are renters. By comparison, the overwhelming majority of those living in all-white neighborhoods are owners. In other words, a majority of those who have some neighborhood contact are not subject to any sense of or threat of economic loss with respect to their housing. And it is this group which has the most favorable attitudes within the large city white manual ranks, 87 per cent of them (N=23) favoring the open-housing option.

It is difficult to draw any firm conclusions about the future. There are a number of contingencies still to be discussed which might affect the situation. For the moment, it may be noted that the actual distribution of attitudes with respect to equal housing is much more positive than is generally realized. Even with respect to a key source of strain, the presumed impact of integration on the value of housing, while we do find a consistent pattern of the home-owning workers being less tolerant than the renters, with equal consistency we find that only a minority of the home-owners behave as commonly predicted. Among the renters and also among the owners in mixed neighborhoods, a higher level of support for equal rights is found. The absence of economic strain for the renters and the influence of personal contact in the case of owners in mixed neighborhoods appear to be the main factors yielding this result. It also appears that a reasonably friendly co-existence prevails in the mixed neighborhoods rather than, as is widely believed, a general antagonism and hostility.

THE JOB QUESTION

Another area of presumed strain and tension is the job sphere. The most frequently heard assumption here is that blacks and whites, particularly those in the working class, are competing for jobs and, consequently, seek to exclude their black competition. The over-view in Table 1 would not appear to support this assumption about the orientations of the white workers. The 1956 question which focused on "jobs and housing" found workers in both Southern and non-Southern regions just as favorably disposed to a government role as the middle class. The same holds for the 1964 question which focused exclusively on "fair treatment in jobs."

Since this "competition" and struggle is likely to be most serious among the poor, a more precise test of the hypothesis would examine the attitudes by income level. Since class is not a factor, we have combined the manuals and nonmanuals for this purpose. Looking first at the non-Southern population in the 1956 study, one finds that the pattern is just the opposite of the conventional expectation. The percentage favoring the government guarantee of equality in jobs and housing is greatest among the poor (Table 6). According to the conventional hypothesis, the poor should be *less* willing than the well-off. They should fall far short of the 81 per cent indicating support for a government role as is shown in this study.

The evidence from the same study for the Southern whites shows the same pattern, the largest percentage in favor of the government guarantee of equality in these two areas again being found among the poor whites. There is, to be sure, no strong relationship with income, but the remarkable fact is that the tolerant response tends to be negatively related to income rather than, as is so frequently assumed, positively.

This accounting focuses on the nonfarm populations. It might be

103

TABLE 6   INCOME AND GOVERNMENT GUARANTEE OF JOB EQUALITY:
BY REGION
(married, active, nonfarm white population)
Family Income

	To $3,999	$4,000 4,999	$5,000 5,999	$6,000 7,499	$7,500 9,999	$10,000 14,999	$15,000 or more
	Per cent favoring government role * (of those with opinion)						
1956							
Non-Southern	81	75	76	72	68	70	
N =	(105)	(124)	(126)	(102)	(111)	(72)	
Southern	70	53	67	67	62	58	
N =	(50)	(38)	(49)	(30)	(24)	(19)	
1964							
Non-Southern	57		41	48	44	45	32
N =	(61)		(53)	(107)	(121)	(102)	(43)
Southern	38		30	25	23	35	48
N =	(39)		(27)	(28)	(26)	(34)	(23)

* See Table 1 for question wordings.

that the "really" poor whites are to be found within the farm populations. An alternative stress has, to be sure, focused on the rednecks, the
peckerwoods, and the crackers as providing the core support for
the racist reaction. Separate consideration of the poor Southern-
white farm population, however, did not support this view. Some 76 per
cent (N=21) of those farmers earning less than $4,000 in 1956 gave
the "tolerant" response to this question.

The results from the 1964 study, a study which has a "purer" question, one focusing exclusively on the job question, are similar to those
already described. In the non-Southern regions, the support for the government intervention is greatest among the poor and least among the
rich. In the South, the pattern is somewhat more complicated this time.
There is a negative relationship with income up to the $10,000 cutting
point. In the higher income ranges there is a sharp increase in the percentage of those favoring a government role. These higher income ranges
are heavily impacted with people raised outside of the South. Looking
only at the Southern-reared, however, the same curvilinear pattern appeared, with both the poor and the rich being most favorable to the
intervention and the "middle-income" groups, those between $6,000 and
$10,000 being the least favorable.

The claims about poor whites, about their struggle for jobs and their consequent hostility toward blacks, are not supported by the data at hand, that is, with respect to these questions on a right to job equality. It is clear that some open and vicious struggle over jobs, housing, etc., does occur. The point suggested by these data is that it would be a mistake to generalize from the fact of street riots in poor working-class neighborhoods and to take such facts as evidence about the outlook of the entire area.

At this point and with the limited resources available, one can do little else but guess at the reasons for this unexpected development. One possibility is that the poor have a strong concern with equality, that they have a greater commitment to the equality value than any other group in the population. Another related possibility is that the very poor know what it means to be unemployed and do not wish that experience on anyone.

This suggestion amounts to a minor doctrinal heresy but it is worthwhile at least considering the possibility—namely that a dominant motivation is one of common decency. A fair quantity of materials are now available which challenge the "ruthless competition" viewpoint (the "hard realistic" outlook). These materials stress patterns of reciprocity, of helping one another out, and of behaving in ways which through cooperation do something to ease the burdens.[10]

It is clear that the survey evidence considered here does not support the standard hypotheses on the subject. Outside of the South there are basically no differences in the proportions of manuals and nonmanuals who affirm an equal-rights position. Even within the South the differ-

[10] Some evidence and discussion of the working-class reciprocity patterns may be found in the following sources: William J. Newman, "The Culture of the 'Proles,'" *Dissent,* V (Spring 1958), 154–61; Richard Hoggart, *The Uses of Literacy* (London: Chatto and Windus, 1957); Michael Young and Peter Willmot, *Family and Kinship in East London* (London: Routledge and Kegan Paul, 1957); Andrée Michel, "Relations parentales et relations de voisinage chez les ménages ouvriers de la Seine," *Cahiers Internationaux de Sociologie,* XVII (July-December 1954), 140–53; Donald E. Muir and Eugene A. Weinstein, "The Social Debt: An Investigation of Lower-Class and Middle-Class Norms of Social Obligation," *American Sociological Review,* 27 (August 1962), 532–39; William F. Whyte, *Street Corner Society,* 2d edition (Chicago: University of Chicago Press, 1955); and Herbert J. Gans, *The Urban Villagers* (New York: The Free Press, 1962).

Some evidence on the concern with equality may be found in William Form and Joan Rytina, "Income and Ideological Beliefs on the Distribution of Power in the United States," *American Sociological Review,* 34 (February 1969), 19–31, and "Income and Stratification Ideology: Beliefs About the American Opportunity Structure," *American Journal of Sociology,* 75 (January 1970), 703–16.

ences prove to be surprisingly small. In the specific conflict areas, in housing and jobs where black-white struggle is expected, the surveys indicate a considerable basis for harmony. The attitudes of whites at the "points of contact" prove to be generally more favorable than is the case with those whites who are more distant, who live and work in all-white settings.

One other aspect deserves some emphasis. The only point at which interracial conflict can occur is where there is some contact. The most likely setting for conflict, in other words, is in those integrated areas where the attitudes toward integration, on the whole, happen to be most favorable. Although the dominant attitude in such areas happens to be positive, there is a minority present which holds opposite orientations. It is obviously possible to draw enough "recruits" from among that intolerant minority to make a sizable "urban disturbance."

The major lesson indicated by this review of the evidence is that the hypothesis of "working-class authoritarianism" has very little support. At least up to the mid-sixties the survey data reviewed here show that outside of the South, that is for the large majority of the American population, there is no support for the hypothesis. Even in the South the evidence favoring the hypothesis is, at best, rather fragmentary. The alarm generated about the sentiments or propensities of the "lower middle class" also appears to be without justification.[11]

[11] An abridged version of a paper which reviews the evidence through to 1968, including evidence on the Wallace support in that year, appears in my "Black Demands, White Reactions, and Liberal Alarms," in Sar Levitan, ed., *Blue-Collar Blues* (forthcoming). The findings reported there are very similar to those reported in this article.

6

HARRY MAGDOFF

The Economic
Aspects of Imperialism

Harry Magdoff has taught economics at the New School for Social Research
and other colleges and now serves as co-editor of *Monthly Review*. He
wrote *The Age of Imperialism* (1969) and a sequel, "Is Imperialism Really
Necessary?" *Monthly Review*, Vol. 22, Nos. 5 and 6, October and November 1970.

Three interrelated views on the New Imperialism, and in particular on
contemporary economic imperialism and United States foreign policy,
prevail today:

1. Economic imperialism *is not* at the root of United States foreign
policy. Instead, political aims and national security are the prime motivators of foreign policy.

2. Economic imperialism *cannot* be the main element in foreign
policy determination, since United States foreign trade and foreign
investment make such relatively small contributions to the nation's overall economic performance.

3. Since foreign economic involvement is relatively unimportant
to the United States economy, it follows that economic imperialism
need not be a motivating force in foreign policy. Hence some liberal and
left critics argue that present foreign policy, to the extent that it is influenced by imperialism, is misguided and in conflict with the best economic interests of this country. If we sincerely encouraged social and
economic development abroad, the argument goes, even to the extent
of financing the nationalization of United States foreign investment, the
rising demand for capital imports by underdeveloped countries would

create a more substantial and lasting stimulus to prosperity than the current volume of foreign trade and foreign investment.

Obscuring economic and commercial interests by covering them up or intermingling them with idealistic and religious motivations is hardly a new phenomenon. Wars have been fought to impose Christianity on heathen empires—wars which incidentally also opened up new trade routes or established new centers of commercial monopoly. Even such a crass commercial aggression as the Opium War in China was explained to the United States public by the American Board of Commissioners for Foreign Missions as "not so much an opium or an English affair, as the result of a great design of Providence to make the wickedness of men subserve his purposes of mercy toward China, in breaking through her wall of exclusion, and bringing the empire into more immediate contact with Western and Christian nations." [1]

John Quincy Adams, in a public lecture on the Opium War, explained that China's trade policy was contrary to the law of nature and Christian principles:

> The moral obligation of commercial intercourse between nations is founded entirely, exclusively, upon the Christian precept to love your neighbor as yourself. . . . But China, not being a Christian nation, its inhabitants do not consider themselves bound by the Christian precept, to love their neighbor as themselves. . . . This is a churlish and unsocial system. . . . The fundamental principle of the Chinese Empire is anti-commercial. . . . It admits no obligation to hold commercial intercourse with others. . . . It is time that this enormous outrage upon the rights of human nature, and upon the first principles of the rights of nations, should cease. [2]

Perhaps the Christian principle of "love thy neighbor" and the more modern ethic that the anti-commercial is also immoral have become so habitual in accepted ways of thought that we have lost the facility to sep-

[1] American Board of Commissioners for Foreign Missions, *32nd Annual Report* (1841), as quoted in Richard W. Van Alstyne, *The Rising American Empire,* Chicago, Quadrangle Books, 1965, p. 171. The latter, originally published in 1960 by Oxford University Press, New York, is highly recommended for a better understanding of the continuity of United States foreign policy. See also Charles A. Beard, *The Idea of National Interest,* reissued in 1966 by Quadrangle Paperbacks with new material; and Lloyd C. Gardner, *Economic Aspects of New Deal Diplomacy,* Madison, University of Wisconsin Press, 1964.

[2] *Niles' National Register,* January 22, 1842, pp. 327–8.

arate the various strands that make up foreign policy. Perhaps the source of the difficulty can be traced to a lack of understanding of what Bernard Baruch called "the essential one-ness of [United States] economic, political and strategic interests." [3]

There will probably be little dispute about the "one-ness" of United States political and national security aims. The only rationale of national security today is "defense" against the Soviet Union and China. To be absolutely safe, it is said, we need also to cope with the "concealed wars" which may appear as internal revolutions or civil war.[4] It is merely coincidental, to be sure, that socialist revolutions destroy the institutions of private ownership of the means of production and thereby violate the Christian precept to love thy neighbor by eliminating freedom of trade and freedom of enterprise in large and important sectors of the earth.

The "one-ness" of the political and national security aims becomes more evident on examination of the political aims, since in this realm of thought our policy-makers and policy-defenders are strict economic determinists. Political freedom is equated with Western-style democracy. The economic basis of this democracy is free enterprise. Hence the political aim of defense of the free world must also involve the defense of free trade and free enterprise. The primary departure from this rigid economic determinism appears when dealing with politically unstable nations where, obviously, the art of self-government is not fully developed. In such cases, for the sake of political stability, we permit and encourage military dictatorships, in full confidence that the people of these countries will eventually learn the art of self-government and adopt a free society just so long as the proper underpinning of free enterprise remains.

While our policy-makers and policy-defenders will identify in the most general terms the "one-ness" of the nation's foreign political and national security goals, they usually become quite shy when it comes to the question of the unity of these goals and economic interests. We have come a long way from the very straightforward bulletin prepared in 1922 by the Office of Naval Intelligence on "The U.S. Navy as an

---

[3] Foreword to Samuel Lubell, *The Revolution in World Trade and American Economic Policy*, New York, Harper and Brothers, 1955, p. XL.

[4] *International Security—The Military Aspect,* Report of Panel II of the Special Studies Project of Rockefeller Brothers Fund, Garden City, N.Y., Doubleday & Co., 1958, p. 24.

Industrial Asset." [5] This report frankly details the services rendered by the Navy in protecting American business interests and in seeking out commercial and investment opportunities which the Navy Department brings to the attention of American businessmen.

But today our national aims are presumably concerned only with political and philosophic ideals. In so far as economic interests are concerned, the tables have been turned: today it is business that is expected to serve the needs of national policy. The problem is how to stimulate private investment abroad. Private foreign investment is considered such a necessary tool of national policy that various forms of investment guaranty programs have been designed to protect foreign investors against losses due to confiscation, wars, and the uncertainties of currency convertibility.

The interrelation between economic interests and foreign policy is seen more clearly by business-minded observers. Thus the former president and chairman of the World Bank, Eugene R. Black, informs us that "our foreign aid programs constitute a distinct benefit to American business. The three major benefits are: (1) Foreign aid provides a substantial and immediate market for U.S. goods and services. (2) Foreign aid stimulates the development of new overseas markets for U.S. companies. (3) Foreign aid orients national economies toward a free enterprise system in which U.S. firms can prosper." [6]

More specifically, an Assistant Secretary of Commerce for Economic Affairs explains to businessmen that "if these [military and economic] aid programs were discontinued, private investments might be a waste because it would not be safe enough for you to make them." [7]

On a much more elevated plane, we are told by a specialist on

[5] The full title reads, *The United States Navy as an Industrial Asset—What the Navy has done for Industry and Commerce,* written by the Office of Naval Intelligence, U.S. Navy, in October, 1922 and published in 1923 by the U.S. Government Printing Office, Washington, D.C. The following excerpt is typical: "In the Asiatic area a force of gunboats is kept on constant patrol in the Yangtse River. These boats are able to patrol from the mouth of the river up nearly 2,000 miles into the very heart of China. American businessmen have freely stated that should the United States withdraw this patrol they would have to leave at the same time. Our Navy not only protects our own citizens and their property, but is constantly protecting humanity in general and frequently actually engages the bands of bandits who infest this region." (p. 4)

[6] *The Domestic Dividends of Foreign Aid* in *Columbia Journal of World Business,* Vol. 1, Fall 1965, p. 23.

[7] Address by Andrew F. Brimmer at a meeting of the Tax Foundation, Inc., as reported in the *New York Times,* December 5, 1965.

international business practice, a teacher at MIT and Harvard: "It would seem that there is a horrible urgency in making Western economic concepts internationally viable if man's dignity is to be preserved—and incidentally, a profitable private business." [8]

And as an indication of how in fact some influential members of the business community see the "one-ness" of economic, political, and security interests, listen to the view expressed in 1965 by the Vice-President of Chase Manhattan Bank who supervises Far Eastern operations:

> In the past, foreign investors have been somewhat wary of the over-all political prospect for the [Southeast Asia] region. I must say, though, that the U.S. actions in Vietnam this year—which have demonstrated that the U.S. will continue to give effective protection to the free nations of the region—have considerably reassured both Asian and Western investors. In fact, I see some reason for hope that the same sort of economic growth may take place in the free economies of Asia that took place in Europe after the Truman Doctrine and after NATO provided a protective shield. The same thing also took place in Japan after the U.S. intervention in Korea removed investor doubts. [9]

But even if we grant the interrelatedness of economic, political, and security interests, how much priority should we assign to economic interests? Specifically, how can one claim that economic imperialism plays a *major* role in United States policy if total exports are less than 5 percent of the gross national product, and foreign investment much less than 10 percent of domestic capital investment?

Let us note first that the size of ratios is not by itself an adequate indicator of what motivates foreign policy. Many wars and military operations were aimed at control over China's markets at a time when those markets represented only one percent of total world trade. Overall percentages need analytical examination: the strategic and policy-influential areas of business activity need to be sorted out.

Above all, it is important to appreciate that the stake of United States business abroad is many times larger than the volume of merchandise exports. The reason for this is that the volume of accumulated capi-

[8] Richard D. Robinson, *International Business Policy*, New York, Holt Rinehart and Winston, 1966, p. 220.
[9] "Economic Considerations in Foreign Relations—An Interview with Alfred Wentworth" in *Political*, Vol. I, No. 1, July 1965, pp. 45–6.

tal abroad controlled by United States business has been increasing at a faster rate than exports. The unique advantage of capital is that it reproduces itself. That is, the output obtained by capital investment produces enough revenue to cover not only costs of labor and raw materials but also the capital and natural resources consumed plus profits. The annual flow of capital invested abroad is therefore additive: increments to capital enlarge the productive base. Even more important, United States firms abroad are able to mobilize foreign capital for their operations. The net result of the flow of capital abroad and the foreign capital mobilized by American firms is that while production abroad arising out of United States investment was 4½ times larger than exports in 1950, by 1964 this had risen to 5½ times exports. These observations are based on estimates made in a recent study conducted by the National Industrial Conference Board.[10]

OUTPUT ABROAD RESULTING FROM U.S. INVESTMENT

	Sales (in Billions)	
	1950	1964
Output from direct investment *	$24	$ 88
Output from other investment **	20	55
Total	44	143
Sales abroad via exports	10	25
Total output abroad plus exports	$54	$168

* As defined by the Department of Commerce, direct investments are branch establishments or corporations in which United States firms own 25 percent or more of the voting stock.

** "Other investment" represents mainly stocks and bonds of foreign firms owned by United States firms and individuals.

When the Department of Commerce measures the economic significance of exports, it compares them with a figure for total domestic production of moveable goods—that is, the sales of agricultural products, mining products, manufactures, and freight receipts. The estimated total of moveable goods produced in the United States in 1964 was $280 billion.[11] There are technical reasons which make it improper to com-

[10] *The Conference Board Record,* Vol. III, No. 5, May 1966, p. 28. See also Judd Polk, Irene W. Meister and Lawrence A. Veit, *U.S. Production Abroad and the Balance of Payments: A Survey of Corporate Investment Experience,* New York, National Industrial Conference Board, 1966.

[11] This total consists of (a) cash receipts from farm marketing plus consumption of farm products in the farm household, (b) value added in manufacturing industries, (c) value of minerals production, and (d) freight receipts.

pare the $168 billion of sales abroad with $280 billion of domestic output of moveable goods. For example, a portion of our exports is shipped to United States-owned companies as components or semi-finished products. Thus, if we add such exports to output of United States-owned foreign business we are double counting. Adjusting for this and other sources of non-comparability, we arrive at a conservative estimate that the size of the foreign market (for domestic and United States-owned foreign firms) is equal to approximately two-fifths the domestic output of farms, factories, and mines.[12]

If this seems surprising to those who are accustomed to think in terms of Gross National Product, remember that the latter includes government expenditures, personal and professional services, trade, and activities of banks, real estate firms, and stock brokers. But as far as the business of farms, factories, and mines is concerned, foreign business amounts to quite a noteworthy volume relative to the internal market. Nor is this the whole story. These data do not include the considerable amount of sales abroad of foreign firms operating under copyright and patent agreements arranged by United States firms. As an example, one firm in the Philippines manufactures the following brand-name products under restricted licenses of United States firms: "Crayola" crayons, "Wessco" paints, "Old Town" carbon paper and typewriter ribbons, "Mongol" lead pencils, "Universal" paints, and "Parker Quink."

The increasing relative importance of foreign economic activity is well illustrated by the experience of the manufacturing industries, as shown in Chart 1 and Table 1. Here we compare total sales of domestic manufactures with exports of manufactures and sales of United States direct investments in foreign manufacturing activity. The data are plotted on a semi-logarithmic scale in the chart. Therefore, the narrowing of the distance between the two lines depicts the more rapid rise of the foreign market as compared with the growth of domestic markets.

Equally significant is the comparison of expenditures for plant and equipment in foreign-based and in domestic manufacturing firms (Chart 2 and Table 2). As in the preceding chart, the narrowing of the distance

---

[12] The Department of Commerce estimates that $6.3 billion of exports was shipped to foreign affiliates of United States companies in 1964. Other sources of non-comparability arise because (a) the estimated $168 billion includes sales of trade organizations, public utilities, and other non-commodity producers, and (b) the date on sales of domestic manufactures are on a value-added basis while the sales of foreign affiliates are on a value-of-shipments basis. Conservative estimates of adjustments to obtain comparability reduce the $168 billion to $110 billion.

113

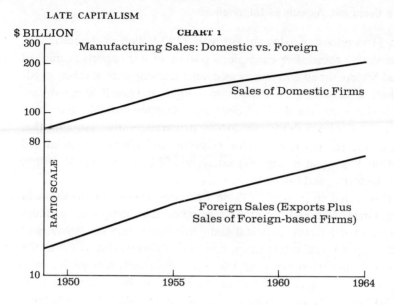

CHART 1
Manufacturing Sales: Domestic vs. Foreign

TABLE 1   MANUFACTURES—FOREIGN AND DOMESTIC SALES
(In Billions)

(1)	(2)	(3)	(4)		(5)	
Year	*Exports*	*Sales by Foreign-based U.S. Firms*	*Total Foreign Sales (2) + (3)*		*Sales of Domestic Manufactures*	
			Absolute	*1950 = 100*	*Absolute*	*1950 = 100*
1950	$ 7.4	$ 8.4	15.8	100	89.8	100
1955	12.6	13.9	26.5	168	135.0	150
1960	16.1	23.6	39.7	251	164.0	183
1964	20.6	37.3	57.9	367	203.0	226

Source: Exports—U.S. Bureau of the Census, *Statistical Abstract of the United States: 1965,* pp. 877, 773. 1964 Sales of Domestic firms—U.S. Bureau of the Census, *Annual Survey of Manufactures, 1964.* Sales of foreign-based U.S. firms—the data for 1950 and 1955 are estimates based on the average relation between sales and investment abroad. (This is the procedure used by the National Industrial Conference Board.) Data for 1960 and 1964—*Survey of Current Business,* September 1962, p. 23, November 1965, p. 18.

Note: The data in columns (4) and (5) are not strictly comparable (see footnote 12). However, the non-comparability does not destroy the validity of comparing the differences in the rates of growth of the two series.

between the two lines is a clear portrayal of the increasing relative importance of business activity abroad. Expenditures for plant and equipment for United States subsidiaries abroad were a little over 8 per cent

114

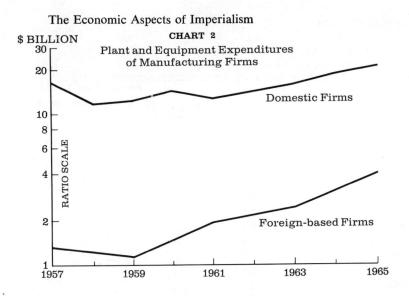

CHART 2
Plant and Equipment Expenditures
of Manufacturing Firms

TABLE 2   PLANT AND EQUIPMENT EXPENDITURES BY U.S. DOMESTIC AND FOREIGN-BASED MANUFACTURING FIRMS

	Domestic Firms		Foreign-based Firms		Foreign as
Year	Billion $ 1957 = 100		Billion $ 1957 = 100		% of Domestic
1957	$16.0	100	$1.3	100	8.1
1958	11.4	71	1.2	92	10.5
1959	12.1	76	1.1	85	9.1
1960	14.5	91	1.4	108	9.7
1961	13.7	86	1.8	139	13.1
1962	14.7	92	2.0	154	13.6
1963	15.7	98	2.3	177	14.7
1964	18.6	116	3.0	231	16.1
1965	22.5	141	3.9	300	17.3

Source: Foreign-based firms—*Survey of Current Business,* September 1965, p. 28; September 1966, p. 30. Domestic firms—*Economic Report of the President,* Washington, D.C., 1966, p. 251.

of such expenditures of domestic firms in 1957. In 1965 this had risen to 17 per cent.

It is not surprising to find, as shown in Chart 3 and Table 3, that profits from operations abroad are also becoming an ever more important component of business profits. In 1950, earnings on foreign investment represented 10 per cent of all after-tax profits of domestic nonfinancial corporations. By 1964, foreign sources of earnings accounted for about

115

TABLE 3   EARNINGS ON FOREIGN INVESTMENT AND DOMESTIC
CORPORATE PROFITS

	Earnings on Foreign Investment (Billions of Dollars)	Profits (After Taxes) of Domestic Nonfinancial Corporations
1950	2.1	21.7
1951	2.6	18.1
1952	2.7	16.0
1953	2.6	16.4
1954	2.8	16.3
1955	3.3	22.2
1956	3.8	22.1
1957	4.2	20.9
1958	3.7	17.5
1959	4.1	22.5
1960	4.7	20.6
1961	5.4	20.5
1962	5.9	23.9
1963	6.3	26.2
1964	7.1	31.3
1965	7.8	36.1

Source: Earnings on foreign investments—U.S. Department of Commerce, *Balance of Payments Statistical Supplement Revised Edition,* Washington, 1963; *Survey of Current Business,* August 1962, August 1963, August 1964, September 1965, June 1966, September 1966. Profits of nonfinancial domestic corporations— *Survey of Current Business,* September 1965, July 1966.

Note: Earnings include (a) earnings on direct investments abroad, (b) fees and royalties on direct investment transferred to parent companies in the U.S., and (c) income from "other" investments (other than direct) transferred to U.S. owners of these assets.

22 per cent of domestic nonfinancial corporate profits. In evaluating the significance of this we should also take into account (a) the understatement of foreign earnings because the latter do not include all the service payments transferred by foreign subsidiaries to home corporations, and (b) the financial advantages achieved in allocating costs between the home firms and foreign subsidiaries so as to minimize taxes. Moreover, we are comparing foreign earnings with earnings of all nonfinancial corporations—those that are purely domestic and those that operate abroad as well as in the United States. If we compared foreign earnings with total earnings of only those industries that operate abroad, the share of foreign earnings would of course be much larger than one fourth.

The significance of the last three tables is their representation of the rapid growth of the foreign sector. During the period when the economy as a whole was experiencing a slowing down in the rate of growth, foreign markets were an important source of expansion. For example, in manufacturing industries during the past ten years domestic sales increased by 50 per cent, while foreign sales by United States-owned factories increased over 110 per cent.

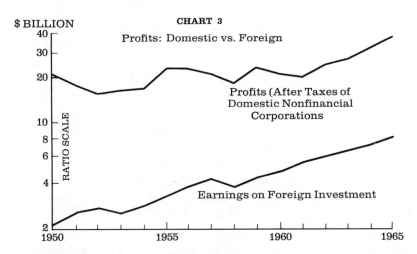

Thus, as far as the commodity-producing industries are concerned, foreign markets have become a major sphere of economic interest and have proven to be increasingly important to United States business as an offset to the stagnating tendencies of the inner markets.

This is quite obvious to American businessmen. The treasurer of General Electric Company put it this way in discussing "the need that American business has to keep expanding its foreign operations":

> In this respect, I think business has reached a point in the road from which there is no turning back. American industry's marvelous technology and abundant capital resources have enabled us to produce the most remarkable run of peacetime prosperity in the nation's history. To keep this going, we have for several years sought additional outlets for these sources in foreign markets. For many companies, including General Electric, these offshore markets offer the most promising opportunities for expansion that we can see.[13]

[13] John D. Locton, "Walking the International Tightrope," address at National Industrial Conference Board, May 21, 1965, published by General Electric Co., Schenectady, N.Y., 1965, pp. 4–5.

It is also quite obvious that if foreign markets are so important to the commodity-producing industries, they are also of prime importance to the other interest groups, those whose profits and prosperity are dependent upon the welfare of the commodity-producers as well as those who benefit from servicing trade and investment in foreign markets: investment and commercial bankers, stock market speculators, transportation, insurance, etc.

For a full measure of economic involvement in foreign markets, the impact of military spending—the "defense" program—must also be reckoned with. The growth of our inner and outer markets has, since the founding of the Republic, been associated with the use (actual or threatened) of military force in peace as well as war. Professor William T. R. Fox states the case quite mildly: "The United States Army in peacetime was, through most of the nineteenth century, extensively used to aid in the winning of the West, and especially in the suppression of Indian opposition to the opening up of new lands for settlement. Our Navy and Marine Corps, beginning with their exploits against the Barbary pirates were also engaged in making it safe for Americans to live and invest in remote places." [14]

While military activity is today presumably subordinated to national security needs, the "one-ness" of the national security and business interests persists: the size of the "free" world and the degree of its "security" define the geographical boundaries where capital is relatively free to invest and trade. The widespread military bases, the far-flung military activities, and the accompanying complex of expenditures at home and abroad serve many purposes of special interest to the business community: (1) protecting present and potential sources of raw materials; (2) safeguarding foreign markets and foreign investments; (3) conserving commercial sea and air routes; (4) preserving spheres of influence where United States business gets a competitive edge for investment and trade; (5) creating new foreign customers and investment opportunities via foreign military and economic aid; and, more generally, (6) maintaining the structure of world capitalist markets not only directly for the United States but also for its junior partners among the industrialized nations, countries in which United States business is becoming ever more closely enmeshed. But even all of this does not

[14] William T. R. Fox, "Military Representation Abroad," in *The Representation of the United States Abroad,* a report of The American Assembly, Graduate School of Business, Columbia University, New York, 1956, pp. 124–125.

118

exhaust the "one-ness" of business interest and military activity, for we need to take into account the stake business has in the size and nature of military expenditures as a well-spring of new orders and profits.

As with exports, the significance of military spending for business and the economy as a whole is usually greatly under-estimated. One often hears that defense expenditures amount to less than 10 percent of the Gross National Product and that with a proper political environment comparable government spending for peaceful uses could accomplish as much for the economy. A crucial weakness of this approach is its uncritical acceptance of Gross National Product as a thing-in-itself. Because GNP is a useful statistical tool and one which has become entrenched in our ways of thought, we tend to ignore the underlying strategic relationships that determine the direction and degree of movement of the economic aggregates. Instead of examining the requirements of the industrial structure and the dynamic elements of economic behavior, we tend to view the economy as blocks of billions of dollars that may be shifted at will from one column to another of the several categories used by statisticians to construct the measurement of GNP.

To appreciate fully the critical influence of foreign markets and military expenditures on the domestic economy, recognition must be given to their exceptionally large impact on the capital goods industries. But first a comment on the capital goods industries and the business cycle. There are diverse explanations of business cycles, but there can be no disputing the fact that the mechanics of the business cycle—the transmission mechanism, if you wish—is to be found in the ups and downs of the investment goods industries. There are cycles which are primarily related to the ebb and flow of inventories, but these are usually short-lived as long as the demand for investment goods does not collapse.

During a cyclical decline, the demand for consumer goods can be sustained for a period by several expedients such as unemployment relief, other welfare payments, and depletion of consumer savings. However, except for the most essential replacement needs, expenditures on investment goods theoretically can go down to zero. Businessmen naturally will not invest unless they expect to make a profit. The result of the diverse behavior of producer goods and consumer goods was classically demonstrated in the depression of the 1930's. During this probably worst depression in our history, purchases of consumer goods declined only 19 percent (between 1929 and 1933). Compare this with the behavior of the two major types of investment goods during the same period: expenditures for residential construction fell by 80 percent and nonresidential fixed investment dropped 71 percent.

With this as background, let us now focus on the post-Second World War relationship between (a) exports and military demand, and (b) a major category of investment, nonresidential fixed investment goods. Table 4 lists the industries producing nonresidential investment goods. It should be noted that a number of these industries also contribute to consumer goods (e.g., steel and machinery for autos) and to residential construction. This table presents the percentages of total demand (direct and indirect) created by exports and purchases of the federal government, which are almost entirely for military needs. These data are for the year 1958, the latest year for which there exists a complete input-output analysis for the United States economy.

As will be noted from Table 4, in only one industry—farm machinery and equipment—did the combined export and military demand come to less than 20 percent of total demand. At the opposite extreme are the military industries par excellence—ordinance and aircraft. For all the other industries, the range of support given in 1958 by exports and military demand is from 20 to 50 percent.

TABLE 4 PERCENT OF TOTAL OUTPUT ATTRIBUTABLE TO EXPORTS AND FEDERAL PURCHASES, 1958

Industry	Going into Exports	Percent of Output Purchased by Federal Government	Total of Exports and Federal Purchases
Iron and ferroalloy ores mining	13.5%	12.8%	26.3%
Nonferrous metal ores mining	9.1	35.6	44.7
Coal mining	19.1	6.3	25.4
Ordnance and accessories	1.7	86.7	88.4
Primary iron and steel manufacturing	10.1	12.5	22.6
Primary nonferrous metal manufacturing	10.1	22.3	32.4
Stamping, screw machine products	7.1	18.2	25.3
Other fabricated metal products	8.6	11.9	20.5
Engines and turbines	14.8	19.7	34.5
Farm machinery and equipment	10.0	2.9	12.9

120

Industry	Going into Exports	Percent of Output Purchased by Federal Government	Total of Exports and Federal Purchases
Construction, mining and oil field machinery	26.9	6.1	33.0
Materials handling machinery and equipment	9.4	17.2	26.6
Metalworking machinery and equipment	14.0	20.6	34.6
Special industry machinery and equipment	17.5	4.3	21.8
General industrial machinery and equipment	13.4	15.3	28.7
Machine shop products	7.0	39.0	46.0
Electric industrial equipment and apparatus	9.8	17.0	26.8
Electric lighting and wiring equipment	5.5	14.5	20.0
Radio, TV and communication equipment	4.8	40.7	45.5
Electronic components and accessories	7.6	38.9	46.5
Misc. electrical machinery, equipment and supplies	8.9	15.1	24.0
Aircraft and parts	6.1	86.7	92.8
Other transportation equipment (not autos)	10.1	20.9	31.0
Scientific and controlling instruments	7.3	30.2	37.5

Source: "The Interindustry Structure of the United States," *Survey of Current Business,* November 1964, p. 14.

While the available statistical data refer to only one year, the postwar patterns of exports and military expenditures suggest that this tabulation is a fair representation of the situation since the Korean War, and surely a gross underestimate during the Vietnam War. More information and study are required for a more thorough analysis. Meanwhile, the available data warrant, in my opinion, these observations:

1. Exports and military spending exert a distinctive influence on the economy because they fortify a strategic center of the existing

industrial structure. This is especially noteworthy because business investment is not, as is too often conceived, a freely flowing stream. There is a definite interdependence between (a) the existing schedule of wage rates, prices, and profits, (b) the evolved structure of industry (the types of interrelated industries, each built to be profitable at the scale of obtainable domestic and foreign markets), and (c) the direction of profitable new investments. To put it in simpler terms, there are sound business reasons why investments flow in the direction they do and not in such ways as to meet the potential needs of this country—for example, to eliminate poverty, to provide the industry which would create equal opportunity to Negroes, to develop the underdeveloped regions of the United States, or create adequate housing. More important, business cannot invest to accomplish these ends and at the same time meet its necessary standards of profit, growth, and security for invested capital. Exports of capital goods and military demand flowing to the capital-goods producers, on the other hand, are uniquely advantageous in that they strengthen and make more profitable the established investment structure; they also contribute to an expansion of the industries that are most harmonious with and most profitable for the existing composition of capital.

2. The support given by foreign economic involvement—both military and civilian commodities—makes a singular contribution by acting as a bulwark against the slippage of minor recessions into major depressions. It has accomplished this by shoring up one of the strategic balance wheels of the economy, the production of investment-type equipment—by supplying, as we have seen, from 20 to 50 percent of the market for these goods.

3. We need also to take into account that it is *monopolistic* industry which dominates the volume and flow of investment and that such monopolistic businesses characteristically gear their investment policies to the "sure thing," where good profits and safety of investment are reliably assured. Here the tie-in of government action and foreign policy is of paramount interest. The military-goods market usually has the decided advantage of supplying long-term contracts, often accompanied by enough guarantees to reduce and even eliminate any risk in building additional plant equipment which may also be used for civilian purposes. In addition, military contracts pay for related research and development expenses, again removing risky aspects of normal investment programs. As for the foreign countries, the United

States military presence, its foreign policy, and its national security commitments provide a valuable protective apparatus for the investments made in foreign markets. These foreign investments together with the demand created by governmental foreign aid, contribute importantly to the demand for the exports of the capital-goods and other manufacturing industries. The confidence in the consistency of governmental foreign policy and its complementary military policy can, and surely must, act as a valuable frame of reference for the domestic as well as foreign investment practices of monopolistic business.

4. The extra 20 to 50 percent of business provided by exports plus military demand (as shown for the key industries in Table 4) provides a much greater percentage of the total profits of these firms. The typical economics of a manufacturing business requires that a firm reach a certain level of productive activity before it can make a profit. Gross overhead costs—depreciation of machinery, use of plant, cost of administration—remain fairly constant at a given level of capacity. Until production reaches a point where at the market price of the final product enough income is produced to meet the overhead and direct costs, a business operates at a loss. Once this "breakeven" point is reached, the profitability of the business surges forward until it hits against the limits of productive capacity. Of course the curve of profitability differs from industry to industry and from firm to firm. But the existence of a breakeven point, and the upward swing of profits after the breakeven point has been passed is a common characteristic of manufacturing industries. What this means is that for many of the firms in the capital goods industries, the overlay of 20 to 50 percent of demand from military purchases and exports probably accounts for the major share of the profits, and in not a few firms perhaps as much as 80 to 100 percent of their profits.

One of the reasons frequently given for believing that economic imperialism is an unimportant influence in foreign and military policy is that only a small segment of American business is vitally concerned with foreign or military economic activities. This might be a meaningful observation if economic resources were widely distributed and the majority of domestic-minded business firms could conceivably be mobilized against policies fostered by the small minority of foreign-oriented businesses. But the realities of economic concentration suggest quite the opposite. In manufacturing industries, 5 corporations own over 15 percent of total net capital assets (as of 1962). The 100 largest corporations own 55 percent of total net capital assets.[15] This means that a small number of firms—with their own strength and that of their allies in finance and mass communication media—can wield an overwhelming amount of economic and political power, especially if there is a community of interest within this relatively small group.

And it is precisely among the giant corporations that we find the main centers of foreign and military economic operations. Just a cursory examination of the 50 largest industrial concerns shows the following types of firms heavily involved in international economic operations and the supply of military goods: 12 in oil, 5 in aviation, 3 in chemicals, 3 in steel, 3 in autos, 8 in electrical equipment and electronics, and 3 in rubber. These 37 companies account for over 90 percent of the assets of the top 50 industrial firms.

The community of interest among the industrial giants in foreign and military operations stems from relations that are not always obvious in terms of the customary statistical categories. First, there is the interrelationship among the firms via the financial centers of power. Second, there are the direct economic ties of business. While only five firms get one fourth of the volume of military contracts and 25 firms account for more than half of such contracts, a large part of this business is distributed to other businesses that supply these chief contractors.[16] Thus, as we saw in Table 4 the primary nonferrous metal manufacturers who receive very few direct military contracts nevertheless get over 22 percent of their business from military demand. And, third, because of the rich growth potential and other advantages of the military and foreign-oriented businesses, the postwar merger movement among industrial giants has intermingled the typically domestic with the typically outer-market directed business organizations. The most unlikely-seeming business organizations are today planted with both feet in foreign and military business. We see, for example, traditional producers of grain mill products and of plumbing and heating equipment acquiring plants that make scientific instruments, meat packing firms

[15] *Hearings, Subcommittee on Antitrust and Monopoly of the Committee on the Judiciary,* U.S. Senate, 88th Congress, 2nd Session, Part I, Washington, D.C., 1964, p. 115.

[16] *Background Material on Economic Aspects of Military Procurement and Supply: 1964,* Joint Economic Committee of Congress, Washington, D.C., 1964, p. 11.

buying up companies in the general industrial machinery field, and many other cross-industry mergers.

The concentration of economic power, so much part of the domestic scene, shows up in even stronger fashion in the field of foreign investment. The basic available data on this are taken from the 1957 Census of foreign investments. (See table 5.) These data refer only to direct

TABLE 5   U.S. DIRECT FOREIGN INVESTMENT BY SIZE OF INVESTMENT (1957)

Value of Direct Investment by Size Classes	Number of Firms	Percent of Total U.S. Investment
$100 million and over	45	57
$ 50–100 million	51	14
$ 25– 50 million	67	9
$ 10– 25 million	126	8
$ 5– 10 million	166	5
Total	455	93

Source: *United States Business Investments in Foreign Countries*, U.S. Dept. of Commerce, 1960, p. 144.

investments and do not include portfolio investments or such economic ties as are created by the licensing of patents, processes, and trademarks. We note from this table that only 45 firms account for almost three fifths of all direct foreign investment. Eighty percent of all such investment is held by 163 firms. The evidence is still more striking when we examine the concentration of investment by industry:

Industry	No. of Firms	Percent of Total Assets Held
Mining	20	95
Oil	24	93
Manufacturing	143	81
Public utilities	12	89
Trade	18	83
Finance and insurance	23	76
Agriculture	6	83

These data are shown from the viewpoint of total United States foreign investment. If we examined the situation from the angle of the recipient countries, we would find an even higher degree of concentration of United States business activities. But from either perspective, the concentration of foreign investment is but an extension of domestic monopolistic trends. The latter provide the opportunity to accumulate the wealth needed for extensive foreign investment as well as the impetus for such investment.

The question of control is central to an understanding of the strategic factors that determine the pattern of foreign investment. In its starkest form, this control is most obvious in the economic relations with the underdeveloped countries—in the role of these countries as suppliers of raw materials for mass-production industries and as a source of what can properly be termed financial tribute.

Let us look first at the distribution of foreign investment as shown in Table 6. We see here two distinct patterns. In Latin America, Asia, and Africa, the majority of the investment is in the extractive industries. Although Canada is an important source of minerals and oil, only 35 percent of United States investment is in these extractive industries, with 45 percent going into manufactures. The investment in extractive industries in Europe is minimal: the data on petroleum represent refineries and distribution, not oil wells.

TABLE 6   PERCENT DISTRIBUTION OF DIRECT FOREIGN INVESTMENT BY AREA AND INDUSTRY, 1964

Industry	All Areas	Canada	Europe	Latin America	Africa	Asia	Oceania
Mining	8.0	12.1	0.4	12.6	21.9	1.1	6.3
Petroleum	32.4	23.4	25.6	35.9	51.0	65.8	28.1
Manufacturing	38.0	44.8	54.3	24.3	13.8	17.5	54.1
Public utilities	4.6	3.3	0.4	5.8	0.1	1.8	0.1
Trade	8.4	5.8	12.2	10.7	5.7	7.8	5.5
Other	8.6	10.6	7.1	10.7	7.5	6.0	5.9
Total	100.0	100.0	100.0	100.0	100.0	100.0	100.0

Source: Calculated from data in *Survey of Current Business,* September 1965, p. 24.

The economic control, and hence the political control when dealing with foreign sources of raw material supplies, is of paramount importance to the monopoly-organized mass production industries in the home country. In industries such as steel, aluminum, and oil, the ability to control the source of raw material is essential to the control over

126

the markets and prices of the final products, and serves as an effective safety factor in protecting the large investment in the manufacture and distribution of the final product. The resulting frustration of competition takes on two forms. First, when price and distribution of the raw material are controlled, the competitor's freedom of action is restricted; he cannot live very long without a dependable source of raw materials at a practical cost. Second, by gobbling up as much of the world's resources of this material as is feasible, a power group can forestall a weaker competitor from becoming more independent as well as discourage possible new competition. How convenient that a limited number of United States oil companies control two thirds of the "free world's" oil! [17]

At this level of monopoly, the involvement of business interests with United States foreign policy becomes ever more close. The assurance of control over raw materials in most areas involves not just another business matter but is high on the agenda of maintaining industrial and financial power. And the wielders of this power, if they are to remain in the saddle, must use every effort to make sure that these sources of supply are always available on the most favorable terms: these foreign supplies are not merely an avenue to great profits but are the insurance policy on the monopolistic position at home.

The pressure to obtain external sources of raw materials has taken on a new dimension during the past two decades, and promises to become increasingly severe. Even though United States business has always had to rely on foreign sources for a number of important metals (e.g., bauxite, chrome, nickel, manganese, tungsten, tin), it has nevertheless been self-reliant and an exporter of a wide range of raw materials until quite recently. This generalization has been a mainstay of those who argued that U.S. capitalism had no need to be imperialistic. But even this argument, weak as it may have been in the past, can no longer be relied on. The developing pressure on natural resources, especially evident since the 1940's, stirred President Truman to establish a Materials Policy Commission to define the magnitude of the problem. The ensuing commission report, *Resources for Freedom*,[18] graphically summarized the dramatic change in the following comparison for all raw materials

---

[17] A George Gols, "Postwar U.S. Foreign Petroleum Investment," in Raymond F. Mikesell, ed., *U.S. Private and Government Investment Abroad,* University of Oregon Books, Eugene, Oregon, 1962, p. 417.

[18] Washington, D.C., 1952.

other than food and gold: at the turn of the century, the U.S. produced on the whole some 15 percent more of these raw materials than was domestically consumed; this surplus had by 1950 turned into a deficit, with U.S. industry consuming 10 percent more than domestic production; extending the trends to 1975 showed that by then the overall deficit of raw materials for industry will be about 20 percent.

Perhaps the awareness of this development was a contributing factor to President Eisenhower's alerting the nation to the unity of political and economic interests in his 1953 inaugural address: "We know . . . that we are linked to all free peoples not merely by a noble idea but by a simple need. No free people can for long cling to any privilege or enjoy any safety in economic solitude. For all our own material might, even we need markets in the world for the surpluses of our farms and our factories. Equally, we need for these same farms and factories vital materials and products of distant lands. This basic law of interdependence, so manifest in the commerce of peace, applies with thousand-fold intensity in the event of war."

As is so often the case, economic interests harmonize comfortably with political and security goals, since so many of the basic raw materials are considered essential to effective war preparedness. Quite understandably the government makes its contribution to the security of the nation as well as to the security of business via diplomatic maneuvers, maintenance of convenient military bases in various parts of the world, military aid to help maintain stable governments, and last but not least a foreign aid program which is a fine blend of declared humanitarian aims about industrialization and a realistic appreciation that such progress should not interfere with the ability of supplying countries to maintain a proper flow of raw materials. To do a real job of assuring an adequate supply of raw materials in the light of possible exhaustion of already exploited deposits, and in view of possible needs for missiles and space programs, the government can make its greatest contribution by keeping as much of the world as possible "free" and safe for mineral development. Clarence B. Randall, president of Inland Steel Co. and adviser on foreign aid to the government, comments on the fortunate availability of uranium deposits in the Belgian Congo as the atom bomb was developed: "What a break it was for us that the mother country was on our side! And who can possibly forsee today which of the vast unexplored areas of the world may likewise possess some unique deposit

128

of a rare raw material which in the fullness of time our industry or our defense program may most urgently need?" [19]

The integration of less developed capitalisms into the world market as reliable and continuous suppliers of their natural resources results, with rare exceptions, in a continuous dependency on the centers of monopoly control that is sanctified and cemented by the market structure which evolves from this very dependency. Integration into world capitalist markets has almost uniform effects on the supplying countries: (1) they depart from, or never enter, the paths of development that require independence and self-reliance; (2) they lose their economic self-sufficiency and become dependent on exports for their economic viability; (3) their industrial structure becomes adapted to the needs of supplying specialized exports at prices acceptable to the buyers, reducing thereby such flexibility of productive resources as is needed for a diversified and growing economic productivity. The familiar symptom of this process is still seen in Latin America where, despite industrialization efforts and the stimulus of two world wars, well over 90 percent of most countries' total exports consists of the export of agricultural and mineral products.[20] The extreme dependence on exports, and on a severely restricted number of export products at that, keeps such economies off balance in their international economic relations and creates frequent need for borrowing. Debt engenders increasing debt, for the servicing of the debt adds additional balance of payments difficulties. And in all such relations of borrowing and lending, the channels of international finance are in the hands of the foreign investors, their business associates, and their government agencies.

The chains of dependence may be manipulated by the political, financial, and military arms of the centers of empire, with the help of the Marines, military bases, bribery, CIA operations, financial maneuvers, and the like. But the material basis of this dependence is an industrial and financial structure which through the so-called normal operations of the marketplace reproduces the conditions of economic dependence.

A critical element of the market patterns which helps perpetuate

[19] *The Communist Challenge to American Business,* Little Brown & Co., Boston, 1959, p. 36.

[20] Joseph Grunwald, "Resource Aspects of Latin American Development," in Marion Clawson, ed., *National Resources and International Development,* Johns Hopkins Press, Baltimore, 1964, p. 315.

the underdeveloped countries as dependable suppliers of raw materials is the financial tribute to the foreign owners who extract not only natural resources but handsome profits as well. The following comparison for the years 1950-1965 is a clear illustration of the process and refers to only one kind of financial drain, the income from direct investments which is transferred to the United States:

INCOME FROM DIRECT INVESTMENTS TRANSFERRED TO U.S.[21]

(Billions of Dollars)

	Europe	Canada	Latin America	All Other Areas
Flow of direct investments from U.S.	$8.1	$6.8	$3.8	$5.2
Income on this capital transferred to U.S.	5.5	5.9	11.3	14.3
Net	−$2.6	−$ .9	+$ 7.5	+$ 9.1

In the underdeveloped regions almost three times as much money was taken out as was put in. And note well that besides drawing out almost three times as much as they put in, investors were able to increase the value of the assets owned in these regions manifold: in Latin America, direct investments owned by United States business during this period increased from $4.5 to $10.3 billion; in Asia and Africa, from $1.3 to $4.7 billion.

The contrasting pattern in the flow of funds to and from Europe indicates a post-Second World War trend. The rapid growth of investments in Europe was in the manufacturing and oil refining fields. The developments in foreign investment in manufacturing are closely related to the normal business drive to (a) control markets and (b) minimize costs of production. The methods used will vary according to the industry and the conditions in each country. The main factors

[21] These are summations of data presented for 1950 to 1960 in U.S. Department of Commerce, *Balance of Payments Statistical Supplement Revised Edition,* Washington, D.C., 1963. The data for 1961 to 1965 appear in the review articles on foreign investment in various issues of the *Survey of Current Business* from 1962 to 1966. The first line in the text table represents net capital outflows of direct investment from the United States. The second line is the sum of dividends, interest, and branch profits, after foreign taxes, produced by direct investments abroad. It does not include the earnings of corporate subsidiaries (as distinguished from branches) which are retained abroad.

involved in relying on capital investment instead of relying on export trade are:

1. If the profit rate obtainable by manufacturing abroad is greater than by increasing domestic production.

2. If it facilitates getting a larger and more secure share of a given foreign market.

3. If it enables taking advantage of the channels of export trade of the country in which investment is made. Thus, United States business firms in England account for 10 percent of Britain's exports.[22]

4. If it is possible to pre-empt a field of industry based on new technological developments, usually protected by exercise of patent rights.

The most dramatic development of our times is the spread of United States industry into the computer, atomic energy, and space technology activities of industrialized countries. The rapid spread of these fields is motivated, to be sure, by immediate profit opportunities. But it most likely also has the aim of helping to maintain, and get full advantage of, the technical edge United States business now has as a result of the vast investment made by the United States government in research and development. The dominant position in this technology may be decisive in achieving wider control of the rest of the economy, when and if the new technology becomes the key to the productive forces of a society.

Such investment as is made by United States capital in manufacturing in underdeveloped countries occurs primarily in Latin America, where the percentage of total United States investment in the field of manufacturing is 24 percent. This investment is mainly in light manufacturing industry, including the processing of native food materials. Manufacturing operations in the durable goods field, such as autos, takes the form of assembly plants. This guarantees the export market of components and parts. It also contributes to stabilizing the market for these United States products. It is much easier for a country faced with severe balance of payments difficulties to prohibit imports of a luxury product than to eliminate the import of raw materials and assembly parts which will create unemployment and shut down local industry.

The postwar foreign economic expansion of United States manufacturing firms has resulted in the transformation of many of the giants

[22] John H. Dunning, *American Investment in British Manufacturing Industry*, G. Allen, London, 1958.

131

of United States business into a new form of multi-national organizations. The typical international business firm is no longer limited to the giant oil company. It is as likely to be a General Motors or a General Electric—with 15 to 20 percent of its operations involved in foreign business, and exercising all efforts to increase this share. It is the professed goal of these international firms to obtain the lowest unit production costs on a world-wide basis. It is also their aim, though not necessarily openly stated, to come out on top in the merger movement in the European Common Market and to control as large a share of the world market as they do of the United States market. To the directors of such organizations the "one-ness" of economic and national interests is quite apparent. The president of General Electric put it succinctly: "I suggest we will perceive: that overriding both the common purposes and cross-purposes of business and government, there is a broader pattern—a 'consensus' if you will, where public and private interest come together, cooperate, interact and become the national interest." [23]

Needless to stress, the term "private interest" refers to private enterprise. Another officer of this corporation grapples with the identity of the private and national interest: "Thus, our search for profits places us squarely in line with the national policy of stepping up international trade as a means of strengthening the free world in the Cold War confrontation with Communism." [24]

Just as the fight against Communism helps the search for profits, so the search for profits helps the fight against Communism. What more perfect harmony of interests could be imagined?

[23] Speech by Fred J. Borch, President of General Electric Company, "Our Common Cause in World Competition," before The Economic Club of New York, November 9, 1964, printed by General Electric Co., Schenectady, N.Y.

[24] Speech by John D. Lockton, Treasurer of General Electric Company, "The Creative Power of Profits," at Macalester College, St. Paul, Minn., April 22, 1964, printed by General Electric Co., Schenectady, N.Y.

NORMAN BIRNBAUM

Late Capitalism
in the United States

Norman Birnbaum is Professor of Sociology at Amherst College, and has
also taught in England and France. His works include *The Crisis of Industrial Society* and a forthcoming collection of essays, *Intellectuals, Culture,
and Politics,* both published by Oxford University Press.

The problem of applying Marxist categories to an analysis of the late
capitalist social order in the United States has now begun to attract a
considerable amount of attention. After a hiatus of some twenty years
(1945-65)—years, to be sure, marked by some honorable exceptions,
represented by C. Wright Mills, Paul Sweezy, and William Appleman
Williams—a growing number of scholars and, most encouragingly,
younger scholars, have begun to ask if there is still something in the
Marxist tradition which may, if properly employed, prove illuminating
with respect to our own social and historical situation. I have employed
the term "Marxist tradition" quite deliberately. A mechanical application of Marxist categories derived from a body of work developed to
deal with the peculiarities of the nineteenth century to contemporary
society is not likely to prove very penetrating. We might just as well
attempt to analyze the military-industrial complex in terms borrowed
from Marx's portrait of Napoleon III—although there may be more
in that analogy than some might think. In any event, our task is a dual
one—to seize the movement of contemporary society in its essentials, and
in so doing, not alone to apply Marxist categories but to revise them

133

in such a way that they can be employed in further intellectual work.

It is quite true that in this respect our colleagues and contemporaries in Europe are appreciably in advance of us. The works of Perry Anderson, Lelio Basso, Jürgen Habermas, Eric Hobsbawm, Henri Lefebvre, Serge Mallet, Ernest Mandel, Rudi Supek, and Alain Touraine bespeak a penetration, a willingness to take intellectual risks, and a historical finality difficult to find in work on America by Americans. Nevertheless, the current situation is rather different from what it was even a half-decade ago, thanks to Eugene Genovese, S. M. Miller, Gabriel Kolko, Herbert Gintis, Herbert Gutman, Christopher Lasch, Harry Magdoff, Barrington Moore, James O'Connor, James Weinstein, and a number of scholars at first grouped around *Studies on the Left* and later extending from the *New York Review of Books* to *Radical America* and *Monthly Review*. The present paper attempts to apply ideas developed in the Western European discussion to American problems.

MARX AND ENGELS ON AMERICA

Marx and Engels devoted most of their theoretical and practical work, of course, to Western Europe. Engels did make a trip to the United States and both Marx and Engels maintained a considerable correspondence with former comrades in the German radical democratic movement who after 1848 took refuge in America. Marx's work (not entirely unaided by Engels) as a European correspondent for the *New York Herald* is well known. In the circumstances, they did give a certain amount of attention to the United States and some of their broad conclusions may be worth repeating in this context. In the first place, they tended to accept theses now quite familiar to us about the peculiarity of the American social system.

Marx and Engels adduced the availability and cheapness of land, in other words the open frontier, as an explanation for the capacity of American capitalism both to expand and to master severe discontent. They adduced the ethnic fragmentation of the American working class as a source of its disunity. They noted that the Anglo-Saxon migrant group, amongst the first to arrive and often highly skilled by contrast with others, developed the status of a labor aristocracy in the American setting. They argued that as long as American capitalism continued in its expansive phase, little could be looked for by way of revolutionary social-ism from a divided American working class, which in any case prospered in relative fashion from American capitalism. They depicted the atheo-reticism of the American working-class movement as both positive and negative. It was positive insofar as the Americans (here Engels in par-ticular who was not above using ethnic analogies with Northern Europe) could learn from experience and would, in fact, only learn from experi-ence. In this respect, Engels and Marx mocked the sectarian European and above all German refugees who imported to the United States their own quarrels as to the revolution. If atheoreticism, in the eyes of Marx and Engels, was a potentially positive factor in the emergence of a distinctively American socialism, it was also, in their view, a hinderance to emergence of a long-term perspective on the part of American working-class leaders.

It is interesting, also, to see that Marx and Engels favored for the American working class something that we would today term a politics of coalition. They held that the working class would have to unite with the smaller farmers against large-scale capitalism. The smaller farmers have by now, of course, virtually disappeared as a powerful and enduring political force in the United States, to be replaced by agricultural en-trepreneurs. The notion, however, that the working class in a differen-tiated social system must seek allies outside of its own boundaries is one which may be applied in the American situation today, even if it is characterized by a different alignment of social forces. They insisted on the strength of the tradition of democracy and representative govern-ment in the United States and asserted that the working-class move-ment as it grew to maturity in America would have to build on this tradition if it was to develop at all. In this connection, it is remarkable that they were the authors of a eulogy to Abraham Lincoln sent by the first International Working Men's Association in 1864. On the whole, Marx and Engels were, if anything, rather too optimistic about the chances for radical discontinuity in America's economic development which could radicalize the working class. They thought that the absence of feudal and aristocratic traditions and the newness of American capitalism would ultimately make the conflict of antagonistic forces in American capitalism that much more profound. They under-esti-mated, in other words, American capitalism's intrinsic capacity for self-renewal and continued expansion. However, they were shrewd enough to see that there were distinctive elements in the American

135

historical experience, and in particular in the American cultural situation, which rendered the tasks of socialist organization and the development of socialist consciousness rather different from those confronted by Europeans. I propose, later, to return to this problem in its modern form.

THE NEW AMERICAN CLASS STRUCTURE

The problem of the new American class structure is specifically an American version of a general problem: how may we conceptualize a class system in which the division between the propertied and the propertyless expresses itself in antagonisms different from those envisaged by Marx? Much of the recent discussion of the "new" working class has been addressed to this question and new political possibilities have been seen in the propertyless status of groups ostensibly remote from the dreadful bottom of modern industrial societies. What is called for is an analysis of the emergent forms of antagonism, a consideration of new mechanisms of the integration of the social classes, in short, an account of the present situation which deals with its extreme differentiation, complexity, and obscurity.

To begin, it is difficult to recognize in the contemporary working class and the white-collar salariat a classical proletariat. We do have a proletariat, in the sense of a group living at the margins of existence, at the mercy of the most minute alterations and cyclical rhythms of capital investment, and suffering from not alone a sense but the reality of exclusion from the general processes of accumulation which characterize the system as a whole. This proletariat in our country is made up of a diversity of groups, commonly designated as the impoverished. This category includes a considerable segment, but by no means the totality of the black population, some, although not all of the aged, the chronically ill without economic support from those relatively well placed in the socio-economic system, the unskilled—in both urban and rural sectors of the economy. It should be pointed out that a not inconsiderable portion of this proletariat can under certain conditions be integrated into the regular labor force of the economy but that this depends upon cyclical movements and social control of the rate of unemployment. No economic policy devised by any American government has been able to bring that rate down permanently and barring changes in our market mechanisms, it does seem that a large proletariat of this sort is a permanent feature of the present American economy. It is clear, of course, that the economic position of this proletariat merges with its racial and cultural attributes. A considerable segment of the black population is incorporated in the proletariat, both in urban and rural areas, and is not yet equipped culturally to enter the industrial labor market on terms of equality with most of the white population. Moreover, it has hitherto lacked incentives to do so in view of the absence of opportunities. Cultural defects of this kind on the part of the blacks is matched by equivalent phenomena on the part of some whites like those who have migrated to the cities from areas of rural poverty and economic decline. A considerable argument has taken place as to whether cultural or economic factors are primary, but from the viewpoint of a structural analysis the argument has a certain remoteness about it. If the black population were culturally equipped to enter the labor force at higher levels, it would not at present find the corresponding employment. (This is quite apart from its encounter with a continuation of the gross prejudice and hatred which is the fate of blacks in America.) On the other hand, if economic opportunities were suddenly made available, the legacy of the system's defects in the past would incapacitate large numbers of those ostensibly eligible and make it impossible for them to seize these opportunities. This last possibility, however, does seem to be an exercise in fantasy for the moment.

We may conclude that modern America does have a proletariat, that it is a minority, if a substantial minority of the labor force, and that its prospects of integration in that labor force, at the moment, appear to be rather low. This by no means entails the assertion that this proletariat is directly and totally exploited by all the other elements in the class structure—even if elements of exploitation are present insofar as cheap services supplied by those recruited from this proletariat keep the general cost of living down, even for the members of the regular working class. Transfer payments for welfare serve to foist the burden for keeping part of this proletariat alive not necessarily on the most advantaged elements in the class structure, but on the working-class group, in itself hard put to maintain a minimal standard of living. Below, I will consider the revolutionary and the general political potential of this proletariat but I wish now to proceed to discuss the manual working class itself.

Much has been made of the recent relative decrease in the size of the manual working group in the labor force. Attention has been given to certain changes in its own inner structure and conditions of work. We may observe, to begin with, that if the manual workers as a category have declined in numbers relative to the newly expanding white-collar sector of the labor force, in absolute terms the manual labor force has indeed expanded in recent decades. Moreover, certain important internal transformations merit attention—notably a decline in the number of unskilled workers relative to an increase in the number of skilled operatives, an increase as well in the number of supervisory manual workers in foreman or supervisory posts. Changes in industrial technology and organization, American capitalism's relentless drive for higher productivity, have clearly accounted for these changes. They have brought with them ostensibly higher wage rates, but also difficult and often exhausting conditions in the workplace. The trade unions have recently purchased higher wages, and in some cases shorter hours and a variety of fringe benefits, at the cost of "productivity." Productivity agreements have made the unions themselves force a more relentless work discipline.

As the technical capacity of the manual labor force has increased, in other words, it has been subjected to increasing supervision and a certain blockage of what might be termed autonomy on the job. This has been accompanied, in certain key industries where the trade unions are strong, by rather different kinds of advantages with respect to medical and retirement benefits, seniority rights in times of economic constriction, in short, an attempt by the unions to turn job rights into a simulacrum of property rights. It may be pointed out in this connection that the tendency of unions to invest their pension funds in stocks, not infrequently the stocks of the corporations for which their members are working, constitute another link between the manual labor force and the maintenance of the present set of economic relationships.

Meanwhile, it may be of interest to consider for a moment the alleged "embourgeoisment" of the American manual work force. It is interesting that this is supposed to have taken place mainly in the private sphere—that is to say, in the acquisition of owner-occupied dwellings, the purchase of consumer-durable goods, the lengthening of vacation periods, and the transmission of certain economic gains to children in the form of expanded educational opportunities which would allow them to move out of the manual working class. No allegation has been made of "embourgeoisment" in terms of career progression on the job, increased

138

autonomy at work, or greatly enlarged cultural perspectives and opportunities for the manual workers themselves.

"Embourgeoisment" refers almost solely to consumption, and not to the productive function itself. It obviously represents a relatively tenuous acquisition by the working class which will certainly prove ephemeral in times of economic constriction—as recent recessions have shown. The political consequences of this "embourgeoisment" are multiple and will be dealt with below in the section on consciousness. The burden of recent critical work on income (especially that of S. M. Miller) is that income must be defined in terms not alone of gross personal revenue but in terms of the capacity to earn (sometimes in kind or fringe benefits) over a lifetime. High levels of disposable wage income for the working class at a given moment in the business cycle do not necessarily continue. The kind of income constituted by the earning capacity attached to a college degree is a more convincing characteristic of a real "embourgeoisement." Here, however, we may note in passing that the notion of "embourgeoisement" may entail a re-definition of property itself.

The future position of the manual working class in the class structure depends upon two factors. The first concerns its technical function, the second entails larger questions of consciousness and politics which will be dealt with subsequently. With respect to its technical function, the increasing technicalization of industrial work, and the introduction of automation and computerization, would appear to entail higher skill qualifications for the manual labor force. A debate between those who argue that this will result in an increase in the number of unskilled operatives or indeed unemployment, and those who argue that this will result in a general elevation of the level of the industrial labor force's qualifications with no necessary diminution of employment, is as yet unresolved. It can be said, however, that the prospect of an increase in the proportion of unskilled operatives with marginal or cyclical employment possibilities does not necessarily represent a "proletarianization" of the working class—much depends upon the political response to this putative development. Equally, an increase in general skilled qualifications, in productivity and presumably wage rates, does not necessarily entail a total "embourgeoisement" of the working class. A development of this sort would depend upon the total system of class relations into which an altered working class would be inserted. An extrapolation from present tendencies would suggest that an increase in skilled qualifications by no means will end the gross, more disguised forms of exploitation of the labor force by corporate capitalism and its social system. We touch again upon problems of political consciousness in the United States, which have proved so intractable from a socialist perspective.

Much of the recent discussion of a "new working class" has referred to the fastest growing sector of the American labor force, those types of employment which require educational qualifications: civil servants, school teachers, semi-professionals and professionals. In brief, those who service the administrative processes of an advanced capitalist society have been increasing in number relative to the manual workers. This greatly expanded white-collar grouping has given rise to a considerable literature (consider C. Wright Mills in 1951). At first considered a social grouping of an extremely labile kind politically, the group has more recently been seen as a new avant-garde, indeed, as having the potential of replacing the manual working class as a revolutionary agency. Surely, not both of these views can be correct. It remains to examine the dimensions of this grouping before analyzing its consciousness, real and potential.

A majority of the recruits to the newly expanded sectors of employment are integrated into one or another form of bureaucratic hierarchy. That is to say, in contrast to the professionals of previous epochs, they must place their educational qualifications at the disposition of those with economic and social power. An orderly career progression in bureaucratic systems for members of this group depends upon a minimum compliance with the imperatives and ideology of the system. The very fact, however, of bureaucratic integration has converted offices, the civil services of federal, state, and local government, and other areas of work into something like modern versions of the nineteenth-century factory. The workplace is cleaner, the mode of discipline is usually far more subtle, the level of autonomy exercised by the individual worker may be greater. Nevertheless, this newly expanded work force in great numbers confronts a small group of controllers or supervisors. The span of control exercised by those in command of the bureaucratic hierarchies has accordingly been widened. John Kenneth Galbraith has written of an "educational and scientific estate." If, in fact, all or most of those in the newly expanded white-collar sector who have educational qualifications are to be included in this estate, we can only say that it resembles the third estate well before the French Revolution. It is not yet ready to assert itself, and its power, vis-à-vis the other and older estates, is limited. Nevertheless, we may point to some sources of contradiction and tension in the occupational existence of those in this grouping. They do exercise a certain autonomy on the job, but that autonomy is severely restricted by commands from above and by the imposition of purposes generated by the organizational imperatives of the capitalist social system as a whole.

In short, those with knowledge may not be able to apply it in terms of their own conception of the social good, but are obliged to take orders from those following narrower and more partial social interests. This is a transposition of the classical case of alienation through the vending of wage labor to a somewhat more spiritualized plane, but it remains a case of alienation. Those with knowledge and competence do not necessarily have the power to apply it. Further, the very imperatives of bureaucratic coordination and of work discipline can produce, and in some cases have already produced, a counter-reaction in the form of the trade unionization of certain occupations within this general grouping. Trade unionization does not necessarily entail a demand for total control of the work process, but it may well entail a demand for regulation of some of its more arduous aspects, in addition to the usual trade-union insistence on improved gross conditions of work in terms of salary, fringe benefits, and hours. The conditions of trade unionization are, clearly, the emergence of a critical mass of new salaried workers, such that an individualistic approach to a career has seemed for many unrealistic and inappropriate. The concentration of these new workers in certain sectors of the economy gives promise of a further progression of trade unionism. However, it should be pointed out that trade unionism can go very far without leading to a qualitative change in class relations; indeed, it can formalize relationships between the classes and act as a regulatory and indeed stabilizing factor. It must be said, in conclusion, that insofar as this group has expanded, it represents—in terms of improved status, relatively agreeable conditions of work, and higher and more consistent levels of remuneration—a decided channel of upward social mobility for the offspring of the working class. This group cannot be ascribed *a priori* a revolutionary or even a very reformist role. Hitherto, many in this social category have accepted their integration in society and the benefits this brought them. In certain countries this group has traditionally been politically on the right. A certain openness on the edges in contemporary America should not lead us to expect its immediate or its total transformation. Much depends upon the total social context in which this group, like the manual working class, has to function.

I have previously referred to Galbraith's use of the concept of an "educational and scientific estate." If this estate does exist, the term can only refer to a relatively small group of persons—appreciably smaller than the census category "professional and technical workers"—who exercise indispensable command or knowledge-producing functions for the society. This elite, which we may refer to as technocratic, would consist of educated managers, higher civil servants, those in effective daily command of the media of communication, those at the top of the knowledge industry. Viewed from this perspective, the "educational and scientific estate," whatever its recent restiveness, is an appendage of the system of power. Insofar as men of knowledge are elevated to power by virtue of their knowledge, they cease to function exclusively as men of knowledge, but function as men of power. If we take account of the fact that there are no purely technical or cognitive criteria for political decisions, if we recall that such decisions always involve choices of political values, that is to say, they alter the balance of power in one or another way (if only by maintaining it), then we can see that the technocrats do not rule in a vacuum. Their exercise of technical capacity in the interests of power follows the present division of power in the society. The existent institutional framework has been modified somewhat by the great importance of knowledge in administration and production, but it has not collapsed before the onslaught of an avant-garde of Ph.D's. Rather, when the Ph.D's have been given a function and rewarded for the performance of services indispensable to the system, a change in the mode of rule from entrepreneurial domination to technocratic manipulation does not alter the locus of rule. The great corporate structures continue to dominate the economy and, via the state, exercise the indispensable function of the political coordination of the social order as a whole. That International Business Machines Corporation, for instance, is able to offer its senior personnel conditions of work as agreeable as those found in a university does not mean that I.B.M. functions according to the ethic of the university. Indeed, we may say that more and more universities have come to function according to the ethic of I.B.M.—or at least, have become increasingly integrated with the sorts of corporate power in the society represented by I.B.M. Many of the assertions made, therefore, about the existence of an autonomous American technocratic elite require severe emendation.

The question of property and of property-owners in American capitalism must now concern us. It is clear that most large-scale industrial property is impersonally owned—by large corporations, by holding companies, by insurance companies, and the like. It is equally clear that those who manage and manipulate this sort of industrial property, do not necessarily own very much of it. (We should not, however, underestimate the proprietary role of managers who benefit from stock options.) A complicating factor is introduced by what we might term administrative property—the capacity to render those administrative and coordinating services without which industrial production and distribution could not proceed. Much of what I have termed administrative property in this country, as in any other, is in the hands of the state, which has become an element in the productive system itself and not outside it. In this complex state of affairs, it is obviously impossible to suppose that *rentiers* actually control the economy (however much they may benefit from it) and we seem to be forced back toward a hypothesis verging on the notion of the direction of the economy and the society by a technocratic or managerial elite—precisely the hypothesis I so strongly criticized some lines above.

Can this dilemma be resolved? We may begin to resolve it by noting that concentrations of impersonal property remain property. Now, even more than in Marx's day, industrial and administrative property organized into large-scale units has assumed something very like a life of its own. Corporations are entities which seem to make midgets or to some extent puppets of the men who direct them. The enormous powers of the state apparatus are such that a John F. Kennedy could respond to the demand for an alteration of federal policy, that he was willing to alter it, but he did not know if the government would agree with him. The concept of bureaucracy gives us the mode of organization of these powers, but not quite its substance or essence. Years of painstaking work by economists, both Marxist and other colleagues with different methodological assumptions, have shown us that the intrinsic or immanent tendencies of the system (occasionally modified by the exercise of political will) do constitute the driving forces which determine the decisions of those in command of large-scale property. In these circumstances, the question of the identity or personification of the owners of

143

property is for immediate analytical purposes less important than the question of control (understood in a short-term sense of control). We may understand control as exercised in such a way that its span of prevision which attaches to it is strictly limited. Decisions are frequently taken with a view to short-term interests in accumulation or in profitability—even if these occasionally add up to long-term developmental tendencies.

Nothing I have asserted is meant to deny, indeed nothing in it can deny, the existence of something like a "power elite." That large-scale *rentiers,* and those who manage large-scale property, are dominant elements in this elite cannot be denied. It does not follow that the power elite, however we describe its composition, reigns sovereign over the workings of the economy and polity with few opposing forces to stay its hand. Quite apart from the amount of direct political opposition its dominant position may generate or evoke, this grouping must reckon with impersonal and structural elements of the situation which shape both the mode and content of its rule. Perhaps we can best deal with these questions if we turn to the next theme, namely, the political integration of late capitalism in America.

POLITICAL INTEGRATION OF CAPITALISM

Employing the term "integration," I by no means imply that all societies are or can be integrated. I do not wish to propound a consensual theory of politics for any society, much less contemporary America. I do wish to begin with the rather obvious proposition that a considerable amount of political integration is a pre-condition for the functioning of a complex system like capitalism. It does not follow that political integration requires consensus; it may require widespread and structural ignorance, apathy, or privatization on the part of its citizenry. Many of these problems were anticipated by Engels in his remarkable conception of "false consciousness"—which has proven rather more of a political force in advanced capitalist societies than the revolutionary consciousness he and Marx so confidently expected to develop. In any event, the political integration of American capitalism must be understood as a general tendency of the system and not as an absolute and fixed state. The extremely large role of government in the function of the economy makes

144

of politics a factor inseparable from the analysis of the control of property.

I have previously introduced the notion of "administrative property." The bureaucratic apparatus which is the modern mode of social integration and of organizational function may be understood as "administrative property" in both its private and state forms. The large industrial organizations and the state do function according to remarkably similar patterns: a formal and legal circumscription of office, a career progression for officials, the application of criteria of efficiency to the workings of the units of the system. It is quite true that the larger corporations measure themselves by their profitability, and that criteria of political profitability for the operations of government agencies are in fact less susceptible of quantitative evaluation. If we consider, however, that most of the functions of government consist in providing an infrastructure for the operations of industrial enterprise, we do find that increasingly explicit notions of social profitability do serve as criteria for governmental decisions.

Much has been made of the oppressiveness and remoteness of bureaucratic forms of organization. There have been demands for "community control" through which a part of the American left has reaffirmed —however unwittingly—some of the traditional American revulsion for impersonality and bigness. Let us be clear: a frontal onslaught on bureaucracy as a social form is not necessarily equivalent to a creative transformation of bureaucratic control, and may indeed represent a desperate rear-guard action. (The American right also claims an anti-bureaucratic ethos.) The remoteness and oppressiveness of bureaucracy in this society is in large measure a function of the remoteness and oppressiveness of political and economic decision in general. That is to say, it is a product of the ends which bureaucracy serves and not of the mere existence of bureaucracy itself. In this connection, efforts to assimilate late capitalism to the state socialist social order prevailing in the Soviet Union are exercises in the avoidance of historical analysis rather than anything else.

What has characterized American capitalism most recently is the enormous growth of a public sector. This public sector has two principal functions. The first is to coordinate the workings of the capitalist system —budgetary and fiscal policy, the control of the level of social investment, above all the tax mechanisms, have been the chosen instruments of control. We have seen symbiotic relationships between government regulatory agencies and the "private" industries they are supposed to regulate. The second function of the expansion of the public sector has been already mentioned—the provision of an infra-structure without which capitalist accumulation could not continue. This includes the provision of essential services like transport, more recently a great expansion of education and health services, and of course the development of an empire to provide a suitably safe world market for American capitalism. We may include the defense industry in the public sector: certainly a remarkable instance of the socialization of loss and the privatization of profit.

What is clear is that the boundaries between "private" and "public" are frequently difficult to establish. The intervention of the state in the sphere of production is so very great as to make dubious the very term intervention. We have to develop new concepts to deal with new historical tendencies and it is here that our conceptual apparatus has fallen rather seriously behind the progression of our empirical knowledge and our political experience. The recent work of James O'Connor, in particular, seems to offer some hope that this deficiency may be made good. At any rate, the deficiencies of critical social analysis in America in this respect seem to parody a more widespread general defect in the society and its political system: our popular and conventional political reflection, and political practice, are not at all adequate to confront the problems of late capitalism. Our society operates with retrograde concepts in a historically advanced situation. It is at this point that we touch the problems of American political and social consciousness to which I now turn.

PROBLEMS OF SOCIAL CONSCIOUSNESS IN AMERICA

If there is one basic American disorder, it certainly entails our inadequate and distorted social consciousness. The sources of defect and distortion are many. Perhaps these go back to the very roots of our culture. It is historically false to argue that the Puritans in New England were without a social ethic: the Mayflower Compact was an exercise in social theology. However, the importation to this country of early bourgeois notions of community and polity combined with the development of a

146

market unrestrained by pre-capitalist institutions and traditions. It eventually resulted in the society's continuing inability to find a social ethic adapted to its real situation. Our social ethic has always evinced a serious lag with respect to the social contradictions it has had to master. It is quite true that no one any longer will promulgate imbecilities like the assertion that the family farm is the backbone of America; the struggle in 1970 over welfare-state institutions which hardly represent an advance over Bismarck's nineteenth-century social policies does suggest that there are still serious historical discrepancies in our public vision.

The first source of these defects must be found in the strange fate of high culture in America. By high culture I mean that tradition of systematic reflection on man, society, and nature developed in the medieval church and the medieval universities and continued at times within and at times without the universities by those intellectuals who assumed the responsibility for the custody of tradition. America has had groups which have manifested a high culture but rarely like the European elite with its community of discourse with their society's intellectual and cultural elite. (Marx's own cultural attitudes would no doubt horrify many dues-paying members of our own New University Conference.) The history of immigration to the United States has been the history of a constant infusion of groups cut off from European high culture. This has been particularly, although not exclusively, true of much of the American working class. The market, therefore, and life goals and life styles derived from the working of market forces, have imposed themselves on most of the American population as an institutional context which could not be imagined away. Critical notions based on other perspectives for human life, as developed by intellectuals who were instinctually anti-capitalist, have met incomprehension, hostility, and even murderous hatred. The secularization of American Protestantism (and of the other American religions) has been so profound that not alone a flattening but a virtual eradication of the metaphysical horizon has reduced most of the American population to the point at which it cannot imagine a concrete transcendence of its conditions of existence. Revising Marx, we may say that precisely the absence of religion has contributed to a state of political quietism in America.

The social classes in America have generally lacked the cultural resources to develop self-conscious and articulated images of their own interests. The southern slaveholders and the New England merchants did for a period develop coherent ideologies. These were not generalized, indeed they could not be generalized, to cover any substantial section of an expanding society—even if they were consonant with the culture, life style, and interests of the groups at issue. It is significant that American liberalism has been a curious fusion of entrepreneurial materialism on the one hand and vulgar egoism on the other—whatever its ideal or more civilizing elements. These last have frequently remained in the realm of moral pronouncement and moral criticism, a realm to which the intellectuals were confined until the emergence, at the beginning of this century, of a true technical intelligentsia. Briefly put, the fragmentation of class struggle in America, the ethnic diversity of the population, have contributed to the prevention of a true cultural homogenization of the population. The homogenization which has now taken place is rather an imposed one and not necessarily an entirely profound one.

Another way of looking at this is to assert that America has developed no political conception of a general will, no genuine notion of a polity and political life. Mills in *White Collar* called our attention to Aristotle's definition of an "idiot" as a private man with no communal or general interests. The reduction of a considerable section of the American population to this sort of idiocy can be seen as due to the interaction of two factors: long-term cultural values (or their absence) and the heavy pressure of a manufactured mass culture. In the circumstances, the wonder is not that America has never had a full-scale or enduring movement of social criticism expressed in political terms, but that so much social criticism and so much radical politics have emerged in our history.

American society, then, lacks the ideological resources to make a correct estimate of its historical situation. Popular notions of social causality remain relatively primitive, however much suspicions and intimations of exploitation move large groups. The targets of popular hostility are frequently displaced. The intellectuals do speak to a larger group—but a good deal of the intellectuals' public is so bound to white-collar or technocratic occupational routine that its perceptions of social contradiction remain, for the moment at least, without serious political consequences. In the circumstances, attacking policemen with lead pipes does not seem to be an entirely appropriate response to the problems of mass political education. I propose in the final section of this essay to turn to questions of contemporary politics and in particular to the question of the possibilities of a development of a new socialist avant-garde.

POLITICAL POSSIBILITIES IN AMERICAN CAPITALISM

The search for a new socialist avant-garde has pre-empted so much of the recent discussion that one might think that we were agreed on the major outlines of our social analysis. The notion of an avant-garde, however, is closely connected with the results of that analysis and, as I have attempted to show, our analysis remains sketchy and far from complete. Let us consider, however, some of the candidacies advanced for the role of political avant-garde.

The first, of course, is youth as a new social category. A general approach insists on the totality of the young as subjected to the vicissitudes and contradictions of late capitalism. The college educated, and those funneled into college, are victims of manpower channeling. Those excluded from college are thrown onto the labor market and excluded from many of the major benefits of the system as presently constituted. All, or so runs the argument, are extremely restive under work discipline and its educational concomitant. The appeal of the new youth culture, of rock music, of drugs and of a certain hedonism in life style, is precisely the appeal of a counter-culture—a form of political protest which ranges from open to covert but which must inevitably bring youth into conflict with the dominant ideologies and agencies of power in the society. These general notions underlie, variously, certain theories of the student revolt and the general doctrine of the existence of a counter-nation argued with such pathos by Abbie Hoffman in his *Woodstock Nation.*

The trouble with the young, however, is that they will have to grow up. Growing up must mean, inevitably, their assuming roles in the occupational system. It may well be that a permanent minority of the young will be encapsulated in counter-cultures or counter-communities. These will either live parasitically off the larger technical-bureaucratic system or entail an increasing reversion to some parody of American pastoral ideals: an implicit dismantlement not alone of capitalism, but of industrialism as a whole. Others may fall permanently under the domination of drugs. Whatever the moral revulsion felt by the Agnewites for this sort of thing, it is indeed a political factor of some importance. Yet it is important to see that the counter-culture movement does not constitute a substitute for a socialist politics in America. If the young are indeed to grow up in the larger sense of the term, perhaps we may be able to

149

characterize what has been happening recently in the universities and elsewhere as an anticipatory strike by the labor force of tomorrow. We have had an inchoate demand for a more humane society, by those who will be called upon to live in it as adults shortly. This, however, will require that they develop political consciousness and political skills, above all the ability to effect short-term and long-term coalitions with other groupings for the sake of common political goals.

The most obvious of these groupings recently has been constituted by the dispossessed—in particular the blacks and the other ethnic minorities excluded from the mainstream of the productive and administrative system. This is not the place to rehearse the familiar debate over black power and black culture. It is difficult for me to see how a black culture compounded of the agrarian experience of the blacks in rural poverty in the south and their experience in the northern ghettos can provide the basis for the emergence of the blacks as a separate power group in a technically advanced society. In any event, a revolutionary strategy based exclusively on the dispossessed must inevitably entail the shifting of revolutionary responsibility from the "mother country" to other external agencies—like the (exceedingly fragmented and disunited) movement of liberation from colonialism and imperialism in the Third World. It may be necessary and honorable for American socialist intellectuals to proclaim their own impotence in this way, but there is nothing in the record of recent history to suggest that the imperial metropolis can be brought down by a tactic of this sort. Unless a socialist politics can enter the mainstream of American political life, deflect it from its previous course and give it a new structure, fadism and sectarianism of the most varied kind will lead to an interminable series of defeats.

We have, finally, to consider the political potential of the so-called "new" working class—particularly in its white-collar and technocratic sectors. I have covered this ground before and can be brief. It is quite true that this grouping experiences the contradictions of capitalism in several ways. It does not exercise autonomy at work despite its high educational and skilled qualifications. The products of its labor are systematically distorted for social purposes other than those which would benefit the collectivity. The fragmentation of existence which distinguishes those members of this somewhat amorphous stratum in their capacities as citizens, as workers, and private persons, seems to continue apace. It is the revulsion for this fragmentation which does seem to motivate their offspring. This grouping cannot be induced to confront the real sources of its own condition and to the beginnings of action to remedy it without a prolonged process of political education and political organization. The unionization of important occupations in this group may be a beginning in this direction, but the history of trade unionism in America again imposes a certain caution upon us. Trade unionism, as we know, may also become a factor which tends to integrate the political system rather than the reverse.

Given the relatively developed general consciousness of the white-collar and technocratic grouping, it may be liable to critical political thought about its situation. As citizens, members of this grouping suffer from the distortion of social priorities entailed in the military-industrial complex and the general unresponsiveness of our electoral and congressional system to changed national requirements. As private persons, they respond already (perhaps too much so, and in exceedingly simple terms) to the issues of environmental degradation. As private persons, as well, they are responsive to the pressures of their children. Finally, as workers, they are both integrated with the system and able to develop critical views of its functioning. The notion of a campaign for the equivalent of "Workers' Councils" at IBM is indeed fantastic—but given the general movement of discontent and criticism in American society, the chances for institutional transformations of this sort do seem higher today than they have been for forty years. Here, a heavy responsibility is incumbent upon the left to devise institutional critiques of advanced capitalism which carry some pragmatic weight: a utilization of some of the propensities of the middle class (admittedly, in its educated sectors) to political organization in conventional terms ought not to be excluded. Finally, given the cultural stratification of American society, the beginnings of radicalization amongst adult members of the middle class may have some influence upon the working class—particularly if the trade unions can be persuaded to take a more radical course.

The contradictions remain. What is lacking are the political mechanisms and a political will to translate these into a coherent and long-term strategy for either revolution or reform. A good many self-designated revolutionary theorists in the United States are unable to distinguish between a revolutionary situation and a situation of simple social decomposition. They do not underestimate the repressive power of the state and of the society, but they certainly underestimate the recuperative power of advanced capitalism. It is entirely possible, after all, that new welfare-state institutions may be developed by the much despised theorists of "corporate liberalism" and that these may well have a stabilizing and integrating effect on the social totality.

What we face is a situation of genuine historical indeterminacy. Analyses of the contradictions of late capitalism predicated on a mechanical or quasi-automatic generation of revolution simply repeat the mistakes of the vulgar Marxism of the late nineteenth century. Our situation is, rather, not unlike that of the first generation of Marxists in the face of new historical forces. A new phase in the existence of bourgeois society calls for new modes of analysis, and above all, new forms of political organization. We do not, however, commence entirely anew. Our harsh judgments on the American political tradition should not lead us to overlook the positive democratic elements within it. A fusion of that tradition with socialism is long overdue. It is striking in this connection that while denunciations of "electoral politics" from radicals rend the air, as reformist a thinker as John Kenneth Galbraith in 1970 called for an explicit socialist program for the Democratic Party. In a society generally affluent, whatever its social impoverishment, old revolutionary rhetoric will not do. Indeed, the dilemma of revolution versus reform may well be out of date. That has been seen by the Italian Communist Party, whose Marxist credentials can hardly be challenged. The task before us is not alone to deepen our analysis of the workings and fatalities of late American capitalism, but to develop a realistic politics based on its inner contradictions. If men make their history, they do so because they possess sufficient political will and political vision to alter their circumstances. The difficulties of American historical consciousness can only be met by a changed consciousness. In this respect, a heavy burden falls upon those intellectuals and not least those intellectuals who have recently renounced critical analysis in favor of a stereotyped recourse to unreflected doctrines about the efficacy of the "counter-culture."

BIBLIOGRAPHY

Perry Anderson, "Components of the National Culture," *New Left Review,* No. 50, 1968.

Lelio Basso *et al.*, contributions to *International Socialist Journal.*

Norman Birnbaum, *The Crisis of Industrial Society,* New York: Oxford University Press, 1969.

152

Norman Birnbaum, "The Crisis of Marxist Sociology," *Social Research*, 2, 1968.

Pual Baran and Paul Sweezy, *Monopoly Capital*, New York: Monthly Review Press, 1966.

John Kenneth Galbraith, *The New Industrial State*, Boston: Houghton Mifflin, 1967.

Eugene Genovese, *Political Economy of Slavery*, New York: Pantheon, 1965.

Herbert Gintis, "The New Working Class and Revolutionary Youth," *Socialist Revolution*, No. 3, 1970.

Jürgen Habermas, *Strukturwandel der Öffentlichkeit*, Neuwied: Luchterhand, 1962.

Tom Hayden, *Trial*, New York: Holt Rinehart, 1970.

Eric Hobsbawn, *Industry and Empire*, New York: Pantheon, 1968.

Abbie Hoffman, *Woodstock Nation*, New York: Random, 1969.

Gabriel Kolko, *Wealth and Power in America*, New York: Praeger, 1962.

Christopher Lasch, *The Agony of the American Left*, New York: Knopf, 1969.

Henri Lefebvre, *La Vie quotidienne dans le monde moderne*, Paris: Gallimard, 1968.

Harry Magdoff, *The Age of Imperialism*, New York: Monthly Review Press, 1969.

Serge Mallet, *La Nouvelle Classe ouvrière*, Paris: rev. ed., Anthropos, 1969.

Ernest Mandel, *Marxist Economic Theory*, New York: Monthly Review Press, 1968.

Herbert Marcuse, *One-Dimensional Man*, Boston: Beacon Press, 1965.

S. M. Miller and Frank Riessman, *Social Class and Social Policy*, New York: Basic Books, 1969.

S. M. Miller and Pamela Roby, *Future of Inequality*, New York: Basic Books, 1970.

C. Wright Mills, *White Collar*, New York: Oxford University Press, 1951.

C. Wright Mills, *The Power Elite*, New York: Oxford University Press, 1956.

Barrington Moore, *Social Origins of Dictatorship and Democracy*, Boston: Beacon Press, 1966.

Pierre Naville, *Le Nouveau Leviathan*, Vols. 1, 2, and 3, Paris: Anthropos, 1967 and 1970.

James O'Connor, "The Fiscal Crisis of the State," *Socialist Revolution*, Nos. 1 and 2, 1970.

Rudi Supek *et al.*, contributions to *Praxis* (published multi-lingually by the Faculty of Philosophy, Zagreb University).

Alain Touraine, *La Société post-industrielle*, Paris: Denoel, 1969.

James Weinstein, *The Corporate Ideal in the Liberal State*, Boston: Beacon Press, 1968.

James Weinstein and David Eakins, editors, *For a New America*, New York: Random, 1970.

William Appleman Williams, *Roots of the Modern American Empire*, New York: Random, 1969.

8

PAUL M. SWEEZY

Workers and the Third World

Paul M. Sweezy is known above all as the author of *The Theory of Capitalist Development* (1942) and as the co-author with Paul A. Baran of *Monopoly Capital* (1966). He writes and lectures widely on Marxist economics, and is a founder and co-editor of *Monthly Review*. He also served for several years as a member of the SSC Steering Committee.

Marx's theory of capitalism was sketched with broad and sweeping strokes in the *Communist Manifesto* and achieved its most comprehensive and polished form in the first volume of *Capital,* published some hundred years ago. The theory holds that capitalism is a self-contradictory system which generates increasingly severe difficulties and crises as it develops. But this is only half the story: equally characteristic of capitalism is that it generates not only difficulties and crises but also its own grave-diggers in the shape of the modern proletariat. A social system can be ever so self-contradictory and still be without a revolutionary potential: the outcome can be—and in fact history shows many examples where it has been—stagnation, misery, starvation, subjugation by a stronger and more vigorous society. In Marx's view capitalism was not such a society; it was headed not for slow death or subjugation but for a thorough-going revolutionary transformation. And the reason was precisely because by its very nature it had to produce the agent which would revolutionize it. This is the crucially important role which the proletariat plays in the Marxian theoretical schema.

154

In the eyes of many people, including not a few who consider themselves to be essentially Marxists, this theory of the revolutionary agency of the proletariat is the weakest point of the whole system. They point to the fact that the English and other Western European proletariats, which Marx considered to be the vanguard of the international revolutionary movement, have actually developed into reformist forces which, by accepting the basic assumptions of capitalism, in fact strengthen it. And they note that the proletariat of what has become the most advanced and powerful capitalist country, the United States of America, has never developed a significant revolutionary leadership or movement, and shows fewer signs of doing so today than at any time in its history.

I do not believe that the empirical observations which support this type of criticism of Marx's theory can be seriously challenged. And yet it certainly will not do to jump from there to the conclusion that Marx's theory is "refuted" and must be abandoned. A more legitimate procedure, I suggest, is to inquire into the inner logic of the theory to discover *why* Marx assigned the role of revolutionary agent to the proletariat. In this way I believe we shall find that it is not the theory itself which is at fault so much as its misinterpretation and misapplication.

First, we must be quite clear that Marx's theory of the revolutionary agency of the proletariat has nothing to do with an emotional attachment to, or blind faith in, the working class as such. He believed that objective forces, generated by the capitalist system, were inexorably molding a revolutionary class, i.e. one which would have both the ability and the will to overthrow the existing order. The ability stemmed from its numerical strength and its indispensable role in the capitalist production process, the will from its being deprived not only of material possessions but of its essential and ultimately irrepressible humanity. Marx's position is perhaps most clearly stated in the following passage from *The Holy Family*:

> When socialist writers ascribe this world-historical role to the proletariat, this is not at all . . . because they take the proletarians for gods. Quite the contrary. Because the abstraction of all humanity, even the appearance of humanity, is practically complete in the fully developed proletariat, because the living conditions of the proletariat represent the focal point of all inhuman conditions in contemporary society, because the human being is lost in the proletariat, but has won a theoretical consciousness of loss and is compelled by unavoidable and

absolutely compulsory need (the practical expression of necessity) to revolt against this inhumanity—all these are the reasons why the proletariat can and must emancipate itself. However, it cannot emancipate itself without abolishing the conditions which give it life, and it cannot abolish these conditions without abolishing all those inhuman conditions of social life which are summed up in its own situation.

It does not go through the hard and hardening school of labor fruitlessly. It is not a question of what this or that proletarian, or even the proletariat as a whole, may imagine for the moment to be the aim. It is a question of what the proletariat actually is and what it will be compelled to do historically as the result of this being. The aim and the historical action of the proletariat are laid down in advance, irrevocably and obviously, in its own situation in life and in the whole organization of contemporary bourgeois society.[1]

The next question is this: What were the processes which molded a proletariat with these particular characteristics? One answer, which I suppose many Marxists would subscribe to, would hold that the revolutionary proletariat is inherent in capitalism and is therefore the creation of the very same processes which originally brought the system into existence and which have subsequently propelled its development. The first step, in this view, was what Marx called primitive accumulation which in one aspect was essentially the violent and bloody process of separating the working people from ownership of their means of production. After that, the expansion of the proletariat to its ultimate position of numerical dominance in capitalist society was the natural result of expanded reproduction on a capitalist basis. Expanded reproduction, as you know, consists of the appropriation by capitalists of surplus value created by wage laborers, and the continuous conversion of part of the surplus value into additional capital.

Now there can be no question that this is an accurate account of Marx's theory of the birth and *quantitative* expansion of the proletariat. But does it explain why he regarded the proletariat as the revolutionary agent destined to overthrow the system? If we say that it does, we necessarily imply that the proletariat was revolutionary from its birth and that only quantitative predominance was required for it to be able to perform its revolutionary function; for there is nothing in the mere me-

[1] Marx/Engels, *Werke*, Vol. 2, p. 38. Except for the first two sentences, the translation is that of the English edition of Franz Mehring's *Karl Marx*, pp. 130–131.

chanics of the expanded reproduction process to bring about a *qualitative* transformation of the proletariat. At this point it is therefore of first importance to recognize that in Marx's view the proletariat was *not* a revolutionary force from its birth but on the contrary acquired this quality in the course of its capitalistic development.

In this connection it is necessary to recall an aspect of Marx's theory of capitalism which is of course known to all students of the subject but which, I believe, is generally considered to have mostly historical interest. This is his division of the capitalist epoch into what Engels, in his editor's preface to the first English edition of the first volume of *Capital,* called "two great and essentially different periods of economic history: the period of manufacture proper, based on the division of manual labor, and the period of modern industry based on machinery." What separated the two periods was the Industrial Revolution, a term much used by Marx, the beginning of which he dated from Wyatt's spinning machine of 1735, and which had worked its transforming effects by 1825, a year of economic crisis in which "modern industry . . . for the first time opens the periodic cycle of its modern life." [2]

From our present point of view there are two fundamental differences between these phases of capitalist development. One relates to the dynamics of the production process itself, the other to the changed character of the proletariat brought about by the transition from the earlier phase to the later. (It should be noted in passing that the formal concepts of Marxian economic theory—constant and variable capital, surplus value, expanded reproduction, etc.—are equally applicable to both phases. At the level of abstraction implied by this conceptual apparatus, there is therefore no difference between the two phases, which is perhaps why many Marxist economists have failed to appreciate the importance of distinguishing between them.)

Manufacture is an extension and adaptation of age-old handicraft methods of production. The chief innovation is the assembling of many craftsmen in a single enterprise, which permits forms and degrees of specialization unthinkable under the medieval guild system. This specialization of crafts—or division of labor, as it was called by Adam Smith, the theorist *par excellence* of the manufacture phase—results in an enormous increase in labor productivity and in this sense marks a great stride forward in human progress. However, it is important to rec-

[2] *Capital,* Kerr ed., Vol. I, p. 18.

ognize that, technologically, manufacture is still an essentially conservative mode of production. The increase of productivity for which it is responsible stems from the more rational utilization of existing technologies, not from the introduction of new technologies. The latter process, often called invention, is no part of the logic of manufacture. Hence, in Marx's words, "History shows how the division of labor peculiar to manufacture, strictly so called, acquires the best adapted form at first by experience, as it were behind the backs of the actors, and then, like the guild handicrafts, strives to hold fast that form when once found, and here and there succeeds in keeping it for centuries." [3] This naturally does not mean that invention was absent or that the culture and ideology of this phase of capitalism did not favor the inventive arts. If such had been the case, there would have been no industrial revolution at the time and in the place where it actually occurred. What it does mean is that invention was not an integral part of the process of production and indeed was often strongly resisted by the practitioners of existing methods of production. This special combination of circumstances, both favoring and inhibiting the progress of invention, found an interesting reflection in Adam Smith who, as Nathan Rosenberg has shown,[4] regarded major inventions as the work of neither laborers nor capitalists but rather of "philosophers" who are totally separated from the productive process.

The labor force of the manufacturing phase corresponded to the requirements of this particular mode of production. It consisted of a multitude of craftsmen possessing a great variety of specialized skills which were characteristically passed on from father to son. Craft consciousness rather than class consciousness was the hallmark of a proletariat so composed. The skilled handworker tended to be bigoted, proud, undisciplined, contentious, capable of waging a bitter and often violent struggle against the constraints of capitalist production and the employer who imposed them upon him. But his vision was necessarily limited: he could not see the system as a whole nor understand his place in it, and he was therefore incapable of sustained revolutionary activity to change it. Capitalism in its manufacturing phase, in addition to being technologically conservative was also highly resistant to political and social change.

[3] *Ibid.,* p. 399.
[4] Nathan Rosenberg, "Adam Smith on the Division of Labor: Two Views or One?," *Economica,* May 1965.

158

The introduction of machinery—which, according to Marx, takes place "from the moment that the tool proper is taken from man and fitted into a mechanism" [5]—changed all that. Having once occurred in one important branch of industry, it literally forced itself on other branches until it finally came to dominate the mode of production as a whole. Marx's account of this process is worth quoting at some length:

> A radical change in the mode of production in one sphere of industry involves a similar change in other spheres. This happens at first in such branches of industry as are connected together by being separate phases of a process, and yet are isolated by the social division of labor in such a way that each of them produces an independent commodity. Thus spinning by machinery made weaving by machinery a necessity, and both together made the mechanical and chemical revolution that took place in bleaching, printing, and dyeing imperative. So too, on the other hand, the revolution in cotton spinning called forth the invention of the gin for separating the seeds from the cotton fibre; it was only by means of this invention that the production of cotton became possible on the enormous scale at present required. But more especially, the revolution in the modes of production of industry and agriculture made necessary a revolution in the general conditions of the social process of production, i.e. in the means of communication and transport. Hence, apart from the radical changes introduced in the construction of sailing vessels, the means of communication and transport became gradually adapted to the modes of production of mechanical industry by the creation of a system of river steamers, railways, ocean steamers, and telegraphs. But the huge masses of iron that had now to be forged, to be welded, to be cut, to be bored, and to be shaped, demanded, on their part, cyclopean machines for the construction of which the methods of the manufacturing period were utterly inadequate.
>
> Modern industry had therefore itself to take in hand the machine, its characteristic instrument of production, and to construct machines by machines. It was not till it did this that it built up for itself a fitting technical foundation, and stood on its own feet. Machinery, simultaneously with the increasing use of it, in the first decades of this century appropriated, by degrees, the fabrication of machines proper. But it was only during the decade preceding 1866 that the construction of railways and ocean steamers on a stupendous scale called into existence the cyclopean machines now employed in the construction of prime movers.[6]

[5] *Ibid.*, p. 408.
[6] *Ibid.*, pp. 419–420.

Whereas capitalism in its manufacturing phase was technologically conservative and immune to the threat of revolutionary change, modern industry based on machinery is the opposite in both respects. Technological progress no longer depends on the ingenuity of the skilled worker or on the genius of the great inventor; it now becomes the province of the rational sciences. This is one of the major themes of Marx's masterful chapter entitled "Machinery and Modern Industry" which alone would be enough to mark the first volume of *Capital* as an epoch-making work. Here we must be content with a couple of brief quotations which convey the gist of his thought:

> The principle, carried out in the factory system, of analyzing the process of production into its constituent phases, and of solving the problems thus proposed by the application of mechanics, of chemistry, and of the whole range of the natural sciences, becomes the determining principle everywhere.[7]
>
> Modern Industry rent the veil that concealed from men their own social process of production, and that turned the various spontaneously divided branches of production into so many riddles, not only to outsiders but even to the initiated. The principle which it pursued of resolving each into its constituent parts without any regard to their possible execution by the hand of man, created the new modern science of technology. The varied, apparently unconnected, and petrified forms of the production process now resolved themselves into so many conscious and systematic applications of natural science to the attainment of given useful effects.[8]

From this the conclusion flowed logically: "Modern Industry never looks upon and treats the existing form of a process as final. The technical base of that industry is therefore revolutionary, while all earlier modes of production were essentially conservative." [9]

With respect to its social base, Marx regarded modern industrial capitalism as no less revolutionary—once again in sharp contrast to capitalism in its manufacturing phase. Machinery progressively abolishes the crafts which are the basis of manufacture and thereby renders obsolete the multitudinous special skills of the craftsmen. In this way it cheapens the labor power of adult males by obviating the need for prolonged and

[7] *Ibid.,* p. 504.
[8] *Ibid.,* p. 532.
[9] *Ibid.*

160

expensive training programs. At the same time, by putting a premium on dexterity and quickness it opens the door to the mass employment of women and children. There followed a vast expansion of the labor supply which was augmented and supplemented by two further factors: (1) Once solidly entrenched in the basic industries, machinery invades ever new branches of the economy, undercutting the old handworkers and casting them onto the labor market. And (2) the progressive improvement of machinery in industries already conquered continuously eliminates existing jobs and reduces the employment-creating power of a given rate of capital accumulation.

The effects of machinery, in short, are on the one hand to extend, homogenize, and reduce the costs of production of the labor force; on the other, to slow down the rate of increase of the demand for labor power. This means a fundamental change in the economic power relation between capital and labor, to the enormous advantage of the former. Wages are driven down to, and often below, the barest subsistence minimum; hours of work are increased beyond anything known before; the intensity of labor is stepped up to match the ever increasing speed of the machinery. Machinery thus completes the process, begun in the period of primitive accumulation, of subjecting labor to the sway of capital. It is the capitalistic employment of machinery, and not merely capitalism in general, which generates the modern proletariat as Marx conceived it.

But the coin has two sides. Economically, the power of the proletariat under modern industry is much reduced compared to that of its predecessor in the period of manufacture. But politically, its potential power is infinitely greater. Old craft and geographical divisions and jealousies are eliminated or minimized. The nature of work in the modern factory requires the organization and disciplining of the workers, thereby preparing them for organized and disciplined action in other fields. The extreme of exploitation to which they are subjected deprives them of any interest in the existing social order, forces them to live in conditions in which morality is meaningless and family life impossible, and ends by totally alienating them from their work, their products, their society, and even themselves. Unlike the skilled craftsmen of the period of manufacture, these workers form a proletariat which is both capable of, and has every interest in, revolutionary action to overthrow the existing social order. These are the ones of whom Marx and Engels had already declared in the *Communist Manifesto*: "The proletarians have nothing to lose but their chains. They have a world to win." In the first volume of *Capital* this bold generalization is supported by a painstaking analysis of the immanent features and tendencies of capitalist "modern industry" as it emerged from the industrial revolution.

So far I have tried to show that Marx's theory of capitalism encompasses two quite distinct phases, separated by the industrial revolution, which can be characterized as follows:

Manufacture

Technology	Conservative
Proletariat	Non-revolutionary

Modern Industry

Technology	Revolutionary
Proletariat	Revolutionary

It must be immediately added, however, that the word "revolutionary" applied to technology has a somewhat different meaning from what it does when applied to the proletariat. A revolutionary technology is one which by its very nature changes continuously and rapidly; a revolutionary proletariat, on the other hand, is one which has the *potential* to make a revolution but which can actually make it only once under favorable conditions (the so-called revolutionary situation). Here a question obviously arises: If, for whatever reason, the emergence of a revolutionary situation is long delayed, what will be the effect in the meantime of modern industry's revolutionary technology on the composition and capabilities of the proletariat?

Marx never asked this question, perhaps because it never occurred to him that the revolution might be long delayed. And yet it is a question which arises quite naturally within the framework of his theory. He had explicitly recognized that modern industry "is continually causing changes not only in the technical basis of production, but also in the functions of the laborer and in the labor-process"; [10] and no one knew better than he that it is the functions of the laborer and the nature of the labor process which determine the character of the proletariat. In the absence of a revolutionary situation, would the proletariat tend to become more or less revolutionary? It would have been a perfectly logical question for Marx to ask when he was writing *Capital;* a hundred

[10] *Ibid.,* p. 533.

years later it seems to be not only a logical but an inescapable question for Marx's followers.

This is obviously not the occasion to attempt a comprehensive answer, and I have to admit that my knowledge of the interrelation between technology and the labor process is far too limited to permit me to speak as an expert on the subject. I will therefore restrict myself to indicating in a very general way why it seems to me that the advance of modern technology must tend to shape a proletariat which is less rather than more revolutionary than that which emerged from the industrial revolution in the middle of the nineteenth century.

I would not put the main emphasis on the consequences of technological change for the workers who actually mind the machines and do functionally similar work, much of it virtually unknown in Marx's time, such as manning assembly lines. These are still for the most part dehumanizing jobs requiring little skill; and speed-up of machinery and increasing work loads certainly do not make them more bearable, not to say attractive. A proletariat dominated by operatives of this general description might well have as great a revolutionary potential as its mid-19th-century predecessor. The point is that relative to the total work force there are so many fewer jobs of this kind than there used to be. Progressive mechanization of particular processes, and more recently the perfection of generally applicable methods of partial or full automation, have reduced this traditional blue-collar segment of the proletariat from what was once a large majority to what is today in the most industrialized societies a small minority. Since the output of this minority has at the same time enormously increased, it is clear that modern technology has multiplied the productivity of labor many times over and put within society's grasp a potential surplus of vast proportions.

The obverse of this development is that a great variety of new categories of jobs has been created. Some of these are integrally related to the new technology—scientists, researchers, engineers, technicians, highly skilled maintenance and repair men, etc.—but many more (both absolutely and relatively) are concerned in one way or another with the manipulation and absorption of the surplus made possible by the increased productivity of the underlying production workers. Under this heading one could list government workers of all kinds, including teachers; those employed in the many branches of the sales apparatus, including most of the personnel of the mass communication media; workers and salaried personnel in finance, insurance, and real estate; and the providers of many different kinds of personal services from beauty treatment to sports spectacles. In the United States today these job categories, taken all together, probably account for close to three quarters of the employed non-agricultural labor force.

In terms of the occupational composition of the labor force, then, the two chief consequences of modern industry's revolutionary technology have been (1) a drastic (and continuing) reduction in the production-worker component, and (2) a vast proliferation of job categories in the distribution and service sectors of the economy. At the same time there has taken place a slow but cumulatively substantial increase in the real wages of both production and non-production workers. In part this reflects an increase in the cost of production of labor power as the educational and training requirements of the new employment categories have risen. And in part it reflects the fact that the workers—and here we mean primarily production workers—have been able through non-revolutionary class struggle to wrest from the capitalists a part of the fruits of increasing productivity.

To sum up: The revolutionary technology of modern industry, correctly described and analyzed by Marx,[11] has had the effect of multiplying by many times the productivity of basic production workers. This in turn has resulted in a sharp reduction in their relative importance in the labor force, in the proliferation of new job categories, and in a gradually rising standard of living for employed workers. In short, the first effects of the introduction of machinery—expansion and homogenization of the labor force and reduction in the costs of production (value) or labor power—have been largely reversed. Once again, as in the period of manufacture, the proletariat is highly differentiated; and once again occupational and status consciousness has tended to submerge class consciousness.

It might be thought that despite these changes the blue-collar proletariat would remain a revolutionary element within the working class as a whole. No doubt there is a tendency for this to happen, and it would be short-sighted in the extreme to overlook the revolutionary potential still remaining in this large body of workers. But one must not go too

[11] As a matter of fact Marx's treatment of the relations among industry, technology, and science was far ahead of his time and has only become fully realistic and applicable a hundred years later.

far in isolating them from the rest of the labor force. As James Boggs says: "Today most workers in the plant [i.e. blue-collar workers] have been to high school and quite a few have even been to college. All either plan or wish to send their sons and daughters to college—their sons so they won't have to work in the factory on what they call a dull and automated job; their daughters . . . so they won't have to marry some bum but can make their own living and be free to decide whether they want to marry or not marry. . . ." [12] In other words, blue-collar workers, being a diminishing minority of the whole working class, do not think of their families as permanently stuck in the stratum which they occupy. As long as this is so, their attitudes and ideology are not likely to be radically different from those of the non-revolutionary majority of the working class which surrounds them.

If we accept these general propositions about the direct and indirect effects of modern technology on the composition and character of the working class, must we conclude that Marx's theory of the proletariat has been refuted? I do not think so. His theory in fact dealt with the early impact of machinery on the proletariat, not with the longer-run consequences of the machine technology for the proletariat. One might perhaps complain that Marx did not attempt to develop a more comprehensive theory; and one could argue, I think persuasively, that he certainly could have done so. Indeed from many remarks scattered throughout his writings, it would probably be possible for a follower of Marx to construct a more or less systematic theory of what the future held in store for the proletariat if capitalism should survive the revolutionary threat inherent in the early period of modern industry. But this is not the occasion for such an effort, and the fact that Marx himself did not make it provides no justification for denying the validity of the theory he did put forward within the limits of its applicability.

In this connection I would go further and argue that the Russian Revolution of 1917 provides extremely strong empirical evidence for the validity of Marx's theory. This revolution occurred in a capitalist country where modern industry was in the process of establishing itself and where it had already created a large and highly revolutionary urban proletariat. Under these circumstances, when the revolutionary situation matured (as it had not done in the Western European countries at a

---

[12] *The American Revolution,* Monthly Review Press, 1963, p. 14.

comparable stage of development), the proletariat played precisely the role attributed to it in Marx's theory. In the social sciences, a theory rarely receives a more striking confirmation.

Here, however, a much more serious question arises: Does the fact that capitalism in Western Europe and North America survived the initial period of modern industry and that its new technology then went on progressively to reduce the revolutionary potential of the proletariat, mean that in the second half of the twentieth century we must abandon the whole idea of a revolutionary agent destined to overthrow the capitalist order? Again, I do not think so.

The belief that the *industrial* proletariat is the only possible revolutionary agent under capitalism stems from focusing attention too exclusively on the advanced capitalist countries where modern industry got its start and where the new technology has had a chance to develop under favorable conditions. But capitalism as a social order has never consisted only of industrialized countries. In fact, as Marx explicitly recognized, the industrialization of some countries had as its counterpart from the outset the non-industrialization of others, with the two sets of countries being integrally tied together in a single system.

> So soon . . . as the general conditions requisite for production by the modern industrial system have been established, this mode of production acquires an elasticity, a capacity for sudden extension by leaps and bounds that finds no hindrance except in the supply of raw material and in the disposal of the produce. On the one hand, the immediate effect of machinery is to increase the supply of raw material in the same way, for example, as the cotton gin augmented the production of cotton. On the other hand, the cheapness of the articles produced by machinery, and the improved means of transport and communications furnish the weapons for conquering foreign markets. By ruining handicraft production in other countries, machinery forcibly converts them into fields for the supply of its raw material. In this way East India was compelled to produce cotton, wool, hemp, jute, and indigo for Great Britain. . . . A new and international division of labor, a division suited to the requirements of the chief centers of modern industry springs up, and converts one part of the globe into a chiefly agricultural field of production for supplying the other part which remains a chiefly industrial field.[13]

[13] *Capital,* Vol. I, pp. 492–493.

Once it is recognized that capitalism is not and never has been confined to one or more industrializing countries, but is rather a global system embracing both the (relatively few) industrializing countries and their (relatively numerous) satellites and dependencies, it becomes quite clear that the future of the system cannot be adequately analyzed in terms of the forces at work in any part of the system but must take full account of the *modus operandi* of the system as a whole.

Lenin was the first Marxist to see this and to begin work on the theoretical extensions and reformulations which it made necessary. His major contribution was his little book *Imperialism: the Highest Stage of Capitalism.* Having been published in 1917, it is exactly half as old as the first volume of *Capital.* There he argued that "Capitalism has grown into a world system of colonial oppression and of the financial strangulation of the overwhelming majority of the people of the world by a handful of 'advanced' countries. And this 'booty' is shared between two or three powerful world pirates armed to the teeth. . . ." He also argued that the capitalists of the imperialist countries could and do use a part of their "booty" to bribe and win over to their side an aristocracy of labor. As far as the logic of the argument is concerned, it could be extended to a majority or even all the workers in the industrialized countries. In any case it is clear that taking account of the global character of the capitalist system provides strong additional reasons for believing that the tendency in this stage of capitalist development will be to generate a less rather than a more revolutionary proletariat.

But once again the coin has two sides. If imperialist exploitation brings wealth to the industrialized countries and enables them to raise further the standard of living of their working classes, it brings poverty and misery to the great mass of the working people—agricultural as well as industrial—in the dependencies. These masses now become an agent of revolutionary change in precisely the sense that Marx believed the industrial proletariat of the mid-19th century to be. Let me quote again what he wrote in the *Holy Family:* "Because the abstraction of all humanity, even the appearance of humanity, is practically complete in the fully developed proletariat, because the living conditions of the proletariat represent the focal point of all inhuman conditions in contemporary society, because the human being is lost in the proletariat, but has won a theoretical consciousness of loss and is compelled by unavoidable and absolutely compulsory need . . . to revolt against this inhumanity

—all these are the reasons why the proletariat can and must emancipate itself."

These words certainly do not apply to the working classes of the United States and Western Europe today. But do they not apply all the more obviously and forcefully to the masses in the much more numerous and populous underdeveloped dependencies of the global capitalist system? And does not the pattern of successful socialist revolutions since the Second World War—highlighted by Vietnam, China, and Cuba— demonstrate beyond any doubt that these masses do indeed constitute a revolutionary agent capable of challenging and defeating capitalism?

In conclusion, let me present a very brief summary of my thesis: In Marx's theory of capitalism, the proletariat is not always and necessarily revolutionary. It was not revolutionary in the period of manufacture, becoming so only as a consequence of the introduction of machinery in the industrial revolution. The long-run effects of machinery, however, are different from the immediate effects. If the revolutionary opportunities of the early period of modern industry are missed, the proletariat of an industrializing country tends to become less and less revolutionary. This does not mean, however, that Marx's contention that capitalism produces its own gravediggers is wrong.

If we consider capitalism as a global system, which is the only correct procedure, we see that it is divided into a handful of exploiting countries and a much more numerous and populous group of exploited countries. The masses in these exploited dependencies constitute a force in the global capitalist system which is revolutionary in the same sense and for the same reasons that Marx considered the proletariat of the early period of modern industry to be revolutionary. And finally, world history since the Second World War proves that this revolutionary force is really capable of waging successful revolutionary struggles against capitalist domination.

9

ERNEST MANDEL

Workers and
Permanent Revolution

Ernest Mandel is a leading European Marxist writer on economics and politics. He has lectured widely in the United States, but in November 1969 was denied a United States visa to take part in the New York conference on "Agencies of Social Change" co-sponsored by the Socialist Scholars Conference. Recently a major work of his, *Marxist Economic Theory* (2 vols., 1969), was published in English.

In the history of class society, the situation of each social class is a unique combination of stability and change. The structure remains the same; conjunctural features are often profoundly modified.

There is a tremendous difference both in standard of living and in social environment between the slave on the patriarchal Greek farms of the sixth century B.C., the slave on Sicilian plantations in the first century B.C., and a clerical or handicraft slave in Rome or the south of France in the fourth century A.D. Nonetheless all three of these were slaves, and the identity of their social status is undeniable. A nobleman living at the court of Louis XV did not have very much in common with a lord of the manor in Normandy or Burgundy seven centuries earlier—except that both lived on surplus labor extracted from the peasantry through feudal or semi-feudal institutions.

When we look at the history of the modern proletariat, whose direct ancestors were the unattached and uprooted wage earners in the medieval towns and the vagabonds of the sixteenth century—so strikingly described by the great story, *Till Eulenspiegel*—we notice the same combination of structural stability and conjunctural change. The proletarian condition is, in a nutshell, the lack of access to means of production or means of subsistence which, in a society of generalized commodity production, forces the proletarian to sell his labor-power. In exchange for this labor-power he receives a wage which then enables him to acquire the means of consumption necessary for satisfying his own needs and those of his family.

This is the structural definition of the wage earner, the proletarian. From it necessarily flows a certain relationship to his work, to the products of his work, and to his overall situation in society, which can be summarized by the catchword "alienation." But there does not follow from this structural definition any necessary conclusion as to the level of his consumption, the price he receives for his labor-power, the extent of his needs or the degree to which he can satisfy them. The only basic interrelationship between structural stability of status and conjunctural fluctuations of income and consumption is a very simple one: Does the wage, whether high or low, whether in miserable Calcutta slums or in the much publicized comfortable suburbs of the American megalopolis, enable the proletarian to free himself from the social and economic obligation to sell his labor-power? Does it enable him to go into business on his own account?

Occupational statistics testify that this is no more open to him today than a hundred years ago. Nay, they confirm that the part of the active population in today's United States which is forced to sell its labor-power is much higher than it was in Britain when Karl Marx wrote *Capital,* not to speak of the United States on the eve of the American Civil War.

Nobody will deny that the picture of the working class under neo-capitalism would be highly oversimplified if it were limited to featuring only this basic structural stability of the proletarian condition. In general, though, Marxists who continue to stress the basic revolutionary role of today's proletariat in Western imperialist society avoid that pitfall. It is rather their critics, who are in error. They commit the opposite error, in fact; they concentrate exclusively on conjunctural changes in the situation of the working class, thereby forgetting those fundamental structural elements which have not changed.

I do not care very much for the term "neo-capitalism" which is ambiguous, to say the least. When one speaks about the "neo-reformism" of the Communist parties in the West, one means, of course,

170

that they are basically reformist; but when the term "neo-socialists" was used in the thirties and early forties to define such dubious figures as Marcel Deat or Henri de Man, one meant rather that they had stopped being socialists. Some European politicians and sociologists speak about "neo-capitalism" in the sense that society has shed some of the basic characteristics of capitalism. I deny this most categorically, and therefore attach to the term "neo-capitalism" the opposite connotation: a society which has all the basic elements of classical capitalism.

Nevertheless I am quite convinced that starting either with the great depression of 1929–32 or with the second world war, capitalism entered into a third stage in its development, which is as different from monopoly capitalism or imperialism described by Lenin, Hilferding and others as monopoly capitalism was different from nineteenth century laissez-faire capitalism. We have to give this child a name; all other names proposed seem even less acceptable than "neo-capitalism." "State monopoly capitalism," the term used in the Soviet Union and the "official" Communist parties, is very misleading because it implies a degree of independence of the state which, to my mind, does not at all correspond to present-day reality. On the contrary, I would say that today the state is a much more direct instrument for guaranteeing monopoly surplus profits to the strongest private monopolies than it ever was in the past. The German term, *Spätkapitalismus,* or late capitalism, seems interesting, but simply indicates a time sequence. So until somebody comes up with a better name—and this is a challenge—we will stick for the time being to "neo-capitalism."

We shall define neo-capitalism as this latest stage in the development of monopoly capitalism in which a combination of factors—accelerated technological innovation, permanent war economy, expanding colonial revolution—have transferred the main source of monopoly surplus profits from the colonial countries to the imperialist countries themselves and made the giant corporations both more independent and more vulnerable.

More independent, because the enormous accumulation of monopoly surplus profits enables these corporations, through the mechanisms of price investment and self-financing, and with the help of a constant buildup of sales costs, distribution costs and research and development expenses, to free themselves from that strict control by banks and finance capital which characterized the trusts and monopolies of

Hilferding's and Lenin's epoch. More vulnerable, because the short-ening of the life cycle of fixed capital, the growing phenomenon of surplus capacity, the relative decline of customers in non-capitalist milieus and, last but not least, the growing challenge of the non-capitalist forces in the world (the so-called socialist countries, the co-lonial revolution and, potentially at least, the working class in the metropolis)—because all these have implanted even in minor fluctua-tions and crises the seeds of dangerous explosions and total collapse.

For these reasons, neo-capitalism is compelled to embark upon all those well-known techniques of economic programming, of deficit financing and pump-priming, of income policies and wage freezing, of state subsidizing of big business and state guaranteeing of monopoly surplus profit, which have become permanent features of most Western economies over the last 20 years. What has emerged is a society which appears both as more prosperous and more explosive than the situa-tion of imperialist countries 30 years ago.

It is a society in which the basic contradictions of capitalism have not been overcome, in which some of them reach unheard-of dimen-sions, in which powerful long-term forces are at work to blow up the system. I will mention here in passing only some of these forces: The growing crisis of the international monetary system; the trend toward a generalized economic recession in the whole capitalist world; the trend to restrict or suppress the basic democratic freedoms of the working class—in the first place, free play of wage bargaining; the trend toward deep and growing dissatisfaction of producers and consum-ers with a system which forces them to lose more and more time producing and consuming more and more commodities which give less and less satisfaction and stifle more and more basic human needs, emotions and aspirations; the contradictions between the accumulation of wasteful "wealth" in the West and the hunger and misery of the colonial peoples; the contradictions between the immense creative and productive potentialities of science and automation and the destructive horror of nuclear war in the shadow of which we are forced to live permanently. All these forces epitomize the basic contradictions of to-day's capitalism.

The question has been posed: Hasn't the role of the working class been fundamentally changed in this changed environment? Hasn't the long-term high level of employment and the rising real wage undercut any revolutionary potential of the working class? Isn't it changing in composition, and more and more divorced from the productive process, as a result of growing automation? Doesn't its relations with other social layers, such as white-collar workers, technicians, intellectuals, students, undergo basic modifications?

Affirmative answers to these questions lead to political conclusions of far-reaching consequence. For some, the stability of the capitalist system in the West cannot be shaken any more, a theory which is nicely fitted to nourish a more material interest and psychological urge of adaptation to that system. For others, that stability could be shaken only from outside: first of all, from the non-industrialized regions of the world—the so-called villages, to repeat Lin Piao's formula —which will have to be revolutionized before revolts could again be envisaged in the imperialist countries themselves (Lin Piao's cities). Others, while not questioning the basic instability of neo-capitalism, see no positive outcome at all because they believe that the system is able to drug and paralyze its victims. Finally, there are those who believe that neo-capitalism raises its gravediggers from within its bosom but see these gravediggers coming from the groups of outcasts: national and racial minorities, super-exploited sections of the population, revolutionary students, the new youth vanguard. All these conclusions share in common the elimination of the proletariat of metropolitan countries from the central role in the worldwide struggle against imperialism and capitalism.

It would be easy to limit oneself to stating an obvious fact: All these theories spring from a premature rationalization of a given situation, the fact that the Western proletariat has receded into the background of the world revolutionary struggle for the past 20 years, between 1948 and 1968. Now that the French May 1968 revolution has shown this phenomenon and period to be a temporary one, we should rather put at the top of the agenda a discussion of revolutionary perspectives in the West from now on.

Such an answer, valid though it may be, would remain insufficient and incomplete. For some of the theories we have just mentioned, while being obvious rationalizations of the *fait accompli,* have enough sophistication and candor not to limit themselves to description pure and simple. They try to draw conclusions about the declining revolutionary role of the proletariat in the West from changes introduced into the very fabric of neo-capitalist society by technological, economic, social and cultural transformations of historic proportions and importance. So we have to meet these arguments on their own ground, and critically reexamine the dynamics of working class struggles, consciousness and revolutionary potential against the background of the changes which neo-capitalism has effected in the classical *modus operandi* of the capitalist system.

Our starting point must be the same as that adopted not only by Karl Marx but also by the classical school of political economy: the study of the place human labor occupies in the economic life of contemporary monopoly capitalism. Three basic facts immediately demand our attention in that respect.

First, contemporary production and distribution of material wealth is more than ever based upon modern industry and the factory. Indeed, one could say that the third industrial revolution at one and the same time both reduces industrial labor in the factory as a result of growing automation and increases industrial labor on a vast scale in agriculture, distribution, the service industries and administration. For the automation revolution must be seen as a vast movement of *industrialization* of these different sectors of economic activity, both economically and socially. We shall have to draw important conclusions from this trend. But what stands out is the fact that industrial labor in the broadest sense of the word—men formed to sell their labor-power to the manufacturing, cotton-growing, data-processing or dream-producing factory!—more than ever occupies the central place in the economy's structure.

Second, whatever the increase in consumption of the working class may have been, neo-capitalism hasn't modified in any sense whatsoever the basic nature of work in a capitalist society as alienated labor. One could even say that in the same way as automation extends the industrialization process into every single corner of economic life, it likewise universalizes alienation to an extent Marx and Engels could only have dimly imagined a hundred years ago. Many passages on alienation in the *Economic-Philosophical Manuscripts,* in the *German Ideology* and in the *Grundrisse* have only been truly realized in the last decades. And one could make the point that Marx's economic analysis of "pure capitalism" is much more a presentiment of what was going to happen during the twentieth century than a description of what was happening under his eyes in the nineteenth century.

In any case, labor under neo-capitalism is more than ever alienated

174

labor, forced labor, labor under command of a hierarchy which dictates to the worker what he has to produce and how he has to produce it. And this same hierarchy imposes upon him what to consume and when to consume it, what to think and when to think it, what to dream and when to dream it, giving alienation new and dreadful dimensions. It tries to alienate the worker even from his consciousness of being alienated, of being exploited.

Third, living labor remains more than ever the sole source of surplus value, the only source of profit, which is what makes the system tick. One can easily reveal the striking contradiction of a productive process heavily pregnant with unlimited potentials of making use-values abundant, but incapable of functioning smoothly and developing steadily because these use-values must first of all slip into the clothing of exchange-values, be sold and meet "effective demand" before they can be consumed. One can note the absurdity of a system in which science, technological progress, humanity's huge accumulated wealth of equipment, are the main basis for material production, but in which the "miserly appropriation of surplus labor," to use Marx's *Grundrisse* phrase, continues to be the only goal of economic growth: "Profit is our business, and business after all only means profit."

But all these contradictions and absurdities are real, living contradictions and absurdities of capitalism. These would attain their absolute limit in universal and total automation which, however, lies completely beyond its reach because living labor is indispensable for the further accumulation of capital. One has only to observe how billion-dollar corporations haggle and shout like fishwives over a 50-cent wage increase here and two hours off the workweek there to see that, whatever ideologies and sociologists might argue, the hard facts of life confirm what Marx taught us: Capital's unlimited appetite for profit is an unlimited appetite for human surplus labor, for hours and minutes of unpaid labor. The shorter the workweek becomes, the higher the actual productivity of labor, the closer and more strictly do capitalists calculate surplus labor and haggle ever more furiously over seconds and fractions of seconds, as in time and motion studies.

Now precisely these three characteristics of modern labor—its key role in the productive process, its basic alienation, its economic exploitation—are the objective roots of its potential role as the main force to overthrow capitalism, the objective roots of its indicated revolutionary mission. Any attempt to transfer that role to other social layers

175

who are unable to paralyze production at a stroke, who do not play a key role in the productive process, who are not the main source of profit and capital accumulation, takes us a decisive step backwards from scientific to utopian socialism, from socialism which grows out of the inner contradictions of capitalism to that immature view of socialism which was to be born from the moral indignation of men regardless of their place in social production.

Here we have to meet an objection often voiced both by so-called dogmatic Marxists and by avowed revisionists or opponents of Marxist theory. Haven't we given too general a definition of the working class under neo-capitalism? Shouldn't we restrict this category to the same group which came under this definition in the classical period of the socialist labor movement, to wit the manual workers actually engaged in production? Isn't it true that this category tends to decline, first relatively and then even in absolute figures, in the most advanced industrial countries of the West? Are not the mass of wage and salary earners to which we have constantly referred too vague and heterogeneous a grouping to be considered a social class in the Marxist sense of the word? And isn't the fading of the revolutionary potential of the working class in the Western metropolitan countries causally linked to this diminution of the manual production workers in the gainfully employed population?

The debate which inevitably arises from an answer to these questions could easily degenerate into a semantic squabble if the qualitative, structural nature of the proletariat is forgotten. Authors like Serge Mallet have correctly argued that the very nature of the productive process, under conditions of semi-automation or automation, tends to incorporate whole new layers into the working class. We do not accept Mallet's political conclusions, which have not at all been confirmed by the May revolt in France. In the forefront of that revolt we did not find only the "new" working class of highly skilled workers and technicians in semi-automated factories like those of the C.S.F. [General Electric] factory in Brest. Equally present were the classical conveyor-belt workers of Renault and Sud-Aviation and even the workers of some declining industrial branches like the shipyard workers of Nantes and Saint-Nazaire. The categories of the "old" and "new" working class created by Mallet do not correspond to the realities of the process.

But what is valid is the fact that the distinctions between the "purely" productive manual production worker, the "purely" unproduc-

176

tive clerical white-collar worker, and the "semi-productive" repairman become more and more effaced as a result of technological change and innovation itself, and that the productive process of today tends more and more to *integrate* manual and non-manual workers, conveyor-belt semi-skilled and data-processing semi-skilled, highly skilled repair and maintenance squads and highly skilled electronics experts. Both in the laboratories and research departments, before "actual" production starts, and in the dispatching and inventory departments, when "actual" production is over, productive labor is created if one accepts the definition of such labor given in Marx's *Capital*. For all this labor is indispensable for final consumption and is not simply waste induced by the special social structure of the economy (as for instance sales costs).

We can return to a point made before and state that just as the third industrial revolution, just as automation, tends to industrialize agriculture, distribution, the service industries and administration, just as it tends to universalize industry, so it tends to integrate a constantly growing part of the mass of wage and salary earners into an increasingly homogeneous proletariat.

This conclusion needs further elucidation. What are the indicators of the enhanced proletarian character of these "new" layers of workers which become progressively integrated into the working class?

We could cite offhand a series of striking facts: reduced wage differentials between white-collar and manual workers, which is a universal trend in the West; increased unionization and union militancy of these "new" layers, which is equally universal (in Brussels as in New York, schoolteachers, electricians, telephone and telegraph workers have been among the militant trade unionists in the last five years); rising similarities of consumption, of social status and environment of these layers; growing similarity of working conditions, i.e., growing similarity of monotonous, mechanized, uncreative, nerve-racking and stultifying work in factory, bank, bus, public administration, department stores and airplanes.

If we examine the long-term trend, there is no doubt that the basic process is one of growing homogeneity and not of growing heterogeneity of the proletariat. The difference in income, consumption and status between an unskilled laborer and a bank clerk or high-school teacher is today incommensurably smaller than it was fifty or a hundred years ago.

But there is an additional and striking feature of this process of integration of new layers into the working class under neo-capitalism:

That is the equalization of the conditions of reproduction of labor-power, especially of skilled and semi-skilled labor-power. In nineteenth century capitalism, there was elementary education for the manual worker, lower-middle-school education for the white-collar worker, high-school education for the technician; the reproduction of agricultural labor-power often didn't need any education whatsoever. Universities were strictly institutions for the capitalist class.

The very technological transformation, of which neo-capitalism is both a result and a motive force, has completely modified the levels of education. Today, outside of entirely unskilled laborers for whom there are very few jobs any more in industry, strictly speaking, and for whom tomorrow there might be no jobs available in the whole economy, conditions of reproduction of skill for industrial workers, technicians, white-collar employees, service workers and clerks are completely identical in generalized high-school education. In fact, in several countries, radicals are fighting for compulsory education up to 18 years in a single type of school, with growing success.

Uniform conditions of reproduction of labor-power entail at one and the same time a growing homogeneity of wages and salaries (value and price of labor-power), and a growing homogeneity of labor itself. In other words, the third industrial revolution is repeating in the whole society what the first industrial revolution achieved inside the factory system: a growing indifference towards the particular skill of labor, the emergence of generalized human labor, transferable from one factory to another, as a concrete social category (corresponding historically to the abstract general human labor which classical political economy found as the only source of exchange-value).

Let it be said in passing that it would be hard to understand the dimensions and importance of the universal student revolt in the imperialist countries without taking into account the tendencies which we have sketched here: growing integration of intellectual labor into the productive process; growing standardization, uniformity and mechanization of intellectual labor; growing transformation of university graduates from independent professionals and capitalist entrepreneurs into salary earners appearing in a specialized labor market—the market for skilled intellectual labor where supply and demand make salaries fluctuate as they did on the manual labor market before unionization, but fluctuate around an axis which is the reproduction cost of skilled intellectual labor. What do these trends mean but the growing proletarianization of

178

intellectual labor, its tendency to become part and parcel of the working class?

Of course students are not yet workers. But it would be as wrong to define them by their social *origin* as it would be to define them by their social *future*. They are a social layer in transition. Contemporary universities are a huge melting pot into which flow youth of different social classes, to become for a certain time a new homogeneous social layer. Out of this interim layer there arises on the one hand an important part of the future capitalist class and its main agents among the higher middle classes, and on the other hand a growing proportion of the future working class.

But since the second category is numerically much more important than the first, since the student milieu, precisely because of its transitional severance of basic bonds with a specific social class and because of its specific access to knowledge not yet excessively specialized, can gain a much sharper and much quicker consciousness than the individual worker of the basic ills of capitalist society and since intellectual labor is increasingly a victim of the same basic alienation which characterizes all labor under capitalism, the student revolt can become a real vanguard revolt of the working class as a whole, triggering a powerful revolutionary upsurge as it did in May 1968 in France.

Let us restate the first conclusion we have arrived at. Neo-capitalism in the long run strengthens the working class much as did laissez-faire capitalism or monopoly capitalism in its first stage. Historically, it makes the working class grow both numerically and in respect to its vital role in the economy. It thereby strengthens the latent power of the working class and underlines its potential capacity to overthrow capitalism and to reconstruct society on the basis of its own socialist ideal.

Immediately new questions arise. If this be so, will not the increased stability of the neo-capitalist system, its wide use of neo-Keynesian and macro-economic techniques, its avoidance of catastrophic economic depressions of the 1929–33 type, its capacity to shape the workers' consciousness through manipulation and the use of mass media, permanently repress these revolutionary potentialities? These questions boil down to two basic arguments which we shall deal with successively. One is the system's capacity to reduce economic fluctuations and contradictions sufficiently to assure enough reforms to guarantee a gradual easing of social tensions between capital and labor. The other is the system's capacity of integrating and engulfing the industrial proletariat

179

as consumers and ideologically conditioned members of the society, to restate Baran and Sweezy's *Monopoly Capital.*

On the economic plane, we can briefly sketch the trends which make long-term "stability in growth" impossible for neo-capitalism. When the growth rate increases, as it did in Western Europe for 15 years from 1950 to 1965, then conditions of near-full employment enable the workers to rapidly increase real wages which, together with the rapidly increasing organic composition of capital, tend to push down the rate of profit. The system must react, and its reactions usually take two forms, or a combination of both. One is rationalization, automation, that is, increased competition between men and machines through reconstitution of the reserve army of labor to keep down the rate of increase of real wages. The other is voluntary or compulsory wage restraints, income policies, anti-strike and anti-union legislation, that is, attempts to prevent labor from utilizing relatively favorable conditions in the labor market in order to increase its share of the new value it creates.

Increased growth rates under neo-capitalist conditions of "administered prices," "investment through prices," state-guaranteed monopoly surplus profits and a permanent arms economy, also mean inflation.

Every attempt to stop inflation strangles the boom and precipitates a recession. Investment fluctuations and monetary disorders combine to increase economic instability, further abetted by stepped-up capital concentration both nationally and internationally, so that the system tends towards a marginal increase in unemployment and a generalized recession in the whole Western world. Both trends push down the rate of growth, as does the system's inability to constantly increase the rate of growth of armaments, that is, their share of the gross national product, without endangering enlarged reproduction, consequently economic growth itself. The accumulation of huge masses of surplus capital and of increasing surplus capacity in the capitalist world industry acts in the same sense of dampening the long-term rate of growth.

What emerges in the end is less the picture of a new type of capitalism successfully reducing overproduction than the picture of a temporary delay in the appearance of overproduction—*"zurückstauen,"* as one says in German—by means of huge debt stockpiling and monetary inflation, which lead towards the crisis and collapse of the world monetary system.

Are these basic economic trends compatible with a secular decrease in social tensions between capital and labor? There is very little reason to believe this. Granted that the phases of rapid economic growth—more rapid in the last 20 years than in any comparable past period in the history of capitalism—create the material possibilities for increasing real wages and expanding mass consumption. But the attempts to base pessimistic predictions about the revolutionary potential of the working class on this trend of rising real wages overlooks the dual effect of the economic booms under capitalism on the working class.

On the one hand, a combination of near-full employment and a rapid rise of productive forces, especially under conditions of rapid technological change, likewise leads to an increase in the needs of the working class. That portion of the value of labor-power which Marx calls historically determined and is attributable to the given level of culture tends to increase most rapidly under such conditions, generally much more rapidly than wages. Paradoxically, it is precisely when wages rise that the gap between the value and the price of labor-power tends to grow, that the socially determined needs of the working class grow more rapidly than its purchasing power. The debate of the past decade in the United States and other imperialist countries on the growing gap between individual consumption and unsatisfied needs of social consumption, publicized by Galbraith as the contrast between private affluence and public squalor, illustrates this point.

Furthermore, rising real wages are constantly threatened by erosion. They are threatened by inflation. They are threatened by structural unemployment generated through technological change and automation. They are threatened by wage restraint and wage-freeze policies. They are threatened by recessions. The more the workers are accustomed to relatively high wages, the more they react against even marginal reductions in their accustomed level of consumption, the more all the just-named threats are potential starting points of real social explosion.

It is no accident that the working class youth is quicker to react and move to the forefront of these revolts. The older generations of workers tend to compare their miseries in the depression and during the war with the conditions of the last 15 years and can even view them as a state of bliss. Younger workers don't make these comparisons. They take for granted what the system has established as a social minimum standard of living, without being at all satisfied, either by the quantity or quality of what they get, and react sharply against any deterioration of conditions. That's why they have been in the front ranks of very militant strikes over the last two years in countries as widely different

181

as Italy, West Germany, Britain and France. That's why they played a key role in the May revolution in France.

Even more important than the basic instability and insecurity of the proletarian condition which neo-capitalism hasn't overcome and cannot overcome is the inherent trend under neo-capitalism to push the class struggle to a higher plane. As long as the workers were hungry and their most immediate needs were unattended to, wage increases inevitably stood in the center of working class aspirations. As long as they were threatened by mass unemployment, reductions in the work-week were essentially seen as means of reducing the dangers of redundancy. But when employment is relatively high and wages are constantly rising, attention becomes gradually transferred to more basic aspects of capitalist exploitation.

The "wage drift" notwithstanding, industry-wide wage bargaining and attempts of neo-capitalist governments to impose income policies tend to focus attention more on the division of national income, on the great aggregates of wages, profits and taxes, than on the division of the value newly created at the factory level. Permanent inflation, constant debates about government fiscal and economic policies, sudden disturbances of the labor market through technological innovation and relocation of whole industries, draw the workers' attention in the same direction.

Classical capitalism educated the worker to struggle for higher wages and shorter working hours in his factory. Neo-capitalism educates the worker to challenge the division of national income and orientation of investment at the superior level of the economy as a whole.

Growing dissatisfaction with labor organization in the plant stimulates this very tendency. The higher the level of skill and education of the working class—and the third industrial revolution leaves no room for an uneducated and unskilled working class!—the more do workers suffer under the hierarchical and despotic work organization at the factory. The stronger the contradiction between the potential wealth which productive forces can create today and the immeasurable waste and absurdity which capitalist production and consumption implies, the more do workers tend to question not only the way a capitalist factory is organized but also what a capitalist factory produces. Recently, these trends found striking expression not only during the May revolution in France, but also at the Fiat plant in Italy where the workers succeeded in preventing an increasing number of different types of high-priced cars from being manufactured.

182

The logic of all these trends puts the problem of workers' control in the center of the class struggle. Capitalists, bourgeois politicians and ideologues, and reformist Social Democrats, understand this in their own way. That is why different schemes for "reform of the enterprises," for "co-management," "co-determination" and "participation" occupy the center of the stage in practically all Western European countries. When de Gaulle launched his "participation" demagogy, even the bonapartist dictatorship of Franco in Spain proclaimed that it was likewise in favor of working class participation in the management of plants. As for Harold Wilson, he didn't wait a month at 10 Downing Street to jump on the same bandwagon.

But parallel to these various schemes of mystification and deception is the growing awareness in working class circles that the problem of workers' control is the key "social question" under neo-capitalism. Questions of wages and shorter working hours are important; but what is much more important than problems of the distribution of income is to decide who should command the machines and who should determine investments, who should decide what to produce and how to produce it. British and Belgian trade unions have started to agitate these questions on a large scale; they have been debated in Italy at the factory level and by many left circles. In West Germany, Sweden, Norway and Denmark they are increasingly subjects of debates in radical working class circles. And the May revolution in France was a clarion call for these ideas emanating from 10 million workers.

There remains the last objection. Have the monopolists and their agents unlimited powers of manipulating the ideology and consciousness of the working class, and can they not succeed in preventing revolt, especially successful revolt, notwithstanding growing socio-economic contradictions?

Marxists have recognized the possibility of "manipulation" for a long time. Marx wrote about the artificially induced needs and consumption of the workers a hundred and twenty-five years ago. Marxists have many times reiterated that the "ruling ideology of each society is the ideology of the ruling class." One of the key ideas of Lenin's *What is to be Done?* is the recognition of the fact that, through their own individual effort and even through elementary class struggle on a purely economic and trade-union level, workers cannot free themselves from the influence of bourgeois and petty-bourgeois ideology.

The classical socialist labor movement tried to achieve such an ideological emancipation through a constant process of organization, education and self-action. But even during its heyday it didn't rally more than a minority fraction of the working class. And if one looks at the extremely modest proportions that Marxist education assumed in mass socialist parties like the German or Austrian Social Democracy before World War I (not to speak of the French Communist Party before World War II), if one looks at the figures of subscribers to the theoretical magazines or students at study camps or workers' universities in those organizations, one can early understand that even then they merely scratched the surface.

Of course things have become worse since the classical labor movement started to degenerate and stopped inoculating the working class vanguard in any consistent manner against the poison of bourgeois ideas. The dikes collapsed, and aided by modern mass media, bourgeois and petty-bourgeois ideology have penetrated deeply into broad layers of the working class, including those organized in mass Social-Democratic and Communist parties.

But one should guard against losing a sense of proportion in respect to this problem. After all, the working class movement arose in the nineteenth century when the mass of workers were far more dominated by the ideas of the ruling class than they are today. One has only to compare the hold of religion on workers in large parts of Europe, or the grip of nationalism on the French working class after the experience of the great French revolution, to understand that what looks like a new problem today is in reality as old as the working class itself.

In the last analysis the question boils down to this: Which force will turn out to be stronger in determining the workers' attitude to the society he lives in, the mystifying ideas he receives, yesterday in the church and today through TV, or the social reality he confronts and assimilates day after day through practical experience? For historical materialists, to pose the question this way is to answer it, although the struggle itself will say the last word.

Finally, one should add that, while "manipulation" of the workers' consciousness and dreams is apparently constant, so after all is the apparent stability of bourgeois society. It goes on living under "business as usual." But a social revolution is not a continuous or gradual process; it is certainly not "business as usual." It is precisely a sudden disruption of social continuity, a break with customs, habits and a traditional way of life.

184

The problems of the revolutionary potential of the working class cannot be answered by references to what goes on every day or even every year; revolutions do not erupt every day. The revolutionary potential of the working class can be denied only if one argues that the sparks of revolt which have been kindled in the working class mass through the experience of social injustice and social irrationality are smothered forever; if one argues that the patient and obstinate propaganda and education by revolutionary vanguard organizations cannot have a massive effect among the workers anywhere, anytime, whatever may be the turn of objective events. After all, it is enough that the flame is there to ignite a combustible mass once every 15 or 20 years for the system ultimately to collapse. That's what happened in Russia. That's what the May revolution in France has shown can happen in Western Europe too.

These epoch-making May events allow us to draw a balance sheet of long-term trends which confirm every proposition I have tried to defend here today. After 20 years of neo-capitalism, functioning under classical conditions, with a "planning board" which is cited as a model for all imperialist countries, with a state television system which has perfected mass manipulation to uphold the ruling class and party, with a foreign policy accepted by a large majority of the masses, in May 1968 there were in France twice as many strikers as ever before in the history of the working class of that country; they used much more radical forms of struggle than in 1936, in 1944-46 or in 1955; they not only raised the slogan of workers' control, workers' management and workers' power more sharply than ever before, but started to put it in practice in a dozen big factories and several large towns. In the face of this experience it is hard to question the revolutionary potential of the working class under neo-capitalism any more. In the face of this experience it is hard to question the prediction that France, which is the politically classical country of bourgeois society, in the same way as Britain and the United States are its economically classical countries, is showing the whole Western world and not least the United States a preview of its own future. *De te fabula narrator!*

We cannot examine here the interconnection between the workers' struggle for socialism in the Western metropolises and the liberation struggle of the colonial and semi-colonial countries as well as the struggle for socialist democracy in the countries of Central and Eastern Europe. These interconnections are manifold and obvious. There are also direct causal links between the upsurge of an independent revolutionary leader-ship in the Cuban and Latin American revolution, the heroic struggle of the Vietnamese people against U.S. imperialist aggression, and the emer-gence of a new youth vanguard in the West, which, at least in Western Europe, through the transmission belt of working class youth, has started to influence directly the development of the class struggle.

The main striking feature here has a more general and abstract character: the reemergence of active internationalism in the vanguard of the working class. The international concentration and centralization of capital, especially through the creation of the "multi-national corpo-ration," gave capital an initial advantage over a working class movement hopelessly divided between national and sectional unions and parties. But now, in France, at one blow, the advanced workers have cleaned the field of the rot accumulated over decades of confusion and defeat. They have cut through the underbrush of bourgeois nationalism and bourgeois Europeanism and have come out into the wide open space of interna-tional brotherhood.

The fraternal unity in strikes and demonstrations of Jewish and Arab, Portuguese and Spanish, Greek and Turkish, French and foreign workers, in a country which has probably been more plagued by xeno-phobia over the last 20 years than any other in Europe, triumphantly culminated in 60,000 demonstrators shouting before the Gare de Lyon: "We are all German Jews." Already a first echo has come from Jeru-salem itself where Jewish students demonstrated with the slogan: "We are all Palestinian Arabs!" Never have we seen anything like this, on such a scale, and these initial manifestations warrant the greatest confidence in the world which will emerge when the working class, rejuvenated after two decades of slumber, will move to take power.

Both through political conviction and as a result of objective analy-sis of present world reality, I firmly believe that we are living in the age of permanent revolution. This revolution is inevitable because there is such a tremendous gap between what man could make of our world, with the power which science and technology have placed in his hands, and what he is making of it within the framework of a decaying, irrational social system. This revolution is imperative in order to close that gap and make this world a place in which all human beings, without dis-tinction as to race, color or nationality, will receive the same care as the rulers today devote to space rockets and nuclear submarines.

What the socialist revolution is all about, in the last analysis, is faith in the unconquerable spirit of revolt against injustice and oppression, and confidence in the ability of mankind to build a future for the human race. Coming from a continent which went through the nightmares of Hitler and Stalin, and emerged hardly a generation later holding high the banner of social revolution, of emancipation of labor, of workers' democracy, of proletarian internationalism, and witnessing in France more youth rallying around that banner than at any time since socialist ideas were born, I believe that faith is fully justified.

10

STANLEY ARONOWITZ

Does the United States Have a New Working Class?

Stanley Aronowitz speaks and writes widely on politics and social change in the United States. He has worked in trade unions and community agencies, and contributed regularly to the *Guardian* and more recently to the *Liberated Guardian*. He also serves on the editorial boards of *Root and Branch* and *Socialist Revolution*.

RECENT DEVELOPMENTS *

The dramatic rise of student radicalism in the past decade, together with the development of new worker militancy in all advanced industrial countries, has put Marxists once more on the offensive in the prolonged ideological debate about the revolutionary potential of the underlying population of advanced industrial societies and of the working class in particular. Events of the past two years have belied the forecasts of "end of ideology" theorists who confidently proclaimed the era of working-class integration into advanced capitalist society at the close of the 1950's. Not only has ideological ferment spread throughout student ranks, but wildcat movements against both union and corporate hierarchies have mushroomed in Great Britain, France, Italy, and, more recently, in the United States. Most widely discussed and novel, perhaps,

* This and later sections of the paper draw on two statistical sources about labor in the United States. Both sources were published in 1969 by the Government Printing Office, Washington, D. C. for the Bureau of Labor Statistics, U. S. Department of Labor: *Handbook of Labor Statistics* and *Manpower Projections, 1960–1975*, 4 vols., especially Vol. 4.

is some evidence of the emergence of a significant political force within working-class ranks: the professional, technical, and scientific workers, within both industry and the university. Among Marxists, this has led to much attention and controversy about a new working class. In this context, can the United States be said to have developed a new working class of that type?

In Europe, discussions of the significance of the growth of technically trained workers within the production process has reached a fairly high level of sophistication. In our country, the debate has barely begun. Despite the great quantity of literature about the subject in Europe, ambiguities remain. Before attempting to answer whether the United States now has a new working class, it is important to provide some basic information, and then to clear up some confusion and undertake some definitions.

European skilled and semi-skilled blue-collar workers have been protesting the decline of living standards and real wages in western capitalist countries for the past few years. Engineers and other technically trained workers are meanwhile raising the problem of control over production, on the one hand, and the content of their work on the other. During and just prior to the May events in France in 1968, technicians in the communications industries demanded workers' control and engaged in struggles to protest the boredom and narrow scope of their work. What stands out is the contradiction between scientific training which prepares them, in part, for broad responsibility in the production process, and the highly rationalized character of their work due to the constraints engendered by the hierarchial organization of production by the managerial bureaucracies. This contradiction is eroding the old professional consciousness of this stratum of workers.

In the United States, there has been a significant rise of white-collar unionism since the mid-sixties. Most of this development is among public employees, where professional and technical workers constitute up to 25 per cent of the nearly 10 million workers in this sector and clerical workers about 35 per cent. But there have been scattered indications that unionism among technical and scientific workers in manufacturing industries is also on the upgrade. Although these developments do not, in themselves, constitute proof of the emergence of a new class-consciousness among members of these strata, it is clear that the old conception of the likelihood of the alliance of the professionals with the ruling class has been severely shaken.

Among engineers in the private sector, starting salaries are usually high for recent graduates. But top rates are reached in a few years, and the range of salary increases is relatively narrow. Engineers starting at $9–11,000 per year rarely earn more than $15–17,000 after ten years in the "profession," unless they leave the technical side of their occupation for management and sales.

It would be equally mistaken, however, to attribute all the recent evidence of militancy among technicians in the United States to quantitative issues alone. Most college-trained workers in both public and private employment feel that they are not working to their competence, that the kind of tasks assigned to them do not measure their training. Contrary to the statement of such writers as Robert Blauner, who speaks of a "secular decline of the workers' class consciousness and militancy," [1] it is precisely because most industries offer few chances for upgrading and enlargement of responsibilities for both manual and mental workers that the new militancy is bursting forth. Increasing evidence shows that teachers do not teach, that planners do not plan, that engineers are limited in their capacity to fulfill their intellectual potential because they are relegated to discrete tasks within a highly rationalized production system.

Marxist Views on the Contemporary Working Class

The Marxist orthodoxy of the Third, Communist International introduced considerable changes in the theory of class among socialists. Instead of deriving its theory from an examination of the actual division of social and technical labor within capitalist production, there was a tendency to regard the working class within a single dimension. The ideal typical revolutionary class was the factory and transportation manual worker, that is, the famous "industrial working class." Workers in basic industries, those which produced means of production, were the critical base of revolutionary class action since they occupied the central position within the production system. Their political power, exercised either at the work place or in the society at large, constituted the sufficient condition for revolutionary activity. The primary task of Marxists was to root themselves among this sector of the working class.

Other working-class strata, particularly those in consumer goods, manufacturing, services, and public employment were secondary reserves

---

[1] Robert Blauner, *Alienation and Freedom: The Factory Worker and His Industry* (Chicago: University of Chicago Press, 1964), p. 182.

of the "industrial working class" of skilled, semiskilled, and unskilled manual workers. Technical, professional, and scientific workers were often regarded as "middle strata," whose significance depended on the particular political situation. In general, however, these groups were adjudged politically unstable, tending toward an alliance with the ruling class as much, if not more than, toward the working class. The classical Leninist notion of the fate of the "employees" was that it depended on the strength of the manual workers within the industrial working class. Presumably, the chances of drawing the "middle strata" into the revolutionary orbit was a function of the hegemony of the communists over the industrial working class, and, in turn, the ability of the manual workers in basic industry to establish their leadership over all oppressed classes and strata of the population. Lenin went so far as to imply that highly skilled workers in imperialist countries constituted a labor aristocracy and thus veered decisively toward the ruling class. Since Marx, "Marxism" has lacked a coherent science of class.

The orthodox Marxian theory of class tended to proceed from the division of labor characteristic of the competitive era of capitalist organization and the technical division under mechanical reproduction. The working class, in theory, was portrayed in undifferentiated terms. Its common ground was that it comprised the great mass of factory and transportation workers from whom surplus value was extracted in the process of the production of commodities. Techncians stood in the middle: between workers and managers. Although American Marxists always disagreed with C. Wright Mills who gave the growing numbers of clerical and administrative workers in the state and corporate bureaucracies "new middle class" designation, the lack of precision in their understanding of these strata was notable.

Part of the difficulty in the Old Left notion of the working class inheres in the broad two-class scheme of Marx himself. In his historical writings, Marx assigned intermediate strata and classes an important role in the unfolding of events. Similarly, personalities are taken into account when describing the course of social struggle. But the concept of the great schism between bourgeois and proletarian constituting the structure of capitalist society found in the *Manifesto* was abstracted from concrete circumstances and transformed into dogma by the Marxism of both the Stalin era and the Social Democrats alike.

The problem comes when this general view of capitalist society becomes the outer analytical limit for a theory of class. Instead of making it a starting point, the Old Left transformed it into a theoretical straight-jacket. Lenin had provided their standard definition:

> Classes are large groups of people which differ from each other by the place they occupy in a historically determined system of social production, by their relation to the means of production, by their role in the social organization of labor, and, consequently by the magnitude and the mode of acquiring the portion of social wealth of which they dispose. Classes are such groups of people, one of which can appropriate the labor of another owing to the different places they occupy in a definite system of social production.[2]

Beyond that standard definition, the Old Left had little to say about the question of class stratification. The burden of the just cited work on the working class, by J. M. Budish of the Labor Research Association was to refute the contemporary notion that the old working class was dissolving in a "middle class" of white-collar workers. The main theme of the work is that white-collar workers and other working-class strata did not constitute a new class at all, much less the "middle class," but were simply salaried, or otherwise occupationally differentiated strata of the working class.

Once again, however, the broad division of classes into two parts is reasserted. The recent writings on the subject take no specific account of the significance of the changing structure of the working class. The neglect is especially true of the rise of workers in the public sector and the increase in the proportion of technical and scientific workers in manufacturing industries.

The virtue of the "new working-class theory" of Serge Mallet, Alain Touraine, and other European Marxists is that, as Marcuse said in December 1968 to a symposium sponsored by the *Guardian* in New York, "it comprehends and anticipates the tendencies that are going on before our own eyes in the material process of production in capitalism, namely that more and more highly qualified salaried employees, technicians, specialists and so on, occupy a decisive position in the material process of production." In general, the Old Left is now prepared to recognize the fact that engineers, scientists, and other employees were part of the productive labor force and are, for the most part, wage and

---

[2] Quoted in J. M. Budish, *The Changing Structure of the Working Class* (New York: International Publishers, 1964), pp. 7–8.

salary workers rather than managers or conventional petit bourgeois. But the question of their centrality to both the work place and their consequent political importance in the working-class movement remains in dispute.

André Gorz has stated the case for the critical significance of the new working class succinctly:

> During the last twenty years the development of the productive forces in the advanced capitalist economies has led . . . to a qualitative change in the character of the labor force, which, at every level, is socially necessary to the advance of the social process of production.[3]

THE THEORY OF THE NEW WORKING CLASS

Four chief characteristics mark the New Working-Class argument:

1. The determining tendency in capitalist production, owing to the vast technological changes which have occurred in the material process of production, is no longer physical labor but knowledge. Knowledge has become the critical productive force in advanced capitalist countries. Technical and scientific workers as the key bearers of knowledge now occupy a central position within socialist strategy and program. The demands of these workers increasingly correspond to the requirements of the new forces of production.

2. Universities have been transformed from institutions which produce managerial and political elites and their teachers into knowledge factories with two distinct but closely related functions: first, to train the vast army of technicians required by the new productive forces, and second, to become important facilities for the conduct of research which constantly revolutionizes production technique.

3. "The contradiction between the growing—latent or actual—autonomy of productive work for an increasing number of workers and its plainly social character and the situation of work within the factory and within capitalist society." [4] More specifically, New Working-Class theorists argue that the requirements of the new productive forces for a worker capable of integrating knowledge comes into conflict with the

---

[3] Gorz, "Capitalist Relations of Production and the Socially Necessary Labour Force," *International Socialist Journal,* Vol. 2, No. 10 (1964), pp. 415–429.
[4] *Ibid.*

limits imposed on his autonomy by the hierarchial organization of work and society. The technician is trained for work of a broad scope. He finds himself rendered both powerless and confined within outmoded relations of production.

Capitalist enterprises still operate within the constraints dictated by the dual criteria of profit and domination. In the end, the highly integrated and social character of advanced technique is subordinated to the bureaucratic organization of capitalism which is unable to permit the full development of the forces of production. This contradiction generates new demands among scientists and engineers, particularly the demand for control over their own work by the technicians, now transformed into a proletariat rather than a managerial elite.

4. The New Working-Class theory gives a new dimension to the concept of alienation. Alienation is understood in the context both of the separation of the highly skilled worker from the product of his work as well as his skill. The creative potential of scientific labor is thwarted by management hierarchies which demand the subordination of knowledge. Workers increasingly find themselves "overtrained," unable to put into practice what they have learned.

In his *Engineers and the Price System,* Thorstein Veblen anticipated the debate which rages in all advanced industrial countries, both capitalist and "state socialist." Nearly fifty years ago, Veblen argued that the technicians as the bearers of technical and scientific knowledge were the crucial element in modern production. Their grasp of the material conditions of industrial technique and organization made them central to the possibility of revolutionary change. ". . . any question of a revolutionary overturn in America or any other of the advanced industrial countries resolves itself in practical fact into a question of what the guild of technicians will do." [5] Veblen was scornful of the possibilities of the organized trade unions, even their revolutionary expression, the IWW, to lead a revolution. The AFL is "officered by safe and sane politicians" and "is a business organization with a vested interest of its own; for keeping up prices and keeping down the supply . . . not for managing productive industry or even for increasing the output of goods produced under any management." [6] The Industrial Workers of the World, made up of "irresponsible wayfaring men of industry, . . . is not organized

[5] Thorstein Veblen, *The Engineers and the Price System* (1921, reprinted New York: Augustus M. Kelley, 1965), p 133.
[6] *Ibid,* pp. 89–90.

to take over the highly technical duties involved in the administration of the industrial system." [7] But the technicians, however endowed with the necessary material requisites for revolutionary takeover, "still are consistently loyal with something more than a hired man's loyalty to the established order of commercial profit and absentee ownership." [8]

Veblen was aware of the necessity of forging an alliance between the technicians and the "underlying population." One of the preliminary moves necessary before an overt uprising could be undertaken would be "the working-out of a common understanding and a solidarity of sentiment between the technicians and the working force engaged in transportation and in the greater underlying industries of the system: to which is to be added as being nearly indispensable from the outset, an active adherence to the plan [of takeover] on the part of the trained workmen in the great generality of mechanical industries." [9]

Veblen was neither an elitist nor a technocrat. He attempted simply to comprehend the sufficient conditions for "popular uprising." These consisted in the "movement effectually meet[ing] the special material requirements of the situation which provokes it." [10] But Veblen was clearly speaking about the managers of capitalist enterprises who were neither owners nor ordinary wage workers. The critical importance of this group derived from their actual control over the production and distribution process. His use of the terms technicians and engineers corresponded to the position of these professions within American industry during the 1920's. The beginning of the separation of ownership from management initiated by corporate capital at the turn of the century was reaching maturity as the corporation became the characteristic form of capitalist enterprise. Veblen acutely recognized that the corporations were centralizing control over production in the hands of a new manager who combined organizational and scientific knowledge.

But the emergence of the distinction between the technocrat, who actually controlled production, and the technician, who performed a specialized task under the direction of a scientifically trained management, had not become visible enough to enter into Veblen's thinking. The New Working-Class theory makes this distinction.

If the New Working-Class theory is understood as describing

[7] *Ibid.*, p. 90.
[8] *Ibid.*, p. 138.
[9] *Ibid.*, p. 168.
[10] *Ibid.*, pp. 86–87.

tendencies in the material process of production rather than accomplished changes, it is a highly useful way of understanding the proletarianization of technical workers in contemporary capitalism. The work of Serge Mallet is particularly welcome because it attempts to provide an empirical base for the theory. Mallet's studies of factories employing advanced techniques have broken new ground toward the development of a contemporary Marxian sociology. The assertion found in Mallet's book, *La Nouvelle Classe ouvrière,* is that the professional, having lost his autonomy during the mechanical phase of industrial capitalist development, can see the possibilities of regaining it in the automation—or third—phase of the industrial revolution when the material process of production demands that he play an integrative role thanks to his grasp of the new technology. Bureaucratic capitalism frustrates this demand, even as it requires that he be the purveyor of technical knowledge. Mallet asserts the separation of knowledge from management in the period of computerization. "The modern conditions of production today offer the objective possibilities for the development of generalized self-management of production and the economy by those who carry the weight within it." [11] Mallet goes on to argue that the possibilities are thwarted by the technobureaucracy which operates on the profit criterion and appears more and more as an obstacle to the harmonious development of the productive forces under workers' control.

In Mallet's conception the scientifically trained workers are the vanguard of the whole working class because they represent the new productive forces. In contrast to Veblen's position, Mallet assumes the wide dissemination of knowledge among larger strata of workers who do not share in the management of the enterprise. Plainly, behind Mallet's view of the new working class as vanguard is the probability that the new technology will become endemic throughout advanced capitalist societies. For the new role of knowledge and those who possess it as a productive force depends on changes within the material process of production—particularly those changes evident already in the most advanced industries such as chemicals, electronics, and oil.

The scientifically trained worker does assume critical importance in the process of social change owing to his centrality in material production, especially those industries marked by the most advanced technologies such as chemicals, aerospace, and electronics. In these industries

[11] Serge Mallet, *La Nouvelle Classe ouvrière* (Paris: Anthropos, revised edition, 1969), p. 41.

the absolute increase in the number of technically trained workers has not only quantitatively transformed the distribution of workers so that professional and technical workers are fast becoming a critical mass within the work place. Also, to the extent that these industries depend on highly complex techniques of production (which in turn are a function of the fact that the application of knowledge has replaced manual labor as the determining element in production), technical workers are absolutely indispensable for the actual production process. Thus, the increase quantitatively of technical workers is intimately related to their qualitative role in the production of goods. In turn, from the point of view of political economy, the appearance of large numbers of technical, professional, and scientific workers in the work force as a whole is an expression of the ever-rising organic composition of capital. The proportion of machinery to labor-hours is itself a consequence of the higher technical composition of capital in many modern industries. Insofar as knowledge has now become an important productive force in advanced industrial societies, to this extent the extreme strategic importance of the technicians is derived.

APPLYING THE THEORY TO THE UNITED STATES

When American writers deal with the New Working-Class theory, they tend to equate the New Working Class with university-trained workers. They note that these are becoming more numerous in the work force in general, largely in consequence of the shift from manufacturing employment to the service sectors, the public bureaucracies, and the university itself. Martin Oppenheimer simply identifies the New Working Class with the skilled sector of white-collar strata. He stresses those who share the experience of having discovered that the modern university instead of being a center of "learning, exploration and self discovery . . . is desanctified as its tie-ins with the military industrial complex . . . are revealed." [12]

Oppenheimer introduces confusion into the observed phenomenon of the growth of the university-trained work force when he uses the term "white collar working class" and implies its existence as a distinct class. He distinguishes himself from European representatives of

[12] Martin Oppenheimer, "The New White Collar Working Class," *Social Policy,* Vol. 1, No. 2, July–August 1970, p. 30.

the New Working-Class theory such as Gorz, Mallet, and Mandel by questioning the revolutionary potential of the university-trained stratum. His first objection is that the "income and life style of the new working class continues at this juncture to be more co-optative than revolt inspiring." He goes on to ask whether the politics of the suburban neighborhood, "the locale of most white collar workers," will generate a left-wing radical development or a sharper move to the right.

Second, Oppenheimer attempts to meet some of the prognoses of theorists such as Mandel, who draw radicalizing conclusions from the alleged "coming crisis" of advanced capitalism.

Oppenheimer speaks from the framework of empiricist sociology. It is apparent that, for him, class is determined in part by education, life style, and income, and that political behavior and ideologies flow from a pluralistic model. Like most academic sociologists, he places much weight on the mediations of social structure in contrast to fundamental developments in the class relations within the production process.

Bogdan Denitch contents himself with repeating the essential elements of the European theory of the New Working Class. He echoes particularly the point that the developments within the forces of production, especially technological change, have called into being a new class of technicians "indispensable to modern economies" and with "a potential social weight greater than its actual numbers, which, in any case, are growing." The fundamental contradiction inherent in the New Working-Class phenomenon is that ". . . promise evoked by higher education clashes with the result, which is often work-compartmentalized to a degree that an older generation of university graduates would find unrecognizable" and that "Whole generations trained to think in terms of societal issues are offered roles as powerless, if well-paid, employees." [13]

According to Denitch, the intellectual training of the New Working Class enables it to raise the demand for autonomy and for workers' control over production and all institutions of social life. Unlike Mills, Marcuse, and others who have advanced, in one form or another, elitist theories of change based on the revolutionary potential of the university-trained portion of the working class, Denitch develops a theory of the alliance of the old and new working classes as the sufficient condition for revolution.

[13] Bogdan Denitch, "Is There a New Working Class?," *Dissent*, Vol. 17, No. 4, July–August 1970, pp. 351–353.

CRITICISMS OF THE THEORY

To anticipate in brief the criticisms of the theory, they reduce themselves to the following:

1. There is no new "class" in contemporary capitalist society. The emergence of the technicians as important elements in the work force is undeniable. But the decline of skills as technology advances, the rise in the general level of education for the whole working class, and the erosion of professionalism by these tendencies has made more apparent the fact that the technicians are merely a differently trained stratum of the industrial working class. The only sense in which the term New Working Class has meaning is by reference to the new generation of workers—not so much by the material processes of production. Yet the rise in the general education level for this new generation *narrows* the differences between various strata of the workink class, rather than making the distinction between technicians and manual workers more sharp.

2. The New Working-Class theorists have tended to overstate the extent of changes within material production. Thus they exaggerate the qualitative aspects of the position of the technicians.

3. The New Working-Class theory does not distinguish sharply enough the technocrats who do control production, but cannot be construed as a new working class, and the technicians who are an important stratum of the working class. This constitutes an all-important distinction.

4. There is not enough attention paid to the origins of occupationally based strata. Does the assignment of highly trained workers in the labor force correspond to new material requirements? Or is it bureaucratically determined? In turn, the question of the role of education in the development of the forces of production is inadequately examined. There seems to be a too-easy assumption that the rise of the qualifications for certain categories of labor is required by new technology. In short, New Working-Class theory has a sociology, but not a political economy.

5. It is doubtful that the tendencies described by Mallet can be universally applied. This is less a criticism of the New Working-Class

199

theory than of those who have attempted to apply the theses to this country. In any case, the role and political significance of technicians must be examined specifically in every context.

The rest of the paper develops the five criticisms just stated and applies them to the United States.

There are several issues left unresolved by Denitch and Oppenheimer as well as the major European writers who advance the New Working-Class thesis. The first issue is the confusion inherent in the term, New Working Class. For Veblen, and implicitly in the work of Serge Mallet, the term refers to the group of technicians within modern industry who actually control elements of the production process, if not the corporate hierarchy itself. In fact, the patterns of domination inherent in corporate organization are presumed to be in conflict with the creative performance of technical work, and beyond production, the development of technology. It is our contention that, with the exception of the most advanced industries in technological terms, the preponderance of American industries do not conform to the notion of the centrality of the working technician within the production process. The leading industries of American capitalism have centralized both knowledge and power within the portion of technicians and scientists who are, at the same time, middle- or upper-level corporate managers.

The use of the concept of the New Working Class to embrace all college-trained workers departs sharply from its most precise importance. In modern industry, the question is whether a section of managers who actually control some processes of the work can be radicalized by making an alliance with the rest of the work force.

This point brings out a second confusion. It appears to me untenable to affix the term "new class" to the rising proportion of mental to physical workers in the labor force as a whole. The rise of the so-called white-collar strata, particularly the technicians, is more complex than the presumed development of technology. The rise of the university-trained worker has sources beyond the changes in material production, although this aspect of the problem has great significance for revolutionary strategy. From the point of view of numerical growth, the service, corporate, and public bureaucracies account for most of the new jobs for university and technically trained workers. Here several issues need clarification. First, the shift from manufacturing employment to nonproductive jobs in the Marxian sense is a consequence of important eco-

200

nomic changes since World War II rather than of significant technical developments. The most important of these is the key role occupied by the state in the political economy, particularly its role as investor and consumer of commodities and regulator of relations within and between classes. Second, the expansion of the service and welfare sectors, especially the distributive industries and health and education, are only qualitatively new developments in relation to the economy. But within these industries technology has not changed so radically that new qualifications for the work force are called into existence.

Especially in the United States, the problem of the relations of technological change to occupational stratification and corporate organization is rarely addressed by proponents of the New Working-Class theory. We will argue that the growth of the state bureaucracies is socially unnecessary and is related more to the requirements of capitalist domination than the development of the productive forces. If anything, work within these bureaucracies has become less complex than within the production sphere. The simplification of tasks is facilitated both by the computerization of many administrative functions and by the rationalization of these functions. No development corresponding to the integrative aspects of continuous flow operations in the oil and chemical industry is widespread within government and corporate offices which, on the contrary, seem to proliferate personnel and functions in an extraordinary irrational pattern.

A further problem with the concept of the New Working Class as it is used in contemporary literature is the ambiguity of the way in which "class" is employed. If the managerial technicians are to be construed as a class, then Victor Fey's concept of *"the wage earning middle class"* [15] seems more appropriate than identifying this group with the working class. Another way of viewing this group is to comprehend it simply as a stratum of the familiar managerial or professional servant class which includes all corporate managers, university presidents and key professors, politicians and other high government officials. This group shares the outlook of the ruling class and serves its interest by running the machinery of government and the corporations, but does not control the fundamental decision-making.

[14] Victor Fey, "Les Classes Moyennes Salariées," in *En Partant du "Capital,"* edited by the author (Paris: Anthropos, 1968), pp. 97–115.

KNOWLEDGE AS A PRODUCTIVE FORCE

It is important to take account of the increase in size and importance of the stratum of college-trained mental workers both in the sphere of material production and in the various bureaucracies. This stratum can only be construed as a class if the model advanced by modern sociologists such as Dahrendorf, Lipset, and others of the pluralistic theories of class is adopted. This is not the place to argue once more the Marxian theory of class, according to which class position is determined by the relationship of the worker to the means of production. There is no dispute that the social weight of university-trained workers in the labor force has increased. In the manufacturing industries they are growing in numbers at twice the rate of any other stratum of workers. In the public, corporate, and service bureaucracies their development has been similarly dramatic. But there is not enough evidence that they share different interests or, in the long run, will develop a different outlook than other strata of wage workers.

Further, the appearance of the university-trained worker is the result of the general rise of the educational level of the whole working class, as much as it depends on changes within industry. Although these developments have historically been closely related, it may be that the rise of mass higher education is only partially a function of the technological requirements of modern industry. The configuration of occupational strata, of credentials and qualifications, is as much a function of social domination as it is of industrial progress. The U.S. labor force is one of the most highly stratified in the capitalist world. Minute stratification is a function of both specialization and the general division of labor and of the impact of trade-union and professional organizations which have assisted corporations to impose complex divisions within the working class.

Mass higher education arose as much from the need of capitalism to prolong the withdrawal of youth from the labor force after the 1950's due to economic stagnation as it did from the need to provide a highly trained labor force for industry. If Marx's thesis that the tendency of modern industry to reduce skills is true, then it would be erroneous to ascribe the development of the university solely in terms of either ma-

202

terial production or the rise of the public sector. Higher education and all schooling now has a broad social function in relation to the distribution of the labor force.

It would be well, at this point, to enter a caveat to the general proposition that knowledge has, in fact, become the decisive productive force in United States capitalism. More accurate is to recognize that U.S. capitalism is characterized by extreme unevenness in the development of both the economy and its technological base. The extent to which machinery has replaced human labor varies widely from industry to industry. In general, in comparison to other capitalist countries, this country's forces of production are retarded in consumer goods industry.[15]

The relatively low proportion of technical and scientific workers to semi-skilled and unskilled production workers is illustrated in the textile industry, where this group constitutes less than 3 per cent of the work force, automobiles, where the percentage is well below 10 per cent, and transportation, where technicians constitute about 3.5 per cent of all workers in the industry. In these industries operatives constitute well over 50 per cent of all workers.

Even in some basic industries, particularly fabricated metals and primary metals, it would be dangerous to overstate the extent of the emergence of the importance of the technical workers. In the basic-steel industry technicians constitute about 6 per cent of the labor force, while the proportion is somewhat larger in metals fabrication. The composition in the pulp and paper industry is somewhat similar, except the growth of the technical labor force is projected to increase by 50 per cent by 1975 due to the rapid technological development of the industry.

The low proportion of technical workers reflects the fact that consumer goods industries have experienced little technological change in the past decade. Most of them are still operating in phase two of industrial capitalism, that is, the period of specialization and rationalization epitomized by the assembly line. The division of labor during the mechanization era was rather minute. Technical processes have not kept pace with industrial expansion. The slow rate of technical development and change in these industries can be attributed to the pre-eminence of the war economy in the post-war period.

The key industries in the defense sector, electronics and chemicals,

[15] See Seymour Melman, *Our Depleted Society* (New York: Harcourt, Brace and World, 1965).

have become leading industries in the American economy, both economically and technologically. Supported by public funds, these industries have been the beneficiaries of tremendous research operations. Ever more the massive development of new weaponry with its concentration on nuclear power and electronic and chemical components has placed these industries at the center of the third industrial revolution. In the third phase of industrial capitalism, automation and computerization reintegrate the labor force under the hegemoney of those who are the possessors of the knowledge required to develop and operate new procsses. If Marx's prediction of the transformation of the forces of production contained in his *Grundrisse* has been fulfilled in contemporary industrial society at all, its primary expression is in chemicals, oils, and electronics. Marx wrote:

> As large-scale industry develops, the creation of real wealth depends less and less upon labor time and the quantity of labor expended and more upon the might of the machines set in motion during labor time. The powerful effectiveness of the machines bears no relationship to the labor time which it cost to produce them. Their power, rather, derives from the general level of science and the progress of technology . . . neither the actual labor expended by man, nor the length of time during which he works, is the great pillar of production and wealth. [16]

According to Marx, labor under the new technology is relegated to the role of bystander and watcher and the concept of productive labor becomes transformed from the application of brute labor power to the production of knowledge. Those institutions involved in the production of knowledge (the universities and the technical schools as well as private corporations) are as much a part of the production system as the factory. The schools now become knowledge factories, not only for the production of managerial elites, but for the production of a large segment of the working class. But to the extent that scientific research is conducted by the universities they also participate in the development of technology and are essential to the changes in the character of large-scale industry, particularly in the war sector of the economy.

[16] Quoted in Michael Harrington, *The Accidental Century* (New York: Macmillan, 1965), pp. 266–268, from Karl Marx, *Grundrisse der Kritik der Politischen Ökonomie* (Berlin: Dietz, 1953), pp. 592, 593.

TECHNICIAN VERSUS TECHNOCRAT

The New Working-Class theory bases itself on the assumption that "the traditional industrial proletariat is gradually diminishing to the point of approaching political insignificance," [18] and being replaced by a stratum of highly trained technicians who perform their productive labor as research, quality control, and organization. In short the character of productive work, it is claimed, has decisively shifted in advanced industrial society to mental rather than physical labor in consequence of the widespread introduction of automation and cybernation into dominant sectors of the American economy.

The strategic implications of this thesis for socialist strategy are evident. The new working class, by virtue of its broader understanding of the production process and its centrality to it, is in a position to challenge the patterns of decision-making by capitalist managers and expose thereby the true despotism of capital. The struggle for workers' control, over the pace and direction of investment, as well as the hierarchial organization of the production process itself, constitutes a crucial transitional demand for exposing the inherent conflict of labor and capital in the modern era. The growing conflict between the broader understanding and control by the technical worker over the production process on one hand and his decreased autonomy in determining the direction of investment and other crucial management decisions constitutes the basis for the potential power of the technical worker in becoming a lever for social transformation.

Here the distinction between the technocrat and the technician is essential. The growing importance of a scientifically trained technocratic elite within United States capitalism is commensurate with the appearance of industries which rely on scientific knowledge for their development. The technocrats are intimately involved in the dominant power system. Often they are the heart of the management stratum. This group is not to be confused with the technical workers who possess knowledge but are bereft of power. Indeed, it is the conflict between their greater knowledge and centrality to the production process and their powerless-

[18] Paul Piccone, "Students' Protest, Class Structure, and Ideology," *Telos,* Vol. 2, No. 1, Spring, 1969, p. 113.

ness which constitutes their revolutionary potential. Technicians have merely become a more important element of the working class. They share the propertylessness and alienation of any other industrial worker. Often the technical worker in the advanced industries replaces the old blue-collar foreman on the production line. The rising qualifications for leading positions in many industries may be a consequence of the rising technical requirements of production. Supervision in the automatic factory carries the requirement that it be of a wider scope. But the fact that an engineer occupies a foreman's role, or that it is technicians rather than craftsmen who are responsible for quality control in a chemical plant, simply comprehends the fact that the similar occupations require a higher level of educational preparation than in more traditional industries. The function of the supervisor remains the same. Plant organization and hierarchy has relegated him to roughly the same position as his predecessor, the manual worker.

The Proletarianization of Technicians

In some industries, the research function is more closely integrated into the production process. The 25 per cent of the work force in chemicals and oils engaged in intellectual labor is largely employed in development activities. But it would be mistaken to draw too broad conclusions from this limited phenomenon. In manufacturing industries as a whole, the decline of the old industrial working class is neither precipitous nor is the rise of the technical worker dramatic. The projected growth of technical, professional, and scientific workers between 1960 and 1975 in manufacturing is only 3.4 per cent and the decline of semi-skilled and skilled workers is only 1.3 per cent. The real change has been the long-term disappearance of the unskilled laborer who has given way to the semi-skilled worker.

Moreover, the relatively slow growth of the technical stratum in manufacturing industries shows no signs of great acceleration. Fundamentally, the New Working-Class theory relies on rapid technical development within the framework of capitalism. There are several reasons why this has not happened. First, the assumption is made of a large surplus of capital which can be invested in technological change in the wake of the sharp curtailment of opportunities for capital investment in the world market. In fact, rapid technological change has occurred in

206

western Europe in precisely those industries where U.S. investment has lagged, the consumer goods sector. The division of labor in world capitalism has forced the United States to become the chief military power, thus limiting its development in other sectors. Second, the reindustrialization on an advanced technological level of U.S. industry seems beyond the present financial capacity of corporations in both the competitive and the monopoly sector. One reason for the deteriorated position of U.S. capital is the inflationary spiral which has afflicted the U.S. economy since 1965. Another is the pre-eminence of investment in western Europe by multi-national corporations controlled by U.S.-based groups.

There are exceptions to the general rule of technological stagnation. It appears that investment plans in the steel industry indicate some expansion of capacity on the basis of new technologies. But the limits to the widespread application of this technology appear as the recession cycle reappears as a regular feature of capitalist stagnation. Another limit is indicated by the amortization problem in computerization of steel processes. The rule of thumb, five-year amortization, seems difficult to realize.

More profoundly, the rising productivity of labor in all mechanical industries since World War II has not resulted in the permanent disemployment of the labor force. Instead, the rise of the public sector, corresponding to the critical role played by the state within the corporate capitalist system, the expansion of retail and other services, and the stabilization of the permanent army at more than 3 million men combined in the 1950's and 1960's successfully to absorb new labor force entrants and re-employ those displaced by technological change, product displacement, and industrial stagnation.

But the short-term prospects for the U.S. economy indicate that the education system has overproduced technical workers in comparison to the pace of technological change within manufacturing industry and the growth of over-all economic activity. The overproduction of technicians has been apparent for some time. Apart from scientifically trained personnel, the glut on the labor market has been apparent among liberal arts and social science fields. Since education and health are not merely ancillary services to manufacturing industries but are industries themselves with a vital role in maintaining capitalist stability, the rise of the public sector was a critical factor in preventing a more apparent surplus of college-trained workers. The dramatic growth of education and health services, together with the rapid increase in corporate and state adminis-

trative bureaucracies, accounted for a greater number of trained technicians than the manufacturing industry during the past two decades.
Twenty-eight per cent of employees in public administration are cate-
gorized as professional and technical workers. Since this sector accounts
for about 15 per cent of the total labor force, or about 11 million
workers, nearly 4 million college-trained workers are employed in these
jobs.

By 1975 there will be more than 3 million health workers, about
1 million of them professionals and technical workers. The rise of the
"new working class" therefore is more apparent in the public and service
sector than in the production of commodities. But in what sense is this
stratum really a "new" working class?

The technicians, including engineers, scientists and non-professional
technical workers, have found their work to be rationalized and atomized
along the lines of the old divisions of labor, rather than sharing in
decision-making or participating globally in control over the production
process.

A good example of the relatively low level of skill and responsibility
assigned to scientific workers is the communications industry, a major
component of electronics. On one hand, professional and technical
workers constitute about one-third of the labor force in giant plants
such as the Western Electric factory in Kearny, New Jersey, or the nearby
International Telegraph and Telephone plant in Clifton. But work is
organized along mechanical lines. The assembly-line model predominates
over integrative patterns of work assignment. Engineers complain bitterly
that they are "overtrained" for the complexity of their tasks. Scientists
holding managerial posts are virtually the only persons occupying strategic positions with research and production spheres. Knowledge in the
factory is concentrated in few hands, rather than diffused among the
highly trained work force.

The proletarianization of technicians is not merely the result of
their growing numerical importance within advanced industries. It is also
a consequence of the relatively low skill required for the performance of
their tasks. Gorz recognizes this development.

> The technical or scientific worker in automated industry is con-
> signed to permanent underemployment. As far as his individual tasks
> go, and hence, as far as his level of consciousness allows, he tends to
> transfer his interest from his purely individual work to his social func-

tion and from his purely individual role in production to the social significance and purpose of management.[19]

The tendency of labor in automated industries is to polarization. Contrary to commonly held belief, the technocrats and not the technicians monopolize both knowledge and power at the work place.

The technician has less autonomy than the skilled worker of fifty years ago, or even many skilled workers in service and technically retarded industries. His degree of control over the production process compares to that of the semi-skilled worker on the assembly line. His qualifications do not match the nature of his labor.

Self-consciousness among technicians employed by large corporations of their position in the corporation no longer corresponds to nineteenth-century professionalism. The mental worker is simply a production worker or low-level supervisor analogous in function and stratification to the industrial proletariat and foremen of the mechanical phase. An indication of a changed consciousness can be measured by the examples of technical unionism—particularly the slow growth of the professional and technical divisions of the electrical and auto workers' unions, and the dramatic rise of public employees' unions corresponding to the growth of the state in the political economy.

EDUCATION OR TRAINING?

The strongest argument for the idea of the New Working Class is that the present and future generations of workers have qualitatively higher educational qualifications than previous generations. We have seen that higher education does not imply greater application of knowledge to the world of work. On one hand, different skills are required by automated industries and the state bureaucracies than the older industries. These skills may be broadly defined as technical and administrative in contrast to mechanical skills of the old journeymen. On the other hand, the level of education possessed by most workers is greater than that required by their jobs.

The contradiction between the rising level of education of larger numbers of workers and the restricted scope of their labor is a form of the conflict between the advance in the forces of production and the

[19] André Gorz, "Capitalist Relations of Production . . . ," cited in Note 3.

fetters put upon them by the old relations of production. The development of the capacity of human labor to transform nature in the service of man and to abolish itself has reached the point where it strains to break out of the confining bourgeois social relations. It is not so much the qualitatively new means of production which have created the crisis, but the level and the scale of knowledge possessed by human labor. This is the heart of the New Working-Class thesis and seems to me its valid core.

There are limits to the idea of the rising general level of education. It involves the distinction between education and training. Education in America has been deteriorating for many decades while training has been broadly disseminated among the underlying population. The proliferation of community colleges and technical schools during the 1950's was fostered by the government to meet a particular cold war need to overcome the shortage of technical and scientific labor for the new means of production in the military sector. The social and political requirements fulfilled by the expansion of higher education facilities were related more to the fact that the rising productivity of labor made early entrance into the labor force unnecessary. The rise of mass higher education became an important means of disguising the rate of employment and simultaneously providing the equivalent of "work" for millions of young people.

The emphasis of the community colleges, second-level state colleges, and the technical institutes is training in a specific task. It is generally acknowledged that the liberal arts curriculum in most of these schools is less than useless. It appears designed, albeit unconsciously in many instances, to discourage interest among students in the arts and humanities. Social science is either taught in the most boring and oppressive manner, or is oriented toward practical tasks in industry. Students, having become disillusioned with the broad objects of education in primary and secondary schools, regard their college experience as a *means* to obtaining the necessary credentials or limited training required by industry or public bureaucracies as prerequisites for employment.

The vocational emphasis of higher education is virtually universal in institutions not specifically mandated to produce managerial, scientific, or educational elites. The instrumental philosophy ensconced in most college curricula is matched by the view of education as a "useful tool" by most students. If school has become a way to stay out of the army, a way to obtain a credential, a method of overcoming the isolation most

210

individuals experience in urban life and finding a new community, then the concept of education as knowledge is clearly peripheral, if not irrelevant, to the university experience.

Yet, the hero of a recent Hollywood film, "Getting Straight," asks a college president exorcized by student radicalism, "If you didn't want them to protest, why did you give them library cards?" The national student strike of May 1970, ostensibly called to protest the entrance of U.S. troops into Cambodia and to protest the killing of four students at Kent State University in Ohio by national guardsmen, was a reflection of a much deeper challenge to capitalist institutions, particularly the higher education factories. Students were not only protesting the particular acts of violence perpetrated by the national administration and its military arms, but were expressing their dissatisfaction with American culture, their protest against the poverty of student life, against the instrumental character of technocratic education. The student movement over the past decade represents the crisis of bourgeois ideology, particularly the breakdown of the socialization of the new generation of workers into the routines of industrial labor. To a large degree, this dissatisfaction has generated a deep chasm between the old liberal values transmitted by culture itself and the growing authoritarian character of all social institutions.

EFFECTS OF THE YOUTH REVOLT

The restiveness of the youth and the collapse of universally accepted values constitutes a massive social challenge to the capitalist order. Not that this generation of workers has opted for an alternative politics or a new set of social values. The situation is in flux. Some young people have chosen to remove themselves from the "straight" world; others have decided to live in communes within urban areas, but are forced to participate in the world of work. The majority of this generation still lives within the confines of industrial routine, whether manifested within the university, the plant, or the state bureaucracy. But explosions are becoming more frequent. These are not only manifested in the form of political protest or in the impulse to unionization among college-trained workers. They appear in the increasing difficulty reported by corporations in recruiting young college graduates for managerial and administrative jobs. This phenomenon has become deeply disturbing to

211

the corporations. They recognize that some of the most brilliant students in the elite universities are no longer directed to careers within industrial or scientific establishments. Students enter the world of work out of need rather than desire. Work is viewed as labor by an increasing number of highly skilled workers who "live" increasingly after their work day has ended—who create a privatized existence outside the work place like their manual worker counterparts.

There are differences between the activities of manual and college-trained workers. The college-trained worker watches television less often, does not spend so much time in his home, does not have the same kinds of social outlets available to manual workers, such as social clubs built around taverns, union halls, or nationality organizations. In many ways, college-trained workers possess fewer social contacts. Unlike manual workers these do not depend on family and the job, but may be based on school contacts, civic activities, or interests. It is not uncommon for these workers to join ski clubs, bridge groups, encounter groups (a sign of their social isolation), and political organizations of various kinds. These "outside" activities are as likely to form their primary social relationships as the job.

The formation of an extramural life outside the job inevitably leads to a weakening of the corporate hold on the individual. Of course, there are still many companies who retain their "family" character. Companies such as IBM attempt to involve their managers and their administrators in a full social life based on the work place. The corporate man has not disappeared; it simply was a phenomenon of the forties and fifties which has been losing ground for at least a decade. The disappearance of the ethos of organization man within the present generation of workers is an implicit anti-capitalist critique. More important, it reveals the deep-seated desire for individual and collective autonomy among young workers.

Thus far, the most visible signs of the youth revolt have been in the form of refusal. There are few signs of a concerted attempt among young workers in skilled and semi-skilled occupations to direct their efforts to challenging the institutions in terms of an attempt to wrest control from the corporate hierarchies, although the fight for student power in the university raged simultaneously with the anti-war protests in the 1960's and the recent May 1970 strike.

Yet the objective conditions for a challenge to the restricted character of mental labor within corporate and state institutions exist. Large numbers of students who have participated in the general denouncement by their generation of bourgeois values now work in research and administrative institutions. These workplaces resemble factories and have reproduced the specialization of tasks characteristic of industrial plants.

If the first impulse of the new generation of skilled mental workers has been to retreat to their own personal lives because they have refused to be incorporated by the bureaucracies, it may not be too long before they recognize privatization as no solution. The next step in some cases has been unionization rather than the demand for control over their own work. It is likely that many mental workers will relive the experiences of their manual worker counterparts of previous periods. Faced with increasingly frustrating and meaningless work, but also with fixed salaries in the face of the inflationary economy, they have begun to organize around their immediate economic needs. It would be an error to regard this development as just another trade-union movement. The advance from the organization man (or its state counterpart the "public servant") to recognition that they are just another group of workers with ordinary working-class demands is a qualitative advance for the mental workers.

A BUREAUCRATIC PROFESSIONALISM

The response of the state and corporate bureaucracies to the proletarianization of the professions has been to encourage professionalism. One example of this has been the demand by government and corporations that job-seekers possess academic credentials far in excess of job requirements. In part, the demand for credentials is a necessary consequence of the overproduction of intellectual and technical labor in the past decade. On the other hand, it represents the effort to reassert the hierarchy of status which was indiginous to the old professionalism. The professional associations have reinforced this tendency. Thus, the struggle against professionalism is a key question of the New Working Class since occupational and professional differentiation bureaucratically rather than technologically determined is a major weapon in the hands of the ruling class for dividing workers.

The unionization of the new generation of mental workers is proceeding in fits and starts. At this juncture it appears that the unions of government employees are acquiescent to the efforts of the bureaucracies

213

to enforce rigid occupational differentiation. Thus the extreme unevenness of the situation is producing, at the same time, an impulse to organization among these workers and a growing tendency toward reaction
by their unions. Even the unions have had to take note of their new
constituency. Teachers', municipal, and federal workers' unions are not
cut from whole cloth. Some of the union leaders have had to pay obei-
sance to the broad anti-war sentiment of their memberships. But this
rhetorical moderate leftism has not prevented the same leaders from
becoming virtual allies of city politicians. It is no secret, for example,
that many local leaders of the huge State, County, and Municipal
Workers' Union are close advisers and political lieutenants of liberal
mayors in several large cities, such as New York, San Francisco, and
Philadelphia. This alliance has meant that public employee unions have
been rendered harmless on everyday job conditions and have tended to
support the maintenance of professional qualifications and standards.

THE VANGUARD UNDER STATE MONOPOLY CAPITALISM

The New Working-Class theory cannot be denied as a broad generalization of the inherent tendencies in advanced capitalist countries to
create a broad stratum of technically and scientifically trained workers
whose interests are similar to the old manual workers. But some
assert their vanguard role in the "long march through institutions"
because they represent the new productive forces whose development is
most fettered by existing social relations. Instead, it appears that to the
extent that the new productive forces are emerging, the whole working
class shares in the rise of educational attainment. If the new means of
production can be developed by capitalism throughout the whole of industrial production, the question of the New Working Class becomes
moot. Nor is it necessarily true that only the college-trained stratum of
the workers will raise qualitative demands, or lead the way toward
workers' control struggles. As the achievement of higher and technical
education becomes the property of the entire generation of new workers,
the characteristics of the current mental workers will be more apparent
in the rest of the population.

In any case, the concept of vanguard is rather ambiguous in the
period of state monopoly capitalism. The integration of the state with
the underlying production of commodities on one hand and the narrow-

ing of the distinctions between mental and physical labor on the other are broad trends which defy the uniqueness of the concept of professions or the special role of scientists, engineers, and technicians. In short, the "new working class" is nothing but this generation and future genera- tions of workers. They will demand, more and more, control over the production of society and autonomy in their own work and lives.

The impetus for this development is as much rooted in the general breakdown of social institutions as it is in the dissonance between qualifications and work. One of the major weaknesses of all New Work- ing-Class theory, except in the writing of Gorz, is the mechanistic frame- work of its analysis: the theory fails to integrate the crisis of institutions and ideologies, within the superstructure, with the observed changes within the base of society. Mallet does not understand the autonomy of superstructure as an important analytic clue to the development of a new consciousness among young, educated workers. The revolt against the technical bureaucracy is more than a function of the critical role of technicians within the most advanced industries and universities. In the United States it is also a consequence of the conflict between the old values of freedom and autonomy and the centralization of all institutions of daily life.

The bourgeoisie has lost claim to its own values. The separa- tion of values from the institutions supposed to embody them can, in the long run, be traced to the underlying irrationality of production re- lations and the thwarting of initiative by the technical bureaucracy. There is no doubt that the struggle of the corporate bourgeoisie to limit the objects of education represents their recognition of the dissonance be- tween knowledge and the interests of the social system of domination. In the United States the fissure penetrates all social layers, even the sons and daughters of the bourgeoisie. The only recourse left to the corpora- tions is to use violence as a method of rule. The increasing tendency among young students and workers is to a global criticism of capitalism rather than a sectoral critique of particular aspects of it. Yet while the New Working-Class theory has a critique of the work place, it is *not* equally prepared to extend its critique to society as a whole. Thus, it tends to syndicalism rather than revolutionary Marxism.

In sum, the idea of the New Working Class is, at best, confusing. At worst it is misleading. In the first place, we have shown that its alleged predominance in the sphere of material production is overstated when applied to U.S. capitalism and the U.S. labor force as a whole.

Second, an examination of material production reveals that few industries employ technical and scientific personnel as controllers of the labor process. In those industries where advanced technologies have become pervasive, a tiny stratum of the labor force, the technocrats, exercises power over the production process. But this group is no different from the corporate managers as a whole and cannot be drawn into the working class.

The answer to our main question, then, is: the United States does *not* have a New Working Class.

11

CHRISTOPHER LASCH

From Culture
to Politics

Christopher Lasch is a professor of history at the University of Rochester
and a frequent contributor to the *New York Review of Books*. His writings
include *The New Radicalism in America* (1965) and *The Agony of the
American Left* (1969).

Culture, not politics, is the principal domain of the intellectual. By culture I mean all those pursuits that nourish and enrich the spirit, enlarge perceptions, quicken sympathy, and expand the capacity to think and feel. Art, philosophy, science, criticism, historical scholarship are activities without which life is narrow and unreflective, bounded wholly by the unarticulated pains and pleasures of the moment. The accumulation of learning, of articulated experience, and of moral awareness is in its own right a social goal of the highest order, and it is the work of intellectuals to defend this position against those who would tie the interests of culture to the interests of the state, the nation, the proletariat, the "revolution," or some other political abstraction. The life of the mind not only does not need to be defended in these terms; such a defense undermines its very foundations by making the defense of culture relative to something else, when in fact the desirability in our lives of enlightenment is absolute and unconditional.

As intellectuals in America, the first thing that ought to engage us as a group is the poverty of American culture. The idea that American culture has finally outgrown its colonial dependence on Europe is a myth, the function of which is to shore up American world power by wrapping

217

imperialism in the guise of cultural maturity. The claim that the United States is culturally mature is preposterous on its face. But it is hard to see this because we are confused and befuddled, even those of us who oppose American imperialism in its more obvious forms, by the cultural xenophobia that has prevailed since the late thirties, by the fascination with things American, and by the emergence of a sort of cultural anti-quarianism, sometimes dignified by the name of American studies, as one of the major branches of academic learning.

The fact is, however, that American culture remains backward and provincial. We have had isolated geniuses but no sustained traditions of cultural expression, not even in the novel, a form in which Americans have excelled. It is highly symptomatic that the best American novels should be what Leslie Fiedler calls novels of masculine protest—books written in defiance of civilization as represented by Aunt Polly, in which men find their souls in combat with nature and in the comradely embraces of other men.[1] The very idea of culture has always been suspect in America, since it has been so closely identified with the spinsterish refinement of elderly ladies; and our best writers have used up their best energies in an unproductive struggle against their own suspicions and inner misgivings about their calling—struggles that usually ended in a flight into the fantasy of boyhood innocence. This fantasy, while it has inspired a few masterpieces, is not enough to nourish a continuing tradition of serious literary work. It is no accident that American writers have typically burned themselves out early in their careers or that the only one who achieved anything like a continuous career—Henry James—did so at the cost of expatriation. The claim of cultural maturity is ironic indeed when one considers that the best American novels have had to be cast in the form of books for boys—children's classics, written by child-men.

The clearest evidence of American cultural backwardness lies not in the novel but in the sphere of social theory and criticism. Indeed it is the poverty of social thought in the United States that underlies the poverty of the novel, in which an awareness of society hardly figures at all. American culture has given rise to idiosyncratic social theorists, like Thorstein Veblen or more recently C. Wright Mills. But it has been unable to produce a body of theory capable of transmission from one generation of intellectuals to the next, which would provide the neces-

[1] Leslie Fiedler, *An End to Innocence* (Boston: Beacon Press, 1955), especially "Come Back to the Raft Again, Huck Honey!"

218

sary framework for an understanding of American society and history. Every serious thinker on social questions has had to start almost from scratch, because the conceptual schemes available to him are so primitive as to be useless for the purposes of critical analysis.

Historical thought, for example, has been dominated by the ideas of Beard and Turner—eccentric geniuses whose valid insights are crusted over with theoretical confusion, faulty methodology, inner contradictions, and by an astonishingly simple-minded conception of the relation between economics and social organization and between social organization and culture. Similarly American Marxism differs from much European Marxism in its rigid dogmatism, its reductionism, its economic determinism, and by its tendency to regard Marxism not as an indispensable foundation for critical thought but as a complete set of answers to every conceivable problem, which one need only "apply" to history in order to produce instant explanation. In the same way, American scholars have tried to "apply" psychoanalysis to history, biography, anthropology, and the study of society, as if to conceal the imperfections of their own thought; just as amateur craftsmen hope to conceal the imperfections of their carpentry by applying thick coats of paint and varnish. American intellectuals, particularly in social theory, have mostly been amateurs working with blunt tools and ignorant of the theoretical foundations of their craft.

The value of culture, of art and learning, needs no extra-cultural defense, and in this sense culture and politics are independent spheres of activity. Yet it goes without saying that the history of culture cannot be understood without reference to politics. I think a strong case can be made for the contention that the failure of American culture is closely related to the failure of mass radical action—that is, to the absence of a revolutionary tradition in American politics.

Lacking a strong challenge to the existing order and the sharp conflicts to which it would have given rise, Americans have lived with a myth of themselves as a people outside history, uniquely favored by fortune, faced with no difficulties that could not be resolved by good will, physical hardihood, and technological virtuosity. They have not had to look deeply into themselves or their situation. The experience of failure, defeat, humiliation, and oppression has not been admitted into their consciousness, because the victims of defeat and oppression had no political or cultural means of becoming articulate. The silence of the victims of progress sustained the optimistic illusion of progress that has

219

always impeded the development of American culture; whereas in Europe, a history of struggle and conflict has made it hard to avoid a tragic sense of the cost of even the most brilliant civilization.

The European revolutionary tradition has itself embodied not only a utopian sense of human possibilities but a tragic sense of the equivocal nature of social and moral progress. One of the best expressions of this awareness occurs in the 1932 manifesto of thirty moderate leaders of the Spanish anarcho-syndicalists who broke away or were expelled from the CNT over the issue of immediate revolution. They stated that "we wish a Revolution born out of the deepest feelings of the people . . . not the Revolution offered us . . . by some individuals who . . . inevitably would convert themselves into dictators the day after their triumph." They went on to accuse those who advocated immediate revolution of "believing in the miracles of the holy revolution as though the revolution were some panacea and not a tragic and cruel event which forms man only through the suffering of his body and the sorrow of his mind." This kind of consciousness is alien to American radicalism and to American culture in general, which reflects not the experience of struggle and defeat but a record of material success over nature and other inarticulate victims.

By reflecting the consciousness of defeat, by contradicting the dominant social myths, by forcing deep questions to the surface, the revolutionary movement in Europe has helped to define the cultural conditions in which even those deeply opposed to the revolution have been obliged to work. And in the United States the only period of important cultural activity on a wide scale—the period roughly from 1890 to the mid-twenties—coincided with the period when mass-based political movements were, for a short time, an essential feature of American politics. It was no coincidence that the years which saw the emergence of populism, socialism, and black nationalism were also years of experimentation and advance in the arts, in architecture, in literary and cultural criticism, and in social thought. In Chicago, Greenwich Village, and Harlem American intellectuals began for the first time to cultivate a systematic awareness of the interdependence of culture and politics. If the political radicalism of the sixties leads to a revival of this awareness, it will have justified itself whatever its other accomplishments.

My general point—that the emergence of a mature American culture probably depends on the emergence of a revolutionary movement for social change—is similar to Arthur Koestler's argument in his 1944 essay "The Intelligentsia": "an intelligentsia deprived of the prop of an alliance with an ascending class must turn against itself." [2] Koestler's own writings often testify to the truth of this observation, since they embody precisely that morbid self-contempt which he correctly identifies as the disease of intellectual classes that have come to doubt the necessity of their own existence. It is important to note that the disease infects not only those who, like Koestler, have become disenchanted with revolutionary movements, but those who embrace them only to announce, with Sartre, that in doing so the intellectuals should regard themselves as commiting suicide as a class.

The New Left in America holds a view similar to Sartre's. Andrew Kopkind declares that "the responsibility of the intellectual is the same as that of the street organizer, the draft resister, the Digger; to talk *to* people, not *about* them." [3] Similarly we find intellectuals attempting to attach themselves to the black-power movement in the hope of losing their identity as intellectuals: they wish to follow the blacks wherever they lead, to "trust them," as one of these fellow-travelers puts it, "like children." Lately we have had the spectacle of people who once preached nonviolence embracing violence, when it is preached by black people, with hardly a qualm; whereas the real job of the intellectual in such a situation, if he believes in nonviolence, is to advance his arguments even more earnestly than before.

Intellectual leadership, however, can come only from intellectuals who have confidence in themselves as a class. For historical reasons, American intellectuals are even more insecure and defensive than most. Not only has the revolutionary movement been weak in America, thereby making it difficult for intellectuals to make class alliances, in Koestler's terms, but the whole idea of culture, as I have indicated, has had a precarious existence from the beginning. Only in the period just before the war did American intellectuals show some signs of collective *élan,* and this quickly collapsed in the twenties, thereby contributing to the collapse of American radicalism.

In the twenties, intellectuals convinced themselves that their proper role in the revolution was to merge their own identity with that of the proletariat. Thus *The Masses* blend of political radicalism and cultural

[2] Arthur Koestler, "The Intelligentsia," *The Yogi and the Commissar,* New York: Macmillan, 1945, p. 82.

[3] Andrew Kopkind, "Soul Power," *The New York Review of Books,* August 24, 1967, p. 3.

modernism gave way to the philistinism of *The Liberator* and *The New Masses*. As early as 1921 Mike Gold was calling for "proletarian art" and denouncing "the mad solitary priests of Dada" and other purveyors of sterile pessimism and "pure art." [4] "Since 1912," Daniel Aaron writes, "a polarizing process had been under way which divided the Bohemian from the revolutionary" [5] and forced writers to choose between art and radical politics. But this polarization, it should be noted, had not become critical so long as American socialism remained a broad and inclusive movement devoted, among other things, to creating a better understanding of life under the existing order—something art is supremely equipped to do. Only when the new Left wing shattered the Socialist party and substituted for long-term efforts to revolutionize American consciousness a mystique of immediate revolution did art and intellectuals come to be suspect in radical circles. The role of intellectuals then came to be defined as dutiful servants of the "revolution"—that is, propagandists for mass culture against the stale and artificial culture, as it had come to be regarded, of the literati.

The Harlem renaissance came to a similar end, and the story of its demise makes timely reading today. In a speech in 1926 on "The Criteria of Negro Art," W. E. B. Du Bois tried to show that Negro art should play a central part in the struggle for political liberation. Organizations like the NAACP, he thought, should address themselves not only to the issue of "civil rights" but to the cultural questions raised by Langston Hughes, Claude McKay, and other spokesmen of the Harlem renaissance. "Some in this audience . . . are thinking . . .: 'How is it that an organization like this, a group of radicals . . . can turn aside to talk about Art? After all, what have we who are slaves and black to do with Art?' " [6] The answer, Du Bois said, was that art alone could capture and preserve those "flashes" of "clairvoyance," so essential to the political movement, "of what America really is. We who are dark can see America in a way that white Americans can not." And this vision could be expressed, he insisted, only in the distinctive forms of a Negro culture.

---

[4] Mike Gold in Daniel Aaron (ed.), *Writers on the Left* (New York: Harcourt, Brace and World, 1961), p. 89.

[5] Aaron, p. 91.

[6] Quoted in Harold Cruse, *The Crisis of the Negro Intellectual,* 2, New York: Morrow, 1967, pp. 41, 43.

In Harlem, it may be seen, the issue was not merely whether art had anything to do with politics but whether black people were to develop their own forms of expression or to continue as cultural dependents of the white community. Because the defense of art implied a defense of ethnic culture and thus ran counter to the integrationist politics then advocated by black socialists, Du Bois's position was denounced even more bitterly in Harlem than the equivalent position came to be denounced, after the war and the Russian revolution, by the new-wave militants of the white Left. A. Philip Randolph's *Messenger*—"the only Radical Negro magazine in America," as it called itself—attacked Du Bois's "cerebration" and made it clear that "with us economics and politics take precedence to 'Music and Art.' " [7]

White radicalism and black radicalism since the twenties have suffered from a common failure to understand that a radical movement needs to proceed along a variety of fronts, political, economic, and cultural, and that no one of these takes precedence over the others. By the "cultural front," I do not refer to the need for propaganda or the creation of a revolutionary myth of virtuous proletarians, resisting slaves, and clear-eyed youth. I refer only to the need for truth; the need to understand, both through art and through analysis, exactly what is wrong with the existing order and also to understand what parts of it are worth preserving. Instead of understanding, the Left in America has relied on denunciations of racism and imperialism and on an escalation of rhetorical militancy that leads nowhere except possibly to violent actions unrelated to any broader strategy for change.

Before the Left can become an effective force in American politics, it needs to demonstrate the superiority of its moral vision and its theoretical understanding. Specifically it needs to work out a theory of advanced society based on historical materialism but capable of explaining phenomena ignored or misunderstood by classical sociology—the role of education in advanced society; the role of the so-called cultural apparatus; the growing hostility between generations; and perhaps most important of all, the unanticipated tenacity of ethnic and national loyalties in a social order which was expected to disintegrate the ties of nationality. All these questions in turn must be related to a program of decentralization addressed to people's real needs, and not to some abstract conception of what their needs ought to be. We must devise new

[7] Quoted in Cruse, p. 41.

institutions capable of meeting those needs. The search for concrete programs, meanwhile, will deepen our theoretical understanding of post-industrial society.

None of these activities mean much in themselves, apart from the struggles of students, black people, and other disfranchised groups. Social change cannot come from pure disembodied criticism. At some periods in our history—in the fifties, for instance—the question of x "class alliances" for intellectuals has been strictly academic, since there were no classes in movement. In the late sixties, however, there were deep forces at work, representing great potential for change. As intellectuals, we can no longer hold ourselves aloof from these forces; but neither can we join them except on our own terms—that is, as intellectuals. To throw ourselves into the movement as followers and fellow-travelers is no service either to ourselves or to the movement.

The movement needs activists and organizers and leaders of "confrontations." But it also needs people who can interpret the meaning and purpose of confrontations, formulate strategies, analyze the strengths and vulnerabilities of the existing system, and more generally, give coherent expression to an otherwise incoherent sense of pain and outrage. If this sounds presumptuous, it will prove to have been presumptuous only if we fail in these things. But if we do fail, it will probably be not because we presumed to give intellectual leadership but because we shrank from asserting ourselves, deferring instead to the blacks and to our students in the hope that out' of their anguish alone would miraculously emerge theory and analysis, a new art and a new consciousness. Since we do not, in general, believe in miracles, why should be believe in this particular miracle?

3

Neo-Marxism

12

IRVING M. ZEITLIN

The Plain Marxism
of C. Wright Mills

Irving M. Zeitlin is professor of sociology at Washington University, St. Louis. He wrote *Ideology and the Development of Sociological Theory* (1968) and *Liberty, Equality, and Revolution in Alexis de Toqueville* (1971).

Western sociology flourished and assumed its peculiar form in the course of a critical encounter with Marxism.[1] Albert Salomon once observed of Max Weber that he "became a sociologist in a long and intense debate with the ghost of Karl Marx," [2] and this is true in varying degrees of most of the outstanding figures of the "golden age" of sociological thinking—that is, the late nineteenth and early twentieth century. Weber, Simmel, Pareto, Mosca, Michels, Durkheim, and Mannheim, to name just a few of the best-known theorists of that period, all engaged in what was sometimes a dialogue and other times a debate with the Marxian legacy.

Some of these thinkers, such as Weber and Mannheim, had been dubbed "bourgeois Marxes." This was supposed to convey that each in his own way had adopted a reconstructed or revised version of "Marxism" conceived not as a critical and revolutionary theory but as a scientific method and system of analysis. Other thinkers, Pareto and

---

[1] Irving M. Zeitlin, *Ideology and the Development of Sociological Theory* (Englewood Cliffs, N.J.: Prentice-Hall, 1968).

[2] See his article on "German Sociology" in George Gurvitch and Wilbert E. Moore (eds.), *Twentieth Century Sociology* (New York: Philosophical Library, 1945), p. 596.

Mosca for instance, thought of their work as a definitive rebuttal of Marxism. Their respective sociologies may be read as elaborate efforts to repudiate and discredit certain essential aspects of the Marxian conception of society and history.

Still other sociologists of that period sought to mediate between Marxism and other systems of thought. Émile Durkheim's sociology, for example, may be regarded as an attempt to reconcile two antithetical models of society, the Marxian and the Comtean. How were social order, unity, and peace possible in the face of an increasingly complex division of labor which brought with it a dispersion of interests, social cleavages, classes, and class conflict? Durkheim thought he saw the key to a reconciliation of order and progress—which had always been viewed as antithetical principles—in the work of Saint-Simon, the common intellectual ancestor of both Comte and Marx. All of Durkheim's major works, therefore, may best be understood as a somewhat more sophisticated elaboration of basically Saint-Simonian principles.

In this perspective Marxism acquires even more importance than one might ordinarily assume. It acquires fundamental importance not only for the immensely rich and insightful ideas which Marx and the Marxists advanced but also because their work provoked a response which accounts in a large measure for the character of Western sociology.

Among contemporary American sociologists C. Wright Mills best understood the significance of the critical encounter with Marxism. Mills realized that the debate with Marx's ghost had given rise to what he called the classical tradition of sociological thinking. This tradition, which included both Marxism and its critics, provided, he believed, an indispensable method for thinking about man, society, and history. In his words:

> Classic sociology contains an enormous variety of conception, value, and method, and its relevance to the life-ways of the individual and to the ways of history-making in our epoch is obvious and immediate. This is why it is central to contemporary cultural work, and among the most valuable legacies of Western civilization.[3]

In these terms, Mills was neither a Marxist nor a non-Marxist but a "plain" Marxist as he chose to call himself. "Included among plain

[3] C. Wright Mills, *Images of Man* (New York: George Braziller, 1960), p. 17.

Marxists," he writes, "although by no means exhausting the list, are such varied thinkers as the late William Morris, Antonio Gramsci, Rosa Luxemburg, G. D. H. Cole, Georg Lukacs, Christopher Cauldwell, Jean-Paul Sartre, the later John Strachey, Georges Sorel, Edward Thompson, Leszek Kolokowski, William A. Williams, Paul Sweezy, and Erich Fromm." [4] With the term "plain," Mills sought to distinguish himself from what he had dubbed, respectively, "vulgar" and "sophisticated" Marxists. The former have a dogmatic commitment to specific features of Marxian thought and "identify these . . . as the whole." The latter, on the other hand, refuse to acknowledge that Marx was wrong about anything. They try to "sophisticate" him by incorporating into his system of thought "the whole tradition of sociology, before and after Marx." [5] For the "sophisticated" Marxist, "there is no 'social science' of much worth; there is only marxist social science. Thus, they tend to stretch and to bend marxist ideas to fit new facts, and to confuse Marx's general model with specific theories. Even when Marx's terminology is obviously ambiguous and plainly inadequate they are often reluctant to abandon it. At its best, this style of thinking is tedious and hampers analysis unnecessarily. At its worst, it becames a substitute for reflection and inquiry, a sophisticated sloganeering." [6]

In contrast, Mills continues, "Plain Marxists (whether in agreement or in disagreement) work in Marx's own tradition. They understand Marx, and many later marxists as well, to be firmly a part of the classic tradition of sociological thinking. They treat Marx like any great nine-teenth-century figure, in a scholarly way; they treat each later phase of marxism as historically specific. They are generally agreed that Marx's work bears the trademarks of the nineteenth-century society, but that his general model and his ways of thinking are central to their own in-tellectual history and remain relevant to their attempts to grasp present-day social worlds." [7] And ". . . in their work, plain marxists have stressed the humanism of marxism, especially of the younger Marx, and the role of the superstructure in history; they have pointed out that to underemphasize the *interplay* of basis and superstructure in the making of history is to transform man into that abstraction for which Marx himself criticized Feuerbach. They have been 'open' (as opposed to

[4] C. Wright Mills, *The Marxists* (New York: Dell, 1962), p. 98.
[5] *Ibid.*, p. 97.
[6] *Ibid.*, p. 98.
[7] *Ibid.*, p. 98.

dogmatic) in their interpretations and their uses of Marxism. They have stressed that 'economic determinism' is, after all, a matter of degree, and held that it is so used by Marx in his own writings, especially in his historical essays. They have emphasized the volition of men in the making of history—their freedom—in contrast to any Determinist Laws of History and, accordingly, the lack of individual responsibility." [8]

For Mills, then, Marx's work was to be viewed as an integral part of the classic tradition of sociological thinking. It was a fundamental element, even the most fundamental element of that tradition. Nevertheless, taken alone without the other, later developments of that tradition, it was inadequate for a comprehension of the social reality of the latter half of the twentieth century. After all, there is no getting around the fact that Marx died in 1883; we must accuse him of dying, as Mills says. And for this reason alone, if for no other, he was wrong about a number of things. He did not live to see certain developments which were to foil his expectations of the revolutionary transformation of capitalist society.

To be sure, though he had no equals among his followers, Marxism did not end with Marx but began with him. It would be a great intellectual loss, Mills emphasizes, to remain ignorant of what the Marxists after Marx have done to develop and refine his system and thereby to enrich the classic tradition. But it would be at least an equal loss if one were to remain ignorant of the non-Marxian contributions to sociological thinking, those of academic social science in general and within that category those of Marx's critics in particular.

Among the thinkers who shaped the classic tradition not all were on the same level. Two of them, Mills believed, stood higher than all the rest: Karl Marx and Max Weber. "Were it necessary," he writes, "to limit ourselves to the works of two sociologists, these two would be my choice." [9] And Mills was, I think, quite accurate here both in his judgment of Weber's stature and in his intellectual introspection. For these two giants contributed most to Mills' intellectual consciousness.

Weber, in his view, was perhaps the greatest revisionist of Marx. And this meant not that Weber had in any sense bested, refuted, or superseded Marx but that his work was an essential refinement and "corrective" of Marx's system. Marx and Weber must not be viewed as antithetical in their conceptual approaches but rather complementary. The model of society which emerged *with* Weber's "corrective" was

[8] *Ibid.,* p. 99.
[9] Mills, *Images of Man,* p. 12.

better than Marx's alone—although taken alone it was still definitely superior to all others. Since Mills consciously employed this Marxian-Weberian model, and emulated both of those mighty thinkers in his own mature work, it may be worthwhile to consider, at least briefly, why Mills had so high a regard for Weber.

My own recent re-examination of Weber's work has confirmed Mills'—or more correctly the Gerth-Mills—view of his relation to Marx. Throughout his life, Weber remained a great admirer of Marx and virtually his entire lifework may be regarded as a gigantic gloss on the work of Marx. The title and subject matter of one of his chief works, *Wirtschaft und Gesellschaft,* his essays for the *Archiv für Sozialwissenschaft und Sozialpolitik,* his concern with the Protestant ethic and the origins of capitalism and even his superb studies of the *Weltreligionen,* all attest to his conscious and continuing dialogue with Marx. And while often this dialogue is only implicit, he returns to remind his reader once in a while that he is considering issues which Marx raised, following his leads, and assessing his judgment of particular questions.

In his studies of the world religions, for instance, where he is concerned among other things with the relevance of religious doctrines for economic development, it is evident that he is addressing himself to the relation of the economic to the other aspects of social life. Yet, there are very few direct references to Marx. His work on India, for example, has but one single reference to that thinker; but in that single reference Weber pauses, suddenly and unexpectedly as it were, to acknowledge his partner in dialogue:

> Karl Marx has characterized the peculiar position of the artisan in the Indian village—his dependence upon fixed payment in kind instead of upon production for the market—as the reason for the specific "stability" of the Asiatic peoples. In this, Marx was correct.[10]

Weber regarded Marx's methodological approach as one of fundamental importance and his own as supplementary to it. In no sense was he developing a method of his own in opposition to that of Marx. Insofar as any refutation of Marxism was intended, it was of certain naïve and vulgar conceptions of Marx's theory held by some of his followers. Mills was therefore quite right in asserting that Weber was "rounding-out"

[10] Max Weber, *The Religion of India* (Glencoe, Illinois: Free Press, 1962), p. 111.

and "revising" Marx's method but not by any stretch of the imagination refuting it.

In his essays for the *Archiv,* some of which have been collected, translated, and published under the title of *The Methodology of the Social Sciences,* Weber refers to Marx as a "great thinker." [11] He says of Marx's conception: ". . . the analysis of social and cultural phenomena with special reference to their economic conditioning and ramifications was a scientific principle of creative fruitfulness and with careful application and freedom from dogmatic restrictions, will remain such for a very long time to come. The so-called 'materialistic conception of history' as a *Weltanschauung* or as a formula for the casual explanation of historical reality is to be rejected most emphatically. The advancement of the economic *interpretation* of history is one of the most important aims of our journal." [12] He had no patience, moreover, with what he called the "clever but fallacious arguments" designed "to 'refute' the 'materialistic conception of history.' . . ." [13] That conception, one of great fecundity, required nonetheless a clarification of its basic terms. Therefore, the term "economic," for instance, which had been used loosely and ambiguously, had to be carefully defined if the analytical power of Marx's method was to be enhanced.

The "strictly economic" events and institutions, "those *deliberately* created or used for economic ends," had to be distinguished from the "economically *conditioned*" events and institutions and these in turn from the "economically *relevant.*" In this way one could introduce greater precision into any discussion of the relation of the economy to the society in general. The stock exchange, for example, could be regarded as a predominantly economic institution. The "state," on the other hand, predominantly non-economic, could be studied as an economically *conditioned* phenomenon. Finally, religious values, clearly non-economic in and of themselves, could become, under certain circumstances, economically *relevant.* This, of course, is what Weber sought to demonstrate—not too successfully according to his own critics—in his studies of ascetic Protestantism and the world religions. By means of this clarification of the concept "economic," Weber was explicitly attributing greater autonomy and greater causal influence to the various non-

[11] Max Weber, *The Methodology of the Social Sciences* (Glencoe, Illinois: Free Press, 1949), p. 103.
[12] *Ibid.,* p. 68.
[13] *Ibid.,* p. 82.

economic institutional orders than Marx seemed to suggest in the *locus classicus* of his so-called materialist conception, i.e., the preface to *A Contribution to the Critique of Political Economy*—though, of course, Marx himself in his historical and journalistic writings, e.g., *The Eighteenth Brumaire of Louis Bonaparte,* and Engels in his celebrated letters on this subject, had also acknowledged the reciprocal influence of the economic and non-economic institutions.

What Weber was suggesting, then, was that although Marx's deliberately "one-sided" perspective provided for insights otherwise unattainable—as in an equivocal and eclectic view, for example—it has nevertheless to be supplemented with other perspectives for a fuller and more adequate understanding of the given reality. There was no getting around the so-called "one-sidedness" of all perspectives and the point was not to abandon Marx's which has proved to be so fruitful but rather to pursue it to the end carefully and systematically. But then one must always remember that this is a partial perspective and be prepared to view the same reality from other angles. In effect, Weber was calling for a more open and empirical approach to the mutual relation of the economic and non-economic than many Marxists were willing to adopt.

Thus Weber was "rounding-out" Marx's view. Precisely because Marx had focused his attention on the economic structure, he did not see, Weber believed, other aspects of the social structure which could be equally important in determining the fate of men in the modern, industrial capitalist system.

One example of Weber's revision is his approach to the institution or phenomenon we call the "state." Quoting Trotsky at Brest-Litovsk, he writes: "Every state is founded on force." [14] And Weber continues: "Today the relation between the state and violence is an especially intimate one. . . . A state . . . (successfully) claims the *monopoly of the legitimate use of physical force* within a given territory. The "state is a relation of men dominating men." And why do men obey those who command? Because they accept as justified the "basic *legitimations* of domination." For Weber, these "legitimations" may be very spurious indeed. The concept is roughly equivalent to Marx's *ideology of the ruling class,* Sorel's *myths,* Pareto's *derivations,* and Mosca's *political formula.*

[14] H. H. Gerth and C. Wright Mills (eds.), *From Max Weber: Essays in Sociology* (New York: Oxford University Press, 1958), p. 78. Emphasis in original.

Now Weber's approach differs from Marx's in certain important respects. The main emphasis which emerges in Marx's work is that the state (political and military power) is in varying degrees determined by, dependent on, and subordinate to, economic power. Control of the means of production by a minority leads to the domination of the majority of men not only in the economic realm but in other social realms as well. That is why he could envision a time when the abolition of private ownership of the means of production could lead to the withering away of the state. This vision was probably quite justified in his time by the empirical-historical evidence: the absolute state had increasingly given way to a more democratic form of state power. The main source of social power for Marx was control of the means of production; political power and its military instrument were subordinate to those with economic power and the former could not prevail for long if they acted contrary to the interests of the latter. And while this may be an oversimplification of Marx's view, there is no denying that this is the main impression one gets from his various discussions of the question. One must add, however, that all of Marx's propositions, including the one under discussion, were historically specific. He never intended to generalize them to cover all times and all places. Weber understood this very well, which was precisely the point of his revision: What may have been true in Marx's time is no longer true or less true in ours.

Today, Weber was saying, Marx's conception is not altogether satisfactory. He does not deny the considerable importance of control over the economic resources. But this is not sufficient for an understanding of social power in general—and of political and military power in particular. He therefore generalizes Marx's theory and argues that disposition of the *means of political administration and means of violence* are no less important than disposition of the economic resources as means of dominating men.

Power is therefore a more general phenomenon for Weber, and it has a number of different aspects. If for Marx the main question was: who controls the means of production? for Weber it was necessary to ask: who disposes of the other strategic means of controlling and dominating men? Weber writes:

> Organized domination, which calls for continuous administration, requires that human conduct be conditioned to obedience towards those masters who claim to be the bearers of legitimate power. On the other

hand, by virtue of this obedience, organized domination requires the control of those material goods which in a given case are necessary for the use of physical violence. Thus, organized domination requires control of the personal executive staff and the material implements of administration.[15]

How he generalized Marx's theory becomes even clearer when he employs the Marxian concept of "separation."

> To maintain a dominion by force, certain material goods are required, just as with an economic organization. All states may be classified according to whether they rest on the principle that the staff of men themselves own the administrative means, or whether the staff is "separated" from these means of administration. This distinction holds in the same sense in which today we say that the salaried employee and the proletarian in the capitalist enterprise are "separated" from the material means of production.[16]

In this way, Weber argued that Marx, by centering his attention on the "separation" of the worker from the means of production, had dramatized a special case—which actually was only one aspect of a much more general social process. There were other strategic areas of the social system in which everyman was increasingly separated from the means of power—not only the economic, political, and military but the *scientific* as well. Again employing Marx's concept of "separation," Weber writes:

> The larger institutes of medicine or natural science are "state capitalist" enterprises, which cannot be managed without very considerable funds. Here we encounter the same condition that is found wherever capitalist enterprise comes into operation: the "separation of the worker from his means of production." The worker, that is, the assistant, is dependent upon the implements that the state puts at his disposal; hence he is just as dependent upon the head of the institutes as is the employee in a factory upon the management.[17]

This general process—"separation"—was increasingly characteristic of Western civilization and was described by Weber as the growing bureaucratization of the modern social structure.

[15] *Ibid.*, p. 80.
[16] *Ibid.*, p. 81.
[17] *Ibid.*, p. 131.

Even the scientists had become wage-laborers dominated by the "masters" of the research institutes. Under these circumstances and after Nietzsche, can we retain, Weber asks, "the naïve optimism in which science . . . has been celebrated as the way to happiness. Who believes in this?—aside from a few big children in university chairs or editorial offices." [18] Thus Weber's mood was one of pessimism, but justified, he believed, by the direction of social change which separated men from the means of controlling their destiny. And for Weber, unlike Marx, this was virtually irreversible. In sharp contrast to Marx's optative mood and philosophy of hope, Weber wrote near the end of his days:

> Not summer's bloom lies ahead of us, but rather a polar night of icy darkness and hardness, no matter which group may triumph externally now. Where there is nothing, not only the Kaiser but also the proletarian has lost his rights. When this night shall have slowly receded, who of those for whom spring apparently has bloomed so luxuriously will be alive? [19]

Weber does not deny the role of classes and class conflict in determining the fate of men. His highly sophisticated discussion of these phenomena is in fundamental agreement with that of Marx—so much so that it could appropriately be appended to the unfinished last chapter of the third volume of *Capital*.

Weber agrees that classes "represent possible, and frequent, bases of communal action," that "we may speak of a 'class' when (1) a number of people have in common a specific causal component of their life chances, insofar as (2) this component is represented exclusively by economic interests in the possession of goods and opportunities for income, and (3) is represented under the conditions of the commodity or labor markets." [20] But he also insists that this must be supplemented by the following considerations:

> "Economically conditioned" power is not, of course, identical with "power" as such. On the contrary, the emergence of economic power may be the consequence of power existing on other grounds. Man does not strive for power only in order to enrich himself economically. Power, including economic power, may be valued "for its

[18] *Ibid.,* p. 143.
[19] *Ibid.,* p. 128.
[20] *Ibid.,* p. 181.

own sake." Very frequently the striving for power is also conditioned by the social "honor" it entails. Not all power, however, entails social honor.[21]

Not that Marx and the Marxists after him did not understand all this. Obviously they did. The point is that Weber saw certain implications which, perhaps, the Marxists in particular and the socialists in general did not see, or at least not adequately: that "socialism" would accelerate and drive to an extreme what already appeared as a frightening degree of bureaucratization in many strategic areas of social life. Weber also emphasized that "class interest" is not an altogether unambiguous concept and that actions and consequences quite different from those Marx expected could flow from the class situation.

In the Marxian scheme political parties, for example, are regarded as vehicles for the expression of the interests of classes and strata. For Weber, on the other hand, "parties live in a house of 'power.' " This means that "their action is oriented toward the acquisition of social 'power,' that is to say, toward influencing a communal action no matter what its content may be." [22] Parties have a certain autonomy: they *may* "represent" classes, strata, or status groups. "In most cases," Weber writes, "they are partly class parties and partly status parties, *but sometimes they are neither.*" [23] Sometimes they represent merely themselves! —and continue to do so for longer than one might have expected, as we see clearly today with military *juntas.*

In short, political and military structures may rest at least in some degree on an economic or class basis and for this reason must not be regarded as totally autonomous institutions. But this basic Marxian proposition should not obscure the fact that often they become sufficiently independent to determine the life-chances and fate of men.

Thus if Marx spoke of the growing concentration of the means of production, Weber applied this concept to means of administration in general:

> The bureaucratic structure goes hand in hand with the concentration of the material means of management in the hands of the master. This concentration occurs, for instance, in a well-known and

[21] *Ibid.,* p. 180.
[22] *Ibid.,* p. 194.
[23] *Ibid.,* p. 194.

237

typical fashion, in the development of big capitalist enterprises, which find their essential characteristics in this process. A corresponding process occurs in public organizations.[24]

And further:

War in our time is a war of machines. And this makes [depots] technically necessary, just as the dominance of the machine in industry promotes the concentration of the means of production and management.[25]

Historically, the bureaucratization of the army has everywhere been realized along with the transfer of army service from the propertied to the propertyless.[26]

In the same way as with army organization, the bureaucratization of administration goes hand in hand with the concentration of the means of organization in other spheres.[27]

And finally,

In the field of scientific research and instruction, the bureaucratization of the always existing research institutes of the universities is a function of the increasing demand for material means of management. Liebig's laboratory at Giessen University was the first example of big enterprise in this field. Through the concentration of such means in the hands of the privileged head of the institute, the mass of researchers and docents are separated from their "means of production," in the same way as capitalist enterprise has separated the workers from theirs.[28]

These, then, were the main revisions or "correctives" of Marx's conception which Weber regarded as essential for an understanding of the social structure of the early twentieth century. And for C. Wright Mills they were even more cogent for an understanding of the latter half of the present century. Particularly in his late works, notably *Power Elite* and *The Marxists,* Mills employed the Weberian guidelines in both his analysis of power in the United States and his critique of Marxism.

[24] *Ibid.,* p. 221.
[25] *Ibid.,* p. 221.
[26] *Ibid.,* p. 222.
[27] *Ibid.,* p. 223.
[28] *Ibid.,* pp. 223–24.

Here, attention will be confined to just a few of the critical observations, derived from Weber's work, which Mills also regarded as essential revisions of Marx's major ideas. Among these ideas, there is the dichotomy: owners and non-owners of the means of production. There are at least two reasons why Marx often worked with a two-class model. In *Capital,* especially the first volume, this was a heuristic device by which he could *begin* to isolate what he considered to be the most essential relationships of the capitalist economic system. But Marx understood very well that if he remained at this high level of abstraction, his model would be a gross oversimplification and hence of very little value when confronting the actual workings of the capitalist system. Following in the footsteps of the English Classical Economists, he therefore employed their well-known method, namely, the method of "successive approximations." In this method one began with a relatively high level of abstraction and moved progressively to more concrete and complex levels of analysis as in fact Marx did in the second and third volumes of *Capital.* Also, in his historical and journalistic writings, Marx obviously took all classes, sub-classes, and strata into his purview. To say, then, that Marx employed *only* a two-class model would be incorrect.

But there is still another reason for the conspicuousness of the capitalist-worker dichotomy in Marx's work. There can be little doubt that as he projected the main tendencies of the capitalist system, he expected the older and intermediate classes and strata increasingly to disappear; as capitalism developed, it would lead to a progressive simplification and polarization of its class structure.

And within the working class Marx tended to underestimate the importance of differences resulting from occupation, income, and status. On balance, he treated the non-owners, particularly in the sphere of industry, as one class. He assumed not only that their existential conditions would lead to a common proletarian consciousness but to a revolutionary consciousness as well. In short, Marx did not adequately consider the complexity of social differentiation and stratification *within* the category of "worker" and hence did not anticipate the consequences of those processes. It is here that Mills criticizes Marx:

> In capitalist societies, among the immense majority who are propertyless, distinctions of status and occupation lead to or away from just those psychological and political consequences of economic stratification expected by Marx. To name only the most obvious,

239

white collar employees, like factory workers, are without property and many receive less income; none the less to treat them together as one stratum, on the criterion of property alone, is to abdicate any real effort to understand one of the most consequential facts of stratification in all advanced capitalist societies.[29]

And later he writes:

From a Marxist point of view, these white collar employees can only be considered "a new proletariat," for they do not own the means of production with which they work, but work for wages or salaries. But to consider them in this category is seriously to limit one's understanding of them as a new set of strata.[30]

Marx's dichotomous view of the class structure of capitalism together with his conception of history as the history of class struggle led him to an emphasis on the conflicting character of capitalist-worker relations. Although this emphasis may have been warranted by the empirical evidence of his time, it became less so after he died. Thus Mills argues:

It is possible within capitalism for considerable periods, to transform class struggle into administrative regulations, just as it is possible to stabilize capitalism itself, subsidizing its deficiencies, defaults, and absurdities, by economic, military and political means.[31]

And further:

Collaboration is as much a fact of class history as is struggle. There are many varieties and many causes of both—historically specific causes which include more than economic conditions.[32]

Still other critical questions which Mills raised relate to Marx's notion of alienation as a form of psychic exploitation rooted in the conditions of capitalism.

Although Marx knew the subtleties of psychic exploitation, he did not know many that we know. The mechanisms, the scope, the

[29] Mills, *The Marxists*, pp. 107–8.
[30] *Ibid.*, p. 110.
[31] *Ibid.*, p. 108.
[32] *Ibid.*, p. 112.

locale, and the effects of modern alienation do not necessarily contradict anything he wrote but he did not describe them. Moreover, psychic exploitations are not, we suspect, rooted in capitalism alone and as such. They are also coming about in non-capitalist and post-capitalist societies. They are not necessarily rooted either in the private ownership or in the state ownership of the means of production; they may be rooted in the facts of mass industrialization itself.[33]

Moreover, the social-psychological condition which Marx described under the rubric of alienation does not lead, it appears, to rebellion and resistance:

> The psychological alternatives for men in capitalist society are no more polarized than is the class structure. Not conservatism *or* insurgency, proletarian *or* bourgeois, but social apathy, a developed and mature political indifference, is often the determining psychological condition. Such apathy is not readily explained in terms of Marx's rationalist model of ideological forms and class consciousness, or by his conception of alienation.[34]

Marx held to an overly rational conception of man and confined rational consciousness rather arbitrarily to "class interest." Mills points to the important implications of the ambiguity of this concept:

> The inadequacy of Marx's notion of "class interests" is of great moral importance. He does not consider the difference between (a) What is to the Interests of Men according to an analysis of their position in society, and (b) What Men Are Interested In according to the men themselves. Nor does he confront fully (as we must since Lenin) the moral meaning of the political uses of this distinction. (This is the moral root of problems of leninism and of the meaning of democracy and freedom.)[35]

Furthermore,

> . . . the fact is that men are often concerned with temporary rather than long-run interests, and with particular interests, of occupational

[33] *Ibid.,* p. 112.
[34] *Ibid.,* p. 113.
[35] *Ibid.,* p. 114.

trades, for example, rather than the more general interests of their class.[36]

This brings us closer to the more explicitly Weberian influence upon Mills and his controversial notion of "power elite," which is now firmly a part of the social-science lexicon. There were important theoretical and empirical reasons which prompted him to coin and work with this concept.

In studying the phenomenon of the "state," for instance, he believed that "power elite" is a more useful concept than "ruling class." The distinction, he insisted, is more than a mere semantic one, more than a mere terminological quibble. That those who own and control the means of production are also those who rule, directly or indirectly, ought to be a hypothesis and not a dogmatic assumption. Lumping together economic and political elements in one concept, as in "ruling class" ("ruling" referring to political power, and class to ownership of property), renders the formulation of a hypothesis more difficult. Mills preferred "power elite" because this concept leaves empirically open "the question of economic determinism and the problem of the relative weight of upper economic classes within the higher [political or ruling] circles." [37]

Following Weber, Mills maintains that Marx had neglected and underestimated in his conception of the state the relative autonomy—how much? is an empirical question—of the non-economic institutions, notably the political and military. "Marx did not see clearly and adequately [writes Mills] the nature of capitalism's monopoly form and the political and military manner of its stabilization. In this monopoly form it has not remained merely 'an anarchy of production.' Vast sectors of it have been highly rationalized by private corporations, trade associations, and state intervention. Capitalism and bureaucracy, in brief, are not polar opposites. They have been integrated. The anarchy of production has not been generalized; to a considerable extent, it has been rationalized." [38] And further: "This does not mean that economic powers are minor, or that they are not translated into effective political and military power. But it does mean that with the expansion of the state, economic

[36] *Ibid.*, p. 115.
[37] *Ibid.*, p. 118.
[38] *Ibid.*, p. 121.

242

powers are now often defensive and limited, and that they are not the all-sufficient key to the understanding of political power or to the shaping of total social structures." [39]

Finally, and this, I think, was Mills' main purpose in *Power Elite*, there is the need to supplement Marx with Weber in order to provide a new and better model with greater analytical power. Here Mills' discussion deserves to be quoted in full:

> In brief, we must generalize Marx's approach to economics. We come then to focus—as did Marx—upon the changing techniques of economic production. But we also focus—as did Max Weber—upon the techniques of military violence, of political struggle and administration, and upon the means of communication—in short upon *all* the means of power, and upon their quite varied relations with one another in historically specific societies.
>
> So we may speak in a thoroughly marxist manner of the appropriation and monopolization of such political and military means. The emphasis upon the economy must be treated as a convenience of method. We must always try to distinguish its causal weight in the society as a whole, but we must leave open the possibilities of more political and more military autonomy than did Marx.
>
> I think this is a necessary and useful refinement and elaboration of the general model of society drawn up by Marx. It then becomes possible to do *whatever* marxists may wish by way of arguing and investigating economic determinism. But economic determinism becomes one hypothesis to be tested in each specific epoch and society. Military determinism and political determinism may also be so tested. Given the present state of our knowledge, no one of the three should automatically be assumed to predominate uniformly among history-making factors in all societies, or even in all types of capitalist societies.[40]

In short, if Marxism is to be a "guide to study, not a lever for construction after the Hegelian," as Marx and Engels insisted, then it must allow itself to be enriched by the insights of the classic tradition of sociological thinking—including the critics of Marxism. This was the view of C. Wright Mills, the "plain" Marxist.

[39] *Ibid.,* p. 125.
[40] *Ibid.,* p. 126.

13

MARTIN JAY

How Utopian Is
Marcuse?

Martin Jay is a graduate student in history at Harvard University and has published several studies on the Frankfurt School of critical sociology.

The rise of Herbert Marcuse from the relative obscurity of his first sixty-five years to a position as one of the media's favorite seducers of the young has not been without its cost. The dissemination of his ideas has brought with it their inevitable dilution. Through what the French, in a delightful phrase, call "la drugstorisation de Marcuse," he has himself become something of a commodity. No article on the New Left is complete without a ritual mention of his name: no discussion of the "counter-culture" dare ignore his message of liberation. What is by and large ignored, however, are the roots of his arguments, which are too deeply embedded in a tradition alien to the thinking of most Americans to make painless comprehension likely. It is far easier, after all, to read the unfortunate essay on "Repressive Tolerance" than to wrestle with the conceptual subtleties and stylistic impenetrability of *Reason and Revolution*. As a result, Marcuse is still to a considerable extent *Cet Inconnu*, as the French journal *La Nef* [1] subtitled its recent issue devoted to him. A complete exploration of the foundations of his thought is of course beyond the scope of this essay. A beginning, however, can perhaps be made by probing one aspect of his thinking which has increasingly come to the fore in recent years: its utopian dimension.

[1] *Marcuse: Cet Inconnu, La Nef,* No. 36, January–March 1969.

How Utopian Is Marcuse?

As has often been observed, Marxist theory has steadfastly refused to offer a blueprint for post-capitalist society. The historicist strain in Marx's own thinking was always in tension with his implicit philosophical anthropology. Occasional attempts to describe "Socialist Man" by his successors have usually been thwarted by the recognition that he will have to define himself in a process of self-creation which cannot be described in advance. Few Marxists or neo-Marxist thinkers have been as sensitive to this historicist ban on positing a normative human nature as those of the so-called "Frankfurt School" of the *Institut für Sozialforschung,* with which Marcuse was associated during the 1930's.

The Institute's reluctance to suggest anything which might be taken as a universal view of man's essence even prevented it from accepting without reservation the anthropological implications of Marx's *Economic and Philosophical Manuscripts* when they were recovered in the early thirties. It is not insignificant that Theodor W. Adorno, who until his death was the Institute's director, chose music, the most unrepresentational of aesthetic modes, as the medium through which he examined bourgeois culture and sought traces of its transcendent negation. In recent years, Max Horkheimer, more than anyone else responsible for the genesis of the Institute's "Critical Theory," has come to believe that this refusal to picture the "other" society beyond capitalism is not unrelated to the Jewish ban on naming or describing God.

Whatever the source of the taboo, only Marcuse of the major figures connected with the Frankfurt School has dared in recent years to break it. Only Marcuse has tried to speak the unspeakable in an increasingly urgent effort to reintroduce a utopian cast to socialist theory. *Eros and Civilization* was his first attempt to outline the contours of the society beyond repressive domination. The *Essay on Liberation* goes even further in explicitly stating the need for a new philosophical anthropology, a frankly "biological foundation" for socialism. The desired transition, he argues, is from Marx to Fourier, from realism to surrealism.[2] The failure of socialism, he seems to be saying, has been the failure of imagination.

By consciously donning the utopian mantle, Marcuse has invited the scorn of "realists" in both the socialist and capitalist camps. Nevertheless, by doing so he has helped give substance and direction to the inchoate yearnings of those dissatisfied with what they see as the present

---

[2] Herbert Marcuse, *An Essay on Liberation* (Boston, 1969), p. 22.

Hobson's Choice between authoritarian socialism and repressive advanced capitalism. While his critiques of both these current societies are well known, the utopian alternative he has projected has been comparatively ignored. Only its psychoanalytic elements—the goal of a society freed from historically grounded "surplus repression" and the "performance principle" (a kind of generalized Protestant Ethic)—have been discussed with any rigor. Far less attention has been paid to its philosophical sources. Only by examining these can the political implications of Marcuse's vision be adequately understood.

Those familiar solely with Marcuse's writings in English are often surprised to learn that before joining the Institute in Frankfurt in 1932, he spent several years with Martin Heidegger at Freiburg. During this period, he attempted to reconcile Heidegger's existential phenomenology with historical materialism,[3] anticipating in a sense what Merleau-Ponty and Sartre were to try to do after the war. The details of his attempt need not concern us now.[4] What is important to note for our purposes is that, as Alfred Schmidt has suggested, Marxism served him as a "positive philosophy" answering Heidegger's question, "What is authentic existence and how is authentic existence possible?" To Marcuse, man can exist authentically only by performing radical deeds, only by engaging in self-creating *praxis*. Man is only man as autonomous subject, never as contingent predicate. The Marxist "fundamental situation," he argued, is that in which the historically conscious man performs radical acts in order to live authentically.

Although abandoning much of Heidegger's terminology and moving away from his ontological approach to history during his tenure at the Institute, Marcuse has never fully relinquished his conviction that the free man is the man who can create himself through radical *praxis*. It might be added parenthetically that Heidegger's influence has persisted in another way as well. Marcuse's much debated attitude toward technology—he has been accused of being everything from a romantic Luddite to a technological determinist—owes much to Heidegger's hostility to the technological logos, which he interpreted as a falling away from the basic insights of the pre-Socratics, a process which began centuries

---

[3] See, for example, Marcuse, "Contributions to a Phenomenology of Historical Materialism" (1928), published in English in *Telos,* No. 4, Fall 1969.

[4] For a discussion of his problem see Alfred Schmidt, "Existential-Ontologie und historischer Materialismus bei Herbert Marcuse," *Antworten auf Herbert Marcuse,* ed. Jürgen Habermas (Frankfurt, Suhrkamp, 1968).

before technology itself achieved its domination over nature and man. In *One-Dimensional Man*,[5] Marcuse openly appropriates a passage from Heidegger's *Holzwege* to attack the "technological a priori."

Still, it would be a grave error to dismiss Marcuse as an existentialist decked out in Marxist trappings, as have some of his critics on the left. Whatever his indebtedness to Heidegger, he has never abandoned his belief in the necessity of rational theory or his conviction in the validity of values beyond experience. Indeed, among his most devastating critiques is an attack on the pro-Nazi political philosopher Carl Schmitt's anti-normative political existentialism.[6] (There is, of course, no necessary connection between the philosophical positions collectively known as existentialist and their political counterpart, although in the sad case of Heidegger, his Nazi sympathies cannot be totally disassociated from his philosophy.)

If there is a leftist parallel to Schmitt and his decisionism, it can be found in those who would collapse theory into an unmediated *praxis*. The most recent manifestation of this basically anarchistic position is the "Weatherman" faction of the Students for a Democratic Society. Although Marcuse has always warned against the complete separation of theory and *praxis,* at no time has he advocated action as sufficient in itself. The goal may be the unity of thought and action, but at this moment in historical time their relationship is necessarily problematical. To declare their unity as already existing is to fall prey to ideology. It is only as a utopian hope that the coordination of self-creating action and rational theory should be understood in Marcuse's work.

If one element of his utopian vision is a stress on radical *praxis* as authentic behavior, there is another, more important strain. Here his distance from existentialism of all types is plainly evident. This is especially clear when compared with the position taken by Sartre in one of the classic existentialist texts, *Being and Nothingness*. The relevant issue here is the possibility of the reconciliation of opposites which anyone who works within a Hegelian framework must confront. In *Being and Nothingness* the dialectic of opposing forces remains inevitably truncated; the redeeming power of synthesis is ultimately denied as a possible end to the historical process. For Itself and In Itself, Sartre's variation on the theme of subject and object, cannot be reconciled. "Conflict,"

[5] *One-Dimensional Man* (Boston: Beacon Press, 1964), pp. 153–54.
[6] "The Struggle Against Liberalism in the Totalitarian View of the State," *Negations* (Boston: Beacon Press, 1969), pp. 31–42.

he writes, "is the original meaning of being-for others." [7] The familiar aphorism of Sartre in *No Exit* makes the same point: "Hell is—other people." Here it might be added, Marcuse's former colleagues at the *Institut für Sozialforschung*, Horkheimer and Adorno, reluctantly reach similar conclusions in their later work, *Negative Dialektik*, Adorno's last great work, stresses non-identity and the importance of negation as the last refuge of freedom. "The totality," he wrote elsewhere, "is the untrue." And in the 1960's, Horkheimer returned to an early interest in Schopenhauer and his pessimistic denial that the world can be made rational.

Marcuse, on the other hand, disagrees both with the gloomy reduction of man to a "useless passion" in *Being and Nothingness* and with the stress on the non-identity of subject and object in the work of the other leading figures of the Frankfurt School. So often taken to task for his "pessimism," he maintains a belief in all his work that true reconciliation, however frustrated in the false harmony of contemporary society, is indeed a possibility. This is not to say, of course, that he believes the synthesis has already been achieved, as Hegelians of the right have always assumed. Firmly grounded in the Marxist tradition as he is, Marcuse is quick to point out that social conditions, behind the façade of one-dimensionality, are still fundamentally contradictory and antagonistic. Class conflict may not be the form in which contradiction now manifests itself, but no universal class has emerged in which all antagonisms have been dialectically resolved. Integration, as he has used it, does not mean true harmony. On the other hand, he does believe that for the first time pre-conditions do exist, created paradoxically by the technology whose other effects he so dislikes, which make the prospects for reconciliation favorable. With the end of scarcity, so runs the familiar argument from *Eros and Civilization*, man's need to repress himself for the sake of productive work is no longer binding. Utopian possibilities are no longer chimerical.

What then does Marcuse mean by reconciliation? What is this true harmony he so fervently seeks? Here more than anywhere else he reveals his roots in the German Idealist tradition. One might even venture the observation that he has succumbed to the lure of Greece and its alleged cultural serenity which had such an enormous influence on German philosophy during its classical period, as E. M. Butler has shown in her

[7] *Being and Nothingness*, trans. Hazel Barnes (New York: Simon and Schuster, 1966), p. 364.

masterful *The Tyranny of Greece over Germany.* The image of the Greeks which was so powerful was not that of a nation of tragedy writers, but rather that of a people in a state of pre-alienated wholeness which Winckelmann introduced to the German mind in the eighteenth century.

In his essay "Philosophy and Critical Theory," first appearing in the journal of the Institute in 1937, Marcuse wrote: [8]

> Under the name of reason [philosophy] conceived the idea of an authentic Being in which all significant antitheses (of subject and object, essence and appearance, thought and being) were reconciled. Connected with this idea was the conviction that what exists is not immediately and already rational but must rather be brought to reason . . . At its highest level, as authentic reality, the world no longer stands opposed to the rational thought of men as mere material objectivity. Rather, it is now comprehended by thought and defined as a concept. That is, the external, antithetical character of material objectivity is overcome in a process through which the identity of subject and object is established as the rational, conceptual structure that is common to both.

Here then is the belief that identity between thought and being—and Marcuse clearly means being-in-the-world, social relations—can be established on the basis of a shared rationality. At no time, however, does he imply that the individual should be sacrificed to the whole in the name of an hypostatized objective reality. In his article "On Hedonism," written for the Institute in 1938, he stresses the function of hedonistic philosophies in preserving the claim of personal human happiness against the demands of over-arching totalities such as the state. Here the stress on sensual gratification which was developed in his post-war work on Freud exists in embryo.

Marcuse has, however, always been careful to avoid advocating simple sexual freedom as the answer to social repression, as Wilhelm Reich on occasion did. "The bogey of the unchained voluptuary," he wrote, "who would abandon himself only to his sensual wants is rooted in the separation of intellectual from material productive forces and the separation of the labor process from the process of consumption. Overcoming this separation belongs to the pre-conditions of freedom." [9] The

[8] *Negations,* pp. 135–36.
[9] "On Hedonism," *Negations,* p. 198.

249

end of the dichotomy between internalized, spiritualized culture and material, sensual activity in the "real" world is thus part of his utopian vision. The stress here on reconciling production and consumption fore-shadows his later use of Schiller's "play drive" in *Eros and Civilization*. Art and technology must ultimately converge; the logos of gratification must be joined with a technology freed from its project of domination.

In Marcuse's thinking, the driving impetus toward harmony is fur-ther demonstrated in his treatment of time. In *Eros and Civilization,* he stresses the function of memory, of "re-membering" that which is asun-der, as a vehicle of liberation. To forget is to forgive the injustices of the past. "From the myth of Orpheus to the novel of Proust," he argues, "happiness and freedom have been linked with the idea of the recapture of time . . . remembrance alone provides the joy without the anxiety over its passing and thus gives it an otherwise impossible duration. Time loses its power when remembrance redeems the past." [10] And in his later essay, "Progress and Freud's Theory of Instincts," he more explicitly outlines a utopian idea of temporality. "Time would not seem linear, as a perpetual line or rising curve, but cyclical, as the return contained in Nietzsche's idea of the 'perpetuity of pleasure.' " [11]

There is more than a little of the tyranny of Greece, or at least the Greek idea of cyclical time, in all of this, not to mention the influence of one of Marcuse's colleagues at the *Institut für Sozialforschung,* Walter Benjamin. In his "Theses on the Philosophy of History," [12] Benjamin developed the ideal of "Jetztzeit" (Nowtime) as a mystical explosion in the continuum of history, a kind of Messianic time qualitatively different from the empty, linear, unfulfilled temporal experience of ordinary men. Marcuse has always been fond of quoting Benjamin's observation that in 1830, the revolutionaries of Paris shot at public clocks to make time stop. The implications of this way of thinking would seem blatantly eschatological. But Marcuse, when questioned on this point, has denied any eschatological intentions. History will go on, he has said, short of a nuclear disaster.

And yet, it would go on in a way very different from the way in which it has been experienced until now. What will be particularly ab-sent is conflict, strife, striving, in short, all the things which have char-

[10] *Eros and Civilization* (Boston: Beacon Press, 1955), p. 213.
[11] Marcuse, *Five Lectures* (Boston, 1970), p. 41.
[12] *Illuminations,* trans., Harry Zohn (New York: Harcourt Brace, 1968), p 263.

acterized Western history for millennia. In his own words, Marcuse desires the "pacification of existence." Gratification and sensual receptivity are the traits of his new aestheticism. Unlike Marx, or at least the mature Marx, Marcuse believes labor can be abolished. Because Marx was more pessimistic on this point, he never believed that the complete identity of the production and consumption processes could be achieved. Indeed, Marx did not even fully accept the Hegelian notion of identity of subject and object to which Marcuse seems to have returned.[13]

The only place in his writings where Marcuse displays similar caution is in his critique of Norman O. Brown, whose mysticism demands the total negation of the *principium individuationis*. ". . . Eros lives in the division and boundary between subject and object, man and nature," he admonished Brown; ". . . the unity of subject and object is a hallmark of absolute idealism; however, even Hegel retained the tension between the two, the distinction." [14] Elsewhere, Marcuse supports an identity theory which, although demanding the preservation of the individual, is scarcely less utopian than Brown's. It is not insignificant that Ernst Bloch, whose animistic belief in the resurrection of a new natural subject marks him as a leading identity theorist, embraced Marcuse at a conference in Yugoslavia in 1968 and welcomed him back to the ranks of the utopian optimists of the 1920's. Indeed, it would be tempting to say that Marcuse has surrendered to what Freud called the "Nirvana Principle," the yearning for the end of tension that is life, if Marcuse were not so sure that life with a minimum of tension is a possibility.[15]

These then are the two strains in Marcuse's vision of the liberated society: first, the stress on radical action, on the deed, on self-creation as the only mode of authentic being; and second, the unity of opposites, the true harmony of pacified existence, the end of conflict and contradiction. The one theme is basically active, one might even say Prome-

[13] See Alfred Schmidt, *Der Begriff der Natur in der Lehre von Marx* (Frankfurt: Europäische Verlagsanstalt, 1962).

[14] *Negations*, p. 238.

[15] In *Eros and Civilization* (pp. 214–15), he writes: "The death instinct operates under the Nirvana principle: it tends toward that state of 'constant gratification' where no tension is felt. . . . If the instinct's basic objective is not the termination of life but of pain—the absence of tension—then paradoxically, in terms of the instinct, the conflict between life and death is the more reduced, the closer life approximates the state of gratification. . . . As suffering and want recede, the Nirvana principle may become reconciled with the reality principle. The unconscious attraction that draws the instincts back to an 'earlier state' would be effectively counteracted by the desirability of the attained state of life."

thean, to use Marx's own favorite metaphor; the other rather more passive, Orphic in the sense Marcuse interprets Orpheus in *Eros and Civilization:* as the singer of joy and fulfillment. And both, he has cogently argued, are denied and frustrated in the contemporary world of repressive capitalism and authoritarian socialism.

Whether or not the two strains are compatible is a problem Marcuse does not seem to have worked out in any detail. It might be said that radical *praxis* is merely the means to achieve the revolutionary breakthrough leading to the pacification of existence. This fails to work, however, because of Marcuse's insistence that self-creating action is the only true authentic mode of being. Another possible solution would be to divide him into an "early" and a "late" Marcuse, as is sometimes done with Marx, with the result that a Heideggerian Marcuse is somehow supplanted by a Hegelianized one under the influence of Horkheimer and the *Institut.* Besides being too schematic, this solution fails to do justice to the mixture of both strains in his work. It seems perhaps best to leave this problem by saying that Marcuse, like so many other thinkers of stature, has unresolved tensions in his thought. As to be expected, the political implications which can be drawn from these conflicting tendencies are no simpler. It is to these that we now turn.

In his treatment of Heidegger's concept of authentic existence, Marcuse was critical of the abstract, undialectical quality of his teacher's idea of history. Not everyone, he argued, was in the position to perform the radical acts constituting authentic behavior. At this stage in man's development, Marcuse claimed, only the proletariat is the true actor on the historical stage because of its crucial role in the production process. To ignore the importance of class differences would be to retreat into Idealism. Heidegger's indifference to the real course of history was not unrelated to the *völkische* ideology of the national *Gemeinschaft* transcending social contradictions.

Since 1928 much of course has happened to emasculate the revolutionary potential of the working class, especially in the America to which Marcuse fled in 1934. To the consternation of those who still romanticize the proletariat, he was among the first to face the implications of its integration. Although he has recently seen evidence of cracks in the one-dimensionality of the system in student protest and the rumblings of what Marx would have dismissed as *Lumpenproletariat,* at no time has he mistaken these forces for a new proletariat or a new historical subject. As a result, he has been the frequent target of other

252

theorists on the left who see the stirring of new "negative" forces in society such as the alienated "new working class" of white-collar workers and technicians. Whoever may be right, it is important to note that Marcuse has always identified the doers of the authentic deed with a specific historical group. To ignore the historical element in his "existentialist" stress on *praxis* is thus to falsify his analysis. Although Marcuse has often been accused of anarchism—such disparate thinkers as Hans Heinz Holz and George Lichtheim have leveled this charge against him,[16] and indeed there is an anarchistic element in his work in the healthy sense of distrusting rigid organizations—it would be a grave error to interpret him as an advocate of indiscriminate activism or political decisionism. That wing of the student movement which takes his name as a justification for such activity is misapplying his teachings, at least insofar as they neglect his stress on present historical possibilities.

And yet, a plausible interpretation of Marcuse on just this level does exist. If the so-called existentialist element in his utopian vision ought not to be interpreted as a justification for the indeterminate negation of the system, what of the other central theme in his work, the yearning for harmony and reconciliation of dialectical contradictions? Here the implications are far more problematical. In his analysis of Marcuse's aesthetics,[17] Herbert Read has argued that the achievement of a rational society would not end the need for art, as Marcuse has implied. If in our own irrational society art provides *une promesse de bonheur,* a promise of unfulfilled happiness, as Marcuse has argued, there is no necessary reason to suppose that a new society, however rational, would satisfy all of men's needs or end all his fears. Above all, the mystery of death and the arbitrariness of suffering would make human existence a continuing subject for the aesthetic imagination. The eternal return is forever bisected by the linear time of mortal men who are born and must ultimately die.

If Marcuse is too quick to assume art would be overcome in a rational society, so too, and this is a vitally important point, is he overly hasty in assuming politics would be overcome in a grand synthesis of differences. The vaunted American system of pluralistic politics may

[16] Hans Heinz Holz, *Utopia und Anarchismus* (Cologne: Pahl-Rugenstein, 1968); George Lichtheim, "From Marx to Hegel: Reflections on Georg Lukacs, T. W. Adorno, and Herbert Marcuse," *Triquarterly,* No. 12, Spring 1968.

[17] Herbert Read, "Rational Society and Irrational Art," *The Critical Spirit,* ed. Kurt Wolff and Barrington Moore, Jr. (Boston: Beacon Press, 1967).

indeed be a mask for manipulation and special interests, as he has always argued, yet pluralism as such is the very essence of politics. The belief that political conflict is an epiphenomenon of economic and social contradictions is a fallacy which ought finally to be laid to rest. What the Czechs were trying in part to say, before they lost the chance to say anything at all, was that politics in the sense of readjusting priorities and working through the competition for power does not end when an economy is socialized. Furthermore, the expectation that international tension would end when the entire world becomes socialist is a hope which drowned in the waters of the Ussuri River with the Sino-Soviet clash.

Thus, in positing a utopia of identity in which all contradictions are overcome, Marcuse displays that basic hostility to politics which has been the curse of too many German thinkers for too many years. Its effects spill over into the only type of political action he sanctions today: the Great Refusal, a complete rejection of the mechanics of political change presented by the system. Although in large measure a response to the sadly true observation that the system all too often fails to do what it promises, it is also a reflection of his more basic rejection of politics as such. The inevitable result of this attitude, if apolitical quietism is to be avoided, is what the French call the politics of making things worse—the apocalyptic hope that out of total chaos will come total change. Metapolitics rather than true political activity becomes the only authentic mode of revolutionary behavior. In the end, it is perhaps all reducible to that "aestheticization" of politics against which Walter Benjamin so earnestly warned.[18] Paradoxically, the radical optimism of Marcuse's utopian vision is the dialectical counterpart of the resignation about the possibilities for change within or growing out of the system which has earned him so much abuse from liberals and the orthodox Left.

It is thus ironic that the existentialist strain in Marcuse's thinking, which is sometimes cited as the source of his anarchistic impulses, is less influential in promoting antipolitical politics than is the Idealist strain. It is almost as if Marcuse has forgotten his tempering of the ahistorical element in Heidegger's thinking in his belief that the metapolitical utopia is just around the corner. Reifying the status quo and rejecting any medium of real change except the sudden and total collapse of the system is to jump out of history. It is no accident that Marcuse has taken more

18 *Illuminations*, p. 244.

and more in his recent works to quoting that other great defector from the mundane course of history, Friedrich Nietzsche.

Perhaps the most unhistorical element in his work is the notion that the abolition of labor and its replacement by play, in Schiller's sense of unrepressed sensuousness reconciled with the "order of freedom," would be the hallmark of the new age. The end of scarcity, a task which is by no means as easily accomplished as he believes, is a thin reed on which to base the end of social, political, and psychological contradictions. Here, curiously, Marcuse shows himself both beyond Marx and beholden to him. He transcends Marx's relatively cautious stance, as mentioned before, by arguing that labor can indeed be abolished. Yet, by giving so much weight to that abolition, he reveals his indebtedness to Marx's conviction that labor is the basic human life activity. Play, it might be argued, is really on the same conceptual axis as labor, if at the other end.[19]

Marcuse's interpretation of Hegel is itself colored by his acceptance of the Marxist centrality of labor. In *Reason and Revolution* he wrote: "The concept of labor is not peripheral in Hegel's system, but is the central notion through which he conceives the development of society." [20] What Marcuse was perhaps forgetting in his desire to demonstrate the closeness of Marx and Hegel has recently been shown by the most gifted second-generation student of the Frankfurt School, Jürgen Habermas. Labor, Habermas has argued in his article "Arbeit und Interaktion," [21]

---

[19] When Marcuse first stressed the ontological centrality of labor in one of his early Heideggerian essays, his attitude toward play was less favorable than in *Eros and Civilization*. In play, he argued, the sway of the objective world over the free subject is suspended. Thus, unlike labor, play produces no permanent objectifications. It has no essential duration, existing in the "inbetween" separating true *praxis*. Nor does it express man's essentially historical nature. "First and only in labor," he wrote, "does man become historically real and win his specific place in historical occurrence." ("Über die philosophischen Grundlagen des Wirtschaftswissenschaftlichen Arbeitsbegriffs," *Archiv für Sozialwissenschaft und Sozialpolitik*, Vol. 69, No. 3, June 1933, p. 279.) Using his own reasoning against him, it might therefore be argued that his recent praise of play as a superior alternative to labor indicates an ahistorical strain in his thinking. I think it is more important to note that Marcuse's discovery of *Homo Ludens* in his recent work occurred against the background of his life-long conviction of the ontological importance of labor. This allows him to see play as resolving contradictions, as he once argued labor did, rather than creating new ones, as is the case when play is understood as related to what Habermas calls "symbolically-mediated interaction."

[20] *Reason and Revolution* (Boston: Beacon, 1966), p. 78.

[21] *Technik und Wissenschaft als "Ideologie"* (Frankfurt: Suhrkamp, 1968).

was not the only category of self-creation in Hegel's thinking. An alternative mode existed in symbolically mediated interaction, i.e. language and expressive gestures, which at least in his early work, Hegel did not see as identical with the dialectic of labor. To Marcuse, however, Hegel was saying that, "Language . . . makes it possible for an individual to take a conscious position *against* his fellows and to assert his needs and desires against those of the other individuals. The resulting antagonisms are integrated through the process of labor, which also becomes the decisive force for the development of culture." [22] Thus, in Marcuse's thinking, the problems of symbolic interaction are contained within the larger framework of the dialectic of labor and the production process. This permits him to give so much emphasis to the utopian possibilities liberated by the abolition of human toil. What he therefore neglects to note is, as Habermas has put it, "Freedom from hunger and toil does not necessarily converge with freedom from slavery and degradation, because an automatic developmental connection between labor and interaction does not exist." [23]

The link between Marcuse's hostility toward politics and his neglect of the problem of symbolic interaction should not be missed. As Hannah Arendt,[24] among others, has so often pointed out, speech and political *praxis* are inseparable. The abolition of labor, even if it were as easily attained as Marcuse thinks it is, would therefore not put an end to all contradictions. Symbolic interaction and the politics with which it is so intimately tied would continue to express the sedimented antagonisms of the past.

Nationalism, for example, is likely to frustrate hopes for a reconciliation of particular and universal interests in the future, as expectations of an internationalist proletariat were frustrated in the past. And, of course, at the center of the national question is the irreducible fact of linguistic differences. This is a reality which Marcuse's utopianism fails to acknowledge, thus allowing him to maintain an implicit faith in the possibility of a Benjamin-like "explosion in the continuum of history." The political imperative which follows from all of this is the cul-de-sac of apocalyptic metapolitics which is really no politics at all.

[22] *Reason and Revolution*, p. 75.
[23] *Technik und Wissenschaft als "Ideologie,"* p. 46.
[24] Hannah Arendt, *The Human Condition* (Chicago: University of Chicago Press, 1958), pp. 155–61.

14

RONALD ARONSON

Dear Herbert

Ronald Aronson received a doctorate in the history of ideas from Brandeis University, and is now an assistant professor at Monteith College, Wayne State University. He has served as an editor of *Studies on the Left* and as a member of the SSC steering committee.

To Herbert Marcuse

Dear   Herbert:

My addressing you in this public way gives me a frightening and exciting chance to come to terms with you—with your effect on me as teacher, with your writings, with you personally. For myself and a few friends, studying with you was one of the decisive experiences of our lives. Your thought, personality, style of teaching, and writings were overpowering. During those years at Brandeis—and in many ways into the present—we were in awe of you. First, your bearing: so self-consciously dignified, distant, demanding. It was clear that your approval, even your notice, had to be won, and we father-tormented graduate students became eager scholars and willing disciples.

You brought us into contact with the central figures in Western thought: Plato, Aristotle, Kant, Hegel, Marx. We didn't learn system-building from the outside, but we learned how to trace the impulses animating the thinking of each man we studied. We learned this, we felt, from someone living inside that movement of ideas, not an academic but

257

someone *of* that tradition. Of that tradition and yet a revolutionary; you helped us to take our stand in Western thought and still be Marxists, to read Plato with warmth and understanding as well as to criticize him on social-historical grounds. You showed that the dilemma was false: Marxism *or* Western culture. So-called "bourgeois" poetry and painting and psychoanalysis and aesthetics are relevant, even central, to revolutionary thought. Your writings on art point this up: nobody I know is as able to appreciate what is going on in modern art, what it *means*.

I recall those classes on Plato's *Meno* and Kant's *Critique of Pure Reason,* we prepared hard and long, read the material two or three times, refused to miss even one class, came expectantly, brought our friends and wives. Something was happening in Marcuse's classes. We all sensed it, we were learning how to read, to think. Above all you emphasized the idea of reason: the capacity of thought to understand the existing social reality, to criticize it, to project alternatives. All this meant disciplined work, mastery, knowledge for the sake of changing the world.

You introduced us to a perspective which was new and revolutionary, which made sense of our lives and helped us to find our way as radicals. In your courses in social and political theory and Marxian theory and in your writings you presented us with a coherent way of seeing history and the role of theory. How to think about history, how to think about thought. Capitalist society became clear as one form of *class* society: the central question became one of domination. And you gave us a way of making the present crisis clear: domination over nature reaches its goal, complete mastery, while domination over man is continued beyond any historical justification, using all of the new capabilities. Perhaps above all, you gave us the message of liberation, in *Eros and Civilization*—a new reality, organized according to different principles, realizing our deepest dreams, breaking with the trend of any past or present society.

You were never humble, and for that I thank you. You insisted that reality *can* be understood, that there is a single decisive issue—liberation—that dialectical thought *is* a valid way to approach the world. And you refused to submit to the authority of doctrine: you have struggled, more than anyone, to understand the present situation in its own terms, without merely reimposing old categories on it, to let thought move with history, freely and imaginatively.

No wonder we felt dominated by you. No wonder we argued after every class about what you meant, read and discussed your books as soon as they came out, quoted you against each other, made "What would Marcuse think?" our major intellectual principle. I think of those days under your tutelage sadly, warmly, so much less secure now that it is time to locate the limits as well as the value of your impact on me. Insecure because as I write this I am not merely drawing myself up to the level of my teacher, declaring equality; I am reopening the intellectual field for myself and those like me, locating our work by spelling out the limits of yours.

Reopening: breaking into the open again. Yes, for a long time it felt closed, my world of radical thought. Why?

It is the intellectual's task and duty, you have said, "to recall and preserve historical possibilities which seem to have become utopian possibilities . . . it is his task to break the concreteness of oppression in order to open the mental space in which this society can be recognized as what it is and does." [1] Take *One-Dimensional Man,* which describes the closed universes of discourse, politics, philosophy, science, and academic concepts. It conveys a sense of suffocation, of totalitarianism at work everywhere. As such it is a major step in our breaking out of that closing universe. By naming it, by helping us to get conscious of it, by conveying its overwhelming power, it helped us to define ourselves in opposition to it—total opposition. Depressing, verging on despair, the almost wholly negative analysis helped me and the movement to find ourselves in a society which integrates and feeds on conventional forms of opposition.

But your thought and teaching could only lead us so far. Secure in our ability to think, we began to see your limitations for our own lives and the historical problems facing us.

I want to talk about your tone: it is abstract and remote. There remains an enormous gulf between your writings and my experience. *Our* experience: the first generation of the New Left. But, strange to say, this weakness is also your strength. The "good" aspects of your writing cannot be rescued by throwing the "bad" overboard. To spell this out is to locate the historical place and limits of your thought—and experience. And define the new prospects and tasks open to those of us young enough to be born into and shaped by postwar America.

The power of your writings goes hand in hand with their weakness.

---

[1] "Repressive Tolerance," in *A Critique of Pure Tolerance* (Boston: Beacon Press, 1965), pp. 81–82.

This can be seen clearly in the opening paragraphs of *One-Dimensional Man:*

> Does not the threat of an atomic catastrophe which could wipe out the human race also serve to protect the very forces which perpetuate this danger? The efforts to prevent such a catastrophe overshadow the search for its potential causes in contemporary industrial society. These causes remain unidentified, unexposed, unattacked by the public because they recede before the all too obvious threat from without—to the West from the East, to the East from the West. Equally obvious is the need for being prepared, for living on the brink, for facing the challenge. We submit to the peaceful production of the means of destruction, to the perfection of waste, to being educated for a defense which deforms the defenders and that which they defend.
>
> If we attempt to relate the causes of the danger to the way in which society is organized and organizes its members, we are immediately confronted with the fact that advanced industrial society becomes richer, bigger, and better as it perpetuates the danger. The defense structure makes life easier for a greater number of people and extends man's mastery of nature. Under these circumstances, our mass media have little difficulty in selling particular interests as those of all sensible men. The political needs of society become individual needs and aspirations, their statisfaction promotes business and the commonweal, and the whole appears to be the very embodiment of Reason.
>
> And yet this society is irrational as a whole. Its productivity is destructive of the free development of human needs and faculties, its peace maintained by the constant threat of war, its growth dependent on the repression of the real possibilities for pacifying the struggle for existence—individual, national, and international. This repression, so different from that which characterized the preceding, less developed stages for our society, operates today not from a position of natural and technical immaturity but rather from a position of strength. The capabilities (intellectual and material) of contemporary society are immeasurably greater than ever before—which means that the scope of society's domination over the individual is immeasurably greater than ever before. Our society distinguishes itself by conquering the centrifugal social forces with Technology rather than Terror, on the dual basis of an overwhelming efficiency and an increasing standard of living.[2]

[2] *One-Dimensional Man* (Boston: Beacon Press, 1964), pp. ix-x. Copyright © by Herbert Marcuse. Reprinted by permission of Beacon Press.

Dear Herbert

In so many ways that statement could not be better. The inseparable and fatally ironic connection is sharply drawn between the society's wealth and well-being and its need to mutilate and possibly destroy us all. We are made to see it as a totality, whose good is born of its evil and vice versa. These passages demand that we think dialectically, that we join rather than separate, that we refuse to accept the logic of social science and detach prospects from problems. The passage is rich with irony, joining terms and concepts kept apart by the mass media; perfection *and* waste, productivity *and* destruction, growth *and* repression, peace *and* war, capabilities *and* domination.

At the same time you force us to think in general terms, we are drawn up from immersion in the immediate and apparently self-justifying particulars of our everyday experience. The general language distances us from that experience, gives us the perspective we need in order to be critical. The charged terms which obstruct and entrap thought, such as communism and capitalism, are replaced by East and West, the various ruling classes become "the forces," their class interests become "particular interests." At once we are lifted beyond the self-enclosed ideological debates of the American center and left and forced to think anew. The general terms, breaking wherever possible with conventional loaded formulations, draw back into themselves current usages for ironic effect: "living on the brink," "facing the challenge," "all sensible men" are juxtaposed with phrases which expose how loaded they are: "business and the commonweal." More, such general formulations as "advanced industrial society" and "contemporary industrial society" place us high above the events—viewing history itself, seeing contemporary society as what it is, the current stage of development. Thus you suggest that we are today living under a *different type* of repression from that in earlier stages. You refuse to let the struggle between socialism and capitalism define the limits of history; it is a longer process, going back at least to the beginnings of Western Civilization, whose future lines are still to be constructed.

Your terminology is rightly uncomfortable to read. It is open, elusive, unfixable. And abstraction of abstractions, Western Capitalism and the Soviet Union, each become "the whole." You speak of "our society" rather than Western Capitalism. It has "capabilities"—what are they? It "dominates"—specifically what does this mean?—through a never clearly defined "efficiency" and rising standard of living. How?

261

Not "war material" but "the means of destruction." And what are those alluded to but never articulated "causes" of the—still so general—"atomic catastrophe"? Aggravating to read, these formulations do what you intend: they re-open meaning, they create the space for thought by destroying our sense that all is set and defined. The high level of generality indicts socialism as well as capitalism: polar and self-evident terms give way to a search for meaning, a suspension of our typical and thoroughly indoctrinated responses.

Reason, Technology, and Terror—all in capital letters—appear almost as semi-autonomous. More distance. Look at this formulation: "the whole appears to be the very embodiment of Reason"—the language of philosophy creates the greatest possible distance. Two separate realms are suggested: the other World of Reason and our apparently rational but false world. Standards for judging this world thus are implied, standards drawn from that second dimension—whose meaning is kept open as it is itself only suggested, never explained. Opening meaning, provoking us to dialectical thought, defeating usual loaded ways of thinking and speaking, your style thus distances us from the world of our immediate experience so as better to see it, while suggesting standards for evaluating it. Truly you succeed in just what you set out to do, breaking "the concreteness of oppression in order to open up the mental space in which this society can be recognized as what it is and does." Anyone who reads you and takes you seriously will sooner or later find himself engaged in one of the most liberating of all acts—thinking.

How many of us have had the experience of discovering the world through *One-Dimensional Man?* But the same paragraphs, the same formulations, the same words—suffocate and deaden. The distance and generality which increase our critical ability in one way destroys it in another for they safeguard us from our own experience. Yes our reason is liberated by your method and tone, drawn and forced upward into the mansions of critical theory—an amazing accomplishment. But the rest of us—our hopes and lives and fears—get left behind.

The tone of remoteness which frees also stifles. I feel a bit lost after reading the introductory passage of *One-Dimensional Man* and completing the book hardly improves the condition. I am restless to get back to the world, to put my feet on the ground of hard and clear examples. Yours is a journey I can take with my intellect only—not with my imagination, my feelings, my guts.

That remote quality of so much of your writing is present in the passage I just quoted. Reason, Terror, Technology in capital letters— what are these self-subsistent, self-moving entities? Elsewhere you put Eros, Self, Beauty, Ego, The Great Refusal, Nature in capitals. Are we back with Plato, sketching a better, more real world but denying this one we live in? Frankly I feel inferior to such a world, to the level of culture which seems to be required for admission to it. After reading your justification for intolerance, some radicals speak of "Marcuse the elitist." And this problem isn't helped by your refusal to translate passages from French and German, your offhand use of terms from Latin and Greek. *Oeuvre* and *technics, Schein,* and *Lebenswelt*—a new vocabulary, taken from and pointing toward the high culture of Western Civilization: remote and intimidating.

High culture truly becomes a realm apart—you speak of *"the* standard literary vocabulary," *"the* classical Marxian theory." You speak of critical theory as if it *is* and *moves: "it elaborates* concepts," *"it continues to insist* that the need for qualitative change" is great, dialectical logic *"insists* that slaves must be free *for* their liberation."

As you move to higher and higher levels of generality the ties with our experience slacken, then loosen. I don't experience "particular interests" but rather very definite forms of oppression. Terms like "domination" and "repression" and "pacification of existence" and "intellectual and material capabilities" are so broad as to be almost emptied of concrete content. How many people read you without understanding, developing only a vague sense of what is wrong! How many well read, thoughtful intellectuals can present the main arguments of *One-Dimensional Man* or *Reason and Revolution?*

Their own fault, you'll say. I disagree. Such formulations neither focus on and illuminate our own experience nor point toward the concrete social experience needed to grasp their meaning.

The passage to which I referred seems so heavy, so dead-serious. Portraying a locked-in social reality, it itself has a locked-in feel. It wholly lacks humor. Gone is Marx's ability to poke fun, to play. The best phrases are grimly ironic: "We submit to the peaceful production of waste, to being educated for a defense which deforms the defenders and that which they defend." Opposites are brought together, but without the satisfaction a Marx shows at having caught the bourgeoise with its pants down, without the biting edge, the passion to expose one finds so often in Lenin, say, or Trotsky. Feeling, yes, but as the play and pleasure are gone, so is the passionate anger. "The game is up," the passage—and its sad depressed tone—seem to say. Opposites are joined, locked-in together. *They* are everywhere: "Don't wait to be hunted to hide." The dialectic is drawn into a circle, from which there is no way out, as everything turns into its opposite. You promote a certain sad style of thought, which many in and out of the movement have imbibed; "Protest only strengthens the established order by showing protest to be possible." Why do so many who read you say this?

Your writing leaves our experience: here is the source of what is exciting in it *and* what is stifling. I think I can make this clearer by a bit of speculation about the historical function of your writing, the experience from which it springs, and how it differs from ours.

Why leave experience? Appeals to the Germanic spirit, the influence of Hegel, the academic environment, are so much nonsense. Look at the character of that experience—yours, the experience of disaster in the West in the fifty years between the beginning of World War I and the mid-sixties. Everyone knows the facts. Workers supported and sacrificed themselves in wars so evidently against their own real interest. Socialist revolutions failed. As the Soviet Union developed, socialism's promise of liberation withered. Then came fascism, wiping out radical opposition and then all opposition, and fascism seemed so evidently popular—war, barbarism, genocide, and all. It is depressing enough for me to think about—what must it have been like to live through it as a partisan of a losing cause, as a potential victim?

And for a moment, the enormous cloud drawn over the West seemed to lift: the war was over, fascism dead. But the chance for revolution in France and Italy passed. American democratic capitalism became the most complete and effective form of totalitarianism. Opposition caved in, the Cold War began. Soon monopoly capitalism extended itself everywhere—around the world, into people's hopes and fears, wants and needs. The complete and systematic triumph of the principle of historical materialism: thought, imagination, feeling, desire became wholly absorbed by the society, accepted it and sang its praises. People actually want the aggressive, guilt-ridden, thing-obsessed American way of life! All of this done "the American way"—without agencies of control, while preserving the feeling of freedom, civil liberties, the right to vote.

What then came out of this half-century of catastrophe? The end of opposition, the onset of a new form of totalitarianism. It seems as if you saw the world close.

How did you respond to these events—how might any revolutionary intellectual? First, by retreating to thought, where the *ideas* of change, of liberation, of socialism can be preserved intact to await and hope for the reopening of opposition. The socialist movement, the chance for liberation seemed temporarily to collapse in the thirties: the theoretical idea of liberation had to be validated and kept alive. But as western totalitarianism spread—as American capitalism came to exploit and organize every conceivable area, and as alternatives and even criticism became linked with the communist Enemy—your refuge, the realm of ideas itself became attacked. Not only the *idea* of socialism or liberation, but the validity of *any idea* which points beyond our immediate experience. Socialism itself was no longer the issue. The issue was the mind's very ability to *think* about socialism. Your response? Meta-theory, the need to validate theory's right to exist, the need to attack a self-enclosed, self-validating ideology on every plane of experience. Thus the strange-sounding formulation I quoted earlier from "Repressive Tolerance": that the intellectual must "recall" and "preserve" possibilities, that he must reopen "the mental space" in which we can recognize this society. A last-ditch defense in the face of overwhelming odds: preserve the force of the Hegelian dialectic, preserve negative thinking, preserve the vigorous depth-character of Freudian theory, preserve the image of liberation, preserve the second dimension, thought itself, preserve the original impulses of Marxian theory in the face of Soviet distortions.

No wonder your writings seem so heavy: was it still possible to feel confidence, and thus lightness and wit, as opposition to capitalism dried up and seemed impossible? No wonder you convey a sense of *Them* closing in everywhere, of paranoia and futility: all the unbelievably bloody battles of the last fifty years seemed only to strengthen capitalism and deepened its terrifying and apparently unbreakable hold over people. No wonder you seem to take no delight in exposing the system and its Masters: Marx could rightly feel he was making fresh revelations which couldn't help but lead to social change, while today the facts are self-evident but everywhere denied by a mystified people. No wonder you seem obsessed with culture, ideology, consciousness: what is this brave new world all about if not the massive falsification of people's experience, their seeing an oppressive world as free?

And no wonder your writings sound so remote, so abstract: if experience seems just fine, if it thus becomes self-justifying, we must lift thought far above it in order to be able to criticize. If a totalitarian world is depicted in our locked-in and uncritical thought, an authentic language must appear unfamiliar and brittle. If everywhere around us the world is falsely known and falsely comfortable and self-validating, we must be made to feel uncomfortable, to see words as strange and suggestive of undreamed-of possibilities.

Marx hardly needed to be remote. Critical thought could merely follow and present experience—in a clear and comprehended form. This is what Marx does in his histories, this is what he does in *Capital*. Nineteenth-century capitalism provided its own, its internal and universally agreed-upon standards for criticizing it: equality, freedom, property, self-interest. Marxism could be an immanent critique—a critique of experience in terms of its own claims—because it merely traces the inner development of the facts and shows how capitalism denies every one of its basic claims. Criticism can immerse itself in social experience when that experience contradicts and thus criticizes itself. And this happened most clearly when a movement developed whose own life was the most thorough indictment of the society, a life in which all the bourgeois promises were denied.

But this has changed—one of the key themes of your writings. Experience has ceased to be critical of itself. Which means that by and large the society fulfills its promises, meets its claims. The American way of life: a constantly increasing standard of living for almost everyone without giving up our abstract and formal freedoms. As it "delivers the goods" to a people who want only the goods and more of them, advanced capitalism minimizes the distance between people's needs and satisfactions. On the political and social scale this means that the working class has come to accept and defend capitalism. Judged by its own standards the society appears to be just fine, although it has some problems left. It is this situation, you argue, which makes an immanent critique impossible. When only colonial outsiders or the black minority stand as the living negation of American capitalism, where can we go to get our standards for judging it? Close description of the facts is no longer root criticism: it is mostly affirmative. What is our basis for criticism if few people really mind waste or a war policy, if productivity is the social goal, if the good life is directly experienced as what the society puts out?

Critical thought must leave experience if experience ceases to be self-critical, self-contradictory. Standards must be found outside the society's own. We must move, as you say, into abstract, speculative thought: "from the critique of political economy to philosophy." Radical criticism no longer stands with a class inside the system—it takes place from outside: a transcendent critique. Critical theory must divorce itself from experience, become remote from it, provide experience with standards, justify those standards. Thus the other-worldly tone, thus my feeling that your analysis is external. And thus your need to return to the remotest regions of speculative thought in order to reshape the very tools and concepts of criticism. Thought must restore the critical distance lost in daily experience. Remote, yes—but for a life and death reason.

Still, I have criticized your writing! How can I do that and yet pay such warm tribute to it?

When I criticize you for leaving experience, I am implying that critical thought can do otherwise today. Not that you were wrong to do it as you did, but that we are wrong to follow you. We are in a different historical situation: our writings respond to a different experience, have different demands built into them, must be different in form and content. It is wholly different to be born into and raised in a totalitarian society than it is to see and struggle against it coming into being. It is a wholly different experience to be raised in a society without opposition than it is to be part of an opposition on the verge of winning the greatest victory of history, to see it lose, and then to watch it collapse entirely.

What is the difference? Just as you start from the most general level, so I would like to reverse that and start from the most specific. Just as you write meta-theory in the language of Hegel and high culture, so I would like to reverse that and speak of my own experience in the language of that experience. I'm fully aware of the theoretical implications of this effort: living in a totalitarian culture, can I grasp my experience from inside? Beginning with my experience can I understand America?

The key fact about growing up in postwar America was my need to reject America. I needed to break, to say and act No, to leave. Why?

Somehow I had gotten on this machine in motion, had become the machine, acting on behalf of some enormous power I couldn't even begin to fathom. To follow out its and my momentum led to the "good life" whose every detail I already knew in some instinctive way: professional work, marrying, the struggling young couple getting set up, vacation trips, a wonderful child, a small house at first, then living better, making more money. My own steps led naturally into the full-fledged American way of life, a life in which I could look good for other people and smile Hello and buy and "live better and better." Phyllis and I called it "the whole bit." Somewhere inside I knew what attitudes and feelings were required for entry into this good life: despair, boredom, the relentless drive to keep moving, being "realistic" by putting society's demands first and my own second, giving up on happiness, lying about pain.

And a layer deeper inside, I know now, was the emotional basis for all this: feeling inferior. Or better, hating myself. What does this psychological fact have to do with the social facts I'm talking about? Everything. Hating myself meant hating all those feelings, needs, reactions which were most truly mine, which were not socially approved in advance: such as weakness, fear, hurt, anger, sexuality, dependency, loving and needing to be loved. But such impulses were *mine,* and being taught to hate them from childhood meant disowning all these dimensions of myself, pretending to myself that they didn't exist, pushing them back. Pushing myself back. And into this vacuum, created ultimately by America I know now, there grew a new self, also created ultimately by America.

I recall how I struck on performance as the way to get falsely what I needed really. Already unhappy, I had learned to get attention by being a bad boy in school and at home—getting into trouble, destroying things, shouting and disrupting, until an ingenious fifth-grade teacher put me in what she called "isolation," separating me from the other boys and girls and depriving me of attention for my misdeeds. She left me without anything to do but get high marks, and so I did. A good student, I stopped being a rowdy: the transformation was complete. The unhappy, angry boy turned himself into a pleasant, courteous performer.

Thus escaping from my real needs and feelings I developed a relentless drive to keep in motion—in order to keep my now-hateful self from catching up with me. Denying myself, I ceased to transfer my center of gravity, my locus of self-definition onto the world outside. And this self-denial meant accepting inferiority as my basic state. Hating my own

268

impulses, I became ready to accept the substitute impulses offered by parents and teachers—all the conscious and unconscious *shoulds*. Frowning at myself and mistrusting my every impulse, I developed a frantic drive to win smiles from other people, the authorities. Since *I* clearly didn't know who I was and what I wanted, *They* would have to tell me. And of course they had been telling me from earliest childhood, so much so that by the time I finished college I had already drawn them into me. I was already "realistic" in that deepest sense. An all-A student, a nice guy, someone who hated to make scenes: I was well-prepared to accept the American way of life, based on striving, others' approval, and acquiring outside things. What America offered expressed and compensated for my misery.

But in a moment of revelation, after talking with a salesman who had once wanted to be an actor but said "well, you just can't live your dreams," I said, "I'll do what *I* want." That was so vague—who knew what *I* wanted? But the "whole bit" was so suffocating, so known in advance.

Could I accept part of it, only what I had to—job, or living in a dreary neighborhood or buying a new car—and avoid the rest? No, no, no: it *felt* like a whole. *A way of life* was given, not separate materials out of which *I* would build *my* life. Either I had to stay on the machine and live that life or jump off altogether.

So we jumped off the machine, stopped the part of ourselves that wanted it. We had to get away and make a life of our own. *Our own—* that is what was suffocated—our own ideas, our own pace, our own love, our own clothes, our own talk, our own sex, our own pain, our own joy.

Could we travel into different parts of America and find the ground where it would grow? But outside of the natural scenery, everywhere in America seemed so much the same—how people look, what they think, what they want and hate, what they do. So we searched out a remote backwater where things were not yet so modern. Teaching in a country schoolhouse, we lived one of our dreams, going off, living our own life, escaping, turning toward the past—old, good ways, humane habits, authentic people. As I drove the school bus over the hills and along the river to the two-room schoolhouse, our students talked about last night's television programs. Still, there was a real country life. Part of it excluded all transients: the natives rarely befriended the schoolteachers, outsiders from the city. But we too could live among trees and hills, with

269

a sense of nature, time, and space, could take slow walks. But how long were we willing to be lonely? It slowly dawned that the America which threatened to suffocate us was also the only real world. It drew us. Even hating it we could hardly live our whole life outside of it and still feel real. And even if we could, the guilt and self-hatred brought tension into the relaxed walks by the river. I wanted to perform, to look good, to make a name. I couldn't simply sit around enjoying myself. Even here I felt driven. How to get free of America inside myself?

First of all I stopped looking outside me, stopped traveling. As I searched around, I carried inside me all the proper attitudes for becoming an envied success, a responsible provider, a mindless vacationer. I was a living performance principle. I was never satisfied, always striving. How could I get away from it? Only by changing myself.

My personality and the American way of life fit into each other so easily, as if by design. To get free of America outside me I had first to get free of America inside me. How to stop performing? Break the self-hatred, the guilt, the obsession with goals, the need for things, the drive to keep moving, the urge to look good. Psychotherapy, yes. Learning to feel good about myself, to accept and live my desires and reactions and impulses. And in the process I discovered that my hated self was not my fault but finally the society's, that this isolated unique individual was really a deeply social and historical being. And that breaking free to live humanely now meant attacking the America which had made me fit only to live inhumanly.

What a leap I just took! An account of a life-search which doesn't once mention politics, and suddenly I proclaim the necessity for revolution. Why? The strictly personal revelation hints: it contains the structure of experience of this peculiar totalitarian society.

One way of life and only one. *The* good life, set out ahead. No other legitimate choices? It seems not: the only other major patterns seemed to be leftovers from the past. I don't want to spell out the evils of a life turning around television, getting ahead, the suburbs, "fine how are you," and shopping centers—liberals can do that well enough. What suffocated was that there was only *one* life to move into—a single, coherent way of life, defined in virtually all of its actions, attitudes, and gestures. Not open-ended but closed, not subject to *my* activity but ready-made, not waiting to be shaped *by* me but given *to* me, not springing from my spontaneity or rational deliberation but imposing itself,

270

inside me and out, not growing from my needs but already there, deciding what they would be. The American way of life: set up, ready and waiting, and we merely need to be realistic to slip into "the whole bit." If we begin by hating ourselves—by feeling guilty, driven, inferior, obsessed with approval—then it is easy to live the system's life as our own. We are already outside ourselves, already eager for a life to be given to us, already respectful of authorities, already relentless toward ourselves, already eager to gain a sense of power by acquiring things.

I came to see that the search for myself was really a struggle to break free from these needs. But recovering the original and hated needs was per se a battle with the society. Dropping into myself meant being angry, making scenes, being peculiar, asking Why, saying No, fighting. I could only change myself while identifying those forces outside which had originally distorted my needs and now stood against my satisfying them. Changing myself *and* becoming political. Liberation *and* revolution.

The only adequate response to being raised in a one-dimensional society is to demand liberation. I felt totally trapped by America—nothing I could have or be seemed to be free from it, to be mine. To have anything at all of my own, to break free in any one place, meant that I had to break free *everywhere*. Because I was trying to overcome a whole way of life imposed inside and out and not merely a few objectionable demands on me, it seemed as if I had to answer by developing a whole way of life of my own, a "new sensibility."

You ask intellectuals to "preserve historical possibilities" which seem to have vanished today, to keep "open the mental space" in which we can see this society for what it is—but these tasks make no sense to me. You were able to begin with a clear and legitimate identity, a sense of being in opposition, a whole set of values, a strong sense of being part of a tradition. That was what it must have meant to be brought up in a two-dimensional society. On the basis of a secure and clear identity you could take refuge in theory when Nazism took power, you could "recall" the image of liberation as the American way of life became total. In a strict sense you were preserving ideas recalling what had once been your own life-possibilities.

In that same strict sense I have nothing to preserve. When times get tough I can hardly fall back on the secure corner of my identity where opposition and real freedom are still possible. What identity? That has had to be built, by a tremendous act of will, of creativity and resistance.

271

America imposed its life on me by separating me from myself, by making my thinking dominate my desires, by keeping my values away from my actions, by giving me roles to live, by making me hate myself and accept what satisfactions I could get. This is what being "realistic" is all about—saying goodbye to much of ourselves, squeezing the rest into the channels offered. Refusing all separation was one of the main ways of locating myself—demanding that values be lived, that thinking not oppose feeling, rejecting roles as traps, refusing to accept any less than being myself in a total, complete way. Not *preserve* the wish for liberation, but *live* it, not keep open *mental* space, but *breathing* and *feeling* and *acting* space for opposition. You retreated, and I think necessarily; living and responding today I have to take the offensive merely to survive. To be myself I must demand everything.

Why isn't your path, retreat into radical thought, enough for me? In my life it is not capitalist values or elitist values which are oppressive, but *values* as such: ideals, separated from my actions, which mock my life. Not bourgeois abstract thought is intolerable, but abstract thought as such: a thought which rejects and withdraws from my experience. Why isn't it enough to be politically radical and leave the rest of my life intact? Because then everything remains the same, locked into America, except that my ideas are radical, and I make my part-time political statements and acts at meetings with radicals. Only the sense of a new way of life will do, being radical in working, in loving, in thinking, in feeling, in eating, in joking. Being radical: being myself. Anything which separates me from myself oppresses, whether it comes from America or its left-wing opposition. Not only bourgeois morality oppresses, but any morality which imposes oughts from outside. Not only the bourgeois contempt for ignorance, but the radical reliance on a higher culture. Not only the bourgeois domination of feeling by reason, but the radical insistence on the priority of theory, the correct position. Not only middle-class role-playing is oppressive, but accepting any kind of role, even the role of radical intellectual. I have become a revolutionary because America, while willing to sell me everything, won't let me be myself. Should I give up any part of myself in order to oppose America?

In saying this, I'm only taking seriously your demand, in *An Essay on Liberation,* for "a political practice which reaches the roots of containment and contentment in the infrastructure of man, a political practice of methodical disengagement from and refusal of the Establishment,

aiming at a radical transvaluation of values." "Such a practice," you
go on to say, "involves a break with the familiar, the routine ways of
seeing, hearing, feeling, understanding things so that the organism may
become receptive to the potential forms of a nonaggressive, nonexploita-
tive world." [3] It's not my politics that are at stake, or my ideas. My whole
being is at stake. My experience is of being lost in the smiling sick sea
and of needing to wrench myself out step by step; my goal is to avoid
and destroy all of *Their* categories in my life, to live joyously, to reject
bullshit in all its disguises, to let America have none of myself, to get
whole, and to become a guerrilla.

You see, I have been sketching an immanent critique of America.
It is possible to confront the promise with the reality which denies that
promise. Theory need not take up a position outside. Trying to spring
loose from within, I am criticizing America from within. Like Marxism?
Yes and no. Marxism was certainly a theoretical description of the experience of capitalism, of the sources of that experience. Yet it rested
on visible, universally acknowledged conditions: hunger amidst plenty,
business cycles, etc. These were facts whose force was not dependent on
the individual worker's willingness to see them. The only questions were
whether and how to struggle. But to say I feel choked, I can't be myself
because American capitalism has created a totalitarian society and has
wedged me into it, is sharply different than saying I'm hungry because
of wage labor. Anyone can deny the first statement, can say, "I'm not
choked, I'm myself, what is all the fuss about?" Proof is impossible,
and I can hardly point to visible facts. Can I convince anyone that he's
not himself? The point is that millions upon millions of personal commitments are needed to keep the system going: to accept the American
way of life, to give up locating oneself, to accept living in bits and pieces,
and to lie about it. If your survival needs are met well and you can keep
busy, self-deception is possible in a way that it's not if you're hungry.
America keeps going as everyone draws a veil over his own life. If so,
to show the truth is no longer merely to locate the structures behind what
everyone admits to be a problem, but rather to tear away the veil.

Yet the veils don't hide only the system—they hide each and every
one of us from ourselves. And each of us distorts his experience in a
different way, according to his own particular situation. Because of this

[3] *An Essay on Liberation* (Boston: Beacon Press, 1969), p. 6.

peculiar historical situation a critique of America which tries to get inside the key place where it affects us must first be personal. It must begin as a series of attempts to reveal the different kinds of experience possible in America. The opposite of remoteness: talking about ourselves. And since tearing away the veil is hardly a matter of convincing people's intellects, revolutionary thought must engage the whole person: his feeling, his imagination, his sense of being lost. Not only tracing the structure of capitalism, but also blowing people's minds. Disrupting, shattering, springing people loose: we need to be personal, poetic, disturbing. To make people want liberation.

Liberation. Unlike *socialism, freedom,* and *happiness,* this term still belongs to us. It means something so deep and total that even American capitalism hasn't yet promised it. *Eros and Civilization* shows how deep and total. What I found there—the most profound and stirring message coming from any book during the years of recovering myself—is that a world is possible in which we can be happy. That my deepest, most forlorn needs can become the organizing principle of a free society.

What would a movement for liberation look like? This you know well, Herbert. Its tone would be one of joy. Affirming, celebrating life, imaginative, playful. It would refuse to become serious, to become heavy, to become abstract. Angry, yes, and determined to overthrow American capitalism, yes, but *equally* determined to develop a new way of life in the process. Spending as much time looking inward as looking out, as much time locating and breaking free of hang-ups as in locating and attacking the enemy. Hang-ups: people would be encouraged to know where they are, to grow, to get strong. To become themselves. Organizational structures would open toward every member's fullest growth. Therapy? Necessarily: attacking America and freeing ourselves from it would be seen as the same goal. Growth and depth would become criteria of political success, not numbers of people involved. Ordinary lines between what is political and what is not would break down. External structures, the need to be led, centralization, ideologies developed from the top would be fought: instead there would develop loose organizations, each determining its own needs, each analyzing its own experience, each refusing outside direction. Any attempt to impose an ideological line or to develop the cult of leaders would be fought: the pain and needs and liberation of each person would be the focal point. It would be made clear that everyone has experienced America all his or her life, that each of us has already developed the most fundamental knowledge, that turning inward to get clear on our experience is the most certain way to know. Such a movement's actions would be free-wheeling and imaginative. It would appeal mainly to people's sense of life against their death-impulses, their sense of freedom against their shame, their feeling of pain against their protective intellects, their need to be themselves against their respect for authority. It would understand the total hold America has over its people and formulate actions designed to break people loose, blow their minds. It would give up the desperate attempts to find the "agent" of revolution and encourage people to work wherever they feel best, and to get strong there, and to live their impulse for liberation.

Is this our movement, is this the New Left? What do you think? These demands haven't just sprung out of my head. At its best the American and European New Left has or has had most of these traits. But only at its best, here and there, and—especially in America—in lesser and lesser degrees. The French students might say "All power to the Imagination," but the American movement seems to be losing most of the imagination it had. Take the Students for a Democratic Society. I began by analyzing the language of the opening paragraphs of *One-Dimensional Man.* I'll close by doing the same with the 1969 statement of the SDS national convention, expelling members of the Progressive Labor Party, reproduced here in full:

THE PRINCIPLES UPON WHICH PL WAS EXPELLED, ADOPTED BY THE NATIONAL CONVENTION

1. We support the struggles of the black and Latin colonies within the U.S. for national liberation, and we recognize those nations' rights to self-determination (including the right to political secession, if they desire it).

2. We support the struggle for national liberation of the people of South Vietnam, led by the National Liberation Front and the South Vietnamese Provisional Revolutionary Government. We also support the Democratic Republic of Vietnam, led by President Ho Chi Minh, as well as the Democratic Republic of China, the People's Republics of Korea and Albania, and the Republic of Cuba, all waging fierce struggles against U.S. imperialism. We support the right of all peoples to pick up the gun to free themselves from the brutal rule of U.S. imperialism.

The Progressive Labor Party has attacked every revolutionary nationalist struggle of the black and Latin peoples in the U.S. as being racist and reactionary. For example, they have attacked open admission, black studies, community control of police and schools, the Black Panther Party and their "breakfast for children" program, and the League of Revolutionary Black Workers.

The Progressive Labor Party has attacked Ho Chi Minh, the National Liberation Front of South Vietnam, the revolutionary government of Cuba—all leaders of the people's struggles for freedom against U.S. imperialism.

The Progressive Labor Party, because of its positions and practices, is objectively racist, anti-communist, and reactionary. PLP has also in principle and practice refused to join the struggle against male supremacy. It has no place in SDS, an organization of revolutionary youth.

For these reasons, which have manifested themselves in practice all over the country, as well as at this convention, and because the groups we look to around the world for leadership in the fight against U.S. imperialism, including the Black Panther Party and the Brown Berets, urge us to do so, SDS feels it is now necessary to rid ourselves of the burden of allowing the politics of the Progressive Labor Party to exist within our organization. Progressive Labor Party members and all people who do not accept the above two principles are no longer members of SDS.[4]

Look at the tone of this statement. How dead! It speaks the frozen language of the bureaucratic left: "We support the struggles," and "waging fierce battles against U.S. imperialism," and "the brutal rule of U.S. imperialism," and "the people's struggles for freedom against U.S. imperialism," and Progressive Labor "is objectively racist, anti-communist, and reactionary." Does this sound like the New Left, like a movement for liberation, like a new sensibility? The language is heavy, ritualized, dull, abstract. Does this sound like a movement growing from the inside out, based on people's needs, capable of direct and honest statement? The statement is tough, deliberately external, evasive; it explains nothing about why the expulsion or how SDS people *feel* about P.L.

P.L. is "objectively racist, anti-communist, and reactionary"—the line has been laid down, and it is a line saying nothing, absolutely

[4] *New Left Notes* (Revolutionary Youth Movement Faction of SDS), June 25, 1969.

276

nothing about the experience of SDS members, their goals, their needs, their reactions. Truth is found outside *us*—"objectively"—and presented in flat and doctrinaire decrees. Objectively!

External, then, in a double sense: what determines the internal politics of SDS? The most ominous note is added almost as an afterthought, that "the groups we look to around the world for leadership in the fight against U.S. imperialism including the Black Panther Party [and] Brown Berets urge us" to expel P.L. This and constant invocation of "U.S. imperialism" indicates what is happening: SDS's major fight is to free the Third World and internal colonies from America. It is not our fight we are fighting, but *theirs*—and only then, and indirectly, is it ours. *They* determine what we do.

No wonder the prose is so heavy and external—the movement is in the process of becoming joyless and external. And in the process it sets up two ideological tenets which we must accept in order to have a "place in SDS, an organization of revolutionary youth." In the process, what has become of liberation, *our* liberation? Where are the original traits of the movement—the humor, the anarchism, the lightness, the openness, its direct person-to-person quality? Are these men and women who, in your words, "have the good conscience of being human, tender, sensuous, who are no longer ashamed of themselves . . ."? [5]

Instead we see America turned inside out, a would-be revolutionary party reproducing some of the worst features of the society it wants to overthrow. In this statement it is not SDS, but those who rule America who have the last laugh. Socialist scholars talk this way, most other groups talk this way, non-affiliated radicals talk this way. SDS merely presents the attitudes in their sharpest form.

My attempts to explain why your writings share some of these traits won't do for the New Left, for SDS was part of my world, the generation raised up by totalitarian America. Why should those whom I would expect to find the "new sensibility" mirror the old sensibility? One of your main themes, which is one of the backbones of everything I say in this letter, is that traditional notions of politics no longer hold, that political liberation cannot be separated from personal liberation—developing new needs, new reactions. I have come to speak of those new needs as *my* needs, to say that I locate them by learning to experience myself.

[5] *An Essay on Liberation,* p. 21.

But this is the opposite of the manly toughness the SDS statement asserts: being open to yourself, stopping to feel, rejecting aggression, being willing to feel fear and danger, being sensitive to your weaknesses, being vulnerable. Politics, on the other hand, has always been the very home of the external—politics traditionally defined. It is a trap: politics must be redefined. The French students are doing this. Cohn-Bendit's book and actions breathe the spirit of liberation. The American New Left began to do this but it seems in the process of undoing its original impulses.

Why? I think it's because of fear, fear which leads people to become external. Notice—an explanation which is not at all a part of "political analysis." Are the politicos afraid? Yes, I think, in the strangest way. Not afraid of clubbed heads or jail or losing jobs, or not being respectable. America has taught us to be terrified of all this, and the movement has broken that terror, has won out over it. But America has also taught us to be terrified of ourselves. Being external, not being ourselves, refusing to be whole: this is supposed to be strength. From being outside ourselves in America to being outside ourselves in the movement. If we accept this way of defining ourselves America wins; America wins and liberation is a sad joke. The early New Left had its finger on something more vital. But it failed to follow through its anarchism and rejection of ideology and demand for a new life. Instead of deepening its demands it abandoned them. Instead of completing its break with America it returned. "A liberal wants to free others; a radical wants to free himself." Whatever became of this New Left slogan? To carry it out would have meant something far more painful, more threatening than all the Chicagos put together.

Which is better, a movement appealing to our built-in sense of guilt and self-sacrifice, and thus easy to become part of—or a movement which threatens our whole identity by asking a commitment to joy? Which is better, a movement which accepts us as is, and then "naturally" develops elitist, hierarchical, manipulative, centralized leadership—or a movement which demands that we grow, search ourselves, make decisions, become responsible? Which is better, a large and centrally organized mass of people committed to the ideas of socialism and democracy —or a loose and chaotic movement, small and building slowly, basing itself in our guts, giving us the room to get ourselves together?

To me the answers are obvious. A movement for liberation must be above all people who are not afraid to drop into themselves, who are learning to be whole. Yes, a total break with America, a total commitment to change.

Your role in this process has been an ambiguous one. You bring the message of liberation, but another, older message as well. One can draw from you a justification for elitism, vanguardism, contempt for those we claim to want to liberate. Radicals reading you have drawn encouragement for their remoteness from real needs and fears, abstract intellectualism, being external, putting theory ahead of reality, and their insistence on the "objective" historical meaning of people's acts. After all, of all your writings, *One-Dimensional Man* and "Repressive Tolerance" are said to be the most widely read among activists. In helping us to get clear about our situation, they maintain the influence over us of some of our worst patterns of thought and feeling and action. But there is also the message of *Eros and Civilization* and *An Essay on Liberation*. To take the idea of liberation seriously means criticizing the other side of Marcuse and its influence. It means letting go of thought and politics as we know them and turning inward to face what we find there. Yes, you've given us tools and ideas for that, for becoming new men and women.

Is it too late in the day to ask this of the New Left? Has America's resistance to change and resort to repression made my demand foolish? After all, Herbert, if I've explained your limitations by the historical situation, mustn't I do the same with the movement? Does it harden as America hardens?

Nonsense. The historical situation makes demands and sets limits, but it certainly doesn't decide how people must respond. You, for example, managed to keep alive a sense of opposition and liberation at the worst times, so that you have vital things to say to us today. The New Left too can rise to the full height permitted and demanded by our historical situation. Growing out of totalitarian America it can be a movement for liberation. After all, something new and profound is happening in America. Children seem to be growing up freer, more whole, less cowed than I was: a spontaneous coming together in reaction to all the oppressive forces I've discussed. Nourished by new currents, oppressed in new ways, the movement need not merely reinstate doctrinaire and external radical politics. Will it break into the open? The French revolution was tremendously encouraging. The Women's Liberation movement seems to be growing. And much of the original liberating impulse remains in local movement groups. Time will tell. Am I forced to end with a characteristic Marcusean question mark?

Well, Herbert, enough of trying to come to grips with you and your influence. No point in recapitulating—or rather, it would probably be impossible. After all, you've been a truly great teacher. You've done all that any teacher worth the name can do: I use the tools you have helped me to acquire in order to place myself in history and explain my differences with you; your message has taken hold so deeply that I use it to criticize even you. You've helped me, that is, to become myself.

Life,
Ron

15

PAUL BREINES

Marcuse and the
New Left

Paul Breines is a graduate student in history at the University of Wisconsin and lives in Cambridge, Massachusetts. He edited *Critical Interruptions, New Left Perspectives on Herbert Marcuse,* and is an associate of *Radical America* and *Telos.*

Critiques and commentaries on Herbert Marcuse abound and they abound because his works have been associated with the global student-youth revolt as have those of no other contemporary Western theorist. The sociology of this conjuncture of theory and practice—and in particular of the spectacular publicity, celebration, and deformation that has accompanied it—is only emerging. But several things are already clear. First, it is evident that "the student movements which he [Marcuse] neither predicted nor inspired, but which, through their primarily cultural and moral demands (secondarily, and in certain countries, economic demands), found in his works and ultimately *in his works alone* the theoretical formulation of their problems and aspirations." [1] Second, there is the apparently mystical dimension to the situation: "it is obvious that most students who cite or proclaim Marcuse ignore the bulk o. . is writings and thought." Whether, on this question, it is sufficient to say that "they are right in doing so [for] social life has its own logic and everywhere possesses means of disseminating thought other than direct reading and the mass media," is open to question, but this cannot be

[1] Lucien Goldmann, "La Pensée de Herbert Marcuse," *La Nef,* No. 36, January–March, 1969, 56. Emphasis in original.

taken up in detail here.[2] Third, given the uniquely pervasive character of his impact, it is nevertheless true that "anyone who considers Marcuse the theorist of the Movement understands neither Marcuse nor the Movement." Yet at the same time it does not follow that Marcuse was "tacked onto the Movement" by the media and the myth-gurus, even though the Madison Avenue-Baroque extremes to which the guru-mythology has been carried often gives this impression.[3]

Rather, and fourth, the extent to which Marcuse has been made into a publicity stunt is a reflection that *both* his work and the Movement are subject to the processes of commodification, reification, and "one-dimensionalization" which they revolted against in the first place. This development exemplifies the political-technological phenomenon noted some thirty years ago by Marcuse's friend, Walter Benjamin: "the bourgeois publication and production apparatus can assimilate and even publicize an astonishing number of revolutionary themes without thereby throwing into question either its own basis or the basis of the class that controls it." [4] The virtually boundless character of this assimilative capacity today is well enough known and need not be summarized in any detail. It is well known not only through Marcuse's own critique of it but, as suggested above, through the subsumption of his critique in it. Thus an ad such as "Don't be a One-Dimensional Man, Spray on Lotion-X" hardly seems particularly far out, since in essence it has already appeared on the scene. Developments such as this occur, partly because in advanced industrial society everyone is reduced to the mode of spectator at the show of his own alienated activity. The appearance of the "Marcuse spectacle" is, then, an issue worthy of analysis in itself: it would open up critical study of the dialectics of cultural revolution and forces one to ask the extent to which the assimilation and integration of Marcuse—as well as of the New Left, the Hippies, youth culture—by the ruling apparatus may be part of the emerging disintegration of the apparatus.

Useful as this might be, this essay will have a different though related focus, one made necessary by recent and fundamental shifts in the New Left Movement itself and therefore in the relationship between

[2] *Ibid,* footnote.

[3] René Viénet, *Enragés et Situationistes dans le mouvement des occupations* (Paris: Gallimard, 1968), 153.

[4] Walter Benjamin, *Versuche über Brecht* (Frankfurt-Main: Suhrkamp, 1966), 105.

282

it and Marcuse's works. Specifically, among the New Left's supposedly more advanced, "political" sectors Marcuse's work is becoming an object of growing resentment, as it always has been for the traditional Marxist or Old Left. Two glimpses into what has been happening: during the mass upheaval in France in May 1968, the identity between many of his main theses and the revolutionary manifestoes and graffiti initiated a new wave of inane speculation on Marcuse as the prime mover of the *enragés*. But from amidst the hullabaloo came reports such as the following from a spokesman of one of the French Trotskyist organizations: at a mass meeting of students in early May a consensus was reached that "the student struggle could only be a part of the struggle for socialism; and the main social force in this struggle was the working class. No remarks of a Marcusean or similar type were listened to." [5] Since our own focus will be on developments in the United States, it is irrelevant whether this report is mere sectarian wish-think or whether it is accurate in the French context: it adequately characterizes the bulk of meetings, writings, and general thinking within the New Left here during the past two years or so. The second glimpse: the charges, levelled by the Progressive Labor Party, that Marcuse is a CIA agent, are not merely psychotic. Nor does the fact that the charges have not been vehemently repudiated by the Movement suggest that the New Left *en masse* believes them. Rather the charges are a psychotic spin-off from an emerging consensus around the idea that the supposedly metapolitical, post-political, utopian, personal liberation, anti-working class stage in the Movement's development—with Marcuse being taken as one of the main symbols of this stage—must be exorcised and surpassed.

This shift away from Marcuse is evident not only in the U.S. but is "Western-wide"; and *in principle* a shift which carried the Movement's pratical theory and conscious practice beyond both Marcuse and its own previous stages *could* be an unquestionable and vital advance. The whole point of Marcuse's work is that it be superseded on all levels, and numerous theorists within and close to the Movement have attempted to specify the lines which the practical and theoretical critique might follow.[6] While such analyses were appearing before the May 1968

[5] Pierre Frank, "From a Student Upheaval Towards a Proletarian Socialist Revolution," in Tariq Ali, ed., *The New Revolutionaries: A Handbook of the International Radical Left* (New York: Morrow, 1969), 180.
[6] See among others: Paul Mattick, "The Limits of Integration," in K. H. Wolff and B. Moore, eds., *The Critical Spirit: Essays in Honor of Herbert Marcuse*

explosion, it gave them additional impetus but also conveyed a rather infantile undertone of "See, Gran'pa, you were wrong, the working class *is* revolutionary, look out there in the streets!" One of the most provocative and serious of these "post-May" criticisms is Henri Lefebvre's and the following excerpt may be taken as a valuable statement of the challenge:

> If the movement of students and intellectuals enlarges a crevice, this means that the wall is cracking. And here we have an *action-crtique* of Marcuse's thesis [that Advanced Industrial Society is closed and impervious to revolutionary transformation], at least as far as France and Europe are concerned. Since it can also be shown in other connections that current social phenomena do not fit in Marcuse's concepts and categories, this indicates that his analysis is inadequate. Theoretical criticism—the formulation of practice—will be continued, but on different ground. The question of acting "subjects," and of objects and projects (of the real and the possible) will be posed in new terms. And should knowledge become able to give form to spontaneity, the acceptable aspect of Marcuse's work will have been determined and delineated: that is, *its utopian function* during a certain period.[7]

Lefebvre's qualifications are as important as his proposition itself; together they establish my premises here. First of all he is correct in restricting himself to France and Europe. Second, he emphasizes that the acceptable aspect of Marcuse's work (which in Lefebvre's view is the argument in *Eros and Civilization* regarding the eroticization of existence which could result from a break with the present linkage of libido to production and consumption and the restriction of desire to the genital and procreative functions, as well as Marcuse's insights into the linkage of politics and eros in the student-youth revolt) will be delineated *if and when* knowledge becomes capable of giving form to spontaneity. Third,

---

(Boston: Beacon, 1967), 347–400; Peter Sedgewick, "Natural Science and Human Theory," *The Socialist Register, 1966* (London: Merlin, 1966), 163–192; the essays in Jürgen Habermas, ed., *Antworten auf Herbert Marcuse* (Frankfurt-Main: Suhrkamp, 1968); Pier Aldo Rovatti, "Marcuse and the 'Crisis of the European Sciences,'" *Telos,* 1:2 (Fall, 1968), 113–115; Jeremy J. Shapiro, "One-Dimensionality: The Universal Semiotic of Technological Experience," in Breines (ed.), *Critical Interruptions* (New York: Herder and Herder, 1970).

[7] Henri Lefebvre, *The Explosion: Marxism and the French Upheaval* (New York and London: Monthly Review Press, 1969), 31. Emphasis in original.

the surpassing of the utopian function of Marcuse's work and the stage of the Movement in the United States to which it corresponded is today being widely announced and it is the extent to which this may be true that we want to examine. Finally, we agree with Lefebvre that the wall is cracking and that a key cause as well as effect of this situation is the revolt of students, youth, and intellectuals: this is what gives the discussion its meaning.

It should be made clear that the Movement, above all in this country, has never been a "Marcusean" movement, and it would be silly to insist that it should have been or should be, whatever that might mean. Aside from the fact that no social movement springs from the head of a theorist, the New Left in this country has been the proud progeny of the isolation and insulation from dialectical social theory which has historically defined American intellectuals in general and Left intellectuals in particular. The situation within the German Movement, for example, where " 'the Frankfurt School' [Max Horkheimer, Marcuse, T. W. Adorno, *et al.*] has been very useful to the young intellectuals . . . for a whole generation of socialist students it was one of the most important starting points," [8] hardly obtained here. But it is precisely within this built-in truncation that the structure of the links between Marcuse and the Movement here took shape: central among the new, liberatory needs generated by the student-youth revolt is the need for dialectical social theory.

Within this general structure Marcuse's thought has been a key component in the Movement's process of self-constitution and self-comprehension in more specific ways. Marcuse's analysis of "one-dimensional man" took hold within wide sections of the New Left because it corresponded to the *experience* of many in or entering the Movement: part of a generation began to perceive that it was living or was supposed to live a one-dimensional existence and could not tolerate it. Further, his analysis of the "new politics" established by advanced industrial society and the new type of opposition it necessitated went to the core of the New Left's situation and activity: the modern technics of production, consumption, administration, and destruction have issued in radically new modes of political-social domination, manipulation, and alienation (intricating the instinctual, sexual, cultural, and linguistic dimensions into society's self-reproductive process), and this requires

[8] Wolfgang Abendroth, in Theo Pinkus, ed., *Gespräche mit Georg Lukács* (Hamburg: Rowohlt, 1967), 80.

that, if possible at all, political-economic revolution must be preceded and shaped by a radical and collective *self*-transformation of men and women—their consciousness, language, values, instincts, desires, needs. And the existing society's incorporation of phantasy, the imagination, the aesthetic into its system of hegemony and the "fantastic" liberatory possibilities created and blocked by the prevailing form of modern technology, makes essential the re-incorporation of phantasy, imagination, and aesthetics into critical theory and practice. Traversing these arguments is a perspective which originated with the "young Marx" and which the "young Marcuse" adopted as the fundament of his conception of revolution: the abolition of private property in the means of production is the mere (and necessary) precondition of socialism and communism, whose *aim* is the liberation of men and society from subjugation to economic-political relationships as such.[9] This perspective has been implicitly and explicitly developed by Marcuse in all of his more recent works. And in these "Marcusean theses" the Movement glimpsed itself, its own self-consciousness.

Marcuse's analysis (particularly several of his revisions of classical Marxian theory) included the argument that the industrial working class has been integrated into the ruling system—as a beneficiary of its productivity and as an active consumer of its commodities and "commodity way of life"—and no longer embodies the "vital need for revolution," but has become part of society's conservative, popular base. It is probably accurate to say that until recently the New Left by and large accepted this argument (which is not Marcuse's alone) or did not particularly care about it, but either way moved ahead on the assumption that the Movement was working in what Marcuse termed the "society without opposition." Thus, simultaneously with the publication of *One-Dimensional Man* (1964), Marcuse found in the Movement both an emerging practical refutation of some of his claims regarding the closed, oppositionless character of the ruling society, and an emerging realization of some of the utopian "political-erotic" concepts formulated in *Eros and Civilization* (1955), and he began to direct his own energies increasingly toward the New Left. By 1966–67 the "spectacle" started to

---

[9] See especially Marcuse's review of the first publication in German of Marx's "Economic and Philosophical Manuscripts" of 1844, "Neue Quellen zur Grundlegung des historischen Materialismus," *Philosophie und Revolution, I: Aufsätze von Herbert Marcuse* (Berlin: Philosophie und Revolution, 1967), 40–142. The essay was originally published in the journal *Die Gesellschaft* in 1932.

erupt: an internationally publicized "return to Berlin" for a meeting with the Movement there, the mass of interviews, reviews, previews, and the rest. In the flurry, Marcuse's insistence that the New Left-student-youth revolt does not represent *the* revolutionary agency, but a catalyst, a "capability" of freedom, and that the present period is barely a pre-revolutionary one of "enlightenment," awakening, and struggle aimed at enlarging the scope of the subjective-instinctual break with the system —these claims, in the flurry, were obscured.

As stated earlier, the always complex, problematic, and truncated links between Marcuse's thought and the Movement are now in a state of rupture. And this particular transformation is important only as a sign and expression of larger changes in the Movement itself. There are, as it happens, far more vivid signs. At present the New Left appears to have utterly and decisively freaked out—and it may have. Normal and intense factional debate has not only suddenly been replaced by a blaring carnival of fetishized and mind-clogging rhetoric, but the rhetoric itself is "new." Actions and theories are now upheld or denounced in the name of Marxism-Leninism, proletarian internationalism, revolutionary discipline, the working class, the Black Panther Party, Chairman Mao, the National Liberation Front of Vietnam, the dictatorship of the proletariat, the seizure of state power, armed struggle, and, here and there, Stalin, Georgi Dimitrov, and the Peoples' Republic of Albania. At least momentarily, genuine *auto-critique* or critical self-reflection is scarce. For example, one faction announces that in the service of revolution there are no "adventurist" actions, and another labels the Democratic Republic of Vietnam "revisionist" and "counter-revolutionary" for participating in the Paris negotiations. Such positions are upheld by recitations of Lenin, Lin Piao, and Mao Tse-tung; in turn, they are denounced by other, apparently less crazed factions with other or often the same recitations from these masters. It is as if there were a self-propelling mechanism which brings everyone into the general reduction of *the entire terrain* of debate and consciousness to the level of retail sanity within wholesale madness. And there is such a mechanism.

Since its origins in the late 1950s the New Left has developed within a permanent and multiple crisis of self-definition and self-consciousness. The Movement has been precisely a movement: a process, a piercing-through the shells of advanced capitalism and traditional socialism, a not-yet and a to-be. It has been a project of discovering and inventing liberatory forms of expression, experience, organization, and

287

struggle in a system of technically prefabricated and administered life: sit-ins, building occupations, mass confrontations with authority, street fighting, disruptions, drugs, guerrilla theater, laughter, communes, and so forth, out of which solidarity, living human groups, and moments of disalienation were forged and lived within the dominant *dureé* of reification, fragmentation, and powerlessness. Beneath and within this project has been the drive toward the *coherence* of critical theory. And right now it appears that the severity of the need for coherence combined with the Movement's long-standing hostility to "theory" (and theorists) as a bad trip, identical to the asphyxiating fragments of non-thought and programmed incoherence met in classrooms and textbooks, is finally turning against the Movement itself. The increasingly pervasive pseudo-coherence of Marxism-Leninism, the factional bedlam, and the new cults of violence (or of workers) suggest that the continuing crisis of self-definition and consciousness has hit a point of *implosion and self-consumption.* Rapidly or gradually additional groups and individuals are pulled into the vortex. Meanwhile, a sense that the Movement is in the deepest trouble in its history is widespread; well-intended but entirely abstract appeals to unity, to an end to internecine warfare, abound. Yet as fundamental alternatives remain seemingly incoherent and fragile in comparison with the new "toughness" and the new ideologies, confusion and despair increase on the margins while the organized factions forge ahead confidently.

The shift from an eclectic and inadequate but relatively experimental and fluid "New Left-student-youth revolt" language to a progressively mechanical and self-ossifying Marxist and Leninist rhetoric is part of a new strategic intention: to transform the New Left-student revolt into (variously) a mass, anti-imperialist movement with working-class leadership; a white, revolutionary youth ally of the Black and Third World revolutionary movements; an anti-capitalist worker-student alliance. While the university and high schools may, in practice, remain the Movement's central arena, the intended focus is on factories and the streets. This shift and the increasingly brutal and systematic repression which much of the Movement as well as the Black Panthers are facing, have led to the adoption of the new rhetoric and the concepts of discipline, organization, and revolution to which it is connected. In addition, progressively apocalyptic notions of the imminence of fascism and/or revolution are both effects and contributing elements in the general hardening of lines. Thus, fairly abruptly the New Left is moving from a consciously decentralist movement with natural historical affinities to the anarchists and the anti-Leninist "workers' councils" tradition to one which begins to view the Leninist vanguard, cadre party as its organizational model. The dual assumption is that in the imperialist era this is *the* model of revolutionary organization, strategy, and theory, and that the era is characterized by one "primary contradiction" (between the industrial workers and capital, or between the Third World-non-white revolutionary movements and the American empire) and thus contains "a" revolutionary class or agent (the proletariat or the anti-imperialist revolts).

Meanwhile, the infrastructure of these developments is infused with masochism, self-flagellation, and often near schizophrenia on the part of the "bourgeois" student radical. This motif has always been constitutive of the life of bourgeois intellectuals in general and radical intellectuals in particular, as well as of the New Left. Historically it has been grounded in conscious or unconscious recognition that within the division of labor in capitalist society intellectuals are parasites on the body of the working class, and this recognition is not without its genuine and progressive aspects. Yet, in the present state of affairs, where the character and function of intellectuals, students, and "mind-workers" has been drastically transformed by the development of advanced capitalism, the adoption of factory-worker, Black Panther, or street-gang ego models is absurd. It is a false and alienated overcoming of one's own alienation as a "bourgeois" student, and a suppression of the most original fact about the New Left itself: that it is not the classical breakaway intellectual vanguard whose role is to serve the impoverished against the affluent but a revolt against capitalist affluence itself, a critique of capitalist abundance as an abundance of alienation. And by denying the legitimacy of the critique of the conditions of his own existence the student radical not only recapitulates his alienation (his "untrue" existence) at a new level, but simultaneously suppresses the peculiarly explosive total critique and demands that arise out of his own alienated life.

What is happening, in its basic configurations, is hardly new; Marx himself perceived the essential element long ago:

> The tradition of all the dead generations weighs like a nightmare on the brain of the living. And just when they [the radicals] seem engaged in revolutionizing themselves and things, in creating something that has never yet existed, precisely in such periods of

revolutionary crisis they anxiously conjure up the spirits of the past to their service and borrow from them names, battle cries, and costumes in order to present the new scene of world history in this time-honored disguise and this borrowed language. Thus Luther donned the mask of the Apostle Paul, the Revolution of 1789 to 1814 draped itself alternately as the Roman republic and the Roman empire, and the Revolution of 1848 knew nothing better to do than to parody, now 1789, now the revolutionary tradition of 1793 to 1795. In like manner a beginner who has learnt a new language always translates it back into his mother tongue, but he has assimilated the spirit of the new language and can freely express himself in it only when he finds his way in it without recalling the old and forgets his native tongue in the use of the new.[10]

Marx goes on to emphasize, and others have pointed out, that this process of conjuring up one's progenitors in struggle can serve as a medium of deepening and illuminating one's present situation and needs. But the dominant thrust of the American New Left's sudden and enthusiastic rediscovery of Marxism and Marxism-Leninism has in actuality been regressive and repressive in precisely the terms Marx states at the same time. The fact of the matter is that in "re-Marxifying" itself, the New Left is engaged in a suppression and flight from its own most basic impulses and implications, as well as from the new scene of world history in which it stands. What has permitted the weight of the "tradition of all the dead generations" to come down on the mind of the Movement as if it were a deliverance is that the weight of its own originality was too great to bear. The Movement's struggle to invent, create, and develop a new language, forms of organization, and a coherent critique of modern society is aborting itself in a "mother tongue" that was sclerosed and mechanical long ago; in organizational ideas that are repressive and authoritarian; and in a pseudo-coherence of abstract dogmas and myths. Concepts such as "working class" and "proletarian revolution," and "revolutionary party" become magical totems whose function is to act as mystical resolutions of real contradictions. Deflected and deformed expressions of radical and critical energy are contained in the revival of Marxism and Marxism-Leninism. The New Left is alienating itself into its own opposite.

This process of self-alienation and self-mystification is true literally, not just figuratively. The tendency, characteristic of vanguard parties and

[10] Karl Marx, "The Eighteenth Brumaire of Louis Bonaparte," *Marx and Engels, Selected Works I* (Moscow: Foreign Languages, 1958), 247.

organizations of the past, to identify the vanguard with "the revolution" and "the revolutionary class" has reappeared in the Movement today. The host onto which the movement latches itself may be the working class, the Black Panther Party, or the Third World revolutionary movements: the political-psychological mechanisms involved are the same. One's own weakness and isolation, a critical apprehension of their sources, and a strategy which deals concretely with them are overcome and bypassed through a leap of faith, a linking of oneself to an apparently world-historic force. If past precedents are any measure, such a leap today amounts to a bad and trite joke, if not to suicide:

> Those intellectuals who fully subordinate themselves to the psychological situation of the class which in itself [appears] to represent the force of transformation and change, are led to a professional optimism and to the euphoric sensation that they are tied to an immense power. When the latter suffers severe setbacks, many of these same intellectuals face the danger of falling into a pessimism and nihilism that would be as unfounded as their optimism was. They cannot bear the fact that in particular periods it happens that the representatives of the most *avantgarde,* and futuristic thought, thought which grasps the historical situation at its roots, are necessarily isolated and forced to rely on themselves.[11]

[11] Max Horkheimer, "Traditionelle und kritische Theorie," in Alfred Schmidt, ed., *Kritische Theorie II* (Frankfurt-Main: Fischer, 1968), 163. The essay was originally published in 1937. The problems contained in the New Left's present enthusiasm for and faith in Third World revolutionary movements in particular are not only strategic in Horkheimer's sense. Rhetorical solidarity often blocks the much-needed concrete analysis of the actual relations (and antagonisms) between movements for socialism in situations of scarcity and colonialism and movements for socialism in situations of abundance and empire. Beyond this, and connected to it, the problems are also "moral." Faith, on the part of the Western New Left, in Third World "peoples' war of liberation" and in the doctrine of imperialism as a "paper tiger" is too often *both* euphorically unrealistic and immoral in the terms outlined by Rudi Dutschke: "We should be asking what difficulties of a political-strategic nature . . . are being faced by the movements in the Third World. Indeed, the forces of the Liberation Front in Vietnam are at present on the political-military offensive, but day by day the best part of the Vietnamese people is destroyed, hundreds and thousands are destroyed. To cash in on this by saying, 'the revolutionary peoples' war will win,' seems to me incorrect. Yes, Lin Piao says, 'strategically, imperialism is a paper tiger,' but tactically—and this is the situation of the Vietnamese people, the Peruvian peasants, the Bolivian fighters—tactically this situation is *miserable,* and tactically this situation is enormously difficult for us to understand." *Der Kampf des vietnamesischen Volkes und die Global-strategie des Imperialismus* (Proceedings of the International Vietnam Congress, February, 1968, West Berlin) (Berlin: Maikowski, 1968), 72.

Now, just when this isolation is beginning to break down, when the deep-freeze of advanced capitalism shows signs of melting, this tendency is all the more destructive because it aborts the process and struggle through which the *avant-garde* comes to itself—the only basis on which it can be of any use to anybody else.

Having begun, as the New Left has, to erect abstract bonds with world-historic forces (or supposedly world-historic forces), it is inevitable that factional lines rigidify and that one or another "deviating" faction is elevated from one that is wrong to the status of an objective agent of the ruling class. Expulsions, charges of fifth columns, "running dogs of imperialism," and the rest of the gobbledygook follow naturally. And it is not merely opposing factions that are expelled, but little bits of genuine critical theory and self-criticism accompany each deviant out of the Movement or organization. A "line" or *Weltanschauung,* that is, an "objective" body of concepts external to the concrete existence of the Movement, displaces critical thought. The dilemma, in this context, was posed sometime ago: "As long as the *avant-garde* can carry on without periodic purges, it keeps alive the hope of a classless society." [12]

The Movement's schizophrenia appears in more concrete and glaring ways. Just in the midst of the explosion of the student revolt onto a planetary scale—a fact which outside the United States has provoked important advances in New Left theory—the American movement is, with much fanfare, rushing to the factories to organize the workers. Significantly, the globalization of the student-youth revolt was not so much as mentioned in any published material relating to the National Convention of Students for a Democratic Society in the Summer of 1969. Just as commodity fetishism, bureaucratization, and alienation are beginning to generate disquiet, dissent, and disruption in nearly all sectors of American society, the New Left is putting forward a "new" critique of capitalism which describes it as a system run by a few rich men who, aided by police and military lackeys, suck the blood of the people. Such a critique is not so much inaccurate—it is not—as it is utterly fragmentary and hardly abreast of the system as a whole. Worse, it is a critique which does not contain *within itself* the germs and idea of a new society adequate to the present technological and social pre-conditions of liberation. Just at this time the movement is beginning to experience increasingly massive and systematic repression and terror. These can

[12] Max Horkheimer, "Autoritärer Staat," *Walter Benjamin zum Gedächtnis* (California: Institute for Social Research, Mimeo. ed., 1942), 149.

be met on their own terms only within the context of a decisive dis-integration of the existing State and its military-counter-insurgency capability, and an equally massive, decentralized, and popular armed uprising; none of these conditions is present today, nor are they im-aginable in the immediate future. Yet the New Left is beginning to dabble in irresponsible mimicry of peasant guerrillas, gun worship, and an elevation of street fighting from a necessary tactic in many situations to the level of a strategy and even a principle of the Movement.

Within this blow-up the most regressive and disastrous element is perhaps the tendency among the Marxified and Leninized sectors of the Movement to repudiate that component of its past which linked it most closely to Marcuse. It is now claimed, for example, that the New Left has surpassed the critique of "the quality of life and culture" of capi-talism, that it has gone beyond the earlier "politics of the unpolitical" to a new realism and critique of political-economy. In this respect the Movement has ironically come around to agree with those other lechers after the practical and necessary—liberals and Old Marxists "sympa-thetic" to the New Left. For the meaning of the Movement's "politics of the unpolitical" lay in its recognition that nothing in modern society is unpolitical; that every detail of daily life is saturated with and repro-duces the hegemony of the ruling system; that the object of critical thought and action is "the system" as a *totality*. In the lifetime of the New Left the commodification and bureaucratization of daily existence —that is, the transformation of life into things, functions of economic and political mechanisms—has been stretched to a breaking point and the Movement was born out of this point. One of the many implications of this fact has been that the New Left was a continual self-criticism, a refusal to recapitulate the ruling forms of life, organization, and social relations within itself. Thus, for example, it brought to the center of its activity and critique a fact previously recognized only by outcasts from the organized Left (e.g., Wilhelm Reich) and small groups of anarchists: capitalism expresses itself as much through the "authoritarian person-ality" it generates, as it does through the bombs it drops. (It remains to be seen whether the former is not an "organizable issue"; it is beyond debating, however, that authoritarian personalities have something to do with those who drop and want to drop bombs on peasant rebels.)

And it recognized that authoritarian and egomaniacal character structures are a deep-seated problem within the New Left itself. The choice is not between a revolutionary movement and a Left-wing

"T-group," but between a libertarian and liberatory movement, and a Left-wing recapitulation of capitalist society. A dreadful legacy of traditional Marxism is the notion that the contradictions of capitalism exist entirely in the "economic base" of society, outside the individual, including the individual Marxist and the Marxist organization. And part of the original definition of the New Left is its rejection of this legacy; its recognition that a coherent and unitary critique of modern society begins with a critique of individual existence. Thus the movement's "politics of the unpolitical" is not a matter of taste but a shift in the "strategy of liberation" made necessary by developments in advanced capitalism itself: it is the attempt to give life to

> new needs, qualitatively different and even opposed to the prevailing aggressive and repressive needs: the emergence of a new type of man, with a vital, biological drive for liberation, and with a consciousness capable of breaking through the material as well as ideological veil of the affluent society.[13]

Apparently the Movement has outgrown such "polymorphously perverse" politics. For example, at its National Conference in the Summer of 1969, Students for a Democratic Society expelled the Progressive Labor Party—the first time in its history that SDS expelled any tendency or faction—and the ground was not that the PLP embodies a repressive, ossified, mechanistic, and puritanical ideology, but that it was objectively an agent of the capitalist state because its particular political positions on the Black Panther Party and North Vietnam were racist and counter-revolutionary. In the process the Movement's original critique of reification, authoritarianism, rote learning, hierarchy, is dropped not only in its perception of the ruling society, but in its perception and critique of itself. And these are precisely the components of the ruling society that have begun clearly to manifest themselves inside the Movement. It appears to be a law of radical politics that when the critique of the quality of life in capitalist society is dropped, the possibility of a self-critique of the quality of the Movement is lost.

The New Left, then, is departing from the soil in which it was nurturing itself. And it is not breaking new ground but is itself being

[13] Herbert Marcuse, "Liberation from the Affluent Society," *To Free a Generation: The Dialectics of Liberation* (New York: Collier, 1968), 177.

294

broken by the crusty and arid terrain it seems to have chosen. That few remarks "of a Marcusean or similar type" are listened to or spoken is a key symptom of these new developments, or of this this return of very old developments. The Movement is "overcoming" its isolation in society (and in the universities) by metaphysical leaps into "world revolutionary" forces and into compulsive fixations on one or another single agent or revolution. That it stands in a situation which is not that of Marx, Lenin, or Mao—the nature of its own gestation and growth, the planetary explosion of student revolt, and the utopian-libertarian-experimental character of its own consciousness and activity have been partial but decisive proofs of this fact—but one in which the nature of class struggle, radical politics and revolution assume radically *original* forms . . . all this is being suppressed by the Movement itself. Snatching up bits and pieces of rhetoric from ideological expressions of already surpassed stages of capitalist development and Left-wing movements, the New Left constructs a cocoon around its own life; it insulates itself from its own originality and desensitizes itself to the dynamic processes of social disintegration and reconstruction in motion around it.

At the time of writing, the tendencies outlined in the preceding pages are not yet closed but they are more than epiphenomenal signs. The only way of preventing their closing is for the Movement, from the bottom up, to develop its own critique of its supposedly more advanced echelons. Signs of such a reversal are present, but it is too early (and would be unjustifiably optimistic) to say that the recent degeneration and implosions are mere passing moments of regression on the road to renewal. By an odd happenstance the Movement's new period coincides with the publication of Marcuse's *An Essay on Liberation* (1969), which focuses on the New Left, among other things, and formulates thoughts of its own on possible higher stages. Marcuse, for example, argues that the present historical period and the development of the Movement in advanced industrial society necessitates a theoretical and practical move from "Marx to Fourier . . . from realism to surrealism." [14] This is a strategic and political conception, one which goes to the core of the cultural revolutionary vortex of the New Left. Its meaning may be summarized in words from the original Surrealists. "if it is realism to prune trees, it is surrealism to prune life." And here we have a perfect scenario:

[14] Herbert Marcuse, *An Essay on Liberation* (Boston: Beacon, 1969), 22.

Marcuse, at seventy, remains true to his own and the Movement's "polymorphous perversity," while the young Movement turns on its youth in anxiety-ridden anger and embraces the maturity of tree-pruning realism. If the New Left is to renew itself, *one* of the paths it will have to travel is the one which the Movement and "ideas of a Marcusean or similar type" first met. It can and will surpass the "utopian function" of Marcuse's work only by realizing it.

16

TRENT SCHROYER

The Critical Theory
of Late Capitalism

Trent Schroyer is an assistant professor of sociology in the Graduate Faculty,
New School for Social Research.

With the help of a prescriptive scientism, a technocratic strategy
today guides and stabilizes the crisis of late capitalism. Orthodox Marxism fails to recognize the uniqueness of late capitalism. Hence tradi-
tionalists on the Left cannot offer a critique of the humanly destructive
dynamics of the technocratic strategy and prescriptive scientism. A critical theory of late capitalism needs to do just that. In the process, a
critical theory must discard the costumes and ghosts of past revolutionary
struggles.

TECHNOCRATIC STRATEGY AND PRESCRIPTIVE SCIENTISM

Contemporary science and technology serve as a new strategy for
legitimating power and privilege. Insofar as the practice of the scientific
establishment is held to be neutral, while actually justifying the extension
of repressive control systems, we can assert that the contemporary self-
image of science functions as a technocratic ideology.[1] Technocratic

[1] Cf. Jürgen Habermas's *Technik und Wissenschaft als "Ideologie"* (Suhrkamp, 1968). This paper constitutes in part my interpretation of the pioneering
work of Habermas. It belongs to a work in process that will be published by
George Braziller, Inc.

legitimation assumes a positivist view of science. This positivist view holds: (1) that knowledge is inherently neutral; (2) that there is a unitary scientific method; (3) that the standard of certainty and exactness in the physical sciences is the only explanatory model for scientific knowledge.

We call this conception of science *prescriptive scientism* [2] and we argue that a critical theory of society must reject and refute each one of these fundamental principles in the scientistic self-image of science. Scientism is the culmination of the positivist tradition and has become dominant in both the established social science of late capitalism and the scientific materialism of orthodox Marxism. In any scientific establishment, prescriptive scientism functions as a societal a priori, which uncritically permits the extension of an exploitive instrumental rationalization.[3] That is, it contributes to the generation of decision-making whose "rationality" is instrumental effectiveness and efficiency. Such mechanisms work against a broader mode of rationalization which would maximize the participation and individuation of affected people.

Scientism has created a crisis in man's knowledge of himself because it mystifies the practice and societal function of science. In so concealing its contemporary research-guiding framework, scientism becomes a self-fulfilling and self-reinforcing force of history. The faith that men will be emancipated through the extension of neutral techniques of science and technology obscures the reality of research serving and justifying control systems which accept power structures as given.

Scientism as the positivistic self-image of science separates the subject and object of knowledge and takes the statements of science as an observational given. Knowledge is thus conceived as a neutral picturing of fact. This denies that there could be any predefinitions of the object of knowledge by the prior organization of our experience. The positivistic

[2] The term "scientism" is used to refer to the contemporary self-image of science. Rather than honor modern forms with the term "neo-positivism," it seems more fitting to recognize a common cause with other anti-positivist methodologists, e.g. Edmund Husserl, Eric Voegelin, etc.

[3] The concept of "instrumental rationalization" is used by Habermas in his critical reconceptualization of Max Weber's unitary concept of rationalization. Habermas is concerned with demonstrating that extension of economic rationality to spheres of symbolically mediated interaction is a surpression of necessary communicative prerequisites for self-reflective consciousness. Habermas therefore reconceptualizes "rationalization" upon a twofold model of instrumental and symbolic interaction, seeing both modes of rationalization necessary for a rational society.

philosophy of science overlooks that the societal framework within which research practice takes place exercises a direct influence in the processing of theory and data. This scientistic trend exemplifies what Edmund Husserl has called the fallacy of objectivism.[4] Thus while more and more able to systematize knowledge, positivistic theory is less and less able to reflect about its own presuppositions and is left without any way of objectifying the structuring framework of this epoch.[5]

Scientism and the positivistic philosophy of history are vestiges of classic ontology in that pure theory and scientific method are held to be historically neutral. The on-going articulation of the scientific method within the establishment, whether by logicians or by practicing scientists, is but a later reconstruction of the results of scientific inquiry, and as such is an idealization of the actual practice of science. Insofar as this reconstructed logic is held to be a guide for inquiry and superimposed upon scientific praxis, it is distortive of both the logic-in-use,[6] i.e. the actual logic of inquiry used by scientists, and the reality investigated.

However, this idealization of science and its method is none the less an active force in history and does transform the human world. Thus the greatest problem that social theory faces is not whether behaviorism, game theory or systems analysis is theoretically valid, but whether it might not become valid through a self-fulfilling prophecy justified by a technocratic ideology.

KNOWLEDGE AS A PRODUCTIVE FORCE

Science and science-based technology have become more basic to the production processes of advanced industrial societies.[7] The institu-

---

[4] Cf. Husserl, *Phenomenology and the Crisis of Philosophy* (New York: Harper paperback, 1966).

[5] This point is developed in numerous ways by Gerald Radnitzky in the second volume of his work *Contemporary Schools of Metascience* (Goteborg: Akademeförlaget, 1968).

[6] The concepts "reconstructed-logic" and "logic-in-use" are used by Abraham Kaplan in the first chapter of *The Conduct of Inquiry* (San Francisco: Chandler Publishing Co., 1964).

[7] On this point there is a growing consensus. O'Connor writes: "With the new, rationalized social organization of technology and the labor process completed, technical knowledge became the main form of labor power and capital." James O'Connor, "The Fiscal Crisis of the State; Part I," *Socialist Revolution*, Vol. 1, No. 1, 1970, pp. 48 ff. According to Birnbaum, ". . . knowledge has be-

tionalization of science and technology as "research and development" has generated a "knowledge industry" which is itself a force of production. Knowledge production units become autonomous structures that are perpetuated beyond their originating goals. They link directly or indirectly (technology transfer from state-financed research, e.g. the space program), to corporate profit-making capacity.[8]

"Knowledge," however, is produced within the context of an instrumentally rationalizing society. Thus scientism increasingly becomes the prescriptive decision-matrix for ever new spheres of society.[9] Insofar as more spheres of decision-making are construed as "technical problems" requiring information and instrumental strategies produced by technical experts, they are removed from political debate.[10]

The increased importance of the "knowledge industry" has led some social theorists to conceptualize "post-industrial" society as a self-regulating system in which information is the crucial input.[11] With this, or related images of contemporary society, we have an infinitely flexible

---

come a factor of production, in the form of the technological derivatives of scientific enquiry and in the indispensable contribution of other forms of knowledge . . . to the organization and maintenance of the productive process. Indeed, the ineluctable development of a fusion of administrative, political and productive processes in neo-capitalism . . . has made it difficult to specify where precisely production stops and the administrative begins, and has rendered virtually impossible a distinction between 'political' and 'economic' decisions." Norman Birnbaum, "On the Idea of a Political Avant-Garde in Contemporary Politics: The Intellectuals and the Technical Intelligentsia," *Praxis,* Nos. 1 and 2, 1969, pp. 234–35. Also see Amitai Etzioni, *The Active Society* (New York: Free Press, 1968), Chapter 9.

[8] At the moment the disproportionate allocation of state resources to the military and space research and development is legitimated by the concept of "technology transfer." Whatever the significance of such "transfer" (this constitutes an important area for research), there is no doubt that it presently legitimates an undiscussed commitment to a "defense economy." For example: "The exacting demands of the space program, which operates at the outermost limits of knowledge, have stimulated advances in almost every discipline of science and engineering. . . . These advances have spun off into business and industry." Wernher von Braun, as quoted in the *Wall Street Journal,* August 9, 1969.

[9] Cf. Radnitzky, *op. cit.,* pp. 133 ff.; Irene Taviss, "The Technological Society: Some Challenges for Social Science," *Social Research,* Vol. 35, No. 3, Autumn 1968.

[10] This broad speculative hypothesis is also shared by Sheldon Wolin, *Politics and Vision* (Boston: Little, Brown and Co. 1960); Hannah Arendt, *The Human Condition* (New York: Doubleday, 1958); Herbert Marcuse, *One-Dimensional Man* (Boston: Beacon Press, 1964).

[11] For example, Etzioni's *The Active Society.*

ideology which can be interpreted in ways which legitimate public or private policy adopted by established power and privilege groups (e.g. theories of "modernization" applied to socio-economic development).[12]

REINTERPRETING MARX

We argue that the scientistic image of science has become the dominant legitimating system of advanced industrial society. It has gradually replaced the ideology of equivalence exchange which performed the legitimating function for early industrial society. Whereas Marx was able to show how the non-equivalence of exchange between labor and capital was the major contradiction in capitalist society, we are now unable to express a later stage of this development in the same way. (This will be discussed below.) The advanced stage of the contradiction between labor and capital involves the distortion of the market by the growth of state interventions. These emergent functions of the state are necessitated for the sake of avoidance of its final disruption.[13]

In order to reproduce Marx's critical-emancipatory analysis for our time we must reconstruct his analytic framework in a way which makes for a more concrete expression of the source of contemporary alienation. Whereas Marx was able to formulate his critical theory as a critique of the purest ideological expression of equivalence exchange, i.e. classical political economy, we are forced to broaden our critique to the positivistic theory of science itself. It is our thesis that the scientistic image of science is the fundamental false consciousness of our epoch. If the technocratic ideology is to loose its hold on our consciousness, a critical theory of science must lay bare the theoretical reifications of the scientistic image of science.[14] That is the concern of this paper.

Some social theorists, such as C. Wright Mills, place Marxism in the classic tradition of social science and then proceed in an eclectic

[12] Cf. André Gundar Frank, "The Sociology of Development and the Underdevelopment of Sociology," *Catalyst,* Summer 1967.

[13] James O'Connor, *op. cit.,* pp. 48–49.

[14] A special panel of the National Academy of Sciences prepared for the United States government a study on the problem of "technology assessment". The panel report observes that the government policy has become "at least as influential as the forces of the ordinary market" in setting directions for technological change. Quoted in the *Wall Street Journal,* October 12, 1969. (The report is summarized in *Scientific American* in February 1970.)

manner to combine Marx with Weber, Veblen, G. H. Mead, and Freud. These eclectic constructions cannot generate an alternative to established theory. They do little more than illuminate historical structures of power and privilege, and function more or less as strain-measuring scales for these same structures. Not until we have a community of critical scientists who perceive social science in a critical manner will we be able to perform the ongoing tasks of research, critique, and political program formulation.

A rethinking of the nature of science and its relation to society has already begun in contemporary European Marxism, especially in the Frankfurt School of critical sociology.[15] This particular attempt to re-interpret Marx consists of searches for the first principles of a critical (or emancipatory) science that can respond in a contemporary manner to the methodology of the established social sciences.'

In this reinterpretation, or this reconstruction of Marxism if you will, science is conceived as part of the materialist model of society. But the materialist model of society is now reinterpreted as three societal systems of action: [16] (1) instead of talking about the substructure, we refer to the systems of purposive rational action; (2) instead of talking about the superstructure, we refer to the systems of symbolic interaction; (3) instead of talking about the forms of social consciousness, we can speak about the reflexive recognition of legitimate authority which is internal to the system of self-reflection.

THREE TYPES OF SCIENTIFIC INTEREST

By considering scientific inquiry as the formalization of the logics-in-action of societal systems, we can generate a new conception of the logics-in-use of science. We can achieve an insight into the prior orientations of

---

[15] The Frankfurt School represents the only *school* of critical scientists in the West. They have been self-consciously trying to generate a combination of critical theory and critical social research for several decades. Crucial statements of this collective project are Max Horkheimer's "Traditionelle und Kritische Theorie" in A. Schmidt (ed.), *Kritische Theorie,* Vols. 1 and 2 (Frankfurt: S. Fischer, 1968); and Jürgen Habermas's *Theorie und Praxis* (Neuwied: Luchterhand Verlag, 1963).

[16] This is my reconstruction of Habermas's work in its continuity with the Marxist tradition.

302

scientific inquiry. We can express predefinitions of the object-of-knowledge in terms of the relation of cognition and interest. By analyzing the transcendental interests of cognition as they are linked to historically determined conceptual schemes and behavioral systems we can arrive at an understanding of the logical rules of the process of inquiry. The procedures of scientific inquiry are rooted in the prescientific processes of everyday life, and the finding and inventing of hypotheses, the deduction of conditional predictions, and the testing of hypotheses are parallel to the practice of life itself. Only within the mode of conceptualizing scientific inquiry and its rootedness in everyday life can we see both the validity of science and relate it to changing historical variables. Only by integrating a logic of inquiry within an empirically transforming life-world can we achieve a dialectical theory of science and society. In so constructing a unified theory of the logics-in-use of scientific practice and the logics-in-action of societal systems we are able to show that cognition is never a neutral fact-picturing. Since knowledge is never neutral, we can demonstrate that there are distinct scientific methods and that each requires a somewhat different explanatory model. In this way we are able to refute the theory of science inherent in scientism.

Our pay-off is a new classification of the sciences and an analysis of the logical *interest* (or transcendental principle) presupposed in each practice. We then see three interests as fundamental to three kinds of science: (a) we conceive of the strict sciences as that mode of analysis which yields information that presupposes the interest of certainty and technical control; (b) we conceive of the hermeneutic sciences (or the historical-interpretive sciences) as that mode of interpretation which yields an understanding of the social-cultural life-world and which presupposes the interest of extending of intersubjective understanding; (c) we conceive of a critical science as that kind of inquiry which is capable of analyzing the supposed and actual "necessity" of historical modes of authority and which presupposes the interest of the emancipation of men from law-like patterns of "nature" and history.

Established, "official" social science understands itself as having the interest of the strict sciences. In practice, that means that established social science, although it conceives itself as neutral, is actually an inquiry which has the theoretical interest and societal consequence of maintaining technical control.

However, within the methodological debates of established social science there has emerged a recognition of a competing interest and a

303

competing logics-in-use of scientific inquiry. To cite a few of these debates in one sphere, sociology, we can see emergent modes of analysis such as phenomenology, ethnomethodology, a priorist sociology deriving from the late Wittgenstein, and symbolic interactionism. These debates are recognition of a competing practical interest within social-science methodology, that of the hermeneutic sciences. Despite these new methodological reflections, the dominant trend is to continue to understand social inquiry in a way which identifies it with the strict sciences.

THE ROOTS OF CRITICAL SCIENCE

At this point let us go back to Marx himself and reconstruct the beginnings of a critical science. Whereas Marx was grounded in classic philosophy and discovered the key to an emancipatory science of man in Hegel, we are often less aware of these foundations. We therefore need to fill in the philosophical dimensions of Marxism as a critical science, seeing it as a product of its time and perhaps being able to reconstruct its main elements more systematically than its founder.

Hegel provided for Marx the foundation of a critical theory of human development in that he formulated a science of the experience of consciousness as a historical self-forming process. Marx extended this analysis to the historical conditions of the self-formation of man by materializing the notion of dialectical synthesis. He thus transformed the critique of knowledge into the critique of society. It is in the reconstruction of this common link between Hegel and Marx that we will find the key to a Marxist theory of science and society, to Marxism as a critical science.[17]

Critical philosophy has always pointed to positivism's inability to account for the possibility of objective knowledge, or even to give an interpretation of its own historical development and practice. The more recent development of positivism has only increased this inability until reflective analysis is reduced to the marginal status of the analysis of scientific language. Positivists hold that philosophic analysis cannot produce "knowledge." In opposition to this, critical science retains philosophic reflection as a mode of the critique of research practice and for the substantive critique of ideologies. Hence a critical science differs

[17] Cf. Trent Schroyer, *Alienation and the Dialectical Paradigm* (Doctoral Dissertation, New School for Social Research), 1968.

from all other sciences in that it employs both logical and empirical analysis in the framework within which it validates knowledge. Since the modes of mediation of the object-of-knowledge will change as the historical subject changes, a critical theory of science holds that an adequate methodology will include a critical theory of knowledge internal to its theory of society.

The recent work of the philosopher-sociologist Jürgen Habermas, the leading younger figure in the Frankfurt School, has focused upon this aspect of the Marxist tradition. In his book *Erkenntnis und Interesse* (1968), he has reinterpreted the Marxist theory of labor in a way which fills in its logical foundations.

Habermas argues that the Marxist notion of work is not only an economic category, but also deals with ways in which the material base of society conditions objectively possible knowledge. In this critical-materialism, the subject of world constitution is not the transcendental consciousness, as in Kant, but the existing human species which reproduces the actual conditions of its life. Thus the Marxian notion of man as *homo faber* fundamentally differs from all previous notions in that work is conceptualized as both the mechanism of human development and as the objective framework through which possible experience is constituted.

When Marx argues that "the history of industry is the open book of the essential human powers," he is speaking of the empirical dynamic *and* the logic by which man objectivates himself. To relate Marx's conception to transcendental logic is not falling into idealism; the theory remains materialistic. Taken this way we see that Marx's theory of work completes Hegel's critique of Kant. Whereas Kant's analysis of knowing places the synthesis of the material perception under the transcendental rules of the pure concepts of the understanding which are internal and unchanging, Marx stresses that the synthesis of the materials of work are unified under the technical rules of the instruments of production and these belong to the historically changing base of society. It is a subtle argument. Marx has taken the transcendental mode of logic and integrated it into an empirical science. So that when we talk about dialectics, under this reconstruction of Hegelian-Marxist theory, we are talking about a reconceptualization of transcendental logic in a way that brings into that mode of analysis empirical historical conditions.

The logical dimension of this dialectical theory of work is that the knowledge we can generate about nature is bound to the limits of the technically possible control over nature. Therefore, and this is a key point, the objectivity of societal experience and of scientific knowledge is possible as a function of the widening sphere of technical control over nature, and specifically within the framework of instrumental systems which form the basis of society. Hence the mode of mediation of subject and object is historically bound on the empirical level as well as the logical; both the material used in work and the living work process are historical variables.

NEW CONCEPTS FOR HISTORICAL MATERIALISM

Instrumental action is a form of purposive rational action which proceeds according to technical rules based on empirical knowledge. It includes predictions about observable events and these are true or false, thus providing us with knowledge whose adequacy depends on how efficiently man controls reality. A more recent variation of instrumental behavior are systems of rational choice which proceed from strategies that are based on analytical knowledge that include deductions from preference rules or general maxims and may be correct or not. Strategic behavior depends upon a correct evaluation of alternative possibilities of action by inferring from a given system of values and maxims. Systems of instrumental action are different forms of technical rules which are universal and not context-based and they can be formulated in context-free language. Thus the truly universal languages are the technologies produced by man.

However, in Marx's model of society he distinguishes the social relations from the revolutionizing means of production. Therein lies a distinction between instrumental and symbolic systems of action. Habermas reconceptualizes this distinction by a logical analysis of the difference between a social norm and a technical rule.

We can see a social norm as defining reciprocal behavior expectations that are shared by at least two persons. They are not true or false and determined by technical success but enforced by sanction. The validity of social norms depends upon the mutual understanding of expectations and common recognition of obligations. As such the meaning of social norms can, as a rule, be understood via ordinary language communication (whereas technical rules are formulated in a formalized language). Hence social norms form context-specific systems of action

306

whose logical status differs from technical rules. Symbolic interaction systems are equivalent to the social-cultural life-world of society and are to be distinguished from systems of instrumental action. The relation of systems of technics to symbolic systems is a historical variable. For example, Marx showed that capitalism is the point in history where there is a reversal of the order of legitimation. This is the beginning of what in our own time has become known as the technological society. In this phase the extension of the systems of purposive rational behavior begins to legitimate itself. In Marx's analysis this is expressed as the point at which the extension of the capitalistic economy produces its own reified culture: the fetishism of the community form.

The work of Herbert Marcuse is primarily a documentation of the ongoing fetishes, or reifications, of possessive individualism, consumer orientation, and the like in the advanced stages of industrial society. Marcuse concretely documents a suggestion made by Marx in *Grundrisse* that the production system can begin to integrate social and cultural needs within its own development. ("Production not only furnishes the object of a need, but it also furnishes the need for an object.") Thus there is a potential for the total inversion of the traditional relationship between the system of instrumental behavior and the system of symbolic interaction. The meaning of "one-dimensionality" (Marcuse) or "instrumental rationalization" (Habermas) implies the objective possibility of the total control of social-cultural change. Systems of instrumental action can be extended to the organization of human responses to a stimulus-response pattern, e.g. the shaping of behavior in behavioral psychoanalysis. The possibility of bringing under technical control systems of symbolically mediated interaction suggests that the practice of life could be reduced to instrumental action. Men would resort to an artificial necessity, guided by the standards of technical success and efficiency; *1984* is technologically feasible.

What this would mean is the reducing of cultural traditions of common symbols to technics of adaptive behavior. Marcuse and Adorno have indeed suggested that human behavior is becoming more and more of a mimetic acting out by an externally conditioned ego.[18] The possibility of this degree of loss of ego-autonomy is, however, an empirical question. But the critical theories of Adorno, Marcuse, and Habermas,

[18] Cf. Herbert Marcuse, *One-Dimensional Man* (Boston: Beacon Press, 1964), especially Chapter 3; Theodore W. Adorno, "Sociology and Psychoanalysis," Parts I and II, *New Left Review*, No. 46, 1967, and No. 47, 1968.

are, at this point, an interpretation of analytical schemes and must not be taken as a factual claim. What it would mean is that the distinction between social action and adaptive behavior, learned and "instinctive behavior," would become more and more meaningless. This historical configuration of instrumental and symbolic interaction systems means that the third system, self-reflection, is reduced to a minimum. Critical reflection about the legitimacy of authority structures is replaced by an immediate identification with the collective ego-ideal.[19]

While Marx kept the instrumental and symbolic action-systems separate in his substantive research, he did not separate them in his theory of society. Thus his later understanding of political economy as an historical natural science suppresses the logical uniqueness of symbolic communication and reconstructs it upon the model of instrumental behavior. This is exactly what most modes of positivist analysis did in the course of their development.

CRITICAL THEORY AND THE SOCIAL SCIENCES

In our time, with its dominant technocratic ideology, the point of a critical theory of society will be to show that instrumental action is not the only interest that guides research practice in the social sciences. More specifically, the concern of a critical theory is to try to formulate a view of practical scientific interests and relate these to the societal action systems. Toward that end we need a reconceptualization such as to the following:

The Logics-in-Use of the Strict Sciences

In this direction we find that the pragmatic philosophy of science, especially that of C. S. Pierce, has already developed an approach to this problem which is consistent with a dialectical epistemology. The pragmatic tradition has focused upon the logical analysis of the procedures and inquiry of science, and has not restricted itself to formal methodology and the analysis of language as have the positivists. Thus

[19] Cf. Adorno, *ibid*. This point is developed most extensively in an essay by Marcuse, which is essentially a theory of social regression. See "The Obsolescence of the Freudian Concept of Man" in Marcuse's *Five Lectures* (Boston: Beacon Press, 1970).

308

pragmatism has conceived of methodological rules as norms guiding the practice of inquiry of a community of investigators. From this analysis we can make a basic distinction between the logics-in-use and the reconstructed logic of science. The former analysis explicates the rules guiding the practice of inquiry; the latter formulates criteria of validity and semantic meaning in relation to the results of science. As we noted at the start, the positivist philosophy of science has worked exclusively with the reconstruction logic of science.

Thus Pierce gives us an analysis of the logical (transcendental) and empirical conditions for the validity of strict science inquiry in the form of a logic-in-use of strict science. Pierce argues that the research interest guiding strict science is that of gaining and expanding control over objects which we have observed. Development of this logical argument cannot be dealt with here. What this means, however, is that in the process of inquiry we ourselves behave *as if* the events of reality were the products of a subject who, under contingent initial conditions, continually draws conclusions from a definite valid set of rules and then decides to act, permanently conforming to the predictions thereby derived. Thus our research praxis is guided by *instrumental actions* which presuppose that reality is also an actor who has internalized a set of habits we call "laws of nature." Pierce's analysis is unique and is parallel to Marx's analysis of the logic of the work process in that both logical and empirical conditions are seen as determining the possibility of successful instrumental action. Whereas Marx's analysis can be construed as a general critique of Kant's notion of the world-constituting powers of human knowing, Pierce's can be seen as a similar critique of Kant but dealing with the instrumental action procedures of the community of strict scientists.

Pierce has shown that the synthetic modes of reasoning, i.e. induction and abduction, are chains of inference whose validity can be accounted for only by referring to the norms of procedure that are sedimented into the research practice of a community of investigators. Within this frame of reference we are able to conceive of scientific reasoning as systems of purposive rational behavior which are essentially the "habits" of research practice. Their function is to fixate belief, to operate as guiding principles for the accumulation of new information, and to be revised when there are failures in anticipated results. Belief is secured again when there is a successful acting upon a new recipe which is repeatedly reconfirmed. Hence the systems of purposive rational behavior embedded in the research practice of a community of investigators functions as the transcendental scheme that constitutes possible cognition. But this transcendental framework is within the system of instrumental action of a given historical context, the framework determines the conditions under which we objectify and experience "reality" as a possible object of purposive rational action, or possible technical control.[20]

We can therefore see that the work process and strict science inquiry are related. Both are constituted through an instrumental logics-in-use and thus objectify reality from the viewpoint of instrumental action linked to the instrumental action system of society. To put it another way we can say that they both presuppose (in the transcendental sense) a model of certainty for the successful control of observed processes. In short the *"interest"* of instrumental action and strict science is one, that of technical control. Thus a social science in this category of science would be interested in recurrent regularities of the social world toward the end of technical control, e.g. behaviorism.

Indeed the most advanced forms of social-science inquiry, such as systems analysis and decision theory, are guided by the interest of technical control. But a critical theory of society can show that this is not the only interest that guides research in the established social sciences. In competition with the technical interest of strict science inquiry we can formulate, from the tradition of the Human Sciences (Geisteswissenschaften), a practical interest—that of the extension of communicative understanding toward the end of the formation of consensus.[21] This interest is presupposed by the historical-interpretive sciences of the social-cultural life-world such as cultural sociology, history of art, etc. We will refer to this category of science as the *hermeneutic* sciences.[22]

[20] Cf. Jürgen Habermas, *Erkenntnis und Interesse* (Suhrkamp, 1968), pp. 116–78.

[21] Habermas, *ibid.*, pp. 178–234.

[22] The modern hermeneutic movement and its foundations is only now becoming known in the Anglo-American world. For a short summary of this development consult R. Palmer, *Hermeneutics* (Evanston: Northwestern University Press, 1968); for its crucial significance for the methodology of a critical science, see Habermas, "Zur Logik der Sozialwissenschaften," Special Issue of *Philosophische Rundschau,* February 1967.

The Logic-in-Use of the Hermeneutic Sciences

Identification of a unique method for the hermeneutic sciences requires a return to the debate about the differences between the natural and human sciences. At the very least we must go back to the theory of science which preceded the neo-Kantian distinction between the empirical and the philosophical, the "is" and the "ought" dimensions.

An important beginning point for the rediscovery of a hermeneutic logics-in-use is the last essays of Wilhelm Dilthey.[23] In these essays, written between 1905 and 1910, Dilthey is putting the distinction between the natural and human sciences in a way which recaptures part of the Hegelian theory while addressing itself to a twentieth-century context. He points to the *logical* differences between perception and explanation in the natural sciences, and interpretation and understanding in the human sciences. The focus then is upon the different logics-in-use of these scientific processes. This focus suggests that concepts, theories, methods, and principles of verification are related to the processes of inquiry for their validity.

Whereas in the strict sciences we are constrained by the range of our technical control over natural processes, in the hermeneutic sciences we are constrained by our socially established conventions which exercise a predefinition of how we understand symbolic communication. In this way the fundamental "communality" we have with others constitutes a transcendental presupposition of hermeneutic understanding. Thus in the systems of common symbols which are sedimented, first in an ordinary language and then in typical action patterns and typical attitudinal orientations, are the rules of the logic-in-use of hermeneutic understanding. In formulating rules of interpretation we are trying to consciously recapture the process of interpretation which enables everyday actors to understand each other. The expression of these logic-in-use rules has been worked out by Dilthey's analysis of the "circle of interpretation" and by what later writers call the Hermeneutic Circle. Recognition of the logical difference of the interpretation of symbolic systems has led to pro-

---

[23] The key essay here is "The Construction of the Historical World of the Human Studies" which appears in a partial translation in *Pattern and Meaning in History* (New York: Harper paperback 1962), or W. Dilthey, *Gesammelte Schriften,* Vol. 7 (Stuttgart, 1958).

grammatic ideals for the social sciences such as phenomenological sociology (e.g. Alfred Schutz); [24] ethnomethodology (e.g. Garfinkel, Cicourel); [25] symbolic interactionism (Herbert Blumer [26] and others). However, the result of hermeneutic inquiry in these paradigms can give us little more than an interpretative sociology's explanation.

But we are not concerned with a defense of the human sciences but with the existence of a competing interest to technical control in social inquiry. The question for critical science is how to develop a mode of analysis which is both explanatory and able to interpret symbolic communication. This form of science would have a still different research guiding interest—that of emancipation.

Established social science is essentially manipulative because it has allowed itself to be conceived as having the same research-guiding interest as the strict sciences. Insofar as technical control is the guiding interest of social science, it is consistent with the technocratic trend and overtly legitimates class or elite exploitation. On the other hand a human science guided only by its practical interest would have very little explanatory power. Thus the need for the synthesis: critical science.

It is now possible to briefly summarize the above arguments. The methods of the strict sciences and the hermeneutic sciences are both but formalizations of the praxis of the everyday systems of instrumental and symbolic interaction. These two types of praxis are not neutral with regard to their "objects" but rather presuppose an inherent teleology of inquiry. Just as instrumental systems constitute the material base of society, symbolic interaction systems change our everyday consciousness about the world. Changes in these sub-systems of society are not passive accumulations; the societal context is transformed in a way which also transforms the subject (men). Thus the extension of these systems are together the processes by which the human species itself is developed historically. This development does not occur by an external necessity in which man is the passive medium through which the "laws" of nature and history are manifested. On the contrary, our conception stresses that men are active in the con-

[24] Cf. Alfred Schutz, *Collected Papers,* 3 Vols. (Hague: Nijhoff, 1962–66).

[25] Cf. Harold Garfinkel, *Studies in Ethnomethodology* (Englewood Cliffs, N.J.: Prentice-Hall, 1967), Aaron Cicourel, *Method and Measurement in Sociology* (New York: Free Press, 1964).

[26] Cf. Herbert Blumer, "Society as Symbolic Interaction" in A. Rose (ed.), *Human Behavior and Social Processes* (Boston: Houghton Mifflin, 1962).

stitution of their own world and of their own "nature." This process of self-formation cannot be conceived within a theory which assumes that knowledge represents "structures" and is neutral in regard to its "object."

Foundations of a Critical Science

Reflection about the sub-systems of society, and their function as transcendental frameworks which link system interests and cognition, requires a unique mode of analysis. Such methodological reflection tries to illuminate both human history and the practice of science as historical self-forming processes, and thereby restores to men an awareness of their position as the active, yet historically limited, subject of history. To recognize the processes of historical self-formation of human history is to become aware of the dialectical mechanisms of negativity and therefore to be able to generate a critique of existing structures by objectifying the historical possibilities of a social totality.[27] Hence the generation of a critical theory of science and society is at the same time the broadest theoretical framework for a revolutionary theory.[28]

A critical science differs from the strict or hermeneutic sciences in that it presupposes that all self-conscious agents can become aware of the self-formative processes of society and self and with this knowledge achieve a historically conditioned autonomy. Thus the character of a critical science is unique insofar as it is concerned with the assessment of the socially unnecessary modes of authority, exploitation, repression.[29] The interest of a critical science is the emancipation of all self-conscious agents from the seemingly "natural" forces of nature and history.

[27] The possibility of a critical science depends upon a theoretical totalization which can function as both a framework for the analysis of contemporary society and at the same time serve as a hypothetical philosophy of history that can guide hermeneutic inquiry. Cf. Marlis Kruger "Sociology of Knowledge and Social Theory" in *Berkeley Journal of Sociology,* Vol. 14, 1969, pp. 152–63.

[28] However, to have a theory broad enough for societal critique is not to have an "instrument to guide praxis." An historical theory must be interpreted with regard to specific historical conditions and hence between theory and praxis there is a crucial mediator of judgment. It is illusory to believe that any critical theory can simply be a "tool" in the hands of any class. Between theory and praxis there is a crucial phase of political program formulation which requires not only theoretical clarity but practical judgment about specific life-worlds.

[29] Schroyer, *op. cit.,* Chapter 3.

How is a critical science related to the history of human society? This linkage is to the capacity of men to be reflective about their own formative process. A critical science is linked to the dialectic of self-reflection that is present in all socialization processes, specifically in the reflective recognition of legitimate authority.[30] From the point of view of the strict or hermeneutic sciences, a critical science is a speculative science in that it tries to reflect about the "necessity" for the conditions of law-like patterns in society and history. It is a science which in reconstructing the dynamic of individual or societal development tries to assess what are necessary norms and which are but remnants of power structures no longer humanly useful. This mode of analysis derives from the historic-genetic mode of conceptualization which is inherent in Hegel's transcendental ontology as developed in his *Phenomenology of Mind*. The mode of analysis is essentially related to the Hegelian concept of reflexive reason which is fundamental to a Marxist science. Hegel conceives of reason as inherently historical, as geared to the "explanation" not of invariant laws (the positivistic fallacy of objectivism) but of self-forming (*Bildung*) processes.[31]

I have elsewhere interpreted Hegel's philosophy as generated by his concern to overcome emergent cultural alienation.[32] Hence his analysis of the French Revolution, despite its rejection of the terror and its critique of one-sided individualism, is an affirmation of the revolution as releasing men from cultural systems that distorted and suppressed thought and emotion. Hence his conception of a philosophy which could illuminate historical contradictions by objectifying cultural symbols as alienated forms of free self-conscious life. By comprehending alienated moments of the necessary movement of *Geist,* Hegel thought that men could be reconciled with their actual potential and not constrained by outmoded systems of thought and action. In this way the *Phenomenology* can be seen as a philosophical form of

---

[30] This distinction is crucial for a critical science. Marcuse's concept of "surplus repression" (*Eros and Civilization,* Boston: Beacon Press, 1955, p. 32) is an attempt to turn it into a category of critical theory. It is also the focus of critical research done by the Frankfurt School, notably *Studien über Autorität und Familie,* edited by Max Horkheimer, 1936. Critical research now being carried on at Frankfurt focuses on the formation of ego-identity and class-specific socialization patterns.

[31] Schroyer, *op. cit.,* Chapter 1.

[32] Schroyer, "The Paradox of Alienation in the Western Image of Man," *Abraxis,* Vol. 1, No. 2, Winter 1970.

a critical science, one that tries to view over 2500 years of human history as a single development in which pivoted movements are represented as alienated cultural forms, e.g. the medieval world-view as depicted by the Unhappy Consciousness. The Marxian critique of Hegel's claim to absolute knowledge, or the deduction of all from the principle of Geist, is but an extension of this dialectic of reflection: Marx's *Capital* is a realization of Hegel's conception of a science of reason. Marx produced, however, not a dialectical ontology but a dialectical empiricism. That is, a science of society which is rooted in critical, reflexive reason but one that can be realized only as a material critique of society.

In so refuting the residue of classical ontology in Hegel, Marx does not thereby banish the praxis of Reason from an empirical science. Instead Marx differs from other empirics in that he retains this mode of historic-genetic conceptualization. The history of Marxist theory and struggle has too often denied or ignored the fact that a Marxist science is based upon a unique logic-in-use—that of Reason in the Hegelian sense. In so suppressing the foundations of a Marxist science or history, "Marxism" has repressed its own logical foundations and has therefore fallen into a sterile distinction between science and philosophy which simply assimilates the scientistic image of science. The problem with much of contemporary "Marxism" is that it is unable to understand itself as a unique critical science. Beginning with Engels, Marxists have fallen into a scientistic understanding of the work of Marx.

Marx's unique contribution to critical science was his labor theory of value which was a self-reflective model for the critical analysis of capitalist society. In the classical form of the labor theory of value Marx discovered the basic ideology of a society based upon economic exchange. By distinguishing between living-labor and labor-power Marx broke the ahistorical equation of labor and value embedded in Ricardo's labor theory. As long as feudal production was organized through status authority it was primarily production for use. However, the emergence of a class society where economic exchange is liberated from status relations results in the gradual deterioration of production for use and its replacement by a universal exchange value. In this epoch the equivalence between labor and value is negated in the exchange between the seller of labor-power and the capitalist who appropriates it. Whereas the seller receives the market price, its exchange value, the capitalist appropriates the value—creating capacity of living labor.[33] Hence Marx demonstrates the non-equivalence of the exchange between labor and capital by working out the developmental laws of capitalism. While being the basic legitimation of capitalist society, the practice of equivalance exchange was also the source of the alienation of all labor.

> . . . thus all the progress of civilization, or in other words, every increase in the production power of labor itself, does not enrich the worker, but capital, and thus increases the power that dominates labor.[34]

Equivalence exchange was then both the principle of justice and the practice of domination. Reflection upon this fundamental contradiction of capitalist society liberated consciousness from the cultural reifications of the "commodity form." In the commodity form is found the record of the alienated work process and the immanent contradiction of capitalist society. To Marx, the dialectical analysis of the commodity form is a *Schein,* or showing forth, of the essence of human production. That is, Marx's analysis in the first chapter of *Capital,* while seemingly couched in visual metaphor, is really attempting to make *transparent* the essential behind the appearance. At every point in *Capital,* Marx tries to keep "the real" (use value) in the foreground while dealing with the exchange-system of capitalism. In identifying the commodity form he has made the real nature of human work "show forth" to all so they can "see through" the appearance of capitalism. "Seeing" the commodity form is to reflexively understand its real nature.[35] The moment of "show" is the moment of negation of the appearance and is the characteristic of a cirtical science. Marx thus restores the historical dimension to a whole social process, capitalist production, thereby enabling men to recognize the reified character of life practice under the domination of the commodity form.

[33] Cf. Martin Nicolaus, "The Unknown Marx," *New Left Review,* No. 48, 1968.

[34] Quoted in Nicolaus, *ibid.*

[35] Insofar as men perceive their work, each other, and themselves through the "phenomenal" commodity form they will be superimposing an abstracted category upon their life activity. Hence the action-reaction character of life activity is broken and skewed by the fixed external standard which reifies the objectification of action. Recognition of the causal source of false consciousness in the capitalist epoch results in a reflexive awareness of the *false necessity* of the reifying structures.

All critical science attempts to restore missing parts of the self-formation process to men and in this way to force a process of self-reflection which will enable them to reinterpret the legitimacy of existing control systems. Insofar as these reconstructions are able to link repressed dimensions of historical structures to both individual and collective self-forming processes, and can be accepted as fitting all available facts, we can be liberated. That is, insofar as men become aware of the structuring of their self-formation they can distinguish between historically necessary modes of control and those that are but unnecessary patterns connected to class privilege and power. In this self-reflective recognition of pseudo-"necessity" the conditions needed to perpetuate unnecessary behavioral orientations are removed and men can enter into a realm of self-discovery.

CRITICAL THEORY TODAY: HOW TECHNOCRATIC STRATEGY SUSTAINS CAPITALISM

Marx's critical theory can be seen as a form of technological utopianism. His theory assumed that the movement toward an automatic system of production would force contradictory trends: socialization of the labor force *and* the implementation of increased labor-saving technology. Hence Marx believed that an extension of the forces of production was incompatible with the continued existence of wage labor. People would be emancipated, indirectly, from the inauthenticity of alienated labor by the power of technological systems. In this residual utopianism of Marx's Enlightenment heritage lie the weaknesses of his critical theory.

Rather than producing the decisive economic crisis, or promoting the growth of leisure ("the real wealth of society"), science and technology have been employed in the service of international control systems, economic stabilizers, and cultural and personality manipulation which creates ever new needs for a consumer oriented capitalism. Marx was simply unable to imagine a stage of technological development where systems of purposive rational action could potentially contain social movements and reify symbolic communication. The complex integration of contemporary state and society has generated a technical-administrative system in which technological rationality has increasingly become a manipulative rationality. This is the essence of the crisis of late capitalist society.

To mediate the crisis, late capitalism must achieve the "necessary" system goals of:

1. economic stability
2. international equilibrium

However, historical practice has revealed that there is a third necessary condition:

3. maintenance of mass loyalty

To repeat, the problems which must be solved by contemporary capitalism are both international control of the "free world" and sustained economic growth. To do this requires a depoliticization of the population.[36]

If we formulate this sociologically, it means that what Weber called rationalization takes place in a way which accepts as given the perpetuation of private capital realization. All institutions have to passively adjust to this, the active, innovating sector of society. This adjustment has had some unintended consequences:

1. In today's society control of inflation and international stabilization at the same time implies a stagnation of public health and educational systems—which are not high on the priority list. To me it is significant that the only nation that can afford to police the world and land on the moon at the same time is unable to provide health services on a par with western Europe.

2. The "public discussion" of issues is taken over by interest groups on the one hand, and parties on the other, and to some extent the mass media. Interest groups try to gain influence in the pre-parliamentary phase and remove the issues from public discussion. Parties can't afford to differ too much from each other and hence narrow the alternatives they debate. The function of the public is hence reduced to a setting of a context of acclamation by passive members of organizations of decisions already made or limited to a narrow choice. The power of the private person is reduced to that of a voter or a consumer of alternatives he has no part in determining. Thus, in the context of a crisis managed society the character of "politics" is reduced to the establishment of a climate of acclamation. Democratic procedure is increasingly replaced by plebiscitary decisions about alternative sets of administrative personnel.[37]

These are some of the unintended trends which result from an un-

---

[36] This point is developed theoretically by Claus Offe's "Politische Herrschaft und Klassenstruktur" in D. Senghass (editor), *Einführung in die Politikwissenschaft* (Frankfurt, 1969).

[37] Cf. Jürgen Habermas, *Strukturwandel der Öffentlichket* (Luchterhand, 1968).

discussed committment to a private structure of power and privilege. But the sociological tradition has shown that every society must render distribution of the surplus to be just and equitable. Hence the problem emerges as to how the depolitization of the public is possible; how can the policy of systems maintenance be made plausible to the masses?

A "RATIONALLY MANAGED" SOCIETY

Under late capitalism, the ideology of equivalence exchange no longer serves as the main ideological scheme of legitimation. Increasingly a new ideology legitimates instrumental rationalization.

Just as in the past the principle of equivalence exchange emerged on a broad front as a critique of absolutism, so now the new legitimating system arises as a critique of liberal capitalism. For example, a recent editorial in the *Wall Street Journal* argues: ". . . the post-World War II technology explosion provided an increasingly powerful motive for imposing conscious guidance upon the *mindless marketplace*." [38]

The motif of "the mindless market" suggests an entire critique of the liberal stage of capitalism. A perspective sees the societal system as determined by the immanent logic of scientific and technological progress. (In a way, all capitalists have now become vulgar Marxists!) Under this viewpoint the intrinsic logics of technical development become the source of societal constraints, and now justify policy decisions. For example, the weapons race has constantly been perpetuated by a rhetoric which speaks of the technical necessities of our national security system.

An indicator to the growth of this ideology is the trend in social sciences toward a policy orientation. For example, the emergence of systems analysis, futurology, the "new political economy", game theory, etc., are all instances of the increasing understanding by social science that they pursue a technical interest. [39]

Another indicator for the new ideology is a growing demand from the knowledge industry and bureaucrats, for a system of social account-

[38] *Wall Street Journal,* October 17, 1969.

[39] A self-congratulatory review of this trend is illustrated by the March 1970 issue of *The Annals of Political and Social Science* which is devoted to a discussion of social indicators and social reports. This focus, the editorial forward reports, "place(s) this journal on the cutting edge of major governmental innovations." The issue must be read to recognize how closely contemporary "policy sciences" have become linked to governmental policy formation.

ing.[40] This demand explicitly acknowledges the above mentioned pre-suppositions of contemporary capitalism. Here too, the guiding principles are that all "budgets must be balanced, investments must be planned in accordance with profit expectations, and thus human needs are still (conceived as satisfiable only) in relation to 'effective demand' of paying customers." That this is as true in the public sector as in the private, is exemplified by the techniques of cost-effectiveness and the Planning, Programming, Budgeting System (P.P.B.S.) that is increasingly used in governmental decision making. A bill called the "full opportunity and social accounting act" has been introduced in two consecutive sessions of Congress. In July 1969, the Nixon administration committed itself to a program of social reports in which the attempt to formulate "national goals" is foremost. (This continues a tradition that began with the 1957 Sputnik-stimulated report *Goals for Americans* which was requested by President Eisenhower.)

These new modes of analysis make very explicit the taken-for-granted system goals of national and international stability, and some are even systematic enough to explicitly state the third one of mass loyalty. For example, a Department of Health, Education and Welfare document entitled *Toward a Social Report,* released January 20, 1969, argues that the management of society is only rational when there exists a *complete consensus on national goals.*

As the critical theory of today must make clear, the new "rational" ideology could be more powerful than that of liberal capitalism. For the ideology of late capitalism conceals the practical questions of daily life and projects no image of the good life. The avowed value neutrality of the new policy sciences presupposes a binding value: the survival and control of a given social system. Insofar as institutions dominant are in fact polarized and rationalized toward the end of crisis management, of sustaining a given social system, these institutions already predetermine the satisfaction of human needs.

The unique present-day crisis of capitalism goes back precisely to this growing trend toward an instrumental rationalization. Ever more, that kind of rationalization dominates and absorbs human activities based on communication between people. Socialization increasingly consists of

---

[40] Cf. Daniel Bell "The Idea of a Social Report," *The Public Interest,* No. 15, Spring 1969. Also see U.S. Congress, Senate Subcommittee on Government Operations, Hearings, *Full Opportunity and Social Accounting Act,* 90th Congress 1st session 1967.

learning the system's technical rules for how to adapt to it, and less and less of internalizing norms emerging from communicative interaction between people.

A technocratic self-understanding of our time—especially the ideal of a "rationally managed" society—now functions as both the principle of justice and the practice of domination. Prescriptive scientism thus becomes part of a powerful ideology which makes the difference so crucial today, between instrumental, technical action and communicative, human interaction. By the same token, the technocratic strategy serves as a self-fulfilling and self-reinforcing scheme; the policies it molds leave little room for democratic choice or participation.

Sources and
Acknowledgments

Each chapter appears in this volume with the kind permission of its author. In addition, their publishers generously gave permission to reprint the papers indicated here.

CHAPTER 1: Martin Nicolaus presented the bulk of his paper to the SSC in 1967. REP, the Radical Education Project, published it the same year as a pamphlet under the title *The Contradictions of Advanced Capitalist Society*. The author wrote the paper's later section in 1970 for this volume.

CHAPTER 2: James R. O'Connor presented this paper to the Town Hall conference in New York in November 1969, co-sponsored by the SSC, on "Agencies of Social Change." A revised version appeared in 1970 as an editorial, "The Making of Socialist Consciousness," in *Socialist Revolution* (Vol. 1, No. 2).

CHAPTER 3: John M. Cammett presented his paper to the SSC in 1967. It is printed here, with a few revisions, for the first time.

CHAPTER 4: Irving Howe presented his paper to the SSC in 1967 and then published it in revised form in *Partisan Review* the same year (Vol. 34, No. 2) and in Jeremy Larner and Irving Howe (eds.), *Poverty: Views from the Left* (Morrow, 1968). Reprinted with permission of *Partisan Review*.

CHAPTER 5: In 1965 Richard F. Hamilton presented to the SSC "Working-Class Authoritarianism: A Reconsideration." The present chapter is a considerably revised and expanded version of that paper. It will appear in the author's *Class and Politics in the United States* (forthcoming). Reprinted with permission of John Wiley and Sons, Inc.

CHAPTER 6: Harry Magdoff presented his paper to the SSC in 1967. The paper appeared in revised form as Chapter 5 of the author's *Age of Imperialism* (1969). Reprinted with permission of Monthly Review Press.

CHAPTER 7: Norman Birnbaum presented his paper to the SSC at its 1969 annual meeting, and revised it for this volume.

CHAPTER 8: Paul M. Sweezy presented his paper to the SSC in 1967 and published it the same year in *Monthly Review* (Vol. 19, No. 7). Reprinted with permission of Monthly Review Press.

CHAPTER 9: Ernest Mandel presented his paper to the SSC in 1968, and published it the same year in the *International Socialist Review* (Vol. 29, No. 6). Reprinted with permission of the *International Socialist Review*.

CHAPTER 10: Stanley Aronowitz spoke at the 1969 annual meeting of the SSC, and expanded his remarks for this volume.

Sources and Acknowledgements

CHAPTER 11: Christopher Lasch presented his paper to the SSC in 1968. It appears here in its original form and for the first time.

CHAPTER 12: Irving M. Zeitlin presented his paper to the SSC in 1967. It appears here in its original form and for the first time.

CHAPTER 13: Martin Jay presented his paper to the SSC at its 1969 annual meeting. It appeared the year after in *Dissent* (Vol. 17, No. 4). Reprinted with permission of *Dissent*.

CHAPTER 14: Ronald Aronson spoke at the 1969 annual meeting of the SSC, and revised his remarks for this volume.

CHAPTER 15: Paul Breines presented his paper to the SSC at the 1969 annual meeting and published it in expanded form in *Critical Interruptions* (1970), edited by him. Reprinted with permission of Herder and Herder.

CHAPTER 16: Trent Schroyer presented his paper to the SSC at its 1969 annual meeting, and revised it considerably for this volume. The paper will appear in the author's forthcoming book, *The Idea of a Critical Science*. Reprinted with permission of George Braziller, Inc.

Index

Index

Index

Liebknecht, Karl, 47
Lipset, S. M., 202
Lin Piao, 173, 287
Lincoln, Abraham, 135
Lukacs, Georg, 229
Luxemburg, Rosa, 47, 229

Monopoly Capital, 10–11, 180
Monthly Review, 134
Moore, Barrington, 134
Morris, William, 229
Mosca, Gaetano, 227–28, 233
Myrdal, Gunnar, 71

McKay, Claude, 222
Magdoff, Harry, 134
Male chauvinism. *See* Sexism
Mallet, Serge, 134, 176, 192, 196–200, 215
Man, Henri de, 171
Mandel, Ernest, 134, 198
Mannheim, Karl, 227
Mao Tse-tung, 287, 295
Marcuse, Herbert, 69, 192, 198, 244–96, 307–8
Marx, Karl, 3–20, 133–36, 143–44, 153–68, 174–81, 191, 202–4, 227–43, 252–57, 263–66, 286–89, 295, 301–4, 308, 315–16
Marxist theory, 6, 9, 12, 38–39, 64, 80, 133–34, 176, 183, 191, 219, 229–31, 237, 245, 258, 273, 290; contemporary, 3–6, 10–11, 15–22, 134, 140, 152, 162–66, 184–88, 215, 227–321; nineteenth-century, 4, 56, 152, 227; orthodox, 8, 12, 18–22, 53, 64–65, 176, 190–93, 229, 254, 288–302; revisionist, 19, 58–59, 176, 183; twentieth-century, 41, 67, 143, 155, 170–71
Marxists, The, 238
Masses, The, 221
Mead, George Herbert, 302
Merleau-Ponty, Maurice, 246
Messenger, The, 223
Michels, Roberto, 3, 227
Middle class, 72, 76, 81–106, 150–51, 177–79, 192, 201, 272. *See also* Bourgeoisie, Capitalist class
Military, 11, 17, 26, 30–34, 51, 68–69, 118–23, 129, 171, 203–10, 234–43, 261–67, 293
Miller, S. M., 134, 139
Mills, C. Wright, 133, 140, 148, 191, 198, 218–43, 301–2

National Association for the Advancement of Colored People, 222
National Socialist Party, 82, 247, 271
Nature. *See* Ecology
Negros, *see* Blacks
Neo-capitalism. *See* Capitalism, contemporary
Neo-Marxism. *See* Marxist theory, contemporary
New Left. *See* Marxist theory, contemporary; Socialist movements, twentieth-century; Youth and students
New Masses, The, 222
New University Conference, 147
New Working Class, 136–40, 150–51, 173–79, 188–216, 253
New York Review of Books, 134
Nietzsche, Friedrich, 254–55
Norway, 183
Nouvelle Classe ouvrière, La, 196

O'Connor, James, 134, 146
One-Dimensional Man, 247, 259–63, 275, 279, 286
Oppenheimer, Martin, 197–98, 200

Pareto, Vilfredo, 227–28, 233
Paris Commune, 16–20
Parties, Communist, 5, 48–49, 54, 170–71, 184; vanguard, 4–5, 42–50, 53–59, 214, 289–91
Phenomenology of the Mind, 314
Philippines, 113
Pierce, Charles Sanders, 308–10
Plato, 257–58
Poland, 49